GRE®
Answers
to the
Real Essay Questions

3rd Edition

Mark Alan Stewart

PETERSON'S

A **nelnet** COMPANY

About Peterson's, a Nelnet company

To succeed on your lifelong educational journey, you will need accurate, dependable, and practical tools and resources. That is why Peterson's is everywhere education happens. Because whenever and however you need education content delivered, you can rely on Peterson's to provide the information, know-how, and guidance to help you reach your goals. Tools to match the right students with the right school. It's here. Personalized resources and expert guidance. It's here. Comprehensive and dependable education content—delivered whenever and however you need it. It's all here.

Petersons.com/publishing

Check out our Web site at www.petersons.com/publishing to see if there is any new information regarding the test and any revisions or corrections to the content of this book. We've made sure the information in this book is accurate and up-to-date; however, the test format or content may have changed since the time of publication.

For more information, contact Peterson's, 2000 Lenox Drive, Lawrenceville, NJ 08648; 800-338-3282; or find us on the World Wide Web at www.petersons.com/about.

© 2009 Peterson's, a Nelnet company

Previous editions © 2002, 2003

Stephen Clemente, President; Bernadette Webster, Director of Publishing; Mark Snider, Editor; Jill C. Schwartz, Production Editor; Ray Golaszewski, Manufacturing Manager; Linda M. Williams, Composition Manager

ISBN-13: 978-0-7689-2821-1
ISBN-10: 0-7689-2821-4

Printed in the United States of America

10 9 8 7 6 5 4 3 2 1   11 10 09

Third Edition

By printing this book on recycled paper (40% post consumer waste) 88 trees were saved.

CONTENTS

We Have All the Answers

All GRE test takers must compose two essays as part of their testing experience. Specifically, the GRE includes the following two "Analytical Writing" tasks.

- Present Your Perspective on an Issue (45 minutes)

- Analyze an Argument (30 minutes)

The computerized testing system will randomly select your GRE essay questions from an official "pool."

Here's the Good News:

Educational Testing Service (ETS), the test maker, has predisclosed its complete pool of GRE essay questions; so you can be ready for any of them—if you're willing to make the effort!

Here's Even Better News:

Top-scoring sample responses to more than 200 official GRE essay questions are right here in this book! (You'll find them in Parts 2 and 3.) In addition, the author has given you all the tools you need to compose your own high-scoring GRE essays in Part 1.

For Online Updates on the GRE Essay Topics

Be sure to check the author's online supplement to this book. From time to time, the test maker (ETS) might alter the sequence of questions in its official pool as well as add new questions and delete others. For updates on the official pool, consult this book's suplemental Web site:

www.west.net/~stewart/grewa

Also visit the author's main GRE page, where you'll find tutorials and mini-tests for every section of the General GRE—plus book reviews, links, and more:

www.west.net/~stewart/gre

How to Match Our Essays to the Topics in the Official Pool

Preceding each essay in Parts 2 and 3 is a brief description of the topic at hand; this description will help you match the two. For additional help in matching each essay in Parts 2 and 3 to its corresponding topic, you can search the official pool's electronic file for our corresponding key phrase. **We've highlighted key phrases in bold.** You'll find the complete pool of GRE essay topics at the testing services' official GRE Web site (www.gre.org).

PART ONE
Getting Ready for GRE Analytical Writing

Analytical Writing has been an integral part of the GRE General Test since 2002. If you plan to take the GRE General Test, this book will teach you everything you need to score your best on this section of the exam. Here in Part 1 you'll learn:

- How to organize and compose a high-scoring Issue essay

- How to organize and compose a high-scoring Argument essay

- What the Analytical Writing computer interface looks like

- What to expect of the exam's special word processor

- How GRE essays are scored and evaluated

- How to make the most of the time you have to prepare for GRE Analytical Writing

In Parts 2 and 3, there are sample essay responses to more than 200 of the questions appearing in the official test pool. It is recommended that you download via the Internet the official pool of GRE essay questions. They're available free of charge at the ETS (Educational Testing Service) Web site. Although you don't need the official question pool to benefit greatly from this book, you'll get more out of the book if you have the official pool of questions in hand.

To obtain the question pool, follow the instructions and links at this book's supplementary Web site (www.west.net/~stewart/grewa), or visit the testing service's official GRE Web site (www.gre.org) directly.

GRE Analytical Writing—At a Glance

What's Covered

GRE Analytical Writing consists of two distinct writing tasks:

Task 1: Present Your Perspective on an Issue (45 minutes). You respond to a statement concerning an issue of broad intellectual interest. (I'll refer to this task simply by the word "Issue" from now on.)

Task 2: Analyze an Argument (30 minutes). You critique a stated argument. (I'll refer to this task simply by the word "Argument" from now on.)

The Pool of Essay Topics

The computerized testing system stores a total of more than 200 Issue topics and more than 200 Arguments in a "pool." During your test, the system will randomly select two of the Issue topics, from which you'll choose either one for your Issue essay (Task 1). However, you won't have a choice when it comes to the Argument task (Task 2); the system will randomly select only one Argument, to which you must respond.

Time Allowed

You will have a total of 75 minutes (45 minutes for the Issue writing task, and 30 minutes for the Argument writing task).

Ground Rules

1. No break is provided between the two writing tasks.

2. The testing system does not allow you to spend more than 45 minutes on the Issue writing task, nor does it allow you to spend more than 30 minutes on the Argument writing task.

3. The testing system does not allow you to return to the first writing task once you've moved on to the second task. (But if you've finished the first one early, you can proceed immediately to the second one, at your option.)

4. Scratch paper and pencils are provided (just as for the multiple-choice sections of the exam).

5. To compose your essays, you must use the word processor built into the testing system. Handwritten responses are not permitted.

Skills Tested

Content   Your ability to present cogent, persuasive, and relevant ideas and arguments through sound reasoning and supporting examples

Organization	Your ability to present your ideas in an organized and cohesive fashion
Language	Your control of the English language, as demonstrated by your vocabulary, diction (word choice), and use of idioms
Mechanics	Your facility with the conventions of standard written English, including grammar, syntax (sentence structure), and word usage

> **NOTE:** Your essays won't be evaluated based on spelling and punctuation, unless you make many such errors and they interfere with your ability to communicate your ideas effectively. (The GRE's built-in word processor does not include a spell-checker or grammar-checker.)

Scoring System

Two readers grade each essay on a scale of 0–6 (0, 1, 2, 3, 4, 5, or 6), 6 being the highest possible score, based on the skill areas listed above; a single Analytical Writing score is then calculated as the average of the four grades (rounded up to the nearest half-point).

> **NOTE:** More details on scoring and evaluation are provided later here in Part 1.

The Issue Writing Task

The Issue task is designed to test your ability to present a position on an issue effectively and persuasively. Your task is to analyze the issue presented, considering various perspectives, and to develop your own position on the issue. In scoring your Issue essay, GRE readers will consider how effectively you:

- Recognize and deal with the complexities and implications of the issue

- Organize, develop, and express your ideas

- Support your ideas (with reasons and examples)

- Control the elements of standard written English (grammar, syntax, and usage)

> **NOTE:** In the Issue section, there is no "correct" answer. In other words, what's important is how effectively you present and support your position, not what your position is.

What GRE Issues Look Like

Your GRE Issue will consist of two elements: a brief *directive* (statement of your task) followed by a one-to-two sentence *topic* (a quotation that is a statement of opinion on an issue). The GRE Issue directive is essentially the same for every Issue topic.

> Present your perspective on the following issue; use relevant reasons and/or examples to support your viewpoint.

GRE Issues cover a broad spectrum of issues of intellectual interest with which college and graduate-level students often deal. Here are four sample topics that are similar to the kinds of topics you'll find in the official GRE Issue pool.

> **NOTE:** These are simulated topics that do not appear among the official GRE topics.

> "Leisure time has become an increasingly rare commodity, largely because technology has failed to achieve its goal of improving our efficiency as we go about our daily lives."

> "In order to achieve greatness in a particular field—whether it be in the arts, sciences, or politics—any individual must challenge tradition as well as the conventional wisdom of the day."

> "The objective of science is largely opposed to that of art; while science seeks to discover truths, art seeks to obscure them."

> "The best way to ensure protection and preservation of our natural environment is through government regulatory measures. We cannot rely on the voluntary efforts of individuals and private businesses to achieve these objectives."

What You Should Know about the Issue Writing Task

Before you begin the timed Issue task, the testing system will present to you one "screen" of directions specific to this task. These directions will indicate the four general scoring criteria listed on pages 2–3, as well as the following guidelines:

- Your time limit is 45 minutes.

- Writing on any topic other than the one presented is unacceptable.

- The topic will appear as a brief statement on an issue of general interest.

- You are free to accept, reject, or qualify the statement.

- You should support your perspective with reasons and/or examples from such sources as your experience, observation, reading, and academic studies.

- You should take a few minutes to plan your response before you begin typing.

- You should leave time to reread your response and make any revisions you think are needed.

The topics in the official Issue pool share many common themes. Although each of the official Issue topics is unique, their basic themes cover a lot of common ground. Here's a list of themes that cover most of the official Issue topics (they're listed here in no particular order):

- Conformity and tradition versus individuality and innovation

- Practicality and utility versus creativity and personal enrichment

- The importance of cultural identity (customs, rituals, and ideals)

- Keys to individual success and progress

- Keys to societal progress, and how we define it

- How we obtain or advance knowledge, and what constitutes knowledge or advancement of knowledge

- The objectives and methods of formal education

- The value of studying history

- The impact of technology on society and on individuals

- The sorts of people society considers heroes or great leaders

- The function and value of art and science (for individuals and for society)

- The proper role of government, business, and individuals in ensuring the well-being of society

Considered collectively, the GRE Issue topics relate to all areas of intellectual inquiry—including sociology, anthropology, history, education, law and government, political science, economics, philosophy, the physical and behavioral sciences, the fine arts, and the performing arts.

NOTE: For research ideas, see pages 60 and 61.

There is no "correct" response to any Issue topic. You won't encounter any statement in the official topic pool that is either clearly irrefutable or clearly wrong. The test makers have written the Issues this way in order to gauge your ability to argue persuasively for or against a position as well as to qualify, or "hedge," your position.

There is no prescribed or "correct" length for an Issue essay. The only limitation on length that the testing system imposes is the practical limitation associated with the 45-minute time limit. So, do GRE graders prefer brief or longer Issue essays? Well, it all depends on the essay's quality. An essay that is concise and to the point can be more effective than a long-winded, rambling one. On the other hand, a longer essay that is nevertheless articulate and that includes many insightful ideas that are well supported by examples will score higher than a brief essay that lacks substance.

A few pages ahead is a sample essay that runs just under 500 words and that meets all the criteria for a top score of 6. The sample essay in Part 2 of this book are a bit longer; on average, they vary from 500 to 750 words in length. The only model ("6") Issue essay that ETS has published is about 700 words in length, and contains seven paragraphs. However, ETS admits that "other '6' responses may not be as eloquent as this essay."

7 Steps to a High-Scoring Issue Essay

To score high on the Issue writing task, you need to accomplish the four basic tasks listed on page 3. To make sure you accomplish all four tasks within the 45-minute time limit, follow the 7-step approach outlined here.

NOTE: The suggested time for each step is merely a guideline. You might find that allocating your time somewhat differently works better for you.

Step 1: Carefully Consider Both Available Issue Topics and Choose Between Them (1 minute)

The testing system will randomly select two Issue topics from the official pool and will require that you choose between them. (There is no "correct" choice as far as the test makers are concerned.) Read both Issue statements carefully. To help you decide which one to select, answer these questions for yourself:

- Does this topic genuinely interest me?

- In the past, have I ever thought about this issue and developed a reasoned viewpoint on it?

- Do I have any specific knowledge from my academic experience or outside reading that I can draw upon to evaluate the statement?

- Have I had any personal experiences that I can draw upon in discussing this topic?

- In reading the statement, did any ideas for either defending or attacking the statement come immediately to mind?

Step 2: Do Some Brainstorming: Jot Down Your Ideas as You Think of Them (2–3 minutes)

List whatever reasons and examples you can think of in support and in opposition to the statement. In brainstorming, try to think of ways to either *limit* or *qualify* your agreement or disagreement with the statement. For example, ask yourself whether the statement's accuracy depends on certain conditions or circumstances, or on how the statement is applied or interpreted. At this stage, don't commit to a position on the issue, and don't filter out what you think might be unconvincing reasons or weak examples. Just let your ideas flow onto your scratch paper.

> **NOTE:** A bit later in Part 1, you'll learn more about different approaches to critiquing an Issue statement and to "hedging" your agreement or disagreement. And in Part 2 you'll find oodles of illustrative Issue essays for each approach.

Step 3: Decide on a Viewpoint and Organize, Prioritize, and Fill Out Your Ideas (1–2 minutes)

Review your notes from step 2, and then decide on the basic point of view you want to adopt and support in your essay. Pick the three or four ideas from your notes that best support your viewpoint. These should be ideas you believe make sense and support your viewpoint reasonably well. Earmark those ideas as the ones you're sure you want to use in your essay. If you don't have enough, take one or two of the ideas you like best and elaborate on them. Think of related ideas, add details or examples, and then use these to fill out your list. Finally, decide on the most natural or logical sequence for presenting your ideas, and number them accordingly in your notes. You now have a good working outline for your essay.

Step 4: Compose the Opening Sentences of Your Essay (2–3 minutes)

An effective way to make a favorable initial impression on the reader is to devote your opening sentences to the following three tasks:

1. Show the reader that you understand the issue raised by the statement.

2. Let the reader know that you have a clear viewpoint on the issue.

3. Forecast the ideas that you intend to present in your essay.

Although there is no "correct" structure for the Issue essay, it is recommended that you add a paragraph break after these opening remarks. You can probably accomplish all three tasks in two to three sentences. Don't waste time repeating the Issue statement verbatim. The reader will already be familiar with the topic and will be interested in your analytical writing skills, not your transcribing abilities.

> **NOTE:** You can also wait until you've completed the rest of your Issue essay to compose your introduction. By using this strategy, you won't need to revise the introduction you wrote earlier in the event that your ideas change as you compose the body of your essay (it could happen).

Step 5: Compose the Body of Your Essay (25–30 minutes)

During this step, your ambition is to get your main points—as well as your supporting reasons and examples—from your brain and scratch paper onto the computer's editing screen. Keep the following suggestions in mind as you compose the body of your essay:

- Begin each paragraph with a distinct train of thought that clearly conveys the essence of the paragraph.

- Arrange your paragraphs so your essay flows logically and persuasively from one point to the next. Stick to your outline, but be flexible.

- Try to devote no more than four or five sentences to any major point from your outline.

- Don't stray from the issue at hand and on the points in your outline. Going off point or, worse yet, off topic will in all likelihood serve to lower your score.

In composing the body of your essay, you might not have time to cover every point from your notes. That's all right, though. The GRE readers understand that the time constraint of the exam prevents most test takers from covering every point they want to make.

Step 6: Compose a Brief Concluding or Summary Paragraph (2 minutes)

This step isn't as crucial as the others. But bear in mind that unless your essay has a clear ending, the reader might think you didn't finish in time, and that's not the impression you want to give. So try to leave time to wrap up your discussion. Convey the main thrust of your essay in a clear, concise, and forceful way. Two or three sentences should suffice. If an especially insightful concluding point occurs to you, the final sentence of your essay is a good place for it.

> **NOTE:** In your closing remarks, be sure that you don't simply repeat your introductory ones. These two bookends should complement each another, each providing its own distinct slant on your thesis. If you need to fine-tune your first paragraph, step 6 is the time to do so.

Step 7: Proofread for Glaring Mechanical Problems (5 minutes)

To score high with your Issue essay, you don't need to compose a flawless work of art. The GRE readers won't reduce your score because of an occasional awkward sentence and minor error in punctuation, spelling, grammar, or diction (word choice and usage). Don't get hung up on whether each sentence is something your English composition professor would be proud of. Instead, use whatever time remains to read your essay from start to finish and fix the most glaring mechanical problems. Here are some suggestions for what you should try to accomplish during this final step:

- Find and rework awkward sentences, especially ones in which the point you're trying to make is unclear.

- Find and correct accidental omissions of words, garbled phrases, and glaring grammatical errors. It doesn't take much time to fix these kinds of mistakes, and doing so will go a long way toward making a positive impression on the reader.

- Correct spelling and other typographical errors only when they might prevent the reader from understanding the point at hand.

- Don't spend valuable time correcting punctuation, removing extra character spaces between words, or correcting minor spelling errors.

- Above all, don't get drawn into drastic rewriting. Accept that your essay is what it is and that you don't have time to reshape it substantially.

Putting It Together—a Sample Issue Essay

Now, take a look at an essay response to the last of the four Issue topics you saw on page 4. In this response, I've underlined certain transitional words and phrases to help you see how I organized my ideas so they flow naturally from one to the next. (On the real exam you won't be able to underline, italicize, or otherwise highlight text.)

As you read the response, keep in mind:

- None of the points I've made are irrefutable, because the issue is far from black-and-white. It's all a matter of perspective. That's what the Issue essay is all about.

- My response is relatively simple in style and language, and it is brief enough (about 500 words) to compose and type in 45 minutes. Yet it meets all the criteria for a top score of 6.

- Don't worry if your practice essays don't turn out quite as polished as this one. An Issue essay can contain minor flaws and still earn a top score.

Sample Response to Issue on Page 4

In asserting that government regulation is the "best" way to ensure environmental protection, the speaker fails to acknowledge certain problems inherent with government regulation. Nevertheless, I agree with the statement to the extent that exclusive reliance on individual or business volunteerism would be naive and imprudent, especially considering the stakes involved.

Experience tells us that individuals and private corporations tend to act in their own short-term economic and political interest, not on behalf of the environment or the public at large. For example, current technology makes possible the complete elimination of polluting emissions from automobiles. Nevertheless, neither automobile manufacturers nor consumers are willing or able to voluntarily make the short-term sacrifices necessary to accomplish this goal. Only government holds the regulatory and enforcement power to impose the necessary standards and to ensure that we achieve these goals.

Admittedly, government penalties do not guarantee compliance with environmental regulations. Businesses often attempt to avoid compliance by concealing their activities, lobbying legislators to modify regulations, or moving operations to jurisdictions that allow their environmentally harmful activities. Others calculate the cost of polluting, in terms of punishment, then budget in advance for anticipated penalties and openly violate the law. However, this behavior only serves to underscore the need for government intervention, because left unfettered this type of behavior would only exacerbate environmental problems.

One must admit as well that government regulation, environmental or otherwise, is fraught with bureaucratic and enforcement problems. Regulatory systems inherently call for legislative committees, investigations, and enforcement agencies, all of which add to the tax burden on the citizens whom these regulations are designed to protect. Also, delays typically associated with bureaucratic regulation can thwart the purpose of the regulations, because environmental problems can quickly become grave indeed. <u>However</u>, given that the only alternative is to rely on volunteerism, government regulation seems necessary. <u>Moreover</u>, such delays seem trivial when we consider that many environmental problems pose not only a real threat to public health but also a potential threat to our very survival as a species.

<u>Finally</u>, environmental issues inherently involve public health and are generally too pandemic for individuals or even businesses to solve on their own. <u>I would concede that</u> a strip miner in Montana or a landfill operator in New Jersey might theoretically be capable of undoing whatever environmental damage it has inflicted. <u>But</u> many of the most egregious environmental violations—especially those involving the pollution of air, oceans, or major rivers—traverse state and sometimes national borders. I seriously doubt that even a large multinational corporation could wield enough power or resources to address these widespread hazards, assuming the corporation's leaders had the will to do so in the first place.

<u>In the final analysis</u>, only the authority and scope of power that a government possesses can ensure the attainment of agreed-upon environmental goals. Because individuals are unable and businesses are by nature unwilling to assume this responsibility, government must do so.

Advanced Tools for Creating a Top-Scoring Issue Essay

In this section, you'll delve more deeply into the process of developing, organizing, and presenting your ideas for the GRE Issue essay. You'll learn more about how to do the following:

- Qualify or limit your agreement or disagreement with an Issue statement
- Debate an Issue statement's pros and cons
- Persuade the reader using effective rhetorical arguments
- Employ a rhetorically effective paragraph structure in your essay response

If you follow the step-by-step approach you learned a few pages earlier, you should earn a better-than-average score of at least 4 on the Issue writing task. Mastering the advanced tools and techniques listed in this section will give you an even better chance at improving your score.

Qualify or Limit Your Agreement or Disagreement with the Statement

In your Issue essay, it's perfectly okay to agree (or disagree) wholeheartedly with the statement at hand. Be aware, however, that in so doing you risk leaving the impression that you've oversimplified the issue. If you decide to adopt a one-sided position, be sure to provide very convincing reasons and highly relevant examples to support that position, and be sure your essay is very polished and well-organized. Otherwise, you probably won't earn a top score.

To be on the safe side, show the readers that you appreciate the issue's complexities by acknowledging at least one argument against your chosen viewpoint. For example, discuss how the Issue statement *may* or *may not be true*, or how the statement is accurate only *to a certain extent* or only *in part*. In other words, try to *qualify* or *limit* your agreement or disagreement. To illustrate this strategy, here are two GRE-style Issue statements, each followed by a viewpoint that expresses only qualified or limited agreement:

> "To truly succeed in life, a person must assert his or her individuality rather than conform to the expectations of others."

Viewpoint: Asserting individuality is important only to an extent. The key is to strike the optimal balance between individuality and conformity, a balance that varies depending on the particular activity or goal involved.

> "The greatest responsibility of a leader—whether in politics, business, or the military—is to serve the interests of his or her followers."

Viewpoint: The statement's accuracy depends on the category. Legitimate political leadership must, by definition, serve the citizenry, but the same can't be said for business or military leadership.

Keep in mind that the test makers designed nearly every one of the Issue statements in the GRE official pool so that they can be qualified or limited in at least one of the following ways:

- The statement has merit but overlooks legitimate competing interests or considerations. (The first of the two Issue statements provided above is a good example.)

- The statement lists or otherwise embraces two or more distinct areas of consideration. (The second Issue statement above is a good example; it lists three different categories that might lend different degrees of support to the statement.)

- The statement might be true or untrue generally, but it fails to account for significant exceptions.

- The statement actually makes two or more distinct claims or raises two or more issues. One might be a so-called "threshold" issue that should be addressed before the main issue is examined.

- The statement is unclear or vague; its accuracy depends upon how you define a particular term or how you interpret the statement as a whole.

- The statement appears credible but misses the point by ignoring an entirely different—and better—way of looking at the issue.

Perhaps you're wondering whether you'll appear wishy-washy or indecisive by qualifying or limiting your agreement or disagreement. To the contrary, you'll impress the reader as being thoughtful and insightful. Just be sure to persuade the reader, using sound reasons and relevant examples, that your hedged position is justifiable.

Debate the Statement's Pros and Cons

A few pages ago, I recommended that you devote at least 4 or 5 minutes before starting to type your essay to brainstorming and jotting down points for and against the Issue statement as the points occur to you. A useful way to approach this process is to view it as a debate in which you formulate points and supporting examples to bolster one side of the issue, and then respond with counterpoints and counterexamples. In fact, you can go a step further and rebut a counterpoint or counterexample.

To organize your debate, try creating two columns on your scratch paper, one for points that support the statement (the "pro" column) and the other for opposing points (the "con" column). To help you see how this might work, let's review the Issue statement related to the essay on pages 10–11:

"The best way to ensure protection and preservation of our natural environment is through government regulatory measures. We cannot rely on the voluntary efforts of individuals and private businesses to achieve these objectives."

Now, here are what the writer's notes looked like after brainstorming and jotting down this statement's pros and cons in separate columns, and then numbering the main points in the order he or she decided to present them in the essay (notice the plan to present two of the "con" points in a single paragraph):

Outline (Issue 1)

<u>PRO</u>

① • self-interest rules
ind. & bus.
  • e.g. auto emissions
  • but nations too

④ • environ problems too
widespread for
ind. & bus.
  • but nations must
cooperate

<u>CON</u>

② • lawmakers pander
  • but accountable
to voters
• enforcement problems
  • e.g. bus. relocate

③ • bureaucratic problems
  • e.g. delays
  • e.g. compromises
  • e.g. admin. expense
  • but must put up with
problems to save
environ.

As you can see, the writer filled out each main point with at least one example ("e.g.") or counterpoint ("but"). Now review the essay on pages 10–11. Notice that the writer didn't have time to include every single idea he had jotted down, but that otherwise the writer stuck to his basic outline. The end result: an essay that demonstrates an ability to recognize an issue's complexities and to articulate and support a position on it—in other words, a thoughtful, well-organized and persuasive essay worthy of a high GRE score.

Persuade the Reader Using Effective Rhetorical Arguments

The word *rhetoric* refers to the art of persuasive argumentation. A rhetorically effective GRE Issue essay does more than merely itemize the best reasons and examples in support of one viewpoint on the issue. It also acknowledges:

- possible problems with the your viewpoint, and then defends that viewpoint by responding to those problems head-on

- at least one other position or viewpoint, and then challenges it directly

As you take notes on your Issue statement, ideas for countering other viewpoints and for responding to possible problems with your own are likely to occur to you naturally. But if you do get stuck for ideas, here's a way to get your rhetorical juices flowing. Draw upon the five tried-and-true techniques we'll introduce here. To illustrate each technique, we'll review examples based on the following two Issue statements—the first of which should be very familiar to you by now:

> "The best way to ensure protection and preservation of our natural environment is through government regulatory measures. We cannot rely on the voluntary efforts of individuals and private businesses to achieve these objectives."

> "Large organizations, whether public or private, should focus on teamwork as the primary means of achieving success."

Turn Around a Weakness (or Strength):

One of the strategies you can adopt in your Issue essay is to argue that an apparent weakness is actually not one, or that an apparent strength isn't a strength, if you view it from a different perspective. The essay on the first Issue statement above provides a good example of this rhetorical technique. The writer first cited evidence that lends apparent support to the opposing position:

Admittedly, businesses . . . often attempt to avoid compliance by concealing their activities. . . . Others calculate the cost of polluting in terms of punishment, then budget in advance for anticipated penalties and openly violate the law.

He then indicated how this point actually undermines that position:

However, this behavior only underscores the need for government intervention, because left unfettered, this type of behavior would only exacerbate environmental problems.

Trivialize a Weakness (or Strength):

You can also argue that an apparent weakness of your position (or an apparent strength in a different position) is trivial, minor, or insignificant. The second Issue statement provides a good opportunity to employ this technique. The writer might first supply examples that lend apparent support to those who disagree with the statement:

Detractors might cite the heavy manufacturing and natural resource industries, where the value of tangible assets such as raw materials and capital equipment are often the most significant determinant of business success.

The writer would then "explain away," or trivialize, these examples:

However, such industries are diminishing in significance as we move from an industrial society to an information age.

Appeal to Broader Considerations:

A third strategy is to argue that any minor problems with your position are insignificant in light of the broad and serious implications that the issue raises. The essay on the first issue above provides a good example. The writer first acknowledged a particular problem with his position:

Delays typically associated with bureaucratic regulation can thwart the purpose of the regulations, because environmental problems can quickly become grave indeed.

He then pointed out the broad societal consideration that puts this minor drawback in its proper perspective:

However, such delays seem trivial when we consider that many environmental problems pose not only a real threat to public health but also a potential threat to our very survival as a species.

Argue for the "Lesser of Two Evils":

Another avenue of attack is to argue that an opposing position is no stronger than yours or is perhaps even weaker in a certain respect. As with the "broader considerations" technique, the writer might first acknowledge a certain weakness in his position, as the writer did in his essay on the first issue:

Delays typically associated with bureaucratic regulation can thwart the purpose of the regulations, because environmental problems can quickly become grave indeed.

Then, the writer can point out an even greater weakness in the opposing position, as you saw in the essay:

However, given that unjustifiable reliance on volunteerism is the only alternative, government regulation seems necessary.

Try the "Greater of Two Virtues" Argument:

This strategy is the flip side of the previous one. Here, you argue that a particular strength of the opposing position is overshadowed by one or more virtues of your position. The second Issue statement above provides a good opportunity to employ this rhetorical device. The writer might first admit that the opposing position has merit:

No reasonable observer of the world of big business or big government could disagree that the leadership and vision of a large organization's key executives is of great importance to its success.

Next, though, the writer would assert that the contrary position has even greater merit:

Yet surely our great political leaders, as well as the chief executives of our most successful Fortune 500 corporations, would all admit that without the cooperative efforts of their subordinates, their personal vision would never become reality.

Choose a Rhetorically Effective Paragraph Structure

There is no "best" structure or "correct" number of paragraphs in a GRE Issue essay—but this doesn't mean that it won't matter whether your essay ideas flow from one to the next. To ensure a high score on your Issue essay, arrange your ideas in a logically and rhetorically effective sequence, with appropriate paragraph breaks that help the reader follow your train of thought. How you structure your ideas can greatly affect your essay's persuasiveness, and hence your Analytical Writing score.

A basic strategy that works well in most cases is to use a four-paragraph structure (not counting introductory and concluding paragraphs) in which you start with your best argument, finish with your second-best one, and sandwich two other arguments—ones for which you've identified strong counterarguments—between your first and last body paragraphs. If you've jotted down a list of pros and cons like the one you saw a few pages previously, you shouldn't have any trouble organizing the body of your essay this way. Here's the basic structure, which is the one used in the essay on page 10, except that the first body paragraph included a counterargument as well:

- **1st paragraph:** The chief argument (a reason and/or examples) in support of your position

- **2nd paragraph:** One counterargument, followed by your rebuttal argument

- **3rd paragraph:** Another counterargument, followed by your rebuttal argument

- **4th paragraph:** The second-strongest argument in support of your position

Of course, this isn't the only effective way to organize an Issue essay. The best structure will depend on how your ideas flow most logically and naturally from one to the next. Here are the means by which you should measure the effectiveness of your essay:

- **The number of reasons and examples you cite in support of each side of the issue.** If you raise only one opposing point, consider dispensing with it before turning to the points that support your stated position. Whatever you do, avoid ending the body of your essay with a good argument against your viewpoint.

- **The extent to which you agree with the statement.** A balanced viewpoint calls for a balanced structure that treats both sides of the issue equally—one side at a time (to avoid confusion).

- **Whether the Issue statement can be broken down into two or more distinct claims or other aspects.** If it can, you should devote at least one separate paragraph to each one in turn.

In any event, be flexible. You might start out with a particular structure in mind, then midway through your essay you might discover that the pieces are not falling into place the way you'd hoped. If you have enough time, switch to a structure that works better and rearrange your paragraphs.

DOs and DON'Ts for the Issue Writing Task

Here's a list of DOs and DON'Ts that recap what you've learned in Part 1 about composing your Issue essay. To reinforce the ideas in this list, refer back to it from time to time as you read the sample essays in Part 2.

DO try to break apart the statement into components or discrete areas of consideration. In fact, many GRE Issue statements are intentionally designed for you to do so.

DON'T waste time second-guessing what the reader might agree (or disagree) with. Instead, just be sure to adopt a clear perspective on the issue and develop a well-supported position on it.

DO try to hedge your position by qualifying your viewpoint and acknowledging others. In doing so, you won't appear wishy-washy, but rather, thoughtful and scholarly.

DON'T be reluctant to take a strong stance on an issue, but avoid coming across as fanatical or extreme. Approach the Issue essay as an intellectual exercise, not as a forum for sharing your personal belief system.

DON'T dwell on the details, but don't try to cover everything. Try to cover as many points in your outline as you have time for, devoting no more than one paragraph to each one. At the same time, don't worry if you're forced to leave the secondary and more tangential points on your scratch paper. GRE readers understand your time constraints.

DON'T overdo it when it comes to drawing on personal experiences to support your position. Try instead to demonstrate a breadth of both real-world experience and academic knowledge.

DON'T approach the Issue task as a trivia contest. By all means, bolster your position with solid evidence. But avoid recounting statistics, quoting obscure sources, or citing little-known historical events as a substitute for thoughtful analysis.

DO explain how each example you mention illustrates your point. Anyone can simply list a long string of examples and claim that they illustrate a point. But the readers are looking for incisive analysis, not fast typing.

The Argument Writing Task

The Argument task is designed to test your critical-reasoning skills as well as your writing skills. Your task is to critique the stated argument in terms of its cogency (logical soundness) and in terms of the strength of the evidence offered in support of the argument. In scoring your Argument essay, GRE readers will consider how effectively you:

- Identify and analyze the key elements of the argument
- Organize, develop, and express your critique
- Support your ideas (with reasons and examples)
- Control the elements of standard written English (grammar, syntax, and usage)

What GRE Arguments Look Like

Each Argument in the official pool consists of a brief *directive* (statement of your task) followed by a paragraph-length passage, which presents an *argument*. The directive is the same for every Argument in the official pool:

Discuss how well reasoned you find this argument.

The Argument itself might take the form of quotation from a fictitious report or article or some other source. Here are two GRE-style Arguments. Keep in mind, however, that neither of these two examples is included in the official pool, so you won't see either on your exam.

The following appeared in an advertisement for United Motors trucks:

"Last year the local television-news program *In Focus* reported in its annual car-and-truck safety survey that over the course of the last ten years United Motors vehicles were involved in at least thirty percent fewer fatal accidents to drivers than vehicles built by any other single manufacturer. Now United is developing a one-of-a-kind computerized crash warning system for all its trucks. Clearly, anyone concerned with safety who is in the market for a new truck this year should buy a United Motors truck."

The following appeared in a memo from the manager of UpperCuts hair salon:

"According to a nationwide demographic study, more and more people today are moving from suburbs to downtown areas. In order to boost sagging profits at UpperCuts, we should take advantage of this trend by relocating the salon from its current location in Apton's suburban mall to downtown Apton, while retaining the salon's decidedly upscale ambiance. Besides, Hair-Dooz, our chief competitor at the mall, has just relocated downtown and is thriving at its new location, and the most prosperous hair salon in nearby Brainard is located in that city's downtown area. By emulating the locations of these two successful salons, UpperCuts is certain to attract more customers."

What You Should Know about the Argument Writing Task

Before you begin the timed Argument task, the testing system will present to you two "screens" of directions specific to this task. In addition to indicating the four general scoring criteria listed on page 19, these directions will indicate essentially the following:

Screen 1 (general guidelines and suggestions):

- Your time limit is 30 minutes.
- You must critique the logical soundness of the argument presented.
- A critique of any other argument is unacceptable.
- You should take a few minutes to plan your response before you begin typing.
- You should develop your ideas fully and organize them in a coherent manner.
- You should leave time to reread your response and make any revisions you think are needed.

Screen 2 (specific guidelines for critiquing the argument):

- You are not being asked to agree or disagree with any of the statements in the argument.
- You should analyze the argument's line of reasoning.
- You should consider questionable assumptions underlying the argument.
- You should consider the extent to which the evidence presented supports the argument's conclusion.

- You may discuss what additional evidence would help strengthen or refute the argument.

- You may discuss what additional information, if any, would help you to evaluate the argument's conclusion.

Your analysis must focus strictly on the Argument's logical features and on its evidence. Do not confuse the Argument writing task with the Issue task. Your Argument essay is not the place to present your own opinions about an issue that the Argument might involve. Consider, for example, the first of the two Arguments you just read (pages 19 and 20). An Issue topic involving advertising claims might call for you to present various viewpoints about the duty of a business or businesses to provide complete and unbiased product information to consumers. But such viewpoints are irrelevant to the Argument task, in which you must focus strictly on the internal cogency (logical soundness) of the Argument.

The test makers have intentionally loaded each Argument with numerous flaws (unstated assumptions and other reasoning problems) that you must address effectively to score high. In contrast to the instructions for the Issue writing task, the instructions for the Argument task do not state: "There is no correct response." Why not? In designing each Argument, the test makers made sure to incorporate into it certain reasoning problems for you to identify and address in your essay. That's what the Argument writing task is all about. Should you fail to identify and address these built-in problems, you won't attain a high score.

A typical GRE Argument will contain three or four discrete reasoning flaws. Here's a list of the seven types of flaws that appear most frequently in the official GRE Arguments:

1. Drawing a questionable analogy between two people, places, or things

2. Confusing a cause-and-effect relationship with a mere correlation or temporal sequence

3. Assuming that all members of a group share the same key attributes

4. Assuming that a certain condition is necessary and/or sufficient for a certain outcome

5. Relying on a potentially unrepresentative statistical sample

6. Relying on a potentially unreliable survey or poll

7. Assuming that all things remain unchanged over time

> **NOTE:** Beginning on page 27 you'll find detailed explanations and illustrations of these flaws.

All GRE Arguments are not created equal. Having composed essays for more GRE Arguments than I care to remember, I can state with authority that some GRE Arguments are tougher to handle than others. Of course, after reading Parts 1 and

3 of this book, you shouldn't have much trouble with any of them. Nevertheless, if you peruse the official pool of Arguments, you'll no doubt notice that in some of them the logical flaws seem to jump out at you, one at a time, while in others the flaws are intertwined or hidden from clear view, making it especially challenging to extract, separate, and organize them. And there are no guarantees that the test will deal you a favorable hand. But at least you have this book to help even the playing field.

There is no prescribed or "correct" length for a high-scoring Argument essay. The length of your Argument essay is limited only by the 30-minute time limit and the number of reasoning flaws that are available to discuss. In my experience composing Argument essays, fewer than 400 words can suffice for a top-scoring response to any GRE Argument. (The essays in Part 3 run longer because in the first paragraph of each one I've recapitulated the entire Argument—for your reference.)

7 Steps to a High-Scoring Argument Essay

To score high on the Argument writing task, you need to accomplish the four basic tasks listed on page 19. To make sure you accomplish all four tasks within the 30-minute time limit, follow the 7-step approach outlined here.

> **NOTE:** The suggested time for each step is merely a guideline. You might find that allocating your time somewhat differently works better for you.

Step 1: Read the Argument and Identify Its Conclusions (1–2 minutes)

Every GRE Argument consists of three basic elements:

1. Evidence (stated premises that the argument does not dispute)

2. Assumptions (unstated premises needed to justify a conclusion)

3. Conclusions (inferences drawn from evidence and assumptions)

As you read an argument for the first time, identify its *final* conclusion and jot it down on your scratch paper. You'll probably find this conclusion in the argument's first or last sentence; the argument might refer to it as a "claim," a "recommendation," or a "prediction." Also look for an *intermediate* conclusion, upon which the final conclusion depends. (Not every argument contains an intermediate conclusion.)

Why is this first step so important? Unless you are clear about the argument's conclusions, it's impossible to evaluate the author's reasoning or the strength of the argument's evidence. And that's what the Argument writing task is all about!

Step 2: Examine the Argument's Evidence and Determine How Strongly It Supports the Argument's Conclusions (1–2 minutes)

Most GRE Arguments contain at least two or three items of information (or evidence) supporting their conclusions. Identify these items, label them, and jot them down on your scratch paper. Then analyze each item to determine how much support it lends to the argument's conclusions. The test directions that you'll view just before your argument prompt will instruct you to look for unsubstantiated or unreasonable assumptions upon which the argument's conclusions depend. For example, an argument might rely on one of the following assumptions but fail to provide evidence to support the assumption:

- An event that occurred after another one was caused by the other (a false-cause problem).

- Two things that are similar in one way are similar in other ways (a false-analogy problem).

- A statistical sample of a group is representative of the group as a whole.

The test's directions will also instruct you to check for problems with the argument's internal logic—for example, the argument might be self-contradictory or employ circular reasoning. Just as with the Issue essay, don't filter your ideas during this crucial brainstorming step. Just put them all down on paper for the time being; you'll sort them out during step 3.

Step 3: Organize and Prioritize Your Points of Critique (1 minute)

Using your notes from step 2 as a guide, arrange your ideas into paragraphs (probably three or four, depending on the number of problems built into the argument). Take a minute to consider whether any of the flaws you identified overlap and whether you can separate them into two distinct problems. In many cases, the way to organize your points of critique is to put them in the same order in which reasoning problems arise in the argument itself. As with the Issue essay, you can probably use your notes as your outline, numbering them according to how they'd most logically arise in discussion.

Step 4: Compose a Brief Introductory Paragraph (1–2 minutes)

Now that you've spent about 5 minutes planning your essay, you have to compose it. Don't waste time repeating the quoted argument; the reader is already familiar with it and is interested in your critique, not your transcribing skills. Here's what you should try to accomplish in your initial paragraph:

1. Identify the argument's final conclusion.

2. Briefly describe the argument's line of reasoning and evidence in support of its conclusion.

3. Allude generally to the problems with the argument's line of reasoning and use of evidence.

You can probably accomplish all three tasks in two to three sentences.

> **NOTE:** Your introductory sentences are the least important component of your essay. So, you might consider holding off on composing them until you've completed your critique of the argument.

Step 5: Compose the Body of Your Response (15–20 minutes)

As with the Issue essay, when you're composing the body of your Argument essay, your chief aim is to peck madly at your keyboard to get your ideas onto the computer's editing screen. Start with whichever points of critique strike you as the most important and easiest to articulate. You can always rearrange your points later using the word processor's cut-and-paste feature. Here's what you need to keep in mind as you compose your body paragraphs:

- Try to devote a separate paragraph to each major point of your critique—but be flexible. Sometimes it makes more sense to discuss related points in the same paragraph.

- Be sure the first sentence of each paragraph conveys the essence of the problem you're dealing with in that paragraph.

- For each of the argument's assumptions, be sure to explain how the argument relies on the assumption. It might help to provide one or two examples or counterexamples (a hypothetical scenario) that, if true, would undermine the assumption.

- Devote no more than three or four sentences to any one point in your outline. Otherwise, you risk running out of time without discussing all of the argument's major assumptions or other problems.

- Arrange your paragraphs so your essay flows logically from one point of critique to the next.

- Don't worry if you don't have time to discuss each and every point of critique or example from your notes. Remember, GRE essay readers understand your time constraint.

Step 6: Compose a Final Paragraph (2–3 minutes)

This step, like step 4, is not as crucial as the others. However, providing a recap at the end of your Argument essay helps demonstrate your control over the writing task. So try to make time to "wrap up" your analysis. This paragraph is not the place to point out additional problems with the argument. Instead, I suggest two alternative approaches. One is to briefly touch on either of the following, which the test's directions indicate you may discuss at your option:

1. How the argument can be strengthened

2. What additional information is needed to evaluate the argument

Another approach to a final paragraph is to simply recapitulate the argument's problems in two or three sentences.

Step 7: Proofread for Mechanical Problems (3–5 minutes)

Be sure to reserve time to check the flow of your essay. Pay special attention to the first sentence of each paragraph, and check to see if you should rearrange paragraphs in a more logical sequence. Also, proofread for mechanical problems. Your Argument essay, like your Issue essay, need not be flawless to earn a high score. GRE readers aren't looking for the occasional awkward sentence, minor punctuation or spelling gaffes, or errors in grammar or diction (word choice and usage). Use whatever time you have left to read your essay from start to finish and fix the most glaring mechanical problems.

Don't bother reworking a sentence or correcting a spelling or punctuation error unless you think the problem will interfere with the reader's understanding of the point at hand. Above all, don't get pulled into drastic rewriting. Accept that your essay is what it is; you don't have time to reshape it.

Putting It Together—a Sample Argument Essay

Now, take a look at a response to the Argument on page 20 about hair salons. In this response certain transitional words and phrases that are used over and over in the essays in Part 3 have been underlined. This should help you see how to formulate the introductory and concluding paragraphs and how to organize and present points of critique so that they flow logically from one to the next. (On the real exam you won't be able to underline, italicize, or otherwise highlight text.)

As you read the following essay, keep in mind:

• This essay meets all the ETS criteria for a top score of 6.

• This essay is brief enough (370 words) to organize and compose in 30 minutes.

• Don't worry if your practice essays don't turn out quite as polished. Rest assured you can earn a top score even if your essay contains some minor flaws.

Sample Response to Argument on Page 20

Citing a general demographic trend and certain evidence about two other hair salons, the manager of UpperCuts (UC) <u>concludes that</u> UC should relocate from suburban to downtown Apton in order to attract more customers and, in turn, improve its profitability. <u>However</u>, the manager's argument <u>relies on a series of unproven assumptions</u> and is <u>therefore unconvincing</u> as it stands.

<u>One such assumption</u> is that Apton reflects the cited demographic trend. <u>The mere fact that</u> one hair salon has moved downtown hardly suffices to show that the national trend applies to Apton specifically. <u>For all we know</u>, in Apton there is no such trend, or perhaps the trend is in the opposite direction, in which event the manager's recommendation would amount to especially poor advice.

<u>Even assuming</u> that downtown Apton is attracting more residents, relocating downtown might not result in more customers for UC, especially if downtown residents are not interested in UC's upscale style and prices. <u>Besides</u>, Hair-Dooz might draw potential customers away from UC, just as it might have at the mall. <u>Without ruling out these and other reasons</u> why UC might not benefit from the trend, the manager can't convince me that UC would attract more customers by moving downtown.

<u>Even if</u> there would be a high demand for UC's service in downtown Apton, an increase in the number of patrons would not necessarily improve UC's profitability. UC's expenses might be higher downtown, in which case it might be no more, or perhaps even less, profitable downtown than at the mall.

<u>As for</u> the Brainard salon, its success might be due to particular factors that don't apply to UC. <u>For example, perhaps</u> the Brainard salon thrives only because it is long-established in downtown Brainard. Or perhaps hair salons generally fare better in downtown Brainard than downtown Apton, due to demographic differences between the two areas. <u>In short</u>, the manager simply <u>cannot justify</u> his proposal on the basis of the Brainard salon's success.

<u>In sum</u>, the argument <u>depends on certain unproven assumptions</u>, which render it dubious at best. <u>To strengthen the argument</u>, the manager should provide better evidence of a demographic shift toward downtown Apton and clear evidence that the shift portends success there for an upscale salon.

Handling the Most Common Reasoning Flaws In GRE Arguments

The test makers intentionally incorporate into each GRE Argument numerous flaws in reasoning and use of evidence that render the Argument vulnerable to criticism. In a typical Argument you can find three or four distinct areas for critique. (Glance through the more than 100 essays in Part 3, and you'll notice that most of them contain three or four body paragraphs—one for each distinct flaw built into the Argument.)

In this section you'll explore the types of reasoning flaws that appear most frequently in GRE Arguments. For each flaw you'll find an Argument that illustrates the problem along with an effective response.

> **NOTE:** The examples in this section are not taken from actual GRE Arguments; but they closely simulate many of the Arguments you'll find in the official Argument pool. Also keep in mind that these examples are a bit briefer than complete GRE Arguments—because each one is intended to isolate one particular reasoning problem.

Drawing a Weak Analogy

A GRE Argument might draw a conclusion about one thing (perhaps a city, school, or company) on the basis of an observation about a similar thing. However, in doing so the Argument assumes that because the two things are similar in certain respects they are similar in all respects, at least as far as the Argument is concerned. Unless the Argument provides sufficient evidence to substantiate this assumption (by the way, it won't), the Argument is vulnerable to criticism.

Here's an argument that contains a questionable analogy, followed by an effective three-sentence analysis:

Argument:

> The following was part of a speech made by the principal of Valley High School:
>
> "Every year Dunston High School wins the school district's student Math SuperBowl competition. The average salary of teachers at Dunston is greater than at any other school in the district. Hence in order for Valley High students to improve their scores on the state's standardized achievement exams, Valley High should begin awarding bonuses to its teachers whenever Valley High defeats Dunston High in the Math SuperBowl."

Response:

The principal's recommendation relies on what might be a poor analogy between Dunston and Valley. Valley teachers might be less responsive than Dunston teachers when it comes to monetary incentives, or Valley students might be less gifted than Dunston students when it comes to math. In short, what might have helped Dunston perform well at the Math SuperBowl would not necessarily help Valley perform better either at the SuperBowl or on the state exams.

Confusing a Cause-and-Effect Relationship with a Mere Correlation or Temporal Sequence

Many GRE Arguments rely on the claim that certain events cause other certain events. A cause-and-effect claim might be based on the following two claims:

1. a significant *correlation* between the occurrence of two phenomena (both phenomena generally occur together), or

2. a *temporal relationship* between the two (one event occurred after another).

A significant correlation or a temporal relationship between two phenomena is one indication of a cause-and-effect relationship between them. However, neither in itself suffices to prove such a relationship. Unless the Argument also considers and eliminates all other plausible causes of the presumed "result" (by the way, it won't), the Argument is vulnerable to criticism. The following example incorporates both claims (1 and 2) listed above.

Argument:

The following appeared in the editorial section of a newspaper:

"Many states have enacted laws prohibiting environmental emissions of nitro carbon byproducts, on the basis that these byproducts have been shown to cause Urkin's Disease in humans. These laws have clearly been effective in preventing the disease. After all, in every state that has enacted such a law the incidence of Urkin's disease is lower than in any state that has not enacted a similar law...."

Response:

Based on a known correlation between laws prohibiting certain emissions and the low incidence of Urkin's Disease, the argument concludes that the latter is attributable, at least partly, to the former. Yet the correlation alone amounts to scant evidence of the claimed cause-and-effect relationship. Perhaps Urkin's disease can be caused by other factors as well, which are absent in these particular states but present in all others. Moreover, the argument overlooks the fact that it is the level of compliance with a law, not its enactment, that determines its effectiveness. The editorial's author has not accounted for the possibility that the laws prohibiting the emissions were never enforced or complied with, and that the emissions have continued unabated. If this is the case, then the conclusion that the laws are effective in preventing Urkin's Disease would lack any merit whatsoever.

Assuming That All Members of a Group Share the Same Key Attributes

A GRE Argument might point out some fact about a general group—such as students, employees, or cities—to support a claim about one particular member of that group. Or, conversely, the argument might point out a fact about a particular member in order to generalize about the entire group. In either scenario, unless the argument supplies clear evidence that the member is representative of the group as a whole (by the way, it won't), the argument is vulnerable to criticism.

Here's an argument that makes the former type of assumption. The accompanying response shows how to handle the problem in one succinct paragraph

Argument:

The following is part of an article that appeared a few years ago in the entertainment section of a local newspaper:

"At the local Viewer Choice video store, the number of available movies in VHS format remains about the same as three years ago, even though the number of available movies on digital video disk, or DVD, has increased tenfold over the past three years. People who predict the impending obsolescence of the VHS format are mistaken, since demand for VHS movie rentals today clearly remains just as strong as ever."

Response:

> This argument assumes that Viewer Choice (VC) is typical of all video stores, as a group. However, this isn't necessarily the case; VC might carry far more VHS tapes, as a percentage of its total inventory, than the average store. If so, then the argument has failed to discredit the prediction for the industry as a whole.

Assuming That a Certain Condition Is Necessary and/or Sufficient for a Certain Outcome

A GRE Argument might recommend a certain course of action, based on one or both of the following claims:

1. The course of action is *necessary* to achieve a desired result.

2. The course of action is *sufficient* to achieve the desired result.

Both claims often occur in the same Argument, and both are potentially vulnerable to criticism. With respect to claim 1, the Argument must provide evidence that no other means of achieving the same result are available (by the way, it won't). With respect to claim 2, the Argument must provide strong evidence that the proposed course of action by itself would be sufficient to bring about the desired result (by the way, it won't). Lacking this sort of evidence, the Argument cannot rely on these claims to support its recommendation. In the following example, the response includes two paragraphs; the first challenges claim 1, while the second challenges claim 2.

Argument:

> The following appeared in a memo from the superintendent of the Cutter County school district:
>
> > "In order to raise the level of reading skills of our district's elementary school students to a level that at least represents the national average, we should adopt the "Back to Basics" reading program. After all, this reading program has a superior record for improving reading skills among youngsters nationwide. By adopting Back to Basics the parents of our young students would be assured that their children will develop the reading skills they will need throughout their lives...."

Response:

The recommendation depends on the assumption that no alternative means of improving the students' reading skills are available. Yet no evidence is offered to substantiate this assumption. Admittedly, the superior record of the Back to Basics (BTB) program is some evidence that no other program is as likely to achieve the desired result. However, it is entirely possible that means other than this or any other reading program would also achieve the desired result. Perhaps the desired improvement could be achieved if the schools instead hired special reading instructors, or encouraged parents to read with their children, or simply devoted more time during school to reading. Without considering and ruling out these and other alternative means of improving reading skills, the superintendent cannot confidently conclude that the schools must adopt the BTB program—or for that matter any reading program—in order to achieve the district's goal.

The recommendation depends on the additional unsubstantiated assumption that adopting BTB would by itself improve students' reading skills to the desired extent. Absent evidence that this is the case, it is equally possible that adopting the program would not suffice by itself. Students must be sufficiently attentive and motivated, and teachers must be sufficiently competent; otherwise, the program will not be effective. In short, unless the superintendent can show that the program will be effectively implemented and received, I cannot accept the recommendation.

Relying on a Potentially Unrepresentative Statistical Sample

A GRE Argument might cite statistical evidence from a study, survey, or poll involving a "sample" group or population, then draw a conclusion about a larger group or population that the sample supposedly represents. But in order for a statistical sample to reliably represent a larger population, the sample must meet two requirements:

1. The sample must be *significant in size* (number), as a portion of the overall population.

2. The sample must be *representative* of the overall population in terms of relevant characteristics.

GRE Arguments that cite statistics from studies, surveys, and polls often fail to establish either of these two requirements. Of course this failure is by design of the test makers, who are inviting you to call into question the reliability of the evidence.

Here's an argument that relies on two potentially unrepresentative sample groups: (1) new graduates from a certain state's undergraduate programs and (2) new graduates from the state's graduate-level programs. The response that follows it provides a brief but effective critique.

Argument:

The following was part of an article appearing in a national magazine:

"Our nation's new college graduates will have better success obtaining jobs if they do not pursue advanced degrees after graduation. After all, more than 90 percent of State X's undergraduate students are employed full-time within one year after they graduate, while less than half of State X's graduate-level students find employment within one year after receiving their graduate degrees."

Response:

The argument fails to consider that State X's new graduates might not be representative of the nation's as a whole, especially if the former group constitutes only a small percentage of the latter group. If it turns out, for example, that State X's undergraduate students are less motivated than the nation's average college student to pursue graduate-level study, then the argument's recommendation for all undergraduate students would be unwarranted.

Relying on a Potentially Unreliable Survey or Poll

As you just learned, a GRE Argument might draw some conclusion involving a group based on statistical data about an *insufficient* or *unrepresentative* sample. However, this is not the only potential problem with statistical data. The process of collecting the data (i.e., the methodology) might be flawed in a way that calls into question the *quality* of the data, rendering the data "tainted" and therefore unreliable for the purpose of drawing any conclusions. In order for survey or poll results to be reliable in quality they must meet two requirements:

1. The survey or poll responses must be *credible* (truthful and accurate). If respondents have reason to provide incomplete or false responses, the results are tainted and therefore unreliable.

2. The method of collecting the data must be *unbiased*. If responses are not mandatory, or if the survey's form predisposes subjects to respond in certain ways, then the results are tainted and therefore unreliable.

The following Argument relies on a survey that poses both problems, and the response addresses both in a single paragraph.

Argument:

> The following appeared in a memo from the director of human resources at Webco:
>
> "Among Webco employees participating in our department's most recent survey, about half indicated that they are happy with our current four-day work week. These survey results show that the most effective way to improve overall productivity at Webco is to allow each employee to choose for himself or herself either a four-day or five-day work week."

Response:

> The survey methodology might be problematic in two respects. First, we are not informed whether the survey required that respondents choose their work-week preference between alternatives. If it did, then the results might distort the preferences of the respondents, who might very well prefer a work-schedule choice not provided for in the survey. Secondly, we are not informed whether survey responses were anonymous, or even confidential. If they were not, then respondents might have provided responses that they believed their superiors would approve of, regardless of whether the responses were truthful. In either event, the survey results would be unreliable for the purpose of drawing any conclusions about Webco employee preferences, let alone about how to improve overall productivity at Webco.

Assuming That All Things Remain Unchanged over Time

A GRE Argument might rely on evidence collected in the past to formulate some conclusion or recommendation concerning the present or future. Similarly, an argument might rely on evidence about present conditions to make a prediction or recommendation for the future. But unless the argument provides clear evidence that key circumstances have remained, or will remain, unchanged over the relevant time period (by the way, it won't), the argument is vulnerable to criticism.

Here's an argument that provides evidence about the past to draw a conclusion about the present as well as the future, followed by a three-sentence paragraph that addresses the problem.

Argument:

The following appeared in a political campaign advertisement:

"Residents of this state should vote to elect Kravitz as state governor in the upcoming election. During Kravitz's final term as a state senator, she was a member of special legislative committee that explored ways the state can reduce its escalating rate of violent crime. Elect Kravitz for governor, and our cities' streets will be safer than ever."

Response:

Assuming that at one time Kravitz was genuinely committed to fighting violent crime, the ad unfairly infers a similar commitment on Kravitz's part today and in the future while Kravitz serves as governor. Kravitz might hold entirely different views today, especially if her participation as a member of the committee occurred some time ago. Lacking better evidence that as governor Kravitz would continue to make crime-fighting a high priority, the ad cannot persuade me to vote for Kravitz based on her committee membership

DOs and DON'Ts for the Argument Writing Task

Here's a list of DOs and DON'Ts that recap what you've learned here in Part 1 about composing your Argument essay. To reinforce the ideas in this list, refer back to it from time to time as you read the sample essays in Part 3.

DON'T merely restate or rehash the stated Argument. The only way to score points is to tell the reader what's wrong with the argument, so keep your introductory remarks brief. (Remember: My essays in Part 3 contain longer introductions for the purpose of recapitulating the Argument—for *your* reference.)

DO analyze the Argument with an eye for uncovering at least three or four flaws in the author's line of reasoning and use of evidence. Remember: Unless you've recognized and discussed at least three major flaws, you've missed something significant—and you won't score a 5 or 6.

DO support each point of your critique with sound reasons and/or relevant examples.

DON'T stray from the Argument at hand. Your personal opinions about the issue discussed in the Argument are irrelevant to the Argument writing task.

DO discuss what is required to make the Argument more persuasive and/or what would help you better evaluate it—if you have time. The last paragraph of your essay is a good place to accomplish this task.

DO try to make time for an introductory and a concluding paragraph, even though niether is required for a high score. Effective "bookends" lend cohesiveness to your essay and help the reader anticipate and review your essay's main points.

DON'T introduce any new flaws in a concluding paragraph. Simply reiterate the main points of your critique and possibly indicate what would be required to make the Argument more convincing or what additional information would help you evaluate it.

DO organize your points of critique in a logical order, and use transition words and phrases to connect the various points of your critique. The sequence in which the flaws appear in the Argument itself is often as good a sequence as any for the points of your critique.

DOs and DON'Ts for Writing Style

According to ETS officials, GRE readers are instructed to place less weight on writing style and mechanics than on content and organization. But this doesn't mean that your writing style won't influence the reader or affect your Analytical Writing score. You can bet that it will! To ensure a high score, your writing should be:

- Articulate and precise (through the use of good diction and clear expression)

- Correct in grammar, mechanics, and usage (conforming to the requirements of standard written English)

- Persuasive in style (using rhetorical devices effectively)

- Varied in sentence length and structure (to add interest and variety as well as to demonstrate maturity and sophistication in writing style)

All of this is easier said than done, of course. Although there's only so much you can do in a few weeks or even a few months to improve your writing, here are some specific style-related guidelines that you can implement right away in your GRE essays.

DO maintain a somewhat formal tone; avoid slang and colloquialisms. Otherwise, instead of hitting a "home run" with your essay, you'll be "out of luck" with the GRE readers, and you'll have to "snake" your way in to a "bottom-barrel" graduate program. Get the idea?

DON'T try to make your point with humor or sarcasm. Not that the GRE readers don't have a sense of humor; it's just that they leave it at the door when they go to work for ETS.

DON'T overuse Latin and other non-English terms. The occasional use of Latin terms and acronyms—such as *per se, i.e.,* and *e.g.*—is perfectly acceptable. Non-English words used commonly in academic writing—such as *vis-à-vis* and *caveat*—are also acceptable. Just don't overdo it. (The GRE word processor won't allow you to include diacritical marks, like the one above the "a" in *"vis-à-vis."* But don't worry about it; again, the GRE readers understand the exam's constraints.)

DON'T try too hard to impress the readers with your vocabulary. By all means, try to demonstrate a strong vocabulary. (Notice the words "imprudent," "unfettered," and "pandemic" in my sample Issue essay on page 10). Just don't overdo it; and avoid technical terminology that only specialists and scholars in a specific field can understand.

DO refer to yourself, at your option. Self-references—singular as well as plural—are perfectly acceptable, though optional. Just be consistent.

DO be sure your references to the source of the statement or argument are appropriate. If no specific source is provided, try using "speaker" or "statement" in your Issue essay and "author" or "argument" in your Argument essay.

The Analytical Writing Computer Interface

As you'll notice in the screen shot below, the Analytical Writing computer interface has a lot in common with the interface for the multiple-choice sections of the exam.

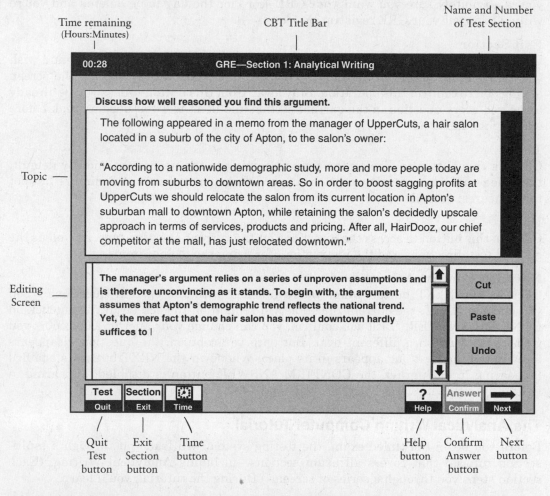

Time remaining (Hours:Minutes)

CBT Title Bar

Name and Number of Test Section

Topic

Editing Screen

Quit Test button

Exit Section button

Time button

Help button

Confirm Answer button

Next button

As the above figure shows, the essay prompt—either the Issue or Argument topic—appears at the top of the screen, and your essay response appears below it as you type. (The editing screen in the figure shows the first of several lines of the response.)

The Toolbar

A series of six buttons appears in a toolbar across the bottom of the computer screen at all times during all test sections. (You cannot hide the toolbar.) Here is a description of each button's function:

Quit Test

Click on this button to stop the test and cancel your scores for the *entire* test. (Partial score cancelation is not allowed in any event.) If you click here, a dialog box will appear on the screen that asks you to confirm this operation. Stay away from this button unless you're absolutely sure you want your GRE score for the day to be deleted and you're willing to forfeit your GRE registration fee.

Exit Section

Click on this button if you finish the section before the allotted time expires and wish to proceed immediately to the next section. A dialog box will appear on the screen asking you to confirm this operation. Stay away from this button unless you've already answered every question in the current section and don't feel you need a break before starting the next one.

Time

Click on this button to display the time remaining to the nearest second. By default, the time remaining is displayed (in the upper-left corner) in hours and minutes but not to the nearest second.

Help

Click on this button to access the directions for the current question type, as well as the general test directions and the instructions for using the toolbar items.

Next and Confirm Answer

Click on the NEXT button when you're finished with the current question. When you click on NEXT, the current question will remain on the screen until you click on CONFIRM ANSWER. Until you confirm, you can change your answer as often as you wish by clicking on a different oval. But once you confirm, the question disappears forever and the next one appears in its place. Whenever the NEXT button is enabled (appearing in dark gray), the CONFIRM ANSWER button is disabled (appearing in light gray), and vice versa.

The Analytical Writing Computer Tutorial

Before you begin the timed exam, the testing system will lead you through a multi-section tutorial that covers all exam sections—including Analytical Writing. (Each section steps you through a series of screens.) During the tutorial, you'll learn:

- How to use the mouse

- How to scroll the screen display up and down

- How to use the toolbar buttons (at the bottom of the screen)

- How to use the built-in word processor

You won't have the option of skipping any section or any screen, and the system will require you to demonstrate competence in using the various computerized features—

including the system's word processor—before you can begin the actual test. You can also practice using the word processor, at your option, before beginning the timed test.

Features and Limitations of the Word Processor

Built into the computerized testing system is a bare-bones word processor. Let's look at its features and limitations.

Navigation and Editing—Available Keyboard Commands

Here are the navigational and editing keys available in the test's built-in word processor:

Backspace	removes the character to the left of the cursor
Delete	removes the character to the right of the cursor
Home	moves the cursor to the beginning of the line
End	moves the cursor to the end of the line
Arrow Keys	move the cursor up, down, left, or right
Enter	inserts a paragraph break (starts a new line)
Page Up	moves the cursor up one page (screen)
Page Down	moves the cursor down one page (screen)

Common Keyboard Commands Not Available

Certain often-used features of standard word-processing programs are not available in the GRE word processor. For example, no keyboard commands are available for:

TAB—disabled (does not function)
Beginning/end of paragraph (not available)
Beginning/end of document (not available)

Mouse-driven Editing Functions

Cut, Paste, and Undo: In addition to editing keys, the GRE word processor includes mouse-driven CUT (but not "copy"), PASTE, and UNDO. To cut text, select the text you wish to cut with your mouse. To paste, position the mouse pointer at the desired insertion spot, then click your mouse. Drag-and-drop cut-and-paste is not available. Also, the GRE word processor stores only your most recent cut, paste, or undo.

The vertical scroll bar: Once you key in ten lines or so, you'll have to scroll up and down to view your entire response.

Spell checking, fonts, attributes, hyphenation, and special characters: The GRE word processor does not include a spell checker, nor does it allow you to choose type-face or point size. Neither manual nor automatic hyphenation is available. Attributes such as bold, italics, and underlining are not available, nor are special characters that do not appear on a standard computer keyboard.

> **NOTE:** As for words you would otherwise italicize or underline (such as titles or certain non-English words), it's okay to leave them as is. To signify an em-dash (—), use either two hyphens (--) or one hyphen with a space both before and after it (-).

Scoring, Score Reporting, and Score Evaluation

Shortly after the exam, both of your essays will be read by qualified ETS "readers," and one single Analytical Writing score (not two separate scores) on a scale from 0 to 6 will be awarded and reported to you and to the schools to which you have directed your score report. In this section I'll explain further this scoring, reporting, and score evaluation process.

> **NOTE:** GRE readers are college and university faculty members experienced in teaching writing and critical thinking skills. ETS trains all readers specifically how to evaluate and grade GRE essays.

How Your Two GRE Essays Are Scored

Within one week after the test, your two essays will be read and graded. Two readers will read and score your Issue essay, and two *other* readers will read and score your Argument essay. Each reader evaluates your writing independently of the other readers, and no reader is informed of the others' scores.

Each reader will employ a "holistic" grading method in which he or she will assign a single score from 0 to 6 (0, 1, 2, 3, 4, 5, or 6) based on the overall quality of your writing. Your final Analytical Writing score is the average of the four readers' grades (in half-point intervals). Average scores falling midway between half-point intervals are rounded up. If scores for an essay differ from each other by more than one point, a third very experienced reader will read the essay and determine its final score.

Just as with the multiple-choice sections, you'll also receive a percentile rank, from 0–99 percent. A percentile rank of 60 percent, for example, indicates that you scored higher than 60 percent of all other test takers. Percentile ranks reflect your performance relative to the entire GRE test-taking population, not just those test takers responding to the same essay topics as you.

The Official Scoring Criteria for GRE Essays

GRE readers follow the official scoring criteria provided in the printed GRE Bulletin and at the official GRE Web site (www.gre.org). Here are the essential requirements for top-scoring ("6") essays (notice that you can attain a top score of 6 even if your essays contain minor errors in grammar, word usage, spelling, and punctuation):

Present Your Perspective on an Issue—
Requirements for a Score of 6 (Outstanding)

- The essay develops a position on the issue through the use of incisive reasons and persuasive examples.

- The essay's ideas are conveyed clearly and articulately.

- The essay maintains proper focus on the issue and is well organized.

- The essay demonstrates proficiency, fluency, and maturity in its use of sentence structure, vocabulary, and idiom.

- The essay demonstrates an excellent command of the elements of Standard Written English, including grammar, word usage, spelling, and punctuation—but it may contain minor flaws in these areas.

Analyze an Argument—Requirements for a Score of 6 (Outstanding)

- The essay identifies the key features of the argument and analyzes each one in a thoughtful manner.

- The essay supports each point of critique with insightful reasons and examples.

- The essay develops its ideas in a clear, organized manner, with appropriate transitions to help connect ideas together.

- The essay demonstrates proficiency, fluency, and maturity in its use of sentence structure, vocabulary, and idiom.

- The essay demonstrates an excellent command of the elements of Standard Written English, including grammar, word usage, spelling, and punctuation—but it may contain minor flaws in these areas.

The criteria for lower scores are based on the ones above; the only difference is that the standard for quality decreases for successively lower scores. Here is how the testing service characterizes the quality of essays at different score levels:

- Score of 6: Outstanding
- Score of 5: Strong
- Score of 4: Adequate
- Score of 3: Limited
- Score of 2: Seriously Flawed
- Score of 1: Fundamentally Deficient

> **NOTE:** An essay that merely copies the stated topic or is indecipherable, completely off topic, or composed in a non-English language will receive a score of 0 (zero).

Reporting of Scores to Test Takers and to the Schools

Within two weeks after testing, ETS will provide you with an official score report that will include your Analytical Writing score. At the same time, ETS will provide a score report to each school that you have designated to receive your score report. Score reports will also include the essay responses themselves.

> **NOTE:** For futher information on score reporting, see the official GRE Web site (www.gre.org).

How the Schools Use GRE Analytical Writing Scores

Each graduate department determines for itself how much weight to place on writing scores relative to other admission criteria (GRE General Test scores, GRE Subject Test scores, GPA, personal statements, recommendation letters, etc.). An admissions committee might use writing scores as a preliminary screen for all applicants; or it might use writing scores to decide between two equally qualified candidates. Contact the individual academic departments for their particular policies.

Evaluating Your Practice Essays

Evaluating Your Issue Essay

In this section, four different essay responses have been provided for the first Issue statement on page 4. These responses will help you understand the official scoring criteria for the Issue writing task, as well as help you to evaluate and score your own practice essays.

> "Leisure time has become an increasingly rare commodity, largely because technology has failed to achieve its goal of improving our efficiency as we go about our daily lives."

The essays range from "outstanding" (worthy of a top score of 6) to "limited" (deserving a score of only 3). Each one is accompanied by commentary explaining why the essay merits its particular score.

> **NOTE:** The following sample essays include many grammatical, word usage, and mechanical errors often committed by GRE test takers.

Essay No. 1 (Score of 6: Outstanding)

Today's world is teeming with time-saving technologies. Computers and internet connections are becoming faster by the day, and there are more gizmos to do our tasks for us more quickly that ever before. Yet Americans constantly complain that they have no time for leisure activities. What explains this paradox? I will argue that we lack free time not because technology has failed to achieve its goal of improving efficiency, but rather, because (1) technology has created more non-leisure pursuits and (2) Americans are subject to a basic ethical drive to do and to have "More."

As a society, most of us get caught up in a schedule of going to work early, coming home late, then taking care of mundane details before finally falling into bed, only to repeat the same routine the next day. Both spouses/partners typically work full-time, which leaves only weekends to take care of household chores. What little free time people do have they spend on their PCs or PDAs or in front of the TV, but this is not really "leisure." You can wile away hours in front of YouTube, Twitter, or a TV, and not come away feeling relaxed because you've spent that entire time keeping up with the constant flash of images, storing information about people, events, and products and other aspects of the media, and all without realizing it. So our so-called "leisurely" pursuits today are not true leisure.

Moreover, technology has created more such pursuits with which the public can easily engage itself. In addition to televisions, we now have blackberries, iPods, cell phones and the Web to occupy our time (to name just a few), all within easy access to the average American. Meanwhile, activities that are traditionally considered relaxing are becoming more expensive and less accessible. For example, for most Americans $100 massages are an unaffordable luxury, and as cities grow larger, nature walks are becoming harder to find. It's easier to just sit down in front of the TV than it is to take the time out to do something special. So people fill their time with mediated technologies and get so caught up in online social networking or their favorite shows that they don't take the time to do things they've been "meaning to do".

This whirlwind of activity is a product of another reason why our society pines for more leisure time. This country was founded on the conservative Protestant ethic that dictates people should work hard now so they may reap the rewards later. While this ethic is essential for effective productivity, it has become detrimental to the American psyche. People push themselves to become more efficient so they can accomplish more, but they end up adding more goals so that in effect the job never gets done. And they also want to buy more things to achieve higher social status, so instead of saving for early retirement, they end up having to work just as long to pay off their debts. Furthermore, people are so busy pushing themselves daily with the vague promise of retirement someday that they forget to stop and enjoy life in the meantime. It's a vicious cycle of foregoing daily enjoyments for the false promise of later rewards.

So while technology has provided the means for greater efficiency, it has also given us more things to deal with and accomplish. As a result, we find ourselves running around endlessly, sometimes forgetting what it is we are running after. In the end, the key to more leisure time is not more or less technology, but a refusal to let technology run our lives.

Commentary

This outstanding essay provides an insightful analysis of the issue at hand, although it deserves what might be termed a "weak 6" (rather than a "strong 6").

The opening paragraph is particularly effective, providing a clear statement of premise (the writer's position or perspective on the issue). In paragraph 2 the writer first establishes that our leisure time is in fact diminishing, and then provides the first of three reasons for this phenomenon. (Paragraphs 3 and 4 provide two more reasons.) The supporting examples given for each reason are ample and relevant. While the reasons and examples given in paragraphs 2 and 3 are not especially insightful, paragraph 4 makes up for it with highly incisive discussion, contributing greatly to the essay's score of 6.

The discussion throughout the three middle paragraphs is not entirely without flaws. Notably, the three reasons (see above) could have been more clearly identified and delineated, and paragraph 2 rambles a bit. Also, the writer should have made more explicit the important point that technology is not the culprit for our diminishing leisure time.

The essay demonstrates a mature, sophisticated writing style virtually free of grammatical, syntax, and language problems. (In the final paragraph the writer exhibits a particularly distinctive, and effective, style and voice.) These strengths contribute greatly to elevating this essay from scoring a 5 to scoring a 6 category.

Essay No. 2 (Score of 5: Strong)

I beg to differ with the speaker's contention which seems to imply that the goal of technology is not only to increase efficiency but also our leisure time. Also interwoven in the speaker's statement is the fallacious assumption that they are connected. So we have three points which need to be considered—technological advances, efficiency & leisure—and how they are related.

The aim of technological advance (progress in applied sciences), as far as I know, is to apply scientific data and discoveries toward practical and beneficial use. For instance we've used new knowledge of Particle Physics in diagnosing medical conditions—eg. through Magneto Resonance Imagery—and also in treatment—eg., radiotherapy. Did this technological advance and the motivation behind it really have anything to do with efficiency? Only in that efficiency might be a by-product of a certain technology , but I do not think it was the primary objective.

Of course the by-product of certain new technologies might be "efficiency" but to what extent? Computers are typically cited as a perfect example. Yes they do help us get more work done without expending as much energy. But we need to factor in the time and energy required in learning how to efficiently operate one, and then expended in keeping our learning up to date with the rapid technological advances in the same. (A person with the energy to compile and critically analyze the data constructively to formulate the answer to that one will definitely need an advanced computer!) So its possible that even computers don't in the end improve the efficiency of our daily lives, in net terms.

And then, there is the question of "leisure". Personally I think it is a matter of choice and not time saving ,technologically advanced, efficient tools. The speaker seems to assume that the time "saved" (we are still waiting for the verdict on that one) will be spent towards leisure. I do not see the connection. Ultimately the motivation of a person, personality & lifestyle choices and circumstances determine how the time that is saved is used. It could be towards leisure in one person's case; in another's towards putting in more hours to make more money to make ends meet or to buy that new car which he/she absolutely must have.

In the end I think there is no clear connection between the three points under consideration. Hence in the absence of the relationship between technology, efficiency & leisure claimed by the speaker I disagree on whole.

Commentary

This essay provides an insightful and organized analysis of the issue's complexities, but is flawed due to problems of syntax, informal expressions, and a weak recapitulation of the essay's premise or conclusion.

The initial paragraph, which anticipates a three-pronged critique, is followed by three body paragraphs addressing each point in turn. This demonstrates a thoughtful approach to the issue and strong organizational skills. The result is a balanced, cohesive, and persuasive essay overall. The reasons and examples in support of each critique are relevant and incisive, and the writer acknowledges differing perspectives on this issue. These features help distinguish this essay from lower-scoring ones. However, the two parenthetical comments (in paragraphs 3 and 4) are inappropriately informal asides that contribute to keeping this essay from scoring a 6.

Also contributing to the essay's less-than-optimal score is the final paragraph, which appears to be an afterthought—a hurried attempt to summarize the essay's arguments. A more effective closing paragraph would provide a clearer statement of premise (thesis or conclusion) and would more clearly recapitulate the writer's line of reasoning.

While the writer demonstrates good overall control of language and written expression, several problems in these areas contribute to keeping this otherwise effectively argued essay from scoring a 6. The problems vary, from redundancy ("apply... toward use") to use of vernacular ("we are still waiting for the verdict on that one") to loose syntax ("A person with the energy to compile and critically analyze the data constructively to formulate the answer to that one will definitely need an advanced computer!"). (There are other instances of syntax problems as well.) The essay's occasional errors in spelling and punctuation did not adversely affect its score.

Essay No. 3 (Score of 4: Adequate)

Leisure time is becoming an increasingly rare commodity in our society. However, this is not due to the failure of technology to improve our efficiency in our daily lives. In fact, improvements in technology have had a positive impact in our daily lives. We live in a consumerist savvy society that thrives on immediate gratification. Our lives depend on the convenience of technology in order that we may continue our busy lifestyles and accomplish simple everyday tasks faster and more efficiently.

Technology is improving the efficiency of our home, school, and work environments everyday. Because of technological improvements, hospitals, schools, libraries, businesses, etc. can look up information and records more efficiently. It is not always necessary to walk down a flood of charts and files to look up basic information. Computer software, such as Excel and Quicken allow us to budget and sort information more quickly and effectively. We do not have to pull out a calculator. The machines do it for us!

Since the invention of the internet, people have been able to accomplish time consuming tasks in short amounts of time. It is no longer necessary to write out a letter and wait for the postman to pick up your mail. Now you can type up a letter and send it instantaneously into cyberspace. We are able to make hotel reservations, book flights, process financial aid applications, and do our Christmas shopping in a matter of minutes. It is no longer necessary to go into the travel agency, shopping mall, or wait on hold for fifteen minutes to accomplish a simple task.

However, with all of these new technological conveniences, how come we find ourselves with even less leisure time? Because it does not matter how many fax machines, cell phones, drive thru windows, and ATM Machines we invent. We will always find some way to use to fill up our leisure time. Unfortunately, it is often through technology that we accomplish this. Just take a look at the stockbroker who takes his cell phone to his son's graduation ceremony. Or the couple that spends an afternoon emailing each other, when they could be out chatting during a nice leisurely hike or bike ride. Technology is not to blame for our lack of leisure time. Technology has made our lives more efficient. It is because of our unfortunate skewing of priorities that technology is not enough to provide us with more leisure time.

Commentary

This response is generally competent; it responds to the topic, recognizes some complexity about the issue, and conveys its ideas clearly and effectively (for the most part). The score of 4 is mainly a reflection of certain substantive and structural problems.

Paragraph 1 is problematic in several respects. First, the writer simply accepts, without providing reasons or examples, that our leisure time is diminishing. Second, the contention that "[w]e live in a consumerist time savvy society that thrives on immediate gratification" does not address the issue at hand, and in any event is not developed or supported in the essay. Thirdly, the paragraph is confusing and rambling overall, suggesting that the writer lacks a clear idea about the direction the essay will take—an organization problem that helps keep this essay from scoring a 5 or 6.

Paragraphs 2 and 3 provide numerous examples of the ways in which technology has enhanced the efficiency of our daily lives. While the examples provide adequate support for this point, they are not especially incisive. It is the writer's undue attention, in these two paragraphs, to a secondary point at the expense of developing the main premise that is primarily responsible for keeping this essay from scoring a 5. The essay fails to adequately develop that premise, provided in paragraph 4—that "our unfortunate skewing of priorities," not technology, is responsible for our diminishing leisure time.

The writer handles language and syntax competently. The essay does contain a few minor language problems, varying from improper references ("institutions can look up...") to improper word usage ("to budget ... information") to questionable idioms ("how come we find out..."). However, these minor and infrequent problems carry little adverse impact on the essay's overall score.

Essay No. 4 (Score of 3: Limited)

Picture this, a family sitting down for breakfast. The father at the head of the table asking everyone what their agenda is for the day. Suddenly he looks at his watch, then with a frantic look on his face, he lets out a bellowing roar of I'm late. Every one looks at each other and scrambles to get thier belongings for the day. Five minutes later everyone meets at the family vehicle and files in. The car speeds away and everyone is off to their busy filled day.

you would think that with today's technology, the family would be able to sit down together and enjoy breakfast without being rushed, but in todays society this is not the case. It seems like the more we are advanced in technology the more we pack into our schedultes eliminating free time. We are trained as children to work as hard as we can, to advance ourseveles in careers or growth and any relaxation could be viewed as laziness by out parents or peers.

Though we do have the technology which could enable us to live stress free lives, we choose to use it to our benefit, but instead of taking advantage of our newly created "spare time", we bog ourselves with more work. Let's take the father of this family who is a well known executive at a prominant accounting firm. He is the man that solves all the problems and has all the answers for his company. During his lunch hour he sits and calculates numbers instead of enjoying himslef and relaxing. "No time for rest" is his motto. When his boss says we're going to give you a half day today, he decides to spend it on the golf course discussin work. He has no time for his family and always seems to be found in his office when at home. This is a very unhealthy way of live and could be damaging to the raising of his children.

The children pick up patterns at a very young age. Grwoing up we are trained by our parents subcounciously. These children from a very young age are taught that leisure time is wrong. At a young age that children are subjected to little league and ballet, as a detourant of cutting into their parents time. In these activities childrn are pushed to their fullest potential, allowing them to accompish the honor roll, class president, or even valedictorian for there graduating class. It is great that the children have such drive, but without relaxation or leisure time it oculd lead to psychological problems or mental breakdowns.

Even though technology has created free or leisure time, we as individuals need to learn to take advantage of it. We have been trained at a very young age always to be busy. When were not working on deadline or have meeting to be at we are often wondering what do we do with ourselves. The fact of the matter is that we do have the technology to make our lives a lot easier, we just need to take advantage of it, if we don't we could end up seriously injured physically, or even more detrminetal psychologically.

Commentary

This essay, which contains 526 words, shows that composing a lengthy essay is not the key to a high score. Although the essay exhibits some competence, it suffers from limited analysis, lack of cohesiveness, and frequent problems in written expression.

Throughout the essay, the writer provides anecdotal support for the claim that as a society we do indeed lack leisure time and that the reason for this phenomenon has to do with how we choose to use our time. However, the writer fails to develop, or even articulate, a position on the extent to which technology is to blame. The writer digresses from the issue, focusing in a rambling fashion on our penchant for busyness and its potential health problems. It is the essay's improper focus and lack of clear structure that are primarily responsible for the essay's limited score of 3.

Frequent grammatical errors and other problems in expression also contribute to keeping this essay out of a higher score category. Examples of grammatical errors include the following:

- Error in choice of relative pronoun ("everyone looks at each other")

- Mixed case ("The children pick up patterns at a very young age. Growing up we are trained...")

- Misplaced modifying words and phrases ("trained by our parents subconsciously" and "These children from a very early age are taught")

- Vague pronoun references ("without relaxation or leisure time it could lead to...")

Here are some examples of other problems in expression:

- Awkward phrases ("It seems like the more we are advanced in technology")

- Awkward use of the passive voice ("seems to be found in his office")

- Lack of sentence sense (first sentence of the third paragraph: "Though we do have the technology...")

- Improper word choice ("Though we do have the technology which could")

- Improper idiom ("accomplish the honor roll...")

Punctuation and spelling errors, while frequent, do not obscure the intended meaning and hence do not contribute to keeping this essay out of a higher score category.

Evaluating Your Argument Essay

In this section, four different essay responses have been provided for the first Argument statement on page 19 about United Motors trucks. These responses will help you understand the official scoring criteria for the Argument writing task, as well as help you to evaluate and score your own practice essays.

The following appeared in an advertisement for United Motors trucks:

"Last year the local television-news program In Focus reported in their annual car-and-truck safety survey that over the course of the last ten years United Motors vehicles were involved in at least 30 percent fewer fatal accidents to drivers than vehicles built by any other single manufacturer. Now United is developing a one-of-a-kind computerized crash warning system for all its trucks. Clearly, anyone concerned with safety who is in the market for a new truck this year should buy a United Motors truck."

The essays range from "outstanding" (worthy of a top score of 6) to "limited" (deserving a score of only 3). Each one is accompanied by commentary explaining why the essay merits its particular score.

> **NOTE:** The following sample essays include many grammatical, word usage, and mechanical errors often committed by GRE test takers.

Essay No. 1 (Score of 6: Outstanding)

A person viewing this ad might at first glance be convinced that a safety-minded truck buyer should choose a new United Motors truck over another brand. Why? United Motors has an ostensibly superior safety record over the past 10 years, and it seems committed to further improving that record. However, if one examines the evidence in the ad closer, one sees that the ad's success turns on consumers blindly accepting numerous assumptions about the statistics and other facts in the ad. I will discuss each one in turn below.

First I turn to the 30% statistic given in the ad. This statistic does not differentiate trucks from cars, yet we are asked to assume that this safety statustic is accurate for trucks in particular. It is also presumed that the 10-year safety record applies to the company's new line of trucks. But is this necessarily so? The ad offers no proof or evidence to back up this implicit claim. An astute consumer would require more information about the safety of United trucks (not cars) compared to other recently manufactured trucks. (However, there might not be enough data yet about this year's models.) Finally, the statistic cannot be relied upon as accurate unless we know that the survey was fair and objective. (What if United is a sponsor of In Focus? Could we trust the truthfulness of accuracy of the statistics? No!)

These are not the only reasons why the statistic in the ad inadequately supports the argument that United has the safest new trucks. The statistic really says nothing explicit about why this is the case. Is it really because United trucks are safer? Or is it becase United truck drivers are better drivers, or because of some other reason? In other words, United must prove that the safety of its trucks is actually the reason why they are in fewer accidents in order for the statistic to be valid to the intelligent consumer deciding which new truck to buy.

Besides the assumptions about the statistic in the ad, another assumption involves the crash warning system. The system is still in development, but the ad tries to convince us to buy a new United truck now based on this evidence, which is illogical. Once United's trucks have the system and it can be proven that the system is effective in improving safety, then I might be swayed toward buying a United truck instead of another brand—but not until then.

In sum, in light of all of the assumptions listed above needed for the argument to "have teeth" but missing from the ad, no consumer should buy a United truck based soley on this ad's false appeal to safety. Consumers should not be hoodwinked by an ad like this one that leaves out important information about how an impressive statistic is arrived at, or that attempts to entice the consumer based on impressive but unproven R&D (especiaaly when today's United Motors truck buyers are the ones who actually paying for the R&D but don't receive the benefits from it.)

Commentary

This outstanding essay exhibits very strong analytical and organizational skills, as well as a firm grasp of language, grammar, and syntax. Ultimately it is the essay's incisive, comprehensive, and well-organized analysis—not its mechanical aspects (grammar, syntax, diction)—that places it squarely in the highest score category.

The essay commences with an introductory paragraph that is rhetorically effective, and then proceeds to identify nearly all of the major problems with the argument. In a logical sequence, each point is connected with the next by helpful transitions. In the three middle paragraphs, the writer challenges the following assumptions underlying the argument:

- The statistical datum is an accurate gauge of the comparative safety level of United Motors trucks (rather than vehicles generally).

- The statistical datum, which involves prior years, is an accurate reflection of current conditions.

- The survey results are unbiased.

- The past fatal-accident record of United Motors trucks is due to the truck's safety feature (rather than to some other factor).

- The new crash-warning system is included in current United Motors trucks and serves its intended purpose.

The only major flaw that this essay neglects to identify and discuss is that the statistic fails to account for nonfatal accidents. However, this single oversight is far outweighed by what is otherwise a comprehensive critique.

The final paragraph serves as a stylistic and rhetorically effective recap. (However, the essay's closing parenthetical remark about R&D is unnecessary and appears to be an afterthought.)

Admittedly, the essay does suffer from various problems in grammar and expression. These problems vary widely:

- Improper idiom ("differentiate trucks from cars")

- Several instances of redundancy ("The ad offers no proof or evidence," "reasons why," and "because of some other reason")

- Faulty parallelism ("deciding between a United truck and another brand" and "safety of United trucks...compared to other trucks")

- Loose syntax ("in light of all of the assumptions listed above needed for the argument to "have teeth" but missing from the ad...")

However, these flaws are neither major nor frequent enough to warrant lowering the essay's score. GRE readers would also overlook this essay's occasional word omissions and other typos, since they are infrequent and do not interfere with the writer's communication.

Essay No. 2 (Score of 5: Strong)

United Motors truck advertisement is weak and misleading. In their advertisement, the company does not provide sufficient evidence and a strong argument for the sale of this year's United Motors trucks. The reports and evidence that United Motors uses to back up this year's trucks is based on past studies and future developments, rather than current research. Not every consumer would be convinced by United Motor's sales pitch. However, the company does use some language that could easily manipulate and convince some unassuming consumers into buying a new United Motors truck.

United Motors' ad is questionable because the only information they provide regarding the safety of their trucks is based on insufficient past and future evidence. The safety survey they mention was reported by In Focus a year ago and was conducted over a period of ten years. This information does not support the safety aspects of this year's United Motors trucks. United Motors mentions that their vehicles were involved in at least thirty percent few fatal accidents to drivers than vehicles built by any other single manufacturer. However, they fail to mention the fatal accidents to passengers and any statistics for non-fatal automotive accidents involving their brand vehicle.

In their ad, the company describes the one-of-a-kind computerized crash warning system they are developing for all of their trucks. However, this new technology is not currently installed in this year's model, so this is not a valid persuasion for a consumer to buy a United Motors truck this year. Consumers would be more likely to buy a future model that included this computerized crash warning feature. In addition, a crash warning system does not make United Motor's vehicles safer. It simply warns the driver that they are about to crash, which most likely would be apparent to the driver without the computerized system in the first place.

However, the United Motor's advertisement does use some manipulative language that could persuade the unquestioning consumer. In their pitch, they use statistics and a safety-survey to convince the consumer. United Motors also mentions that the survey was reported by a local television- news program, and many people believe what they see or read in the news. The automotive manufacturer also states that it is "clear" that this year's car buyers should purchase a United Motors truck. However, despite the effectiveness this advertisement may have on some car buyers, analytically United Motors ad is weak and unconvincing.

Commentary

This strong response demonstrates solid analytical and organizational abilities, as well as a solid control of language, grammar, and syntax.

In paragraphs 2 and 3 the writer identifies the following problematic aspects of the argument:

- The statistics do not necessarily indicate current safety levels.

- The statistics fail to account for nonfatal accidents.

- The new crash-warning system is not included in current United Motors trucks.

- The new crash-warning system might not actually enhance safety.

The writer's critique of each but the last aspect (which is weak and unpersuasive) is adequate. However, the writer neglects to identify any of the three additional, and important, potential problems with the argument:

- The survey encompassed cars as well as trucks, possibly undermining the statistic's relevance.

- The argument provides no evidence that the survey sample was of sufficient size and representativeness to provide a reliable indication of United Motors vehicles' comparative safety record.

- The stellar past safety record of United Motors trucks might be due to some factor other than their safety.

These omissions contribute significantly to keeping this essay from scoring a 6. Also contributing to this essay's sub-optimal score is the essay's final paragraph, which is not a critique of the argument itself (either its line of reasoning, use of evidence, or internal logic), but rather little more than a claim about consumer gullibility.

The essay contains a scant few diction problems ("not a valid persuasion" and "despite the effectiveness this advertisement may have..."). The essay's otherwise clear expression and complete absence of grammatical, syntax, language, spelling, or punctuation errors help distinguish it from lower-scoring essays.

Essay No. 3 (Score of 4: Adequate)

The argument presented is an advertsiement trying to convince people to buy a United Motors truck based on safety record. There are two "exhibits" used in this argument in evidence of the conlcuion that a safety-concious person should "clearly" buy a United Motors truck instead of another make. The first exhibit is the survey that claims to prove that United Motors "vehicles" were involved in 30% fewer fatal accidents during the last 10 years than other vehicles were. To base the given conclusion on this stitistic is faulty reasoning for three reasons:

1) the survey only covered fatal accidents. It should also cover accidents that caused injuries but no one died. This would also help to prove the safety of one type of truck vs. other trucks.

2) "Vehicles" includes more than trucks. They also includes cars. Therefore, the survey is only vaild to help prove the company's argumnet for trucks, and therefore is not very convincing on this basis. It's also not clear whether "trucks" inlcudes SUVs, crossovers, etc. So the term as used in the ad needs to be further defined.

3) In Focus could be paid by United Motors to conduct a survey in a wya that shows what the company wants consumers to see to help sell their trucks. We cannot trust the numbers. If its a show like 60 Minutes then maybe the survey would be believable. We need more information about this to evaluate the argument. Today there are many

websites for consumers to get free information comparing safety records of vehicles. A simple Google search would be a better way to go than simply believing a potentially biased TV ad.

The second exibit is the crash warning system, which is in current development. This fact is also not convincing to prove the argument. There are two questionable assumptions that underlie this evidence:

1) The system is installed on the trucks available now from truck dealers. (If not, then the conclusion that "anyone in the market for a new truck this year should buy a United track" is invalid. A future feature is irrelevant for consumers this year.

2) We are asked to assume that the warning system will perform its purpose— namely, to help prevent accidents. (The argument contains no evidence to support this assumption.)

In conclusion, the evidence might persuade some consumers to to buy a truck from United because the evidence sounds convincing, like many advertisements. However, upon further analysis the questionable assumptions need to be proven before a more skeptical consumer could accept the argument and justify buying a United truck on the basis of safety. The argument would be strengthened by pointing out other features that make United trucks better than other trucks (price, comfort, cargo space, reliability, etc). The argument would be more logically sound if In Focus provided more facts to help prove the assumptions listed in this essay (above): the crash warning system is available this year and makes United trucks even safer than before.

Commentary

This essay exhibits better-than-average organizational skills but is barely adequate in developing an analytical critique and in overall written expression.

The essay shows that the writer recognizes most problematic aspects of the argument:

- The survey failed to account for nonfatal accidents.
- The survey encompassed data on cars as well as trucks, possibly undermining the survey's relevance.
- The survey is potentially biased.
- The new crash-warning system might not be included in current United Motors trucks.
- The new crash-warning system is not shown to actually enhance safety.

When it comes to developing each point of critique, however, the essay is not especially effective. (The writer's second numbered point of critique is particularly inarticulate.) Although the essay fails to identify certain other problems with the argument (see the foregoing commentary on the higher-scoring essays), these omissions do not contribute significantly to keeping this essay from scoring a 5 or a 6.

The essay's final paragraph is a barely adequate attempt to recapitulate the essay's salient points. More importantly, the additional types of evidence listed in this paragraph as means of strengthening the argument are in fact irrelevant to it. This problem leaves the reader with a distinctively negative impression of the writer's analytical ability and contributes to keeping the essay from scoring a 5.

The essay is well organized into a two-prong analysis with enumerated points of critique under each prong. (The writer's enumeration of these points is a useful device but does not in itself serve to enhance the essay's score.) The essay's clear structure helps keep this essay from receiving a lower score.

The essay demonstrates adequate control of language, grammar, and other aspects of written expression. Nevertheless, the essay suffers from numerous problems in these areas, ranging from awkward strings of prepositional phrases (e.g., "...in this argument in evidence of the conclusion" and "what the company wants consumers to see to help sell their trucks") to vague and unclear pronoun references (e.g., "The second exhibit is the crash warning system, which is in current development. This fact..." and "We cannot trust the numbers. If it's a show like 60 Minutes") to questionable parallelism ("to base the given conclusion on this statistic is faulty reasoning"). Such problems are frequent and bothersome enough to help keep this essay from receiving a higher score. Spelling and punctuation problems, although frequent, do not interfere with meaning and hence do not adversely impact the essay's score.

Essay No. 4 (Score of 3: Limited)

As a prospective buyer this advertisement is not very convincing to me. The thread of reasoning is broken right in the middle. It cites a TV programme's survey based on the past 10yrs and then jumps to talking about the future installment of a crash warning system in their trucks, which by the way is still in it's developmental stage. The survey is based on the past and the argument for convincing the buyer is based on the future. The omission of the present is glaring.

On rereading the advertisement I can conclude that the cars and trucks were under consideration and that the trucks definitely did not get a clean bill of health compared to the cars hence they are trying to develop a computerised system to warn the driver in advance of the crashes their trucks seem to be prone to. Till they work out a way to make them less prone to accidents and not just warn me of the accident I am headed towards , as a buyer I'd just focus on the cars.

It is true that fatal-crash-statistics incline buyers towards the manufacturer but to cement the deal I think the manufacturer needs to focus on their R&D contribution towards making their cars safer than the competitors. How are the United Motors' cars safer ? By what means provided by them are the fatalities reduced? Is it extra air bags? Is it the design? Could it be all time on headlights? The advertiser should be careful to not presume that the buyer has seen the TV programme and is already aware of all this. This is an advertisement where United Motors should focus on reiterating the facts which make their vehicles on sale now a safer bet for the discriminating buyer.

Commentary

This limited essay provides some reasoned analysis of the argument but suffers from bothersome problems with the presentation and development of its critique as well as with grammar, syntax, and diction.

The essay identifies four questionable assumptions underlying the argument:

- A past safety record provides a reliable indication of a current one.
- A future development is relevant to the truck's current safety level.
- A statistic about all vehicles (cars and trucks) applies to trucks only.
- The crash-warning system currently under development will be effective in enhancing safety.

However, none of the points of critique is stated articulately, and none is fully developed. Also, the essay's conclusion (in paragraph 2) about United Motors' truck safety record is unjustified. Moreover, the essay fails to identify certain other key problems with the argument. (See the foregoing commentary on the higher-scoring essays.)

The essay is not well organized; the ideas do not flow logically and naturally from one point to the next. Also, the essay demonstrates less-than-adequate control of expression. Such problems are frequent, ranging from misplaced modifying phrases ("As a prospective buyer this advertisement") to awkward or inappropriate idioms ("jumps to talking about," "a clean bill of health," and "cement the deal") to loose and confusing syntax (the first sentence of paragraph 2). These and other problems of expression contribute to keeping this essay from scoring a 4. Frequent punctuation problems interfere somewhat with meaning and hence further contribute to a score that is lower than it might otherwise be.

Making the Most of the Time You Have to Prepare for the GRE Essays

With hundreds of possible GRE essay questions, it would seem a daunting, if not impossible, task to prepare for all of them. Of course, by reading Part 1 of this book you've already made significant strides toward attaining your optimal Analytical Writing score. But what about Parts 2 and 3 of this book? What about doing research for the Issue essays? What about composing practice essays? In this section are my recommendations for making the best use of the time you have to get ready for GRE Analytical Writing.

Don't Try To Memorize My Sample Essays

If you actually were to memorize all of the sample essays in Parts 2 and 3 of this book and reproduce any two of them on the actual exam, you would well deserve some sort of an award, just for the effort! But don't expect the testing service to reward you with a high GRE score. Be forewarned: GRE readers will have access to this book. What's more, every GRE essay is scrutinized by a sophisticated computer program designed to detect plagiarism. There's nothing wrong with borrowing ideas, reasons, and transitional phrases from my sample essays. Do try, however, to include your own specific examples, especially in your Issue essay; and be sure that in both essays you express your ideas in your own words.

Practice, Practice, and Practice!

You could read this book cover to cover ten times and still perform poorly on the actual exam. There's no substitute for putting yourself to the task under simulated exam conditions, especially under the pressure of time. Compose as many practice essays as you reasonably have time for, responding to the official essay topics. As you do so, keep in mind the following points of advice:

- Always practice under timed conditions. I cannot overemphasize this point. Unless you are put under the pressure of time, you really won't be ready for the test.

- Always use a word processor for your practice tests. Restrict your use of editing functions to the ones provided on the real exam.

- Evaluate your practice essays. Practicing isn't all that helpful if you make the same blunders again and again. After composing an essay, use the official scoring criteria to evaluate it. (Better yet, ask an English professor to evaluate it for you.) Then reflect on your weaknesses, and concentrate on improving in those areas the next time. Don't worry if your essays don't turn out as polished as the samples in Parts 2 and 3 of this book. Concentrate instead on improving your own performance.

Take Notes on a Variety of Issue Topics and Arguments from the Official Pool

Download the complete pool via this book's supplementary Web site (www.west.net/~stewart/grewa), or go directly to the official GRE Web site (www.gre.org) to view them. Select some Issue topics covering diverse themes, as well as several Argument topics. For each one, perform the pre-writing steps you learned about here in Part 1. Limit your time to my recommended limits, and keep your mind as well as your pencil moving!

Take Notes on Essays from Parts 2 and 3 of This Book

For the Issue writing task, study at least some essays from each category in Part 2. For each essay:

- Pick up *thesis* ideas from the first and last paragraphs.

- Focus on how the essay is organized to support its thesis in a clear and convincing way.

- Highlight *transition* and *rhetorical* phrases. (Then, as you compose practice essays, make a special effort to incorporate similar phrases so that they become part of your natural writing style.)

For the Argument writing task, study at least some essays from each category in Part 3. For each essay:

- Identify each type of *reasoning problem* that the essay discusses and that you learned about earlier in Part 1.

- Pay special attention to the type of reasoning flaw featured in the particular category.

- Highlight *transition* phrases, which connect the essay's points of critique. (Make a special effort to incorporate similar phrases into your practice essays.)

- Although you don't need the official essay topics for studying the essays in Parts 2 and 3, ideally you should keep them at hand for this purpose.

Consult Peterson's Other GRE Analytical Writing Book

If your analytical writing skills need significant improvement, further help is available in Peterson's complementary book: *Writing Skills for the GRE/GMAT Tests*. The book places special emphasis on building rhetorical writing skills, organizing your two GRE essays, and avoiding or correcting common language, grammar, and other mechanical problems. To help improve and polish your analytical writing skills, the book also contains a variety of reinforcement exercises for each writing task.

Dig Even Further for Issue Ideas and Examples

Referring to the list of Issue themes earlier in Part 1 (page 5) roll up your sleeves and hit the proverbial stacks for Issue ideas. All forms of media are fair game.

Magazines

The periodicals listed below feature articles that cover common Issue themes:

U.S. News & World Report: notable current events

The Economist: political and economic ideology

Reason: ideology and culture (loads of "cross-discipline" articles)

The New Yorker: arts, humanities, sociology, popular culture

The Futurist: cultural and technological trends

With this list in hand, head to your local library or the magazine's Web site and rifle through some back issues or archived articles. You'll come away brimming over with ideas for Issue essays.

Books

Check out books that survey key people, events, and developments in various areas of human endeavor. Here are two useful ones to start with:

A History of Knowledge: Past, Present, and Future, by Charles van Doren (Birch Lane Press, 1991)

The World's Greatest Ideas: An Encyclopedia of Social Inventions, ed. by Nicholas Alberly, et al (New Society Publications, 2001)

Your notes from college course work

Try dusting off your notes from college survey courses in art, science, history, politics, and sociology. You might surprise yourself with what you'll find that you can recycle into a GRE Issue essay.

The Web

Take advantage of the Internet to brush up on common Issue themes. The supplementary Web site for Peterson's *Writing Skills for the GRE/GMAT Tests* (www.west.net/~stewart/ws) provides links to a variety of Web sites that are useful for this purpose. (Go to the "Expanded Table of Contents," then click "Online Resources for Issue Topics.")

Television and Video

If you're a couch potato, tune in to the History Channel or to your local PBS station for Issue essay ideas. Also consider purchasing (or borrowing from a library) "Biography of the Millennium," a 3-hour A&E (Arts & Entertainment) channel production, which surveys the 100 most influential people of the most recent millennium (1000–1999). Zero in on a few of the featured artists, scientists, political leaders, and philosophers, and you'll be ready with good Issue examples.

Keep Your Perspective

The strategies listed above can be time-consuming. If you have ample time before exam day, then go the extra mile (or kilometer). But what if you don't have time for additional reading and brainstorming? Take heart: The specific reasons and supporting examples you cite in your Issue essay are only one of several scoring criteria, and by no means are they the most important. Your primary concern should be with:

- developing a position that accounts for the statement's complexity and implications, and that acknowledges other viewpoints, and

- expressing that position clearly in a balanced, well-organized essay.

Also keep in mind: During your exam the testing system will present to you two Issue topics, and you can choose for your response the topic with which you are more familiar or comfortable.

PART TWO
Answers to the Real GRE Issue Questions

Part 2 contains sample responses to more than 100 official Issue questions, grouped into various catergories. As you study the responses here in Part 2, keep in mind:

- These essays are *not* responses that actual GRE test takers composed; they are written responses provided by Peterson's. And, they are not "the" answers; after all, there is no one "correct" response to any GRE Issue question.

- These essays were not composed under timed conditions. Moreover, they were fine-tuned to make them better models for you to study. So don't be concerned if your essays aren't as polished, or as lengthy, as these. Be realistic about what *you* can produce in 45 minutes.

- These essays are intended to provide you with substantive, organizational, and style ideas for composing your Issue essay; but they are *not* for copying word-for-word. Be forewarned: GRE readers will be on the lookout for plagiarism.

How to Match Our Essays to the Topics in the Official Pool

Preceding each essay here in Part 2 is a brief description of the topic at hand; this description will help you match the two. For additional help in matching each essay here in Part 2 to its corresponding topic, you can search the official pool's electronic file for our corresponding key phrase. **We've highlighted key phrases in bold.**

Answers That Express Unqualified Agreement or Disagreement with an Issue Statement

In your Issue essay, it's perfectly acceptable to express wholehearted agreement or disagreement with the statement at hand. Be assured that you can limit your discussion to just one side of an issue and still produce an essay worthy of a top score of 6, as the sample essays in this section illustrate.

However, should you decide to take this approach, your essay must be *very* well-written and well-organized, and it must provide compelling reasons and examples to support your position. Otherwise, the reader might suspect that you were reluctant to address possible problems with your viewpoint or to acknowledge other perspectives on the issue.

Issue:
Advancements in a **field of study** and outside experts

I strongly agree with the assertion that significant advances in knowledge require expertise from various fields. The world around us presents a seamless web of physical and anthropogenic forces, which interact in ways that can be understood only in the context of a variety of disciplines. Two examples that aptly illustrate this point involve the fields of cultural anthropology and astronomy.

Consider how a cultural anthropologist's knowledge about an ancient civilization is enhanced not only by the expertise of the archeologist—who unearths the evidence—but ultimately by the expertise of biochemists, geologists, linguists, and even astronomers. By analyzing the hair, nails, blood, and bones of mummified bodies, biochemists and forensic scientists can determine the life expectancy, general wellbeing, and common causes of death of the population. These experts can also ensure the proper preservation of evidence found at the archeological site. A geologist can help identify the source and age of the materials used for tools, weapons, and structures—thereby enabling the anthropologist to extrapolate about the civilization's economy, trades and work habits, lifestyles, extent of travel and mobility, and so forth. Linguists are needed to interpret hieroglyphics and extrapolate from found fragments of writings. And an astronomer can help explain the layout of an ancient city as well as the design, structure and position of monuments, tombs, and temples—since ancients often looked to the stars for guidance in building cities and structures.

An even more striking example of how expertise in diverse fields is needed to advance knowledge involves the area of astronomy and space exploration. Significant advancements in our knowledge of the solar system and the universe require increasingly keen tools for observation and measurement. Telescope technology and the measurement of celestial distances, masses, volumes, and so forth, are the domain of astrophysicists. These advances also require increasingly sophisticated means of exploration. Manned and unmanned exploratory probes are designed by mechanical, electrical, and computer engineers. And to build and enable these technologies requires the acumen and savvy of business leaders, managers, and politicians. Even diplomats might play a role—insofar as major space projects require international cooperative efforts among the world's scientists and governments. And ultimately it is our philosophers whose expertise helps provide meaning to what we learn about our universe.

In sum, no area of intellectual inquiry operates in a vacuum. Because the sciences are inextricably related, to advance our knowledge in any one area we must understand the interplay among them all. Moreover, it is our non-scientists who make possible the science, and who bring meaning to what we learn from it.

Issue:
Are mistakes necessary for **discovery or progress**?

The speaker contends that discovery and progress are made only through mistakes. I strongly agree with this contention, for two reasons. First, it accords with our personal experiences. Secondly, history informs us that on a societal level trial-and-error provides the very foundation for discovery and true progress, in all realms of human endeavor.

To begin with, the contention accords with our everyday experience as humans from early childhood through adulthood. As infants we learn how to walk by falling down again and again. As adolescents we discover our social niche, and develop self-confidence and assertiveness, only by way of the sorts of awkward social encounters that are part-and-parcel of adolescence. Through failed relationships not only do we discover who we are and are not compatible with, we also discover ourselves in the process. And, most of us find the career path that suits us only through trying jobs that don't.

This same principle also applies on a societal level. Consider, for example, how we progress in our scientific knowledge. Our scientific method is essentially a call for progress through trial-and-error. Any new theory must be tested by empirical observation, and must withstand rigorous scientific scrutiny. Moreover, the history of theoretical science is essentially a history of trial-and-error. One modern example involves two contrary theories of physics: wave theory and quantum theory. During the last quarter-century scientists have been struggling to disprove one or the other—or to reconcile them. As it turns out, a new so-called "string" theory shows that the quantum and wave theories are mistakes in the sense that each one is inadequate to explain the behavior of all matter; yet both so-called "mistakes" were necessary for physics to advance, or progress, to this newer theory.

The value of trial-and-error is not limited to the sciences. In government and politics, progress usually comes about through dissension and challenge—that is, when people point out the mistakes of those in power. In fact, without our challenging the mistaken notions of established institutions, political oppression and tyranny would go unchecked. Similarly, in the fields of civil and criminal law, jurists and legislators who uphold and defend legal precedent must face continual opposition from those who question the fairness and relevance of current laws. This ongoing challenge is critical to the vitality and relevance of our system of laws.

In sum, the speaker correctly asserts that it is through mistakes that discovery and true progress are made. Indeed, our personal growth as individuals, as well as advances in science, government, and law, depends on making mistakes.

Issue:
Are **politics and morality** mutually exclusive?

Should politics and morality be treated as though they are mutually exclusive? I strongly agree with the speaker that any person claiming so fails to understand either the one or the other. An overly narrow definition of morality might require complete forthrightness and candidness in dealings with others. However, the morality of public politics embraces far broader concerns involving the welfare of society, and recognizes compromise as a necessary, and legitimate, means of addressing those concerns.

It is wrong-headed to equate moral behavior in politics with the simple notions of honesty and putting the other fellow's needs ahead of one's own—or other ways that we typically measure the morality of an individual's private behavior. Public politics is a game played among professional politicians—and to succeed in the game one must use the tools that are part-and-parcel of it. Complete forthrightness is a sign of vulnerability and naiveté, neither of which will earn a politician respect among his or her opponents, and that opponents will use to every advantage against the honest politician. Moreover, the rhetoric of a successful politician eschews rigorous factual inquiry and indisputable fact while appealing to emotions, ideals, and subjective interpretation and characterizations. For example, the politician who claims his opponent is "anti-business," "bad for the economy," or "out of touch with what voters want" is not necessarily behaving immorally. We must understand that this sort of rhetoric is part-and-parcel of public politics, and thus kept in perspective does not harm the society—as long as it does not escalate to outright lying.

Those who disagree with the statement also fail to understand that in order to gain the opportunity for moral leadership politicians must engage in certain compromises along the way. Politics is a business born not only of idealism but also of pragmatism—insofar as in order to be effective a politician must gain and hold onto political power. In my observation, some degree of pandering to the electorate and to those who might lend financial support for reelection efforts is necessary to maintain that position. Modern politics is replete with candidates who refused to pander, thereby ruining their own chance to exercise effective leadership.

Finally, those who claim that effective politicians need not concern themselves with morality fail to appreciate that successful political leadership, if it is to endure, ultimately requires a certain measure of public morality—that is, serving the society with its best interests as the leader's overriding concern. Consider the many leaders, such as Stalin and Hitler, whom most people would agree were egregious violators of public morality. Ultimately, such leaders forfeit their leadership as a result of the immoral means by which they obtain or wield their power. Or consider less egregious examples such as President Nixon, whose contempt for the very legal system that afforded him his leadership led to his forfeiture of that leadership. It seems to me that in the short term amoral or immoral public behavior might serve a political leader's interest in preserving power; yet in the long term such behavior invariably results in that leader's downfall.

In sum, I fundamentally agree with the statement. It recognizes that the "game" of politics calls for a certain amount of disingenuousness that we might associate with dubious private morality. And it recognizes that such behavior is a necessary means to the final objective of moral political leadership. Besides, at the end of the political game any politician failing to exercise moral leadership ultimately forfeits the game.

Issue:
Does our education change how **we perceive the world**?

I strongly agree that by studying any particular academic discipline we alter the way we perceive the world. As intellectual neophytes we tend to polarize what we see as either right or wrong, or as either good or bad. We also tend to interpret what we see by way of our emotions. Once educated, we gain the capacity to see a broader spectrum of opinion and perspective, and to see our own culture and even ourselves as a tapestry-like product of history.

Through the earnest pursuit of knowledge—particularly in history and literature—we reveal to ourselves the flaws and foibles of other humans whose lives we study and read about. History teaches us, for example, that demagogues whom society places on pedestals often fall under the weight of their own prejudices, jealousies, and other character flaws. And, any serious student of Shakespeare comes away from reading King Lear and Hamlet with a heightened awareness of the tragically flawed ironic hero, and of the arbitrariness by which we distinguish our heroes from our villains.

Through education we begin to see flaws not only in people but also in ideologies that we had previously embraced on pure faith. A student of government and public policy learns that many of the so-called "solutions" which our legislatures and jurists hand down to us from atop their pedestals are actually Band-Aid compromises designed to appease opponents and pander to the electorate. A philosophy student learns to recognize logical fallacies of popular ideas and the rhetoric of our political parties, religious denominations, and social extremists. And, a law student learns that our system of laws is not a monolithic set of truths but rather an ever-changing reflection of whatever the society's current mores, values, and attitudes happen to be.

While education helps us see the flawed nature of our previously cherished ideas, paradoxically it also helps us see ideas we previously rejected out of hand in a different light—as having some merit after all. Through education in public policy and law, once-oppressive rules, regulations, and restrictions appear reasonable constraints on freedom in light of legitimate competing interests. Through the objective study of different religious institutions, customs, and faiths, a student learns to see the merits of different belief systems, and to see the cultural and philosophical traditions in which they are rooted.

Education also helps us see our own culture through different eyes. As cultural neophytes we participate unwittingly in our culture's own customs, rituals, and ceremonies—because we see them as somehow sacrosanct. A student of sociology or cultural anthropology comes to see those same customs, rituals, and ceremonies as tools which serve our psychological need to belong to a distinct social group, and to reinforce that sense of belonging by honoring the group's traditions. And, by reading the literary works of writers from bygone eras, a literature student comes to see his or her own culture as a potential treasure trove of fodder for the creative literary mind. For example, by studying Twain's works a student learns that Twain saw nineteenth-century life along the Mississippi not as a mundane existence but as a framework for the quintessential adventure story, and that we can similarly transform the way we see our own culture.

Finally, education in the arts alters forever the way we perceive the aesthetic world around us. Prior to education we respond instinctively, emotionally, and viscerally to the forms, colors, and sounds of art. Post education we respond intellectually. We seek to appreciate what art reveals about our culture and about humanity. We also seek to understand the aesthetic principles upon which true art is founded. For instance, an earnest art student learns to see not just pigments and shapes but also historical influences and aesthetic principles. An informed listener of popular music hears not just the same pleasing sounds and pulsating rhythms as their naive counterparts, but also the rhythmic meters, harmonic structure, and compositional forms used by the great classical composers of previous centuries, and which provided the foundation of modern music.

To sum up, through education we no longer see our heroes, leaders, and idols through the same credulous eyes, nor do we see other humans and their ideas through the black-and-white lens of our own point of view. In the final analysis, through education we come not only to perceive the world differently but also to understand the subjective, and therefore changeable, nature of our own perceptions.

Issue:
Progress through discourse **among people**

The speaker contends that progress is best made through discourse among people with opposing opinions and viewpoints. I strongly agree with this contention. In all realms of human endeavor, including the behavioral and natural sciences as well as government and law, debate and disagreement form the foundation for progress.

Regarding the physical sciences, our scientific method is essentially a call for progress through opposition. Any new theory must withstand rigorous scientific scrutiny. Moreover, the history of theoretical science is essentially a history of opposing theories. A current example involves two contrary theories of physics: wave theory and quantum theory. During the last 20 years or so scientists have been struggling to disprove one or the other, or to reconcile them. By way of this intense debate, theorists have developed a new so-called "string" theory which indeed reconciles them—at least mathematically.

Although "strings" have yet to be confirmed empirically, string theory might turn out to provide the unifying laws that all matter in the universe obeys.

The importance of opposing theories is not limited to the purely physical sciences. Researchers interested in human behavior have for some time been embroiled in the so-called "nature-nurture" debate, which involves whether behavioral traits are a function of genetic disposition and brain chemistry ("nature") or of learning and environment ("nurture"). Not surprisingly, psychologists and psychiatrists have traditionally adopted sharply opposing stances in this debate. And it is this very debate that has sparked researchers to discover that many behavioral traits are largely a function of the unique neurological structure of each individual's brain, and not a function of nurture. These and further discoveries certainly will lead to progress in dealing effectively with pressing social issues in the fields of education, juvenile delinquency, criminal reform, and mental illness. The outcomes of the debate also carry important implications about culpability and accountability in the eyes of the law. In short, the nature-nurture debate will continue to serve as a catalyst for progress across the entire social spectrum.

The value of discourse between people with opposing viewpoints is not limited to the physical and behavioral sciences. In government and politics, progress in human rights comes typically through dissension from and challenges to the status quo; in fact, without disagreement among factions with opposing viewpoints, political oppression and tyranny would go unchecked. Similarly, in the fields of civil and criminal law, jurists and legislators who uphold and defend legal precedent must face continual opposition from those who question the fairness and relevance of current laws. This ongoing debate is critical to the vitality and relevance of our system of laws.

History informs us of the chilling effect suppression of free discourse and debate can have on progress. Consider the Soviet Refusenik movement of the 1920s. During this time period the Soviet government, attempted not only to control the direction and the goals of scientific research but also to distort the outcomes of that research. During the 1920s the Soviet government quashed certain areas of scientific inquiry, destroyed research facilities and libraries, and caused the sudden disappearance of scientists who were engaged in research that the state viewed as a potential threat. Not surprisingly, during this time period no significant advances in scientific knowledge occurred under the auspices of the Soviet government.

In sum, the speaker correctly asserts that it is through discourse, disagreement, and debate between opposing viewpoints that true progress can best be made. Indeed, advances in science, social welfare, government and law depend on the debate.

Issue:
Do people prefer constraints on **absolute freedom**?

Do people prefer constraints on absolute freedom of choice, regardless of what they might claim? I believe so. And I would go even further, to assert that, paradoxically, people demand such constraints to preserve their freedom.

History informs us that attempts to quell basic individual freedoms—of expression, of opinion and belief, and to come and go as we please—invariably fail. People ultimately rise up against unreasonable constraints on freedom of choice. The desire for freedom seems to spring from our fundamental nature as human beings. But does this mean that people would prefer absolute freedom of choice to any constraints whatsoever? No. Reasonable constraints on freedom are needed to protect freedom—and to prevent a society from devolving into a state of anarchy where life is short and brutish.

To appreciate our preference for constraining our own freedom of choice, one need look no further than the neighborhood playground. Even without any adult supervision, a group of youngsters at play invariably establish mutually agreed-upon rules for conduct—whether or not a sport or game is involved. Children learn at an early age that without any rules for behavior the playground bully usually prevails. And short of beating up on others, bullies enjoy taking prisoners—i.e., restricting the freedom of choice of others. Thus our preference for constraining our freedom of choice stems from our desire to protect and preserve that freedom.

Our preference for constraining our own freedom of choice continues into our adult lives. We freely enter into exclusive pair-bonding relationships; during our teens we agree to "go steady," then as adults we voluntarily enter into marriage contracts. Most of us eagerly enter into exclusive employment relationships—preferring the security of steady income to the "freedom" of not knowing where our next paycheck will come from. Even people who prefer self-employment to job security quickly learn that the only way to preserve their "autonomy" is to constrain themselves in terms of their agreements with clients and customers, and especially in terms of how they use their time. Admittedly, our self-inflicted job constraints are born largely of economic necessity. Yet even the wealthiest individuals usually choose to constrain their freedom by devoting most of their time and attention to a few pet projects.

Our preference for constraining our own freedom of choice is evident on a societal level as well. Just as children at a playground recognize the need for self-imposed rules and regulations, as a society we recognize the same need. After all, in a democratic society our system of laws is an invention of the people. For example, we insist on being bound by rules for operating motor vehicles, for buying and selling both real and personal property, and for making public statements about other people. Without these rules, we would live in continual fear for our physical safety, the security of our property, and our personal reputation and dignity.

In sum, I agree with the fundamental assertion that people prefer reasonable constraints on their freedom of choice. In fact, in a democratic society we insist on imposing these constraints on ourselves in order to preserve that freedom.

Answers That Express Qualified Agreement with an Issue Statement

Perhaps you essentially agree with the Issue statement at hand, and you've come up with some solid reasons and examples to support your position. Although you can write a high-scoring essay based just on these ideas (see the first section in Part 3), I recommend that you try to think of at least one way to *qualify* your agreement. You can do so in a variety of ways:

- By adding a caveat (a warning) against extending the statement or its logic too far

- By acknowledging one or two minor exceptions to the overall accuracy of the statement

- By adding a proviso that conditions your agreement on certain assumptions

- By conceding or admitting a valid but relatively trivial objection (a mere quibble)

The sample essays in this section implement these and other methods of qualifying your overall agreement with an Issue statement. As you read these essays, pay particular attention to rhetorical techniques that are used to make ideas that weaken an Issue statement subordinate to those that support it.

Issue:
Do we learn the most from people whose **views we share**?

Do we learn more from people whose ideas we share in common than from those whose ideas contradict ours? The speaker claims so, for the reason that disagreement can cause stress and inhibit learning. I concede that undue discord can impede learning. Otherwise, in my view we learn far more from discourse and debate with those whose ideas we oppose than from people whose ideas are in accord with our own.

Admittedly, under some circumstances disagreement with others can be counterproductive to learning. For supporting examples, one need look no further than a television set. On today's typical television or radio talk show, disagreement usually manifests itself in meaningless rhetorical bouts and shouting matches, during which opponents vie to have their own message heard, but have little interest either in finding common ground with or in acknowledging the merits of the opponent's viewpoint. Understandably, neither the combatants nor the viewers learn anything meaningful. In fact, these battles only serve to reinforce the predispositions and biases of all concerned. The end result is that learning is impeded.

Disagreement can also inhibit learning when two opponents disagree on fundamental assumptions needed for meaningful discourse and debate. For example, a student of paleontology learns little about the evolution of an animal species under current study by debating with an individual whose religious belief system precludes the possibility of evolution to begin with. And, economics and finance students learn little about the dynamics of a laissez-faire system by debating with a socialist whose view is that a centralized power should control all economic activity.

Aside from the foregoing two provisos, however, I fundamentally disagree with the speaker's claim. Assuming common ground between two rational and reasonable opponents willing to debate on intellectual merits, both opponents stand to gain much from that debate. Indeed it is primarily through such debate that human knowledge advances, whether at the personal, community, or global level.

At the personal level, by listening to their parents' rationale for their seemingly oppressive rules and policies, teenagers can learn how certain behaviors naturally carry certain undesirable consequences. At the same time, by listening to their teenagers concerns about autonomy and about peer pressures parents can learn the valuable lesson that effective parenting and control are two different things. At the community level, through dispassionate dialogue an environmental activist can come to understand the legitimate economic concerns of those whose jobs depend on the continued profitable operation of a factory. Conversely, the latter might stand to learn much about the potential public-health price to be paid by ensuring job growth and a low unemployment rate. Finally, at the global level, two nations with opposing political or economic interests can reach mutually beneficial agreements by striving to understand the other's legitimate concerns for its national security, its political sovereignty, the stability of its economy and currency, and so forth.

In sum, unless two opponents in a debate are each willing to play on the same field and by the same rules, I concede that disagreement can impede learning. Otherwise, reasoned discourse and debate between people with opposing viewpoints is the very foundation upon which human knowledge advances. Accordingly, on balance the speaker is fundamentally correct.

Issue:
Should political leaders **withhold information from the public**?

I agree with the speaker that it is sometimes necessary, and even desirable, for political leaders to withhold information from the public. A contrary view would reveal a naiveté about the inherent nature of public politics, and about the sorts of compromises on the part of well-intentioned political leaders necessary in order to further the public's ultimate interests. Nevertheless, we must not allow our political leaders undue freedom to withhold information; otherwise, we risk sanctioning demagoguery and undermining the philosophical underpinnings of any democratic society.

One reason for my fundamental agreement with the speaker is that in order to gain the opportunity for effective public leadership, a would-be leader must first gain and maintain political power. In the game of politics, complete forthrightness is a sign of vulnerability and naiveté, neither of which earn a politician respect among his or her opponents, and which those opponents will use to every advantage to defeat the politician. In my observation, some measure of pandering to the electorate is necessary to gain and maintain political leadership. For example, were all politicians to fully disclose every personal foibles, character flaw, and detail concerning personal life, few honest politicians would ever by elected. While this view might seem cynical, personal scandals have in fact proven the undoing of many a political career; thus, I think this view is realistic.

Another reason why I essentially agree with the speaker is that fully disclosing to the public certain types of information would threaten public safety and perhaps even national security. For example, if the President were to disclose the government's strategies for thwarting specific plans of an international terrorist or a drug trafficker, those strategies would surely fail, and the public's health and safety would be compromised as a result. Withholding information might also be necessary to avoid public panic. While such cases are rare, they do occur occasionally. For example, during the first few hours of the new millennium the U.S. Pentagon's missile defense system experienced a Y2K-related malfunction. This fact was withheld from the public until later in the day, once the problem had been solved; and legitimately so, since immediate disclosure would have served no useful purpose and might even have resulted in mass hysteria.

Having recognized that withholding information from the public is often necessary to serve the interests of that public, legitimate political leadership nevertheless requires forthrightness with the citizenry as to the leader's motives and agenda. History informs us that would-be leaders who lack such forthrightness are the same ones who seize and maintain power either by brute force or by demagoguery—that is, by deceiving and manipulating the citizenry. Paragons such as Genghis Khan and Hitler, respectively, come immediately to mind. Any democratic society should of course abhor demagoguery, which operates against the democratic principle of government by the people. Consider also less egregious examples, such as President Nixon's withholding of information about his active role in the Watergate cover-up. His behavior demonstrated a concern for self-interest above the broader interests of the democratic system that granted his political authority in the first place.

In sum, the game of politics calls for a certain amount of disingenuousness and lack of forthrightness that we might otherwise characterize as dishonesty. And such behavior is a necessary means to the final objective of effective political leadership. Nevertheless, in any democracy a leader who relies chiefly on deception and secrecy to preserve that leadership, to advance a private agenda, or to conceal selfish motives, betrays the democracy—and ends up forfeiting the political game.

Issue:
Do **luxuries** prevent our becoming **strong and independent**?

Do modern luxuries serve to undermine our true strength and independence as individuals? The speaker believes so, and I tend to agree. Consider the automobile, for example. Most people consider the automobile a necessity rather than a luxury; yet it is for this very reason that the automobile so aptly supports the speaker's point. To the extent that we depend on cars as crutches, they prevent us from becoming truly independent and strong in character as individuals.

Consider first the effect of the automobile on our independence as individuals. In some respects the automobile serves to enhance such independence. For example, cars make it possible for people in isolated and depressed areas without public transportation to become more independent by pursing gainful employment outside their communities. And teenagers discover that owning a car, or even borrowing one on occasion, affords them a needed sense of independence from their parents.

However, cars have diminished our independence in a number of more significant respects. We've grown dependent on our cars for commuting to work. We rely on them like crutches for short trips to the corner store, and for carting our children to and from school. Moreover, the car has become a means not only to our assorted physical destinations but also to the attainment of our socioeconomic goals, insofar as the automobile has become a symbol of status. In fact, in my observation many, if not most, working professionals willingly undermine their financial security for the sake of being seen driving this year's new SUV or luxury sedan. In short, we've become slaves to the automobile.

Consider next the overall impact of the automobile on our strength as individuals, by which I mean strength of character, or mettle. I would be hard-pressed to list one way in which the automobile enhances one's strength of character. Driving a powerful SUV might afford a person a feeling and appearance of strength, or machismo. But this feeling has nothing to do with a person's true character.

In contrast, there is a certain strength of character that comes with eschewing modern conveniences such as cars, and with the knowledge that one is contributing to a cleaner and quieter environment, a safer neighborhood, and arguably a more genteel society. Also, alternative modes of transportation such as bicycling and walking are forms of exercise that require and promote the virtue of self-discipline. Finally, in my observation people who have forsaken the automobile spend more time at home, where they are more inclined to prepare and even grow their own food, and to spend more time with their families. The former enhances one's independence; the latter enhances the integrity of one's values and the strength of one's family.

To sum up, the automobile helps illustrate that when a luxury becomes a necessity it can sap our independence and strength as individuals. Perhaps our society is better off, on balance, with such "luxuries"; after all, the automobile industry has created countless jobs, raised our standard of living, and made the world more interesting. However, by becoming slaves to the automobile we trade off a certain independence and inner strength.

Issue:
Should **public figures** expect to lose their privacy?

This statement is fundamentally correct; public figures should indeed expect to lose their privacy. After all, we are a society of voyeurs wishing to transform our mundane lives; and one way to do so is to live vicariously through the experiences of others whose lives appear more interesting than our own. Moreover, the media recognize this societal foible and exploit it at every opportunity. Nevertheless, a more accurate statement would draw a distinction between political figures and other public figures; the former have even less reason than the latter to expect to be left alone, for the reason that their duty as public servants legitimizes public scrutiny of their private lives.

The chief reason why I generally agree with the statement is that, for better or worse, intense media attention to the lives of public figures raises a presumption in the collective mind of the viewing or reading public that our public figures' lives are far more interesting than our own. This presumption is understandable. After all, I think most people would agree that given the opportunity for even fleeting fame they would embrace it without hesitation. Peering into the private lives of those who have achieved our dreams allows us to live vicariously through those lives.

Another reason why I generally agree with the statement has to do with the forces that motivate the media. For the most part, the media consist of large corporations whose chief objective is to maximize shareholder profits. In pursuit of that objective the media are simply giving the public what they demand—a voyeuristic look into the private lives of public figures. One need look no further than a newsstand, local-television news broadcast, or talk show to find ample evidence that this is so. For better or worse, we love to peer at people on public pedestals, and we love to watch them fall off. The media know this all too well, and exploit our obsession at every opportunity.

Nevertheless, the statement should be qualified in that a political figure has less reason to expect privacy than other public figures. Why? The private affairs of public servants become our business when those affairs adversely affect our servants' ability to serve us effectively, or when our servants betray our trust. For example, several years ago the chancellor of a university located in my city was expelled from office for misusing university funds to renovate his posh personal residence. The scandal became front-page news in the campus newspaper and prompted a useful system-wide reform. Also consider the Clinton sex scandal, which sparked a debate about the powers and duties of legal prosecutors vis-à-vis the chief executive. Also, the court rulings about executive privilege and immunity, and even the impeachment proceedings, all of which resulted from the scandal, might serve as useful legal precedents for the future.

Admittedly, intense public scrutiny of the personal lives of public figures can carry harmful consequences, for the public figure as well as the society. For instance, the Clinton scandal resulted in enormous financial costs to taxpayers, and it harmed many individuals caught up in the legal process. And for more than a year the scandal served chiefly to distract us from our most pressing national and global problems. Yet, until as a society we come to appreciate the potentially harmful effects of our preoccupation with the lives of public figures, they can expect to remain the cynosures of our attention.

Issue:
Is image more important than the **truth behind** it?

Has creating an image become more important in our society than the reality or truth behind the image? I agree that image has become a more central concern, at least where short-term business or political success is at stake. Nevertheless, I think that in the longer term image ultimately yields to substance and fact.

The important role of image is particularly evident in the business world. Consider, for example, today's automobile industry. American cars are becoming essentially identical to competing Japanese cars in nearly every mechanical and structural respect, as well as in price. Thus, to compete effectively auto companies must now differentiate their products largely through image advertising, by conjuring up certain illusory benefits—such as machismo, status, sensibility, or fun. The increasing focus on image is also evident in the book-publishing business. Publishers are relying more and more on the power of their brands rather than the content of their books. Today mass-market books are supplanted within a year with products that are essentially the same—except with fresh faces, titles, and other promotional angles. I find quite telling the fact that today more and more book publishers are being acquired by large media companies. And the increasing importance of image is especially evident in the music industry, where originality, artistic interpretation, and technical proficiency have yielded almost entirely to sex appeal.

The growing significance of image is also evident in the political realm, particularly when it comes to presidential politics. Admittedly, by its very nature politicking has always emphasized rhetoric and appearances above substance and fact. Yet, since the invention of the camera presidential politicians have become increasingly concerned about their image. For example, Teddy Roosevelt was very careful never to be photographed wearing a tennis outfit, for fear that such photographs would serve to undermine his rough-rider image that won him his only term in office. With the advent of television, image became even more central in presidential politics. After all, it was television that elected J.F.K. over Nixon. And our only two-term presidents in the television age were elected based largely on their image. Query whether Presidents Lincoln, Taft, or even F.D.R. would be elected today if pitted against the handsome leading man Reagan, or the suave and politically correct Clinton. After all, Lincoln was homely, Taft was obese, and F.D.R. was crippled.

In the long term, however, the significance of image wanes considerably. The image of the Marlboro man ultimately gave way to the truth about the health hazards of cigarette smoking. Popular musical acts with nothing truly innovative to offer musically eventually disappear from the music scene. And anyone who frequents yard sales knows that today's best-selling books often become tomorrow's pulp. Even in politics, I think history has a knack for peeling away image to focus on real accomplishments. I think history will remember Teddy Roosevelt, for example, primarily for building the Panama Canal and for establishing our National Park System—and not for his rough-and-ready wardrobe.

In the final analysis, it seems that in every endeavor where success depends to some degree on persuasion, marketing, or salesmanship, image has indeed become the central concern of those who seek to persuade. And as our lives become busier, our attention spans briefer, and our choices among products and services greater, I expect this trend to continue unabated—for better or worse.

Issue:
The importance of pursuing **idiosyncratic** research interests

Should academic scholars and researchers be free to pursue whatever avenues of inquiry and research interest them, no matter how unusual or idiosyncratic, as the speaker asserts? Or should they strive instead to focus on those areas that are most likely to benefit society? I strongly agree with the speaker, for three reasons.

First of all, who is to decide which areas of academic inquiry are worthwhile? Scholars cannot be left to decide. Given a choice they will pursue their own idiosyncratic areas of interest, and it is highly unlikely that all scholars could reach a fully informed consensus as to what research areas would be most worthwhile. Nor can these decisions be left to regulators and legislators, who would bring to bear their own quirky notions about what would be worthwhile, and whose susceptibility to influence renders them untrustworthy in any event.

Secondly, by human nature we are motivated to pursue those activities in which we excel. To compel scholars to focus only on certain areas would be to force many to waste their true talents. For example, imagine relegating today's preeminent astrophysicist Stephen Hawking to research the effectiveness of affirmative-action legislation in reducing workplace discrimination. Admittedly, this example borders on hyperbole. Yet the aggregate effect of realistic cases would be to waste the intellectual talents of our world's scholars and researchers. Moreover, lacking genuine interest or motivation, a scholar would be unlikely to contribute meaningfully to his or her "assigned" field of study.

Thirdly, it is "idiosyncratic" and "unusual" avenues of inquiry that lead to the greatest contributions to society. Avenues of intellectual and scientific inquiry that break no new ground amount to wasted time, talent, and other resources. History is laden with unusual claims by scholars and researchers that turned out stunningly significant—that the sun lies at the center of our universe, that time and space are relative concepts, that matter consists of discrete particles, that humans evolved from other life-forms, to name a few. One current area of unusual research is terraforming—creating biological life and a habitable atmosphere where none existed before. This unusual research area does not immediately address society's pressing social problems. Yet, in the longer term, it might be necessary to colonize other planets in order to ensure the survival of the human race; and after all, what could be a more significant contribution to society than preventing its extinction?

Those who would oppose the speaker's assertion might point out that public universities should not allow their faculty to indulge their personal intellectual fantasies at taxpayer expense. Yet as long as our universities maintain strict procedures for peer review, pure quackery cannot persist for very long. Other detractors might argue that in certain academic areas, particularly the arts and humanities, research and intellectually inquiry amount to little more than a personal quest for happiness or pleasure. This specious argument overlooks the societal benefits afforded by appreciating and cultivating the arts. And, earnest study in the humanities affords us wisdom to know what is best for society, and helps us understand and approach societal problems more critically, creatively, and effectively. Thus, despite the lack of a tangible nexus between certain areas of intellectual inquiry and societal benefit, the nexus is there nonetheless.

In sum, I agree that we should allow academic scholars nearly unfettered freedom of intellectual inquiry and research—within reasonable limits as determined by peer review. Engaging one's individual talents in one's particular area of fascination is most likely to yield advances, discoveries, and innovations that serve to make the world a better and more interesting place in which to live.

Issue:
Preparing **young people for leadership**

Which is a better way to prepare young people for leadership: developing in them a spirit of competitiveness or one of cooperation? The speaker favors the latter approach, even though some leaders attribute their success to their keenly developed competitive spirit. I tend to agree with the speaker, for reasons having to do with our increasingly global society, and with the true keys to effective leadership.

The chief reason why we should stress cooperation in nurturing young people today is that, as tomorrow's leaders, they will face pressing societal problems that simply cannot be solved apart from cooperative international efforts. For example, all nations will need to cooperate in an effort to disarm themselves of weapons of mass destruction; to reduce harmful emissions that destroy ozone and warm the Earth to dangerous levels; to reduce consumption of the Earth's finite natural resources; and to cure and prevent diseases before they become global epidemics. Otherwise, we all risk self-destruction. In short, global peace, economic stability, and survival of the species provide powerful reasons for developing educational paradigms that stress cooperation over competition.

A second compelling reason for instilling in young people a sense of cooperation over competition is that effective leadership depends less on the latter than the former. A leader should show that he or she values the input of subordinates—for example, by involving them in decisions about matters in which they have a direct stake. Otherwise, subordinates might grow to resent their leader and become unwilling to devote themselves wholeheartedly to the leader's mission. In extreme cases they might even sabotage that mission, or even take their useful ideas to competitors. And after all, without other people worth leading a person cannot be a leader—let alone an effective one.

A third reason why instilling a sense of cooperation is to be preferred over instilling a sense of competition is that the latter serves to narrow a leader's focus on thwarting the efforts of competitors. With such tunnel vision it is difficult to develop other, more creative means of attaining organizational objectives. Moreover, such means often involve synergistic solutions that call for alliances, partnerships, and other cooperative efforts with would-be competitors.

Those who would oppose the speaker might point out that a thriving economy depends on a freely competitive business environment, which ensures that consumers obtain high-quality goods and services at low prices. Thus, key leadership positions, especially in business, inherently call for a certain tenacity and competitive spirit. And, a competitive spirit seems especially critical in today's hyper-competitive technology-driven economy, where any leader failing to keep pace with ever-changing business and technological paradigms soon falls by the wayside. However, a leader's effectiveness as a competitor is not necessarily inconsistent with his or her ability to cooperate with subordinates or with competitors, as noted above.

In sum, if we were to take the speaker's advice too far we would risk becoming a world without leaders, who are bred of a competitive spirit. We would also risk the key benefits of a free-market economy. Nevertheless, on balance I agree that it is more important to instill in young people a sense of cooperation than one of competition. The speaker's preference properly reflects the growing role of cooperative alliances and efforts in solving the world's most pressing problems. After all, in a world in which our very survival as a species depends on cooperation, the spirit of even healthy competition, no matter how healthy, is of little value to any of us.

Issue:
Imaginative works vs. factual accounts

Do imaginative works hold more lasting significance than factual accounts, for the reasons the speaker cites? To some extent the speaker overstates fiction's comparative significance. On balance, however, I tend to agree with the speaker. By recounting various dimensions of the human experience, a fictional work can add meaning to and appreciation of the times in which the work is set. Even where a fictional work amounts to pure fantasy, with no historical context, it can still hold more lasting significance than a factual account. Examples from literature and film serve to illustrate these points.

I concede that most fictional works rely on historical settings for plot, thematic, and character development. By informing us about underlying political, economic, and social conditions, factual accounts provide a frame of reference needed to understand and appreciate imaginative works. Fact is the basis for fiction, and fiction is no substitute for fact. I would also concede that factual accounts are more "accurate" than fictional ones—insofar as they are more objective. But this does not mean that factual accounts provide a "more meaningful picture of the human experience." To the contrary, only imaginative works can bring a historical period alive—by way of creative tools such as imagery and point of view. And, only imaginative works can provide meaning to historical events—through the use of devices such as symbolism and metaphor.

Several examples from literature serve to illustrate this point. Twain's novels afford us a sense of how nineteenth-century Missouri would have appeared through the eyes of 10-year old boys. Melville's "Billy Budd" gives the reader certain insights into what travel on the high seas might have been like in earlier centuries, through the eyes of a crewman. And the epic poems "Beowulf" and "Sir Gawain and the Green Knight" provide glimpses of the relationships between warriors and their kings in medieval times. Bare facts about these historical eras are easily forgettable, whereas creative stories and portrayals such as the ones mentioned above can be quite memorable indeed. In other words, what truly lasts are our impressions of what life must have been like in certain places, at certain times, and under certain conditions. Only imaginative works can provide such lasting impressions.

Examples of important films underscore the point that creative accounts of the human experience hold more lasting significance than bare factual accounts. Consider four of our most memorable and influential films: Citizen Kane, Schindler's List, The Wizard of Oz, and Star Wars. Did Welles' fictional portrayal of publisher William Randolph Hearst or Spielberg's fictional portrayal of a Jewish sympathizer during the holocaust provide a more "meaningful picture of human experience" than a history textbook? Did these accounts help give "shape and focus" to reality more so than newsreels alone could? If so, will these works hold more "lasting significance" than bare factual accounts of the same persons and events? I think anyone who has seen these films would answer all three questions affirmatively. Or consider The Wizard of Oz and Star Wars. Both films, and the novels from which they were adapted, are pure fantasy. Yet both teem with symbolism and metaphor relating to life's journey, the human spirit, and our hopes, dreams, and ambitions—in short, the human experience. Therein lies the reason for their lasting significance.

In sum, without prior factual accounts fictional works set in historical periods lose much of their meaning. Yet only through the exercise of artistic license can we convey human experience in all its dimensions, and thereby fully understand and appreciate life in other times and places. And it is human experience, and not bare facts and figures, that endures in our minds and souls.

Issue:
Should college faculty also work **outside the academic world**?

Whether college faculty should also work outside academia, in professional work related to their academic fields, depends primarily on the specific academic area. With respect to fields in which outside work is appropriate, I strongly agree with the statement; students and faculty all stand to gain in a variety of respects when a professor complements academic duties with real-world experience.

As a threshold matter, the statement requires qualification in two respects. First, in certain academic areas there is no profession to speak of outside academia. This is especially true in the humanities; after all, what work outside academia is there for professors of literature or philosophy? Secondly, the statement fails to consider that in certain other academic areas a professor's academic duties typically involve practical work of the sort that occurs outside academia. This is especially true in the fine and performing arts, where faculty actively engage in the craft by demonstrating techniques and styles for their students.

Aside from these two qualifications, I strongly agree that it is worthwhile for college faculty to work outside academia in professional positions related to their field. There are three clear benefits of doing so. First, in my experience as a student, faculty who are actively engaged in their fields come to class with fresh insights and a contagious excitement about the subject at hand. Moreover, they bring to their students practical, real-world examples of the principles and theories discussed in textbooks, thereby sparking interest, and even motivating some students to pursue the field as a career.

Secondly, by keeping abreast with the changing demands of work as a professional, professors can help students who are serious about pursuing a career in that field to make more informed career decisions. The professor with field experience is better able to impart useful, up-to-date information about what work in the field entails, and even about the current job market. After all, college career-planning staff are neither equipped nor sufficiently experienced to provide such specific advice to students.

A third benefit has to do with faculty research and publication in their areas of specialty. Experience in the field can help a professor ferret out cutting-edge and controversial issues—which might be appropriate subjects for research and publication. Moreover, practical experience can boost a professor's credibility as an expert in the field. For example, each year a certain sociology professor at my college combined teaching with undercover work investigating various cults. Not only did the students benefit from the many interesting stories this professor had to tell about his experiences, the professor's publications about cults catapulted him to international prominence as an expert on the subject, and justifiably so.

In sum, aside from certain academic areas in which outside work is either unavailable or unnecessary, students and faculty alike stand everything to gain when faculty enrich their careers by interspersing field work with academic work.

Issue:
What is required to become "**truly educated**"?

I fundamentally agree with the proposition that students must take courses outside their major field of study to become "truly educated." A contrary position would reflect a too-narrow view of higher education and its proper objectives. Nevertheless, I would caution that extending the proposition too far might risk undermining those objectives.

The primary reason why I agree with the proposition is that "true" education amounts to far more than gaining the knowledge and ability to excel in one's major course of study and in one's professional career. True education also facilitates an understanding of oneself, and tolerance and respect for the viewpoints of others. Courses in psychology, sociology, and anthropology all serve these ends. "True" education also provides insight and perspective regarding one's place in society and in the physical and metaphysical worlds. Courses in political science, philosophy, theology, and even sciences such as astronomy and physics can help a student gain this insight and perspective. Finally, no student can be truly educated without having gained an aesthetic appreciation of the world around us—through course work in literature, the fine arts, and the performing arts.

Becoming truly educated also requires sufficient mastery of one academic area to permit a student to contribute meaningfully to society later in life. Yet, mastery of any specific area requires some knowledge about a variety of others. For example, a political-science student can fully understand that field only by understanding the various psychological, sociological, and historical forces that shape political ideology. An anthropologist cannot excel without understanding the social and political events that shape cultures, and without some knowledge of chemistry and geology for performing fieldwork. Even computer engineering is intrinsically tied to other fields, even non-technical ones such as business, communications, and media.

Nevertheless, the call for a broad educational experience as the path to becoming truly educated comes with one important caveat. A student who merely dabbles in a hodge-podge of academic offerings, without special emphasis on any one, becomes a dilettante—lacking enough knowledge or experience in any single area to come away with anything valuable to offer. Thus, in the pursuit of true education students must be careful not to overextend themselves—or risk defeating an important objective of education.

In the final analysis, to become truly educated one must strike a proper balance in one's educational pursuits. Certainly, students should strive to excel in the specific requirements of their major course of study. However, they should complement those efforts by pursuing course work in a variety of other areas as well. By earnestly pursuing a broad education one gains the capacity not only to succeed in a career, but also to find purpose and meaning in that career as well as to understand and appreciate the world and its peoples. To gain these capacities is to become "truly educated."

Issue:
Should colleges emphasize courses in **popular** culture?

The speaker asserts that the curriculum of colleges and universities should emphasize popular culture—music, media, literature, and so forth—rather than literature and art of the past, for the reason that the former is more relevant to students. I strongly disagree. Although courses in popular culture do play a legitimate role in higher education, formal study of the present culture at the expense of studying past cultures can undermine the function of higher education, and ultimately provide a disservice to students and to society.

Admittedly, course work in popular culture is legitimate and valuable for three reasons. First, popular culture is a mirror of society's impulses and values. Thus, any serious student of the social sciences, as well as students of media and communications, should take seriously the literature and art of the present. Secondly, in every age and culture some worthwhile art and literature emerges from the mediocrity. Few would disagree, for example, that the great modern-jazz pioneers such as Charlie Parker and Thelonius Monk, and more recently Lennon and McCartney, and Stevie Wonder, have made just as lasting a contribution to music as some of the great classical musicians of previous centuries. Thirdly, knowledge of popular films, music, and art enables a person to find common ground to relate to other people. This leads to better communication between different subcultures.

Nevertheless, emphasizing the study of popular culture at the expense of studying classical art and literature can carry harmful consequences for students, as well as for society. Without the benefit of historical perspective gained through the earnest study of the art and literature of the past, it is impossible to fully understand, appreciate, and critique literature and art of the present. Moreover, by approaching popular culture without any yardstick for quality it is impossible to distinguish mediocre art from worthwhile art. Only by studying the classics can an individual develop fair standards for judging popular works. Besides, emphasis on the formal study of popular culture is unnecessary. Education in popular culture is readily available outside the classroom—on the Internet, through educational television programming, and through the sorts of everyday conversations and cross talk that occur at water coolers and in the coffee houses of any college campus.

In sum, while the study of popular literature and art can be worthwhile, it has to be undertaken in conjunction with an even greater effort to learn about the literature and art of the past. In the absence of the latter, our universities will produce a society of people with no cultural perspective, and without any standards for determining what merits our attention and nurtures society.

Issue:
The benefits of televising **government proceedings**

I strongly agree that the more government proceedings—debates, meeting, and so forth—that are televised, the more society will benefit overall. Nevertheless, undue emphasis on this means of informing a constituency has the potential for harm— which any society must take care not to allow.

Access to government proceedings via television carries several significant benefits. The main benefit lies in two useful archival functions of videotaped proceedings. First, videotapes are valuable supplements to conventional means of record keeping. Although written transcripts and audiotapes might provide an accurate record of what is said, only videotapes can convey the body language and other visual clues that help us understand what people say, whether they are being disingenuous, sarcastic, or sincere. Secondly, videotape archives provide a useful catalogue for documentary journalists.

Televised proceedings also provide three other useful functions. First, for shut-ins and people who live in remote regions, it might be impracticable, or even impossible, to view government proceedings in person. Secondly, with satellite television systems it is possible to witness the governments of other cities, states, and even nations at work. This sort of exposure provides the viewer a valuable sense of perspective, an appreciation for other forms of government, and so forth. Thirdly, in high schools and universities, television proceedings can be useful curriculum supplements for students of government, public policy, law, and even public speaking.

Nevertheless, televising more and more government proceedings carries certain risks that should not be ignored. Watching televised government proceedings is inherently a rather passive experience. The viewer cannot voice his or her opinions, objections, or otherwise contribute to what is being viewed. Watching televised proceedings as a substitute for active participation in the political process can, on a mass scale, undermine the democratic process by way of its chilling effect on participation. Undue emphasis on telegovernment poses the risk that government proceedings will become mere displays, or shows, for the public, intended as public relations ploys and so-called "photo opportunities," while the true business of government is moved behind closed doors.

In sum, readier access to the day-to-day business of a government can only serve to inform and educate. Although undue reliance on televised proceedings for information can quell active involvement and serve as a censor for people being televised, I think these are risks worth taking in the interest of disclosure.

Issue:
Is society better off when many **people question authority**?

The speaker asserts that when many people question authority society is better off. While I contend that certain forms of disobedience can be harmful to any society, I agree with the speaker otherwise. In fact, I would go further by contending that society's well-being depends on challenges to authority, and that when it comes to political and legal authority, these challenges must come from many people.

Admittedly, when many people question authority some societal harm might result, even if a social cause is worthy. Mass resistance to authority can escalate to violent protest and rioting, during which innocent people are hurt and their property damaged and destroyed. The fallout from the 1992 Los Angeles riots aptly illustrates this point. The "authority" that the rioters sought to challenge was that of the legal justice system, which acquitted police officers in the beating of Rodney King. The means of challenging that authority amounted to flagrant disregard for criminal law on a mass scale—by way of looting, arson, and even deadly assault. This violent challenge to authority resulted in a financially crippled community and, more broadly, a turning back of the clock with respect to racial tensions across America.

While violence is rarely justifiable as a means of questioning authority, peaceful challenges to political and legal authority, by many people, are not only justifiable but actually necessary when it comes to enhancing and even preserving society's well-being. In particular, progress in human rights depends on popular dissension. It is not enough for a charismatic visionary like Gandhi or King to call for change in the name of justice and humanity; they must have the support of many people in order to effect change. Similarly, in a democracy citizens must respect timeless legal doctrines and principles, yet at the same time question the fairness and relevance of current laws. Otherwise, our laws would not evolve to reflect changing societal values. It is not enough for a handful of legislators to challenge the legal status quo; ultimately, it is up to the electorate at large to call for change when change is needed for the well-being of society.

Questioning authority is also essential for advances in the sciences. Passive acceptance of prevailing principles quells innovation, invention, and discovery, all of which clearly benefit any society. In fact, the very notion of scientific progress is predicated on rigorous scientific inquiry—in other words, questioning of authority. History is replete with scientific discoveries that posed challenges to political, religious, and scientific authority. For example, the theories of a sun-centered solar system, of humankind's evolution from other life forms, and of the relativity of time and space, clearly flew in the face of "authoritative" scientific as well as religious doctrine of their time. Moreover, when it comes to science a successful challenge to authority need not come from a large number of people. The key contributions of a few individuals—like Copernicus, Kepler, Newton, Darwin, Einstein, and Hawking—often suffice.

Similarly, in the arts, people must challenge established styles and forms rather than imitate them; otherwise, no genuinely new art would ever emerge, and society would be worse off. And again, it is not necessary that a large number of people pose such challenges; a few key individuals can have a profound impact. For instance, modern ballet owes much of what is new and exciting to George Balanchine, who by way of his improvisational techniques posed a successful challenge to established traditions. And modern architecture arguably owes its existence to the founders of Germany's Bauhaus School of Architecture, which challenged certain "authoritative" notions about the proper objective, and resulting design, of public buildings.

To sum up, in general I agree that when many people question authority the wellbeing of society is enhanced. Indeed, advances in government and law depend on challenges to the status quo by many people. Nevertheless, to ensure a net benefit rather than harm, the means of such challenges must be peaceful ones.

Issue:
Should laws be **rigid or** flexible?

Some measure of consistency and stability in the law is critical for any society to function. Otherwise, I strongly agree with the speaker's assertion that laws should be flexible enough to adapt to different circumstances, times and places. The law of marital property aptly illustrates this point.

On the one hand, a certain measure of consistency, stability, and predictability in our laws is required in order for us to understand our legal obligations and rights as we go about our day-to-day business as a society. For example, in order for private industry to thrive, businesses must be afforded the security of knowing their legal rights and obligations vis-à-vis employees, federal regulatory agencies, and tax authorities—as well as their contractual rights and duties vis-à-vis customers and suppliers. Undue uncertainty in any one of these areas would surely have a chilling effect on business. Moreover, some measure of consistency in the legal environment from place to place promotes business expansion as well as interstate and international commerce, all of which are worthwhile endeavors in an increasingly mobile society.

On the other hand, rigid laws can result in unfairness if applied inflexibly in all places at all times. The framers of the U.S. Constitution recognized the need both for a flexible legal system and for flexible laws—by affording each state legal jurisdiction over all but interstate matters. The framers understood that social and economic problems, as well as standards of equity and fairness, can legitimately change over time and vary from region to region—even from town to town. And our nation's founders would be pleased to see their flexible system that promotes equity and fairness as it operates today.

Consider, for example, marital property rights, which vary considerably from state to state, and which have evolved considerably over time as inflexible, and unfair, systems have given way to more flexible, fairer ones. In earlier times husbands owned all property acquired during marriage as well as property brought into the marriage— by either spouse. Understandably, this rigid and unfair system ultimately gave way to separate-property systems, which acknowledged property rights of both spouses. More recently certain progressive states have adopted even more flexible, and fairer, "community property" systems, under which each spouse owns half of all property acquired during the marriage, while each spouse retains a separate-property interest in his or her other property. Yet even these more egalitarian community-property systems can operate unfairly whenever spouses contribute unequally; accordingly, some community-property states are now modifying their systems for even greater flexibility and fairness.

Thus, the evolution of state marital-property laws aptly illustrates the virtue of a legal system that allows laws to evolve to keep pace with changing mores, attitudes, and our collective sense of equity. This same example also underscores the point that inflexible laws tend to operate unfairly, and properly give way to more flexible ones— as our nation's founders intended.

Issue:
Is practicality our idol **in today's world**?

In today's world is practicality our idol—one which all powers and talents must serve? While this claim has considerable merit with respect to most areas of human endeavor— including education, art, and politics—I take exception with the claim when it comes to the direction of scientific research today.

Practicality seems clearly to be the litmus test for education today. Grade-schoolers are learning computer skills right along with reading and writing. Our middle and high schools are increasingly cutting arts education, which ostensibly has less practical value than other course work. And, more and more college students are majoring in technical fields for the purpose of securing lucrative jobs immediately upon graduation.

Admittedly, many college students still advance to graduate-level study; yet the most popular such degree today is the MBA; after all, business administration is fundamentally about practicality and pragmatism—that is, "getting the job done" and paying attention to the "bottom line."

Practicality also dictates what sort of art is produced today. Most new architecture today is driven by functionality, safety, and cost; very few architectural masterpieces find their way past the blueprint stage anymore. The content of today's feature films and music is driven entirely by demographic considerations—that is, by pandering to the interests of 18-35 year olds, who account for most ticket and CD sales. And, the publishing industry today is driven by immediate concern to deliver viable products to the marketplace. The glut of how-to books in our bookstores today is evidence that publishers are pandering to our practicality as well. It isn't that artists no longer create works of high artistic value and integrity. Independent record labels, filmmakers, and publishing houses abound today. It's just that the independents do not thrive, and they constitute a minuscule segment of the market. In the main, today's real-estate developers, entertainment moguls, and publishing executives are concerned with practicality and profit, and not with artistic value and integrity.

Practicality is also the overriding concern in contemporary politics. Most politicians seem driven today by their interest in being elected and reelected—that is, in short-term survival—rather than by any sense of mission, or even obligation to their constituency or country. Diplomatic and legal maneuverings and negotiations often appear intended to meet the practical needs of the parties involved— minimizing costs, preserving options, and so forth. Those who would defend the speaker might claim that it is idealists—not pragmatists—who sway the masses, incite revolutions, and make political ideology reality. Consider idealists such as the America's founders, or Mahatma Gandhi, or Martin Luther King. Had these idealists concerned themselves with short-term survival and immediate needs rather than with their notions of an ideal society, the United States and India might still be British colonies, and African Americans might still be relegated to the backs of buses. Although I concede this point, the plain fact is that such idealists are far fewer in number today.

On the other hand, the claim amounts to an overstatement when it comes to today's scientific endeavors. In medicine the most common procedures today are cosmetic; these procedures strike me as highly impractical, given the health risks and expense involved. Admittedly, today's digital revolution serves a host of practical concerns, such as communicating and accessing information more quickly and efficiently. Much of chemical research is also aimed at practicality—at providing convenience and enhancing our immediate comfort. Yet, in many other respects scientific research is not driven toward immediate practicality but rather toward broad, long-term objectives: public health, quality of life, and environmental protection.

In sum, practicality may be our idol today when it comes to education, the arts, and politics; but with respect to science I find the claim to be an unfair generalization. Finally, query whether the claim begs the question. After all, practicality amounts to far more than meeting immediate needs; it also embraces long-term planning and prevention aimed at ensuring our future quality of life, and our very survival as a species.

Issue:
Are nations **necessarily connected** when it comes to their well-being?

I strongly agree that each nation's progress and well-being are now tied to the progress and well-being of other nations. In the pursuit of its citizens' economic and social welfare, as well as their safety, security, and health, each nation today creates a ripple effect—sometimes beneficial and sometimes detrimental—felt around the globe. And, although I disagree that our global interconnectedness is necessary, in all likelihood it is with us to stay.

Turning first to economic progress and well-being, the economic pursuits of any nation today are not merely connected to but actually interwoven with those of other nations. In some cases one nation's progress is another's problem. For instance, strong economic growth in the U.S. Attracts investment in U.S. equities from foreign investors, to the detriment of foreign business investments, which become less attractive by comparison. Or consider the global repercussions of developed nations' over-consumption of natural resources mined from emerging nations. Having been exploited once for the sake of fueling the high standard of living in the developed world, emerging nations are now being pressured to comply with the same energy conservation policies as their exploiters—even though they did not contribute to the problems giving rise to these policies, and cannot afford to make the sacrifices involved. Finally, although international drug trafficking provides an economic boon for the rogue nations supplying the drugs, it carries deleterious economic, social, and public health consequences for user nations.

In other cases the economic connection between nations is synergistic—either mutually beneficial or detrimental. A financial crisis—or a political crisis or natural disaster—in one country can spell trouble for foreign companies, many of which are now multinational in that they rely on the labor forces, equipment, and raw materials of other nations. And, as trade barriers and the virtual distance between nations collapse, the result is economic synergies among all trading nations. For instance, the economic well-being of Middle East nations relies almost entirely on demand from oil-consuming nations such as the United States, which depend on a steady supply from the Middle East.

Nations have also become interconnected in the pursuit of scientific and technological progress. And while it might be tempting to hasten that the ripples generally benefit other nations, often one nation's pursuit of progress spells trouble for other nations. For example, the development of nuclear weapons and biological and chemical agents affords the nation possessing them political and military leverage over other nations. And, global computer connectivity has served to heighten national-security concerns of all connected nations—who can easily fall prey to Internet espionage.

Finally, the world's nations have become especially interconnected in terms of their public health. Prior to the modem industrial age, no nation had the capacity to inflict lasting environmental damage on other nations. But, as that age draws to a close it is evident that so-called industrial "progress" has carried deleterious environmental consequences worldwide. Consider, for instance, the depletion of atmospheric ozone, which has warmed the earth to the point that it threatens the very survival of the human species. And, we are now learning that dear-cutting the world's rainforests can set into motion a chain of animal extinction that threatens the delicate balance upon which all animals—including humans—depend.

In closing, I take exception to the statement only insofar as a nation can still pursue progress and the well-being of its own citizens in relative isolation from other nations. And I concede that in the future the world's nations might respond to the health and security risks of the ripple effect that I've described by adopting isolationist trade, communications, and military policies. Yet, having benefited from the economic synergies which free trade and global financial markets afford, and having seen the potential for progress technological revolution has brought about, I think that the world's nations will be willing to assume those risks.

Issue:
Do **technologies** interfere with "real" learning?

The speaker asserts that innovations such as videos, computers, and the Internet too often distract from "real" learning in the classroom. I strongly agree that these tools can be counterproductive in some instances, and ineffectual for certain types of learning. Nevertheless, the speaker's assertion places too little value on the ways in which these innovations can facilitate the learning process.

In several respects, I find the statement compelling. First of all, in my observation and experience, computers and videos are misused most often for education when teachers rely on them as surrogates, or baby-sitters. Teachers must use the time during which students are watching videos or are at their computer stations productively—helping other students, preparing lesson plans, and so forth. Otherwise, these tools can indeed impede the learning process.

Secondly, passive viewing of videos or of Web pages is no indication that any significant learning is taking place. Thus teachers must carefully select Internet resources that provide a true interactive learning experience, or are highly informative otherwise. And, in selecting videos teachers must be sure to follow up with lively class discussions. Otherwise, the comparatively passive nature of these media can render them ineffectual in the learning process.

Thirdly, some types of learning occur best during face-to-face encounters between teacher and student, and between students. Only by way of a live encounter can a language teacher recognize and immediately correct subtle problems in pronunciation and inflection. And, there is no suitable substitute for a live encounter when it comes to teaching techniques in painting, sculpture, music performance, and acting. Moreover, certain types of learning are facilitated when students interact as a group. Many grade-school teachers, for example, find that reading together aloud is the most effective way for students to learn this skill.

Fourth, with technology-based learning tools, especially computers and the Internet, learning how to use the technology can rob the teacher of valuable time that could be spent accomplishing the teacher's ultimate educational objectives. Besides, any technology-based learning tool carries the risk of technical problems. Students whose teachers fail to plan for productive use of unexpected down-time can lose opportunities for real learning.

Finally, we must not overlook the non-quantifiable benefit that personal attention can afford. A human teacher can provide meaningful personal encouragement and support, and can identify and help to solve a student's social or psychological problems that might be impeding the learning process. No video, computer program, or Web site can begin to serve these invaluable functions.

Acknowledging the many ways that technological innovations can impede "real" learning, these innovations nevertheless can facilitate "real" learning, if employed judicially and for appropriate purposes. Specifically, when it comes to learning rote facts and figures, personal interaction with a teacher is unnecessary, and can even result in fatigue and burnout for the teacher. Computers are an ideal tool for the sorts of learning that occur only through repetition—typing skills, basic arithmetical calculations, and so forth. Computers also make possible visual effects that aid uniquely in the learning of spatial concepts. Finally, computers, videos and the Internet are ideal for imparting basic textbook information to students, thereby freeing up the teacher's time to give students individualized attention.

In sum, computers and videos can indeed distract from learning—when teachers misuse them as substitutes for personal attention, or when the technology itself becomes the focus of attention. Nevertheless, if judicially used as primers, as supplements, and where repetition and rote learning are appropriate, these tools can serve to liberate teachers to focus on individual needs of students—needs that only "real" teachers can recognize and meet.

Issue:
Should all so-called facts **be mistrusted**?

The speaker contends that so-called "facts" often turn out to be false, and therefore that we should distrust whatever we are told is factual. Although the speaker overlooks certain circumstances in which undue skepticism might be counterproductive, and even harmful, on balance I agree that we should not passively accept whatever is passed off as fact; otherwise, human knowledge would never advance.

I turn first to so-called "scientific facts," by which I mean current prevailing notions about the nature of the physical universe that have withstood the test of rigorous scientific and logical scrutiny. The very notion of scientific progress is predicated on such scrutiny. Indeed the history of science is in large measure a history of challenges to so-called "scientific facts"—challenges which have paved the way for scientific progress. For example, in challenging the notion that the earth was in a fixed position at the center of the universe, Copernicus paved the way for the corroborating observations of Galileo a century later, and ultimately for Newton's principles of gravity upon which all modern science depends. The staggering cumulative impact of Copernicus' rejection of what he had been told was true provides strong support for the speaker's advice when it comes to scientific facts.

Another example of the value of distrusting what we are told is scientific fact involves the debate over whether human behavioral traits are a function of internal physical forces ("nature") or of learning and environment ("nurture").Throughout human history the prevailing view has shifted many times. The ancients assumed that our behavior was governed by the whims of the gods; in medieval times it became accepted fact that human behavior is dictated by bodily humours, or fluids; this "fact" later yielded to the notion that we are primarily products of our upbringing and environment. Now researchers are discovering that many behavioral traits are largely a function of the unique neurological structure of each individual's brain. Thus only by distrusting facts about human behavior can we advance in our scientific knowledge and, in turn, learn to deal more effectively with human behavioral issues in such fields as education, juvenile delinquency, criminal reform, and mental illness.

The value of skepticism about so-called "facts" is not limited to the physical sciences. When it comes to the social sciences we should always be skeptical about what is presented to us as historical fact. Textbooks can paint distorted pictures of historical events, and of their causes and consequences. After all, history in the making is always viewed firsthand through the eyes of subjective witnesses, then recorded by fallible journalists with their own cultural biases and agendas, then interpreted by historians with limited, and often tainted, information. And when it comes to factual assumptions underlying theories in the social sciences, we should be even more distrusting and skeptical, because such assumptions inherently defy deductive proof, or disproof. Skepticism should extend to the law as well. While law students, lawyers, legislators, and jurists must learn to appreciate traditional legal doctrines and principles, at the same time they must continually question their correctness—in terms of their fairness and continuing relevance.

Admittedly, in some cases undue skepticism can be counterproductive, and even harmful. For instance, we must accept current notions about the constancy of gravity and other basic laws of physics; otherwise, we would live in continual fear that the world around us would literally come crashing down on us. Undue skepticism can also be psychologically unhealthy when distrust borders on paranoia. Finally, common sense informs me that young people should first develop a foundation of experiential knowledge before they are encouraged to think critically about what they are told is fact.

To sum up, a certain measure of distrust of so-called "facts" is the very stuff of which human knowledge and progress are fashioned, whether in the physical sciences, the social sciences, or the law. Therefore, with few exceptions I strongly agree that we should strive to look at facts through skeptical eyes.

Answers That Express a Balanced Perspective on the Issue

To attain a high score on your Issue essay, you need not assert better and more arguments for one side on an issue than the other. It's perfectly okay to "straddle" the issue, as long as you defend your middle ground by presenting cogent arguments and relevant examples in support of each side. In fact, by adopting a balanced perspective, you'll likely impress the reader as someone who is able to see both sides of a complex issue—and making this sort of impression can only help your score.

That said, I strongly recommend that you conclude a balanced analysis by at least leaning toward one or the other side of the issue, and explain why you tend in that direction. To see what I mean, as you read the following essays pay special attention to their closing paragraphs.

Issue:
The benefits of a **global university**

I agree that it would serve the interests of all nations to establish a global university for the purpose of solving the world's most persistent social problems. Nevertheless, such a university poses certain risks that all participating nations must be careful to minimize—or risk defeating the university's purpose.

One compelling argument in favor of a global university has to do with the fact that its faculty and students would bring diverse cultural and educational perspectives to the problems they seek to solve. It seems to me that nations can only benefit from a global university where students learn ways in which other nations address certain social problems—successfully or not. It might be tempting to think that an overly diversified academic community would impede communication among students and faculty. However, in my view any such concerns are unwarranted, especially considering the growing awareness of other peoples and cultures that the mass media, and especially the Internet, have created. Moreover, many basic principles used to solve enduring social problems know no national boundaries; thus, a useful insight or discovery can come from a researcher or student from any nation.

Another compelling argument for a global university involves the increasingly global nature of certain problems. Consider, for instance, the depletion of atmospheric ozone, which has warmed the Earth to the point that it threatens the very survival of the human species. Also, we are now learning that clear-cutting the world's rainforests can set into motion a chain of animal extinction that threatens the delicate balance upon which all animals—including humans—depend. Also consider that a financial crisis—or a political crisis or natural disaster—in one country can spell trouble for foreign companies, many of which are now multinational in that they rely on the labor forces, equipment, and raw materials of other nations. Environmental, economic, and political problems such as these all carry grave social consequences—increased crime, unemployment, insurrection, hunger, and so forth. Solving these problems requires global cooperation—which a global university can facilitate.

Notwithstanding the foregoing reasons why a global university would help solve many of our most pressing social problems, the establishment of such a university poses certain problems of its own that must be addressed in order that the university can achieve its objectives. First, participant nations would need to overcome a myriad of administrative and political impediments. All nations would need to agree on which problems demand the university's attention and resources, which areas of academic research are worthwhile, as well as agreeing on policies and procedures for making, enforcing, and amending these decisions. Query whether a functional global university is politically feasible, given that sovereign nations naturally wish to advance their own agendas.

A second problem inherent in establishing a global university involves the risk that certain intellectual and research avenues would become officially sanctioned while others of equal or greater potential value would be discouraged, or perhaps even proscribed. A telling example of the inherent danger of setting and enforcing official research priorities involves the Soviet government's attempts during the 1920s to not only control the direction and the goals of its scientists' research but also to distort the outcome of that research—ostensibly for the greatest good of the greatest number of people. Not surprisingly, during this time period no significant scientific advances occurred under the auspices of the Soviet government. The Soviet lesson provides an important caveat to administrators of a global university: Significant progress in solving pressing social problems requires an open mind to all sound ideas, approaches, and theories—irrespective of the ideologies of their proponents.

A final problem with a global university is that the world's preeminent intellectual talent might be drawn to the sorts of problems to which the university is charged with solving, while parochial social problem go unsolved. While this is not reason enough not to establish a global university, it nevertheless is a concern that university administrators and participant nations must be aware of in allocating resources and intellectual talent.

To sum up, given the increasingly global nature of the world's social problems, and the escalating costs of addressing these problems, a global university makes good sense. And, since all nations would have a common interest in seeing this endeavor succeed, my intuition is that participating nations would be able to overcome whatever procedural and political obstacles that might stand in the way of success. As long as each nation is careful not to neglect its own unique social problems, and as long as the university's administrators are careful to remain open-minded about the legitimacy and potential value of various avenues of intellectual inquiry and research, a global university might go a long way toward solving many of the world's pressing social problems.

Issue:
Government's duty to preserve **lesser-known languages**

The speaker asserts that governments of countries where lesser-known languages are spoken should intervene to prevent these languages from becoming extinct. I agree insofar as a country's indigenous and distinct languages should not be abandoned and forgotten altogether. At some point, however, I think cultural identity should yield to the more practical considerations of day-to-day life in a global society.

On the one hand, the indigenous language of any geographical region is part-and-parcel of the cultural heritage of the region's natives. In my observation, we humans have a basic psychological need for individual identity, which we define by way of our membership in distinct cultural groups. A culture defines itself in various ways— by its unique traditions, rituals, mores, attitudes, and beliefs, but especially language. Therefore, when a people's language becomes extinct the result is a diminished sense of pride, dignity, and self-worth.

One need look no further than continental Europe to observe how people cling tenaciously to their distinct languages, despite the fact that there is no practical need for them anymore. And on the other side of the Atlantic Ocean, the French Canadians stubbornly insist on French as their official language, for the sole purpose of preserving their distinct cultural heritage. Even where no distinct language exists, people will invent one to gain a sense of cultural identity, as the emergence of the distinct Ebonic cant among today's African Americans aptly illustrates. In short, people resist language assimilation because of a basic human need to be part of a distinct cultural group.

Another important reason to prevent the extinction of a language is to preserve the distinct ideas that only that particular language can convey. Certain Native American and Oriental languages, for instance, contain words symbolizing spiritual and other abstract concepts that only these cultures embrace. Thus, in some cases to lose a language would be to abandon cherished beliefs and ideas that can be conveyed only through language.

On the other hand, in today's high-tech world of satellite communications, global mobility, and especially the Internet, language barriers serve primarily to impede cross-cultural communication, which in turn impedes international commerce and trade. Moreover, language barriers naturally breed misunderstanding, a certain distrust and, as a result, discord and even war among nations. Moreover, in my view the extinction of all but a few major languages is inexorable—as supported by the fact that the Internet has adopted English as its official language. Thus, by intervening to preserve a dying language a government might be deploying its resources to fight a losing battle, rather than to combat more pressing social problems—such as hunger, homelessness, disease, and ignorance—that plague nearly every society today.

In sum, preserving indigenous languages is, admittedly, a worthy goal; maintaining its own distinct language affords a people a sense of pride, dignity, and self-worth. Moreover, by preserving languages we honor a people's heritage, enhance our understanding of history, and preserve certain ideas that only some languages properly convey. Nevertheless, the economic and political drawbacks of language barriers outweigh the benefits of preserving a dying language. In the final analysis, government should devote its time and resources elsewhere, and leave it to the people themselves to take whatever steps are needed to preserve their own distinct languages.

Issue:
Should society place more **emphasis on the intellect**?

The speaker asserts that society should place more emphasis on intellect and cognition. While the speaker might overlook the benefits of nurturing certain emotions and feelings, on balance I agree that it is by way of our heads rather than our hearts that we can best ensure the well-being of our society.

I concede that undue emphasis on cultivating the intellect at the expense of healthy emotions can harm an individual psychologically. Undue suppression of legitimate and healthy desires and emotions can result in depression, dysfunction, and even physical illness. In fact, the intellect can mask such problems, thereby exacerbating them. To the extent they occur on a mass scale these problems become societal ones—lowering our economic productivity, burdening our health-care and social-welfare systems, and so forth. I also concede that by encouraging and cultivating certain positive emotions and feelings—such as compassion and empathy—society clearly stands to benefit.

In many other respects, however, emphasizing emotions and de-emphasizing intellect can carry negative, even dangerous, consequences for any society. Our collective sense of fairness, equity, and justice can easily give way to base instincts like hate, greed, and lust for power and domination. Thus, on balance any society is better off quelling or at least tempering these sorts of instincts, by nurturing reason, judgment, tolerance, fairness, and understanding—all of which are products of the intellect.

The empirical evidence supporting this position is overwhelming; yet one need look no further than a television set. Most of us have been witness to the current trend in trashy talk shows, which eschew anything approaching intellectual discourse in favor of pandering to our baser urges and instincts—like jealousy, lust, and hate. Episodes often devolve into anti-social, sometimes violent, behavior on the part of participants and observers alike. And any ostensible "lessons learned" from such shows hardly justify the anti-social outbursts that the producers and audiences of these shows hope for.

The dangers of a de-emphasis on intellect are all too evident in contemporary America. The incidence of hate crimes is increasing at a startling rate; gang warfare is at an all-time high; the level of distrust between African Americans and white America seems to be growing. Moreover, taken to an extreme and on a mass scale, appeal to the emotions rather than the intellect has resulted in humanity's most horrific atrocities, like the Jewish holocaust, as well as in nearly every holy war ever waged throughout history. Indeed, suppressing reason is how demagogues and despots gain and hold their power over their citizen-victims. In contrast, reason and better judgment are effective deterrents to despotism, demagoguery, and especially to war.

Those opposed to the speaker's position might argue that stressing cognition and intellect at the expense of emotion and feeling would have a chilling effect on artistic creativity, which would work a harm to the society. However, even in the arts students must learn theories and techniques, which they then apply to their craft— whether it be music performance, dance, or acting. And creative writing requires the cognitive ability to understand how language is used and how to best communicate ideas. Besides, creative ability is itself partly a function of intellect; that is, creative expression is a marriage between cognitive ability and the expression of feelings and emotions.

In sum, emotions and feelings can serve as important catalysts for compassion and for creativity. Yet behaviors that are most harmful to any society are also born of emotions and instincts, which the intellect can serve to override. The inescapable conclusion, then, is that the speaker is fundamentally correct.

Issue:
Our responsibility to **save endangered species**

What are the limits of our duty to save endangered species from extinction? The statement raises a variety of issues about morality, conscience, self-preservation, and economics. On balance, however, I fundamentally agree with the notion that humans need not make "extraordinary" efforts—at the expense of money and jobs—to ensure the preservation of any endangered species.

As I see it, there are three fundamental arguments for imposing on ourselves at least some responsibility to preserve endangered species. The first has to do with culpability. According to this argument, to the extent that endangerment is the result of anthropogenic events such as clear-cutting of forests or polluting of lakes and streams, we humans have a duty to take affirmative measures to protect the species whose survival we've placed in jeopardy.

The second argument has to do with capability. This argument disregards the extent to which we humans might have contributed to the endangerment of a species. Instead, the argument goes, if we are aware of the danger, know what steps are needed to prevent extinction, and can take those steps, then we are morally obligated to help prevent extinction. This argument would place a very high affirmative duty on humans to protect endangered species.

The third argument is an appeal to self-preservation. The animal kingdom is an intricate matrix of interdependent relationships, in which each species depends on many others for its survival. Severing certain relationships, such as that between a predator and its natural prey, can set into motion a series of extinctions that ultimately might endanger our own survival as a species. While this claim might sound far-fetched to some, environmental experts assure us that in the long run it is a very real possibility.

On the other hand are two compelling arguments against placing a duty on humans to protect endangered species. The first is essentially the Darwinian argument that extinction results from the inexorable process of so-called "natural selection" in which stronger species survive while weaker ones do not. Moreover, we humans are not exempt from the process. Accordingly, if we see fit to eradicate other species in order to facilitate our survival, then so be it. We are only behaving as animals must, Darwin would no doubt assert.

The second argument, and the one that I find most compelling, is an appeal to logic over emotion. It is a scientific fact that thousands of animal species become extinct every year. Many such extinctions are due to natural forces, while others are due to anthropogenic factors. In any event, it is far beyond our ability to save them all. By what standard, then, should we decide which species are worth saving and which ones are not? In my observation, we tend to favor animals with human-like physical characteristics and behaviors. This preference is understandable; after all, dolphins are far more endearing than bugs. But there is no logical justification for such a standard. Accordingly, what makes more sense is to decide based on our own economic self-interest. In other words, the more money and jobs it would cost to save a certain species, the lower priority we should place on doing so.

In sum, the issue of endangered-species protection is a complex one, requiring subjective judgments about moral duty and the comparative value of various life forms. Thus, there are no easy or certain answers. Yet it is for this very reason I agree that economic self-interest should take precedence over vague notions about moral duty when it comes to saving endangered species. In the final analysis, at a point when it becomes critical for our own survival as a species to save certain others, then we humans will do so if we are fit—in accordance with Darwin's observed process of natural selection.

Issue:
The limits of the responsibility of **corporate executives**

Should the only responsibility of a business executive be to maximize business profits, within the bounds of the law? In several respects this position has considerable merit; yet it ignores certain compelling arguments for imposing on businesses additional obligations to the society in which they operate.

On the one hand are two convincing arguments that profit maximization within the bounds of the law should be a business executive's sole responsibility. First, imposing on businesses additional duties to the society in which they operate can, paradoxically, harm that society. Compliance with higher ethical standards than the law requires—in such areas as environmental impact and workplace conditions—adds to business expenses and lowers immediate profits. In turn, lower profits can prevent the socially conscious business from creating more jobs, and from keeping its prices low and the quality of its products and services high. Thus, if businesses go further than their legal duties in serving their communities, the end result might be a net disservice to those communities.

Secondly, by affirming that profit maximization within legal bounds is the most ethical behavior possible for business, we encourage private enterprise, and more individuals enter the marketplace in the quest of profits. The inevitable result of increased competition is lower prices and better products, both of which serve the interests of consumers. Moreover, since maximizing profits enhances the wealth of a company's stakeholders, broad participation in private enterprise raises the wealth of a nation, expands its economy, and raises its overall standard of living and quality of life.

On the other hand are three compelling arguments for holding business executives to certain responsibilities in addition to profit maximization and to compliance with the letter of the law. First, a growing percentage of businesses are related to technology, and laws often lag behind advances in technology. As a result, new technology-based products and services might pose potential harm to consumers even though they conform to current laws. For example, Internet commerce is still largely unregulated because our lawmakers are slow to react to the paradigm shift from brick-and-mortar commerce to e-commerce. As a result, unethical marketing practices, privacy invasion, and violations of intellectual-property rights are going unchecked for lack of regulations that would clearly prohibit them.

Secondly, since a nation's laws do not extend beyond its borders, compliance with those laws does not prevent a business from doing harm elsewhere. Consider, for example, the trend among U.S. businesses in exploiting workers in countries where labor laws are virtually non-existent—in order to avoid the costs of complying with U.S. labor laws. Thirdly, a philosophical argument can be made that every business enters into an implied social contract with the community that permits it to do business, and that this social contract, although not legally enforceable, places a moral duty on the business to refrain from acting in ways that will harm that community.

In sum, I agree with the statement insofar as in seeking to maximize profits a business serves not only itself but also its employees, customers, and the overall economy. Yet, today's rapidly changing business environment and increasing globalization call for certain affirmative obligations beyond the pursuit of profit and mere compliance with enforceable rules and regulations. Moreover, in the final analysis any business is indebted to the society in which it operates for its very existence, and thus has a moral duty, regardless of any legal obligations, to pay that debt.

Issue:
Imagination vs. experience

The speaker asserts that imagination is "sometimes" more valuable than experience because individuals who lack experience can more freely imagine possibilities for approaching tasks than those entrenched in established habits and attitudes. I fundamentally agree; however, as the speaker implies, it is important not to overstate the comparative value of imagination. Examples from the arts and the sciences aptly illustrate both the speaker's point and my caveat.

One need only observe young children as they go about their daily lives to appreciate the role that pure imagination can play as an aid to accomplishing tasks. Young children, by virtue of their lack of experience, can provide insights and valuable approaches to adult problems. Recall the movie Big, in which a young boy magically transformed into an adult found himself in a high-power job as a marketing executive. His inexperience in the adult world of business allowed his youthful imagination free reign to contribute creative—and successful—ideas that none of his adult colleagues, set in their ways of thinking about how businesses go about maximizing profits, ever would have considered. Admittedly, Big was a fictional account; yet, I think it accurately portrays the extent to which adults lack the kind of imagination that only inexperience can bring to solving many adult problems.

The speaker's contention also finds ample empirical support in certain forms of artistic accomplishment and scientific invention. History is replete with evidence that our most gifted musical composers are young, relatively inexperienced, individuals. Notables ranging from Mozart to McCartney come immediately to mind. Similarly, the wide-eyed wonder of inexperience seems to spur scientific innovation. Consider the science fiction writer Jules Verne, who through pure imagination devised highly specific methods and means for transporting humans to outer space. What makes his imaginings so remarkable is that the actual methods and means for space flight, which engineers settled on through the experience of extensive research and trial-and-error, turned out to be essentially the same ones Verne had imagined nearly a century earlier!

Of course, there are many notable exceptions to the rule that imagination unfettered by experience breeds remarkable insights and accomplishments. Duke Ellington, perhaps jazz music's most prolific composer, continued to create new compositions until late in life. Thomas Edition, who registered far more patents with the U.S. patent office than any other person, continued to invent until a very old age.Yet, these are exceptions to the general pattern. Moreover, the later accomplishments of individuals such as these tend to build on earlier ones, and therefore are not as truly inspired as the earlier ones, which sprung from imagination less fettered by life experience.

On the other hand, it is important not to take this assertion about artistic and scientific accomplishment too far. Students of the arts, for instance, must learn theories and techniques, which they then apply to their craft—whether music performance, dance, or acting. And, creative writing requires the cognitive ability to understand how language is used and how to communicate ideas. Besides, creative ability is itself partly a function of intellect; that is, creative expression is a marriage of one's cognitive abilities and the expression of one's feelings and emotions. In literature, for example, a rich life experience from which to draw ideas is just as crucial to great achievement as imagination. For example, many critics laud Mark Twain's autobiography, which he wrote on his deathbed, as his most inspired work. And, while the direction and goals of scientific research rely on the imaginations of key individuals, most scientific discoveries and inventions come about not by sudden epiphanies of youthful star-gazers but rather by years and years of trial-and-error in corporate research laboratories.

In sum, imagination can serve as an important catalyst for artistic creativity and scientific invention. Yet, experience can also play a key role; in fact, in literature and in science it can play just as key a role as the sort of imagination that inexperience breeds.

Issue:
Is **complete honesty** a useful virtue in politics?

Is complete honesty a useful virtue in politics? The speaker contends that it is not, for the reason that political leaders must sometimes lie to be effective. In order to evaluate this contention it is necessary to examine the nature of politics and to distinguish between short-term and long-term effectiveness.

On the one hand are three compelling arguments that a political leader must sometimes be less than truthful in order to be effective in that leadership. The first argument lies in the fact that politics is a game played among politicians—and that to succeed in the game one must use the tools that are part-and-parcel of it. Complete forthrightness is a sign of vulnerability and naiveté, neither of which will earn a politician respect among his or her opponents, and which those opponents will use to every advantage against the honest politician.

Secondly, it is crucial to distinguish between misrepresentations of fact—in other words, lies—and mere political rhetoric. The rhetoric of a successful politician eschews rigorous factual inquiry and indisputable fact while appealing to emotions, ideals, and subjective interpretation and characterizations. Consider, for example, a hypothetical candidate for political office who attacks the incumbent opponent by pointing out only certain portions of that opponent's legislative voting record. The candidate might use a vote against a bill eliminating certain incentives for local businesses as "clear evidence" that the opponent is "anti-business," "bad for the economy," or "out of touch with what voters want." None of these allegations are outright lies; they are simply the rhetorical cant of the effective politician.

Thirdly, politics is a business born not only of idealism but also of pragmatism; after all, in order to be effective a politician must gain and hold onto political power, which means winning elections. In my observation, some degree of pandering to the electorate and to those who might lend financial support in reelection efforts is necessary to maintain that position. Modern politics is replete with candidates who refused to pander, thereby ruining their own chance to exercise effective leadership.

Although in the short term being less-than-truthful with the public might serve a political leader's interest in preserving power, would-be political leaders who lack requisite integrity ultimately forfeit their leadership. Consider Richard Nixon, whose leadership seemed born not of ideology but of personal ambition, which bred contempt of the very people who sanctioned his leadership in the first place; the ultimate result was his forfeiture of that leadership. In contrast, Ronald Reagan was a highly effective leader largely because he honestly, and deeply, believed in the core principles that he espoused and advocated during his presidency—and his constituency sensed that genuineness and responded favorably to it. Moreover, certain types of sociopolitical leadership inherently require the utmost integrity and honesty. Consider notable figures such as Gandhi and King, both of whom were eminently effective in leading others to practice the high ethical and moral standards which they themselves advocated. The reason for this is simple: A high standard for one's own personal integrity is a prerequisite for effective moral leadership.

To sum up, I concede that the game of politics calls for a certain measure of posturing and disingenuousness. Yet, at the end of the game, without a countervailing measure of integrity, political game-playing will serve to diminish a political leader's effectiveness—perhaps to the point where the politician forfeits the game.

Issue:
The proper **use of public resources**

The speaker asserts that using public resources to support the arts is unjustifiable in a society where some people go without food, jobs, and basic survival skills. It might be tempting to agree with the speaker on the basis that art is not a fundamental human need, and that government is not entirely trustworthy when it comes to its motives and methods. However, the speaker overlooks certain economic and other societal benefits that accrue when government assumes an active role in supporting the arts.

The implicit rationale behind the speaker's statement seems to be that cultural enrichment pales in importance compared to food, clothing, and shelter. That the latter needs are more fundamental is indisputable; after all, what starving person would prefer a good painting to even a bad meal? Accordingly, I concede that when it comes to the use of public resources it is entirely appropriate to assign a lower priority to the arts than to these other pressing social problems. Yet, to postpone public arts funding until we completely eliminate unemployment and hunger would be to postpone arts funding forever; any informed person who believes otherwise is envisioning a pure socialist state where the government provides for all of its citizens' needs— a vision which amounts to fantasy.

It might also be tempting to agree with the speaker on the basis that arts patronage is neither an appropriate nor a necessary function of government. This argument has considerable merit, in three respects. First, it seems ill conceived to relegate decision and choices about arts funding to a handful of bureaucrats, who are likely to decide based on their own quirky notions about art, and whose decisions might be susceptible to influence peddling. Second, private charity and philanthropy appear to be alive and well today. For example, year after year the Public Broadcasting System is able to survive, and even thrive, on donations from private foundations and individuals. Third, government funding requires tax dollars from our pockets—leaving us with less disposable dollars with which to support the arts directly and more efficiently than any bureaucracy ever could.

On the other hand are two compelling arguments that public support for the arts is desirable, whether or not unemployment and hunger have been eliminated. One such argument is that by allocating public resources to the arts we actually help to solve these social problems. Consider Canada's film industry, which is heavily subsidized by the Canadian government, and which provides countless jobs for film-industry workers as a result. The Canadian government also provides various incentives for American production companies to film and produce their movies in Canada. These incentives have sparked a boon for the Canadian economy, thereby stimulating job growth and wealth that can be applied toward education, job training, and social programs. The Canadian example is proof that public arts support can help solve the kinds of social problems with which the speaker is concerned.

A second argument against the speaker's position has to do with the function and ultimate objectives of art. Art serves to lift the human spirit and to put us more in touch with our feelings, foibles, and fate—in short, with our own humanity. With a heightened sensitivity to the human condition, we become more others-oriented, less self-centered, more giving of ourselves. In other words, we become a more charitable society—more willing to give to those less fortunate than ourselves in the ways with which the speaker is concerned. The speaker might argue, of course, that we do a disservice to others when we lend a helping hand—by enabling them to depend on us to survive. However, at the heart of this specious argument lies a certain coldness and lack of compassion that, in my view, any society should seek to discourage. Besides, the argument leads inexorably to certain political, philosophical, and moral issues that this brief essay cannot begin to address.

In the final analysis, the beneficiaries of public arts funding are not limited to the elitists who stroll through big-city museums and attend symphonies and gallery openings, as the speaker might have us believe. Public resources allocated to the arts create jobs for artists and others whose livelihood depends on a vibrant, rich culture—just the sort of culture that breeds charitable concern for the hungry, the helpless, and the hapless.

Issue:
Are we facing increasingly **complex and challenging** problems?

Is any sense that the problems we face are more complex and challenging than those which our predecessors faced merely an illusion—one that can be dispelled by way of knowledge and experience? The speaker believes so, although I disagree. In my view, the speaker unfairly generalizes about the nature of contemporary problems, some of which have no analog from earlier times and which in some respects are more complex and challenging than any problems earlier societies ever confronted. Nevertheless, I agree that many of the other problems we humans face are by their nature enduring ones that have changed little in complexity and difficulty over the span of human history; and I agree that through experience and enlightened reflection on human history we grow to realize this fact.

I turn first to my chief point of contention with the statement. The speaker overlooks certain societal problems unique to today's world, which are complex and challenging in ways unlike any problems that earlier societies ever faced. Consider three examples. The first involves the growing scarcity of the world's natural resources.

An ever-increasing human population, together with over-consumption on the part of developed nations and with global dependencies on finite natural resources, have created uniquely contemporary environmental problems that are global in impact and therefore pose political and economic challenges previously unrivaled in complexity.

A second uniquely contemporary problem has to do with the fact that the nations of the world are growing increasingly interdependent—politically, militarily, and economically. Interdependency makes for problems that are far more complex than analogous problems for individual nations during times when they were more insular, more self-sustaining, and more autonomous.

A third uniquely contemporary problem is an outgrowth of the inexorable advancement of scientific knowledge, and one that society voluntarily takes up as a challenge. Through scientific advancements we've already solved innumerable health problems, harnessed various forms of physical energy, and so forth. The problems left to address are the ones that are most complex and challenging—for example, slowing the aging process, replacing human limbs and organs, and colonizing other worlds in the event ours becomes inhabitable. In short, as we solve each successive scientific puzzle we move on to more challenging and complex ones.

I turn next to my points of agreement with the statement. Humans face certain universal and timeless problems, which are neither more nor less complex and challenging for any generation than for preceding ones. These sorts of problems are the ones that spring from the failings and foibles that are part-and-parcel of human nature. Our problems involving interpersonal relationships with people of the opposite sex stem from basic differences between the two sexes. The social problems of prejudice and discrimination know no chronological bounds because it is our nature to fear and mistrust people who are different from us. War and crime stem from the male aggressive instinct and innate desire for power. We've never been able to solve social problems such as homelessness and hunger because we are driven by self-interest.

I agree with the statement also in that certain kinds of intellectual struggles— to determine the meaning of life, whether God exists, and so forth—are timeless ones whose complexities and mystery know no chronological bounds whatsoever. The fact that we rely on ancient teachings to try to solve these problems underscores the fact that these problems have not grown any more complex over the course of human history.

And, with respect to all the timeless problems mentioned above I agree that knowledge and experience help us to understand that these problems are not more complex today than before. In the final analysis, by studying history, human psychology, theology, and philosophy we come to realize that, aside from certain uniquely contemporary problems, we face the same fundamental problems as our predecessors because we face the same human condition as our predecessors whenever we look in the mirror.

Issue:
Is **moderation in all things** poor advice?

Should we strive for moderation in all things, as the adage suggests? I tend to agree with the speaker that worthwhile endeavors sometimes require, or at least call for, intense focus at the expense of moderation.

The virtues of moderation are undeniable. Moderation in all things affords us the time and energy to sample more of what life and the world have to offer. In contrast, lack of moderation leads to a life out of balance. As a society we are slowly coming to realize what many astute psychologists and medical practitioners have known all along: we are at our best as humans only when we strike a proper balance between the mind, body, and spirit. The call for a balanced life is essentially a call for moderation in all things.

For instance, while moderate exercise improves our health and sense of wellbeing, over-exercise and intense exercise can cause injury or psychological burnout, either of which defeat our purpose by requiring us to discontinue exercise altogether. Lack of moderation in diet can cause obesity at one extreme or anorexia at the other, either of which endangers one's health, and even life. And when it comes to potentially addictive substances—alcohol, tobacco, and the like—the deleterious effects of over-consumption are dear enough.

The virtues of moderation apply to work as well. Stress associated with a high-pressure job increases one's vulnerability to heart disease and other physical disorders. And over-work can result in psychological burnout, thereby jeopardizing one's job and career. Overwork can even kill, as demonstrated by the alarmingly high death rate among young Japanese men, many of whom work 100 or more hours each week.

Having acknowledged the wisdom of the old adage, I nevertheless agree that under some circumstances, and for some people, abandoning moderation might be well justified. Query how many of the world's great artistic creations—in the visual arts, music, and even literature—would have come to fruition without intense, focused efforts on the part of their creators. Creative work necessarily involves a large measure of intense focus—a single-minded, obsessive pursuit of aesthetic perfection.

Or, consider athletic performance. Admittedly, intensity can be counterproductive when it results in burnout or injury. Yet who could disagree that a great athletic performance necessarily requires great focus and intensity—both in preparation and in the performance itself? In short, when it comes to athletics, moderation breeds mediocrity, while intensity breeds excellence and victory. Finally, consider the increasingly competitive world of business. An intense, focused company-wide effort is sometimes needed to ensure a company's competitiveness, and even survival. This is particularly true in today's technology-driven industries where keeping up with frantic pace of change is essential for almost any high-tech firm's survival.

In sum, the old adage amounts to sound advice for most people under most circumstances. Nevertheless, when it comes to creative accomplishment, and to competitive success in areas such as athletics and business, I agree with the speaker that abandoning or suspending moderation is often appropriate, and sometimes necessary, in the interest of achieving worthwhile goals.

Answers That Apply an Issue Statement Separately to Two or More Categories

Be on the lookout for Issue statements that embrace two or more distinct fields, endeavors, or realms; for example, both science and art or both government and private enterprise. Some Issue statements actually provide a list of categories that virtually invite you to apply the statement separately to each one.

As the essays in this section illustrate, the extent of your agreement with the statement may or may not differ from one category to another. In any event, in your opening remarks you may wish to identify each category and indicate whether your agreement depends on the category under consideration.

Issue:
Can only history determine an individual's **greatness**?

Can a person's greatness be recognized only in retrospect, by those who live after the person, as the speaker maintains? In my view the speaker unfairly generalizes. In some areas, especially the arts, greatness is often recognizable in its nascent stages. However, in other areas, particularly the physical sciences, greatness must be tested over time before it can be confirmed. In still other areas, such as business, the incubation period for greatness varies from case to case.

We do not require a rear-view mirror to recognize artistic greatness—whether in music, visual arts, or literature. The reason for this is simple: art can be judged at face value. There's nothing to be later proved or disproved, affirmed or discredited, or even improved upon or refined by further knowledge or newer technology. History is replete with examples of artistic greatness immediately recognized, then later confirmed. Through his patronage, the Pope recognized Michelangelo's artistic greatness, while the monarchs of Europe immediately recognized Mozart's greatness by granting him their most generous commissions. Mark Twain became a best-selling author and household name even during his lifetime. And the leaders of the modernist school of architecture marveled even as Frank Lloyd Wright was elevating their notions about architecture to new aesthetic heights.

By contrast, in the sciences it is difficult to identify greatness without the benefit of historical perspective. Any scientific theory might be disproved tomorrow, thereby demoting the theorist's contribution to the status of historical footnote. Or the theory might withstand centuries of rigorous scientific scrutiny. In any event, a theory may or may not serve as a springboard for later advances in theoretical science. A current example involves the ultimate significance of two opposing theories of physics: wave theory and quantum theory. Some theorists now claim that a new so-called "string" theory reconciles the two opposing theories—at least mathematically. Yet "strings" have yet to be confirmed empirically. Only time will tell whether the string theory indeed provides the unifying laws that all matter in the universe obeys. In short, the significance of contributions made by theoretical scientists cannot be judged by their contemporaries—only by scientists who follow them.

In the realm of business, in some cases great achievement is recognizable immediately, while in other cases it is not. Consider on the one hand Henry Ford's assembly-line approach to manufacturing affordable cars for the masses. Even Ford could not have predicted the impact his innovations would have on the American economy and on the modern world. On the other hand, by any measure, Microsoft's Bill Gates has made an even greater contribution than Ford; after all, Gates is largely responsible for lifting American technology out of the doldrums during the 1970s to restore America to the status of economic powerhouse and technological leader of the world. And this contribution is readily recognizable now—as it is happening. Of course, the DOS and Windows operating systems, and even Gates' monopoly, might eventually become historical relics. Yet his greatness is already secured.

In sum, the speaker overlooks many great individuals, particularly in the arts and in business, whose achievements were broadly recognized as great even during their own time. Nevertheless, other great achievements, especially scientific ones, cannot be confirmed as such without the benefit of historical perspective.

Issue:
Teamwork as the key to productivity

The speaker asserts that because teamwork requires cooperative effort, people are more motivated and therefore more productive working in teams than working individually as competitors. My view is that this assertion is true only in some cases. If one examines the business world, for example, it becomes clear that which approach is more effective in motivating people and in achieving productivity depends on the specific job.

In some jobs productivity clearly depends on the ability of coworkers to cooperate as members of a team. For businesses involved in the production of products through complex processes, all departments and divisions must work in lock-step fashion toward product roll-out. Cooperative interaction is even essential in jobs performed in relative isolation and in jobs in which technical knowledge or ability, not the ability to work with others, would seem to be most important. For example, scientists, researchers, and even computer programmers must collaborate to establish common goals, coordinate efforts, and meet time lines. Moreover, the kinds of people attracted to these jobs in the first place are likely to be motivated by a sense of common purpose rather than by individual ambition.

In other types of jobs individual competition, tenacity, and ambition are the keys to productivity. For example, a commissioned salesperson's compensation, and sometimes tenure and potential for promotion as well, is based on comparative sales performance of coworkers. Working as competitors a firm's individual salespeople maximize productivity—in terms of profit—both for themselves and for their firm. Key leadership positions also call, above all, for a certain tenacity and competitive spirit. A firm's founding entrepreneur must maintain this spirit in order for the firm to survive, let alone to maximize productivity. Moreover, in my observation the kinds of people inclined toward entrepreneurship and sales in the first place are those who are competitive by nature, not those who are motivated primarily by a sense of common purpose.

On balance, however, my view is that cooperation is more crucial for an organization's long-term productivity than individual competition. Even in jobs where individual competitiveness is part-and-parcel of the job, the importance of cooperation should not be underestimated. Competition among sales people can quickly grow into jealousy, backstabbing, and unethical behavior—all of which are counterproductive. And even the most successful entrepreneurs would no doubt admit that without the cooperative efforts of their subordinates, partners, and colleagues, their personal visions would never become reality.

In sum, individual competitiveness and ambition are essential motivating forces for certain types of jobs, while in other jobs it is a common sense of mission that motivates workers to achieve maximum productivity. In the final analysis, however, the overall productivity of almost every organization depends ultimately on the ability of its members to cooperate as a team.

Issue:
Monitoring our progress with the **use of logic** and measurement

Do we need careful measurements and logic to determine whether and to what extent we are progressing or regressing? I agree that in certain endeavors quantitative measurements and logical analysis of data are essential for this purpose. However, in other realms objective data provide little guidance for determining progress. My view applies to individuals as well as society as a whole.

As for monitoring individual progress, the extent to which careful measurement and logical analysis of data are required depends on the specific endeavor. In the area of personal finance, objective measurements are critical. We might feel that we are advancing financially when we buy a new car or a better home, or when our salary increases. Yet these signs of personal economic success can be deceptive. Cars depreciate quickly in value, and residential real estate must appreciate steadily to offset ownership expenses. Even a pay raise is no sure sign of personal financial progress; if the raise fails to keep pace with the cost of living then the real salary is actually in decline.

In the area of one's physical well-being, however, quantitative measurement might be useful yet insufficient. Quantitative data such as blood pressure, cholesterol level, and body weight are useful objective indicators of physical health. Yet quantitative measurement and logic can only take us so far when it comes to physical well-being. Levels of physical discomfort and pain, the most reliable indicators of physical wellbeing, cannot be quantified. And of course our emotional and psychological wellbeing, which can have a profound impact on our physical health, defy objective measurement altogether.

On a societal level, as on a personal level, the extent to which careful measurement and logic are needed to determine progress depends on the endeavor. In macroeconomics, as in personal finance, objective measurements are critical. For example, a municipality, state, or nation might sense that things are improving economically when its rate of unemployment declines. Yet, if new jobs are in poor-paying positions involving unskilled labor, this apparent advance might actually be a retreat. And, a boom in retail sales might amount to regress if the goods sold are manufactured by foreign firms, who benefit from the boom at the expense of domestic business expansion. Technological progress also requires careful measurement. Advances in computer technology can only be determined by such factors as processing and transfer speeds, numbers of installations and users, amounts of data accessed, and so forth. And, advances in biotechnology are determined by statistical measurements of the effectiveness of new drugs and other treatments, and by demographic statistics regarding the incidence of the ailments that the technology seeks to ameliorate.

In contrast, socio-political progress is less susceptible to objective measurement. For instance, progress in social welfare might be measured by the number of homeless people, incidence of domestic violence, or juvenile crime rate. Yet, would an increase in the number of single mothers on welfare indicate that our society is becoming more compassionate and effective in helping its victims, or would it indicate regress by showing that our private sector and education systems are failing? Moreover, when it comes to our legal system and to politics, progress has little to do with numbers, or even logic. For example, to what extent, if any, would more lenient gun ownership laws indicate progress, considering the competing interests of individual freedom and pubic safety? Do anti-abortion laws indicate a sociological advance or retreat? Or, when a political party gains greater control of a legislature by sweeping a particular election, is this progress or regress?

In sum, although the statement has merit, it unfairly generalizes. In areas such as finance, economics, and computing technology, all of which involve nothing but quantifiable data, nothing but careful measurement and logic suffice to determine the extent of progress. In other areas, such as health care and social welfare, determining progress requires both objective measurement and subjective judgment. Finally, progress in politics and law is an entirely subjective matter—depending on each individual's values, priorities, and interests.

Issue:
The beneficiaries of **global networks**

I agree that the globalization of economic and communication networks will heighten international influences in all four of the areas listed. However, while those influences will no doubt benefit education and the sciences, the nature of those influences on the arts and on politics will probably be a mixed one—beneficial in some respects yet detrimental in others.

The clearest and most immediate beneficiaries of international influences are students. When students learn more about other cultures, systems of government, religions, and so forth, they advance their knowledge and grow in their understanding of humanity—which is, after all, the final objective of education. Emerging distance-learning technologies, made practicable now by the Internet, will no doubt carry an especially profound international influence on education. Distance learning will permit a class of students located all over the world to videoconference simultaneously with a teacher and with one other, thereby enlivening and enriching educational experiences.

The sciences clearly benefit from international influences as well. After all, principles of physics, chemistry, and mathematics know no political boundaries; thus, a useful insight or discovery can come from a researcher or theorist anywhere in the world. Accordingly, any technology that enhances global communication can only serve to advance scientific knowledge. For example, astronomers can now transmit observational data to other scientists throughout the world the instant they receive that data, so that the entire global community of astronomers can begin interpreting that data together—in a global brainstorming session. The sciences also benefit from multi-national economic cooperation. Consider, for instance, the multi-national program to establish a human colony on the Moon. This ambitious project is possible only because participating nations are pooling their economic resources as well as scientific talents.

With respect to the arts, however, the speaker's claim is far less convincing. It might seem that if artists broaden their cultural exposure and real-world experience their art works would become richer and more diverse. However, the logical consequence of increasing international influence on the arts is a homogenous global culture in which art becomes increasingly the same. The end result is not only a chilling effect on artistic creativity, but also a loss of cultural identity, which seems to be an important sociological and psychological need.

The impact of global networking on political relations might turn out to be a mixed one as well. Consider, for instance, the current unification of Europe's various monetary systems. Since Europe's countries are becoming economically interdependent, it would seem that it would be in their best interests to cooperate politically with one another. However, discord over monetary policy might result in member countries withdrawing from the Community, and in a political schism or other falling out. Consider also the burgeoning global communications network. On the one hand, it would seem that instant face-to-face communication between diplomats and world leaders would help avert and quell political and military crises. By the same token, however, global networking renders any nation's security system more vulnerable. This point is aptly illustrated by a recent incident involving a high-ranking Pentagon official who stored top-secret files on his home computer, which was connected to the Internet without any firewall precautions. Incidents such as this one might prompt the world's governments to become more protective of their sovereignty, more insular, and even paranoid.

In sum, growing international influences that result naturally from global communications and economic networks can only serve to facilitate education and to advance scientific knowledge. However, although the same influences no doubt will have an impact on the arts and on international politics, the speaker's claim that those influences will be beneficial is dubious, or at least premature, given that global networking is still in its nascent stages.

Issue:
Do the arts reveal society's **hidden ideas and impulses**?

The speaker asserts that the arts reveal society's hidden ideas and impulses. While this assertion has merit, I think it unfairly generalizes about art. Consider two particular art forms: architecture and painting. In more important architecture one consistently sees a refection of society's ideas and urges. However, in more important paintings of the most recent century one sees instead the artists' personal and idiosyncratic visions of an aesthetic ideal.

Turning first to public architecture, one sees in ancient and Renaissance forms an impulse to transcend the human condition. Clearly, the most important architecture of these periods was built to honor deities and to propel humans into the afterlife. Consider, for example, the ancient pyramids and the great cathedrals of Europe, which rise upward toward the stars and heavens. During the Medieval period the most important architectural form was the castle, which reflected an overriding concern for military security and brute strength during a time of comparative anarchy. During the twentieth century it was first the steel-forged art deco forms and then the sky-scraping office building that dominated public architecture. These forms reflect modern, more mundane concerns for industrial and technological progress.

Turning next to important paintings and painters, it seems to me that the art of previous centuries reflected the attitudes and ideas of the prevailing culture to a far greater extent than today's art. The cynosures of the Medieval and Renaissance artists, for instance, were certain Christian themes—the Trinity, virgin birth of Christ, the Resurrection, and so forth—with which the society at large was also preoccupied. Later, during the eighteenth and nineteenth centuries, an emerging genteel class saw itself reflected in the bourgeois themes of impressionists such as Renoir and Monet.

But in the most recent century the picture has been much different. Consider three of the twentieth century's most influential painters: Picasso, Dali, and Pollock. Picasso's style underwent a series of radical changes throughout his career. Was the reason for Picasso's diverse "periods" a quick series of radical changes in society's ideas and impulses, or perhaps a reflection of society's hidden impulse for constant change? Or did Picasso's varied styles merely reflect the complex psychological profile of one eccentric artist? Dali is known for his surrealistic images; but do these images reveal some kind of existential angst on a societal level, or just the odd aesthetic vision of one man? Pollock's penchant was for dripping paint on the floor in order to create abstract images that would have the sort of visceral impact he was after. In fact, Pollock turned to this technique only after he tried but failed as a conventional painter, using brush and easel. So are Pollock's striking abstract murals a reflection of some mid-twentieth-century societal impulse, or merely the result of one struggling artist stumbling onto something he was good at? In all three cases, it seems that the art reflected the artist but not the society.

In sum, in the art of painting one can observe a shift from styles and themes reflecting broad societal impulses to a more recent concern for expressing personal impulses and creative urges. In contrast, the more public art form of architecture has always mirrored society's ideas and impulses, and probably always will—because architecture is so much more public than the art of painting.

Issue:
Does **personal economic success** require **conformity**?

Personal economic success might be due either to one's investment strategy or to one's work or career. With respect to the former, non-conformists with enough risk tolerance and patience invariably achieve more success than conformists. With respect to the latter, while non-conformists are more likely to succeed in newer industries where markets and technology are in constant flux, conformists are more likely to succeed in traditional service industries ensconced in systems and regulations.

Regarding the sort of economic success that results from investing one's wealth, the principles of investing dictate that those who seek risky investments in areas that are out of favor with the majority of investors ultimately reap higher returns than those who follow the crowd. It is conformists who invest, along with most other investors, in areas that are currently the most profitable, and popular. However, popular investments tend to be overpriced, and in the long run their values will come down to reasonable levels. As a result, given enough time conformists tend to reap lower rewards from their investments than nonconformists do.

Turning to the sort of economic success that one achieves by way of one's work, neither conformists nor non-conformists necessarily achieve greater success than the other group. In consumer-driven industries, where innovation, product differentiation, and creativity are crucial to lasting success, non-conformists who take unique approaches tend to recognize emerging trends and to rise above their peers. For example, Ted Turner's departure from the traditional format of the other television networks, and the responsiveness of Amazon's Jeff Bezos to burgeoning Internet commerce, propelled these two non-conformists into leadership positions in their industries. Particularly in technology industries, where there are no conventional practices or ways of thinking to begin with, people who cling to last year's paradigm, or to the status quo in general, are soon left behind by coworkers and competing firms.

However, in traditional service industries—such as finance, accounting, insurance, legal services, and health care—personal economic success comes not to non-conformists but rather to those who can work most effectively within the constraints of established practices, policies and regulations. Of course, a clever idea for structuring a deal, or a creative legal maneuver, might play a role in winning smaller battles along the way. But such tactics are those of conformists who are playing by the same ground rules as their peers; winners are just better at the game.

In conclusion, non-conformists with sufficient risk tolerance and patience are invariably the most successful investors in the long run. When it comes to careers, however, while non-conformists tend to be more successful in technology- and consumer-driven industries, traditionalists are the winners in system-driven industries pervaded by policy, regulation, and bureaucracy.

Issue:
Effective leadership and commitment to **particular principles**

Whether effective leadership requires that a leader consistently follow his or her principles and objectives is a complex issue—one that is tied up in the problem of defining effective leadership in the first place. In addressing the issue it is helpful to consider, in turn, three distinct forms of leadership: business, political, and social-spiritual.

In the business realm, effective leadership is generally defined, at least in our corporate culture, as that which achieves the goal of profit maximization for a firm's shareholders or other owners. Many disagree, however, that profit is the appropriate measure of a business leader's effectiveness. Some detractors claim, for example, that a truly effective business leader must also fulfill additional duties—for example, to do no intentional harm to their customers or to the society in which they operate. Other detractors go further—to impose on business leaders an affirmative obligation to yield to popular will, by protecting consumers, preserving the natural environment, promoting education, and otherwise taking steps to help alleviate society's problems.

Whether our most effective business leaders are the ones who remain consistently committed to maximizing profits or the ones who appease the general populace by contributing to popular social causes depends, of course, on one's own definition of business success. In my observation, as business leaders become subject to closer scrutiny by the media and by social activists, business leaders will maximize profits in the long term only by taking reasonable steps to minimize the social and environmental harm their businesses cause. Thus, the two definitions merge, and the statement at issue is ultimately correct.

In the political realm the issue is no less complex. Definitions of effective political leadership are tied up in the means a leader uses to wield his or her power and to obtain that power in the first place. Consider history's most infamous tyrants and despots—such as Genghis Khan, Stalin, Mao, and Hitler. No historian would disagree that these individuals were remarkably effective leaders, and that each one remained consistently committed to his tyrannical objectives and Machiavellian principles. Ironically, it was stubborn commitment to objectives that ultimately defeated all except Khan. Thus, in the short term, stubborn adherence to one's objectives might serve a political leader's interest in preserving his or her power; yet, in the long term such behavior invariably results in that leader's downfall—if the principles are not in accord with those of the leader's would-be followers.

Finally, consider social-spiritual leadership. Few would disagree that through their ability to inspire others and lift the human spirit Mahatma Gandhi and Martin Luther King were eminently effective in leading others to effect social change through civil disobedience. It seems to me that this brand of leadership, in order to be effective, inherently requires that the leader remain steadfastly committed to principle. Why? It is commitment to principle that is the basis for this brand of leadership in the first place. For example, had Gandhi advocated civil disobedience yet been persuaded by close advisors that an occasional violent protest might be effective in gaining India's independence from Britain, no doubt the result would have been immediate forfeiture of that leadership. In short, social-spiritual leaders must not be hypocrites; otherwise, they will lose all credibility and effectiveness.

In sum, strict adherence to principles and objectives is a prerequisite for effective social-spiritual leadership—both in the short and long term. In contrast, political leadership wanes in the long term unless the leader ultimately yields to the will of the followers. Finally, when it comes to business, leaders must strike a balance between the objective of profit maximization—the traditional measure of effectiveness—and yielding to certain broader obligations that society is now imposing on them.

Issue:
Can only inside experts judge **work in any given field**?

The speaker's assertion that work in any field can be judged only by experts in that field amounts to an unfair generalization, in my view. I would concur with the speaker when it comes to judging the work of social scientists, although I would strongly disagree when it comes to work in the pure physical sciences, as explained in the following discussion.

With respect to the social sciences, the social world presents a seamless web of not only anthropogenic but also physical forces, which interact in ways that can be understood only in the context of a variety of disciplines. Thus, experts from various fields must collectively determine the merit of work in the social sciences. For example, consider the field of cultural anthropology. The merits of researcher's findings and conclusions about an ancient civilization must be scrutinized by biochemists, geologists, linguists, and even astronomers.

Specifically, by analyzing the hair, nails, blood, and bones of mummified bodies, biochemists and forensic scientists can pass judgment on the anthropologist's conjectures about the life expectancy, general well-being, and common causes of death of the population. Geologists are needed to identify the source and age of the materials used for tools, weapons, and structures—thereby determining whether the anthropologist extrapolated correctly about the civilization's economy, trades and work habits, lifestyles, extent of travel and mobility, and so forth. Linguists are needed to interpret hieroglyphics and extrapolate from found fragments of writings. And, astronomers are sometimes needed to determine whether the anthropologist's explanations for the layout of an ancient city or the design, structure and position of monuments, tombs, and temples is convincing—because ancients often looked to the stars for guidance in building cities and structures.

In contrast, the work of researchers in the purely physical sciences can be judged only by their peers. The reason for this is that scientific theories and observations are either meritorious or not, depending solely on whether they can be proved or disproved by way of the scientific method. For example, consider the complex equations that physicists rely upon to draw conclusions about the nature of matter, time, and space, or the origins and future of the universe. Only other physicists in these specialties can understand, let alone judge, this type of theoretical work. Similarly, empirical observations in astrophysics and molecular physics require extremely sophisticated equipment and processes, which only experts in these fields have access to and who know how to use reliably.

Those who disagree that only inside experts can judge scientific work might point out that the expertise of economists and pubic-policy makers is required to determine whether the work is worthwhile from a more mundane economic or political viewpoint. Detractors might also point out that ultimately it is our philosophers who are best equipped to judge the ultimate import of ostensibly profound scientific discoveries. Yet, these detractors miss the point of what I take to be the speaker's more narrow claim: that the integrity and quality of work—disregarding its socioeconomic utility—can be judged only by experts in the work's field.

In sum, in the social sciences no area of inquiry operates in a vacuum. Because fields such as anthropology, sociology, and history are so closely intertwined and even dependent on the physical sciences, experts from various fields must collectively determine the integrity and quality of work in these fields. However, in the purely physical sciences the quality and integrity of work can be adequately judged only by inside experts, who are the only ones equipped with sufficient technical knowledge to pass judgment.

Issue:
To what extent is **originality** truly original?

Does "originality" mean putting together old ideas in new ways, as the speaker contends, rather than conjuring up truly new ideas? Although I agree that in various realms of human endeavor, such as linguistics, law, and even the arts, so-called "new" or "original" ideas rarely are. However, when it comes to the physical sciences originality more often entails chartering completely new intellectual territory.

The notion that so-called "originality" is actually variation or synthesis of existing ideas finds its greatest support in linguistics and in law. Regarding the former, in spite of the many words in the modern English language that are unique to Western culture, modern English is derived from, and builds upon, a variety of linguistic traditions—and ultimately from the ancient Greek and Latin languages. Were we to insist on rejecting tradition in favor of purely modern language we would have essentially nothing to say. The same holds true for all other modern languages. As for law, consider the legal system in the United States, which is deeply rooted in traditional English common-law principles of equity and justice. The system in the U.S. requires that new, so-called "modern" laws be consistent with—and indeed build upon—those traditional principles.

Even in the arts—where one might think that true originality must surely reside—so-called "new" ideas almost always embrace, apply, or synthesize what came earlier. For example, most "modern" visual designs, forms, and elements are based on certain well-established aesthetic ideals—such as symmetry, balance, and harmony. Admittedly, modern art works often eschew these principles in favor of true originality. Yet, in my view the appeal of such works lies primarily in their novelty and brashness. Once the ephemeral novelty or shock dissipates, these works quickly lose their appeal because they violate firmly established artistic ideals. An even better example from the arts is modern rock-and-roll music, which upon first listening might seem to bear no resemblance to classical music traditions. Yet, both genres rely on the same 12-note scale, the same notions of what harmonies are pleasing to the ear, the same forms, the same rhythmic meters, and even many of the same melodies.

When it comes to the natural sciences, however, some new ideas are truly original while others put established ideas together in new ways. One striking example of truly original scientific advances involves what we know about the age and evolution of the Earth. In earlier centuries the official Church of England called for a literal interpretation of the Bible, according to which the Earth's age is determined to be about 6,000 years. If Western thinkers had simply put these established ideas together in new ways the fields of structural and historical geology might never have advanced further. A more recent example involves Einstein's theory of relativity. Einstein theorized, and scientists have since proven empirically, that the pace of time, and possibly the direction of time as well, is relative to the observer's motion through space. This truth ran so contrary to our subjective, linear experience, and to previous notions about time and space, that I think Einstein's theory can properly be characterized as truly original.

However, in other instances great advances in science are made by putting together current theories or other ideas in new ways. For example, only by building on certain well-established laws of physics were engineers able to develop silicon-based semiconductor technology. And, only by struggling to reconcile the quantum and relativity theories have physicists now posited a new so-called "string" theory, which puts together the two preexisting theories in a completely new way.

To sum up, for the most part originality does not reject existing ideas but rather embraces, applies, or synthesizes what came before. In fact, in our modern languages, our new laws, and even our new art, existing ideas are reflected, not shunned. But, when it comes to science, whether the speaker's claim is true must be determined on a case-by-case basis, with each new theory or innovation.

Issue:
The **impetus for innovation**: individual enterprise or teamwork?

The speaker claims that individual enterprise, energy, and commitment, and not teamwork, provide the impetus for innovation in every case. In my view, although the claim is not without merit, especially when it comes to business innovation, it overlooks the synergistic relationship between individual effort and teamwork, particularly with respect to scientific innovations.

With respect to business innovation, I agree that it is the vision and commitment of key individuals—such as a firm's founder or chief executive—from which businesses burgeon and innovative products, services, and marketing and management strategies emerge. One notable example involves the Apple Computer debacle following the departure of its founding visionary Steve Jobs. It wasn't until Jobs reassumed the helm, once again injecting his unique perception, insight, and infectious fervor, that the ailing Apple was able to resume its innovative ways, thereby regaining its former stature in the computer industry. Admittedly, the chief executives of our most successful corporations would no doubt concede that without the cooperative efforts of their subordinates, their personal visions would never become reality. Yet, these efforts are merely the carrying out of the visionary's marching orders.

Nevertheless, the speaker would have us accept a too narrow and distorted view of how innovation comes about, particularly in today's world. Teamwork and individual enterprise are not necessarily inconsistent, as the speaker would have us believe. Admittedly, if exercised in a self-serving manner—for example, through pilfering or back stabbing—individual enterprise and energy can serve to thwart a business organization's efforts to innovate. However, if directed toward the firm's goals these traits can motivate other team members, thereby facilitating innovation. In other words, teamwork and individual enterprise can operate synergistically to bring about innovation.

We must be especially careful not to understate the role of teamwork in scientific innovation, especially today. Important scientific innovations of the previous millennium might very well have been products of the epiphanies and obsessions of individual geniuses. When we think of the process of inventing something great we naturally conjure up a vision of the lone inventor hidden away in a laboratory for months on end, in dogged pursuit of a breakthrough. And this image is not entirely without empirical support. For example, Thomas Edison's early innovations—including the light bulb, the television, and the phonograph—came about in relative isolation, and solely through his individual persistence and commitment.

However, in today's world, scientific innovation requires both considerable capital and extensive teams of researchers. Admittedly, in all likelihood, we will continue to encounter the exceptional case—like Hewlett and Packard, or Jobs and Wozniak, whose innovations sprang from two-man operations. But for the most part, scientific breakthroughs today typically occur only after years of trial-and-error by large research teams. Even Thomas Edison relied more and more on a team of researchers to develop new innovations as his career progressed. Thus the statement flies in the face of how most modern scientific innovations actually come about today.

To sum up, I agree that, when it comes to the world of business, true innovation is possible only through the imagination of the individual visionary, and his or her commitment to see the vision through to its fruition. However, when it comes to scientific innovation, yesterday's enterprising individuals have yielded to today's cooperative research teams—a trend that will no doubt continue as scientific research becomes an increasingly expensive and complex undertaking.

Issue:
Can **moral behavior** be legislated?

The speaker asserts that many laws are ineffective in solving society's problems because moral behavior cannot be legislated. I agree with this assertion insofar as it relates to constraints on certain personal freedoms. However, when it comes to the conduct of businesses, I think that moral behavior not only can but must be legislated for the purpose of alleviating societal problems.

Morality laws that impinge upon freedom of choice about our personal lives—to control what we do with and to ourselves—simply do not work in a democratic society. People always find ways to circumvent such laws, which ultimately give way to more lenient laws that acknowledge personal freedom of choice. The failed Prohibition experiment of the 1930s is perhaps the paradigmatic example of this. And we are slowly learning history's lesson, as aptly demonstrated by the recognition of equal rights for same-sex partners, and current trends toward legalization of physician-assisted suicide and the medicinal use of marijuana. In short, history informs us that legislating morality merely for morality's sake simply does not work.

Morality laws impinging on personal freedoms are not made any more useful or effective by purporting to serve the greater good of society, because on balance their costs far outweigh their benefits. For instance, those who defend the criminalization of drug use cite a variety of harms that result from widespread addiction: increased incidence of domestic violence, increased burden on our health-care and social-welfare systems, and diminished productivity of addicts. However, these defenders overlook the fact that outlawing addictive substances does not prevent, or even deter, people from obtaining and using them. It only compels users to resort to theft and even violent means of procuring drugs, adding to the economic costs of enforcement, prosecution, and punishment. In short, the costs of proscription outweigh the benefits.

In sharp contrast to personal behavior, the behavior of businesses can and must be controlled through legislation. Left unfettered, businesses tend to act on behalf of their own financial interest, not on behalf of the society at large. And when excessive business profits accrue at the expense of public health and safety, in my view business has behaved immorally.

Examples of large-scale immoral behavior on the part of businesses abound. For example, although technology makes possible the complete elimination of polluting emissions from automobiles, auto manufacturers are unwilling to voluntarily make the short-term sacrifices necessary to accomplish this goal. Tobacco companies have long known about the health hazards of smoking cigarettes; yet they weigh the costs of defending law suits against the profit from cigarette sales, and continue to cater to nicotine addicts. And when given the chance, many manufacturers will exploit underage or underprivileged workers to reduce labor costs, thereby enhancing profits. In short, only government holds the regulatory and enforcement power to impose the standards needed to ensure moral business behavior.

In sum, whether legislating morality is effective or even appropriate depends on whether the behavior at issue involves personal freedom or public duty. Legislating personal moral behavior is neither practicable nor proper in a democratic society. On the other hand, legislating business morality is necessary to ensure public health and safety.

Issue:
Accepting **innovations** and **new ideas**

The speaker maintains that it is easy to accept innovation and new ideas, yet difficult to accept how they are put to use. In my view the speaker has it backward when it comes to socio-political ideas, at least in our democratic society. Nevertheless, I tend to agree with the speaker insofar as scientific innovation is concerned.

In the areas of politics and law, new ideas are not often easily accepted. More often than not, the status quo affords people a measure of security and predictability in terms of what they can expect from their government and what rights and duties they have under the law. The civil-rights movement of the 1960s aptly illustrates this point. The personal freedoms and rights championed by leading civil-rights leaders of that era threatened the status quo, which tolerated discrimination based on race and gender, thereby sanctioning prejudice of all kinds. The resulting civil unrest, especially the protests and riots that characterized the late 1960s, was clear evidence that new ideas were not welcome. And today those who advocate gay and lesbian rights are encountering substantial resistance as well, this time primarily from certain religious quarters.

Yet once society grows to accept these new ideas, it seems that it has an easier time accepting how they are put into practice. The explanation for this lies in the fact that our system of laws is based on legal precedent. New ideas must past muster among the government's legislative, judicial, and executive branches, and ultimately the voters, before these ideas can be codified, implemented and enforced. Once they've passed the test of our democratic and legal systems, they are more readily welcomed by the citizenry at large.

In contrast, consider innovations in the natural sciences. It seems that we universally embrace any new technology in the name of progress. Of course there are always informed dissenters with legitimate concerns. For example, many scientists strongly opposed the Manhattan Project, by which nuclear warfare was made possible. Innovations involving alternative energy sources meet with resistance from those who rely on and profit from fossil fuels. Some sociologists and psychologists claim that advances in Internet technology will alienate society's members from one another. And opponents of genetic engineering predict certain deleterious social and political consequences.

Yet the reasons why these dissenters oppose certain innovations have to do with their potential applications and uses, not with the innovations themselves. Edward Teller, the father of the atom bomb, foresaw the benefits of atomic energy, yet understood the grave consequences of applying the technology instead for destruction. Innovations involving alternative energy sources meet with resistance from many businesses because of their potential application in ways that will threaten the financial interests of these businesses. And those who would impede advances in Internet technology fear that consumers and businesses will use the technology for crass commercialism, exploitation, and white-collar crime, rather than for the sorts of educational and communication purposes for which it was originally designed. Finally, opponents of genetic engineering fear that, rather than using it to cure birth defects and prevent disease, the technology will be used instead by the wealthy elite to breed superior offspring, thereby causing society's socioeconomic gap to widen even further, even resulting in the creation of a master race.

In sum, when it comes to new social and political ideas, the power and security afforded by the status quo impedes initial acceptance, yet by the same token ensures that the ideas will be applied in ways that will be welcome by our society. On the other hand, it seems that scientific innovation is readily embraced yet meets stronger resistance when it comes to applying the innovation.

Issue:
Success: the **ability to survive in** and adapt and alter one's environment

Do academic and professional success both involve surviving in a new environment and eventually changing it, as the speaker claims? Regarding academic success, in my view the speaker overstates the significance of environment. Regarding professional success the speaker's threshold claim that adaptation is necessary has considerable merit; however, the extent to which professional success also entails shaping the environment in which the professional operates depends on the type of profession under consideration.

Turning first to academic success, I concede that as students advance from grade school to high school, then to college, they must accustom themselves not just to new curricula but also to new environments—comprised of campuses, classmates, teachers, and teaching methods. The last item among this list is proving particularly significant in separating successful students from less successful ones. As computers and the Internet are becoming increasing important tools for learning academic skills and for research, they are in effect transforming our learning environment—at every educational level.

Students who fail to adapt to this change will find themselves falling behind the pace of their peers.

Otherwise, the speaker's prescription for academic success makes little sense. Aside from the environmental variables listed above, academia is a relatively staid environment over time. The key ingredients of academic success have always been, and will always be, a student's innate abilities and the effort the student exerts in applying those abilities to increasingly advanced course work. Besides, to assert that academic success involves changing one's environment is tantamount to requiring that students alter their school's teaching methods or physical surroundings in order to be successful students—an assertion that nonsensically equates academic study with educational reform.

Turning next to professional success, consider the two traditional professions of law and medicine. A practicing lawyer must stay abreast of new developments and changes in the law, and a physician must adapt to new and improved medical devices, and keep pace with new and better ways to treat and prevent diseases. Otherwise, those professionals risk losing their competency, and even their professional licenses. However, this is not to say that success in either profession also requires that the practitioner help shape the legal, medical, technological, or ethical environment within which these professions operate. To the contrary, undue time and energy devoted to advancing the profession can diminish a practitioner's effectiveness as such. In other words, legal and medical reform is best left to former practitioners, and to legislators, jurists, scientists, and academicians. Thus the speaker's claim unfairly overrates the ability to change one's professional environment as a key ingredient of professional success.

In contrast, when it comes to certain other professions, such as business and scientific research, the speaker's claim is far more compelling. Our most successful business leaders are not those who merely maximize shareholder profits, but rather those who envision a lasting contribution to the business environment and to society, and realize that vision. The industrial barons and information-age visionaries of the late nineteenth and twentieth centuries, respectively, did not merely adapt to the winds of business and technological change imposed upon them. They altered the direction of those winds, and to some extent were the fans that blew those winds. Similarly, ultimate success in scientific research lies not in reacting to new environments but in shaping future ones— by preventing disease, inventing products that transform the ways in which we live and work, and so forth. Perhaps the most apt example is the field of space exploration, which has nothing to do with adapting to new environments, and everything to do with discovering them and making them available to us in the first place.

To sum up, the speaker's claim has merit insofar as any individual must adapt to new environments to progress in life and to survive in a dynamic, ever-changing world. However, the speaker's sweeping definition of success overlooks certain crucial distinctions between academics and the professions, and between some professions and others.

Issue:
Does technology threaten our **quality of life**?

Whether technology enhances or diminishes our overall quality of life depends largely on the type of technology one is considering. While mechanical automation may have diminished our quality of life, on balance, digital automation is doing more to improve life than to undermine its quality.

First consider mechanical automation, particularly assembly-line manufacturing. With automation came a loss of pride in and alienation from one's work. In this sense, automation both diminished our quality of life and rendered us slaves to machines in our inability to reverse "progress." Admittedly, mechanical automation spawned entire industries, creating jobs, stimulating economic growth, and supplying a plethora of innovative conveniences. Nevertheless, the sociological and environmental price of progress may have outweighed its benefits.

Next consider digital technology. Admittedly, this newer form of technology has brought its own brand of alienation, and has adversely affected our quality of life in other ways as well. For example, computer automation, and especially the Internet, breeds information overload and steals our time and attention away from family, community, and coworkers. In these respects, digital technology tends to diminish our quality of life and create its own legion of human slaves.

On the other hand, by relegating repetitive tasks to computers, digital technology has spawned great advances in medicine and physics, helping us to better understand the world, to enhance our health, and to prolong our lives. Digital automation has also emancipated architects, artists, designers, and musicians, by expanding creative possibilities and by saving time. Perhaps most important, however, information technology makes possible universal access to information, thereby providing a democratizing influence on our culture.

In sum, while mechanical automation may have created a society of slaves to modern conveniences and unfulfilling work, digital automation holds more promise for improving our lives without enslaving us to the technology.

Issue:
Do a society's **heroes or its heroines** reflect its character?

The speaker claims that the character of a society's heroes and heroines ('heroes' hereafter) reflects the character of that society. I tend to disagree. In my observation a society chooses as its heroes not people who mirror the society but rather people whose character society's members wish they could emulate but cannot—for want of character. Nevertheless, I concede that one particular type of hero—the sociopolitical hero— by definition mirrors the character of the society whose causes the hero champions.

First consider the sports hero, whom in my observation society chooses not merely by virtue of athletic prowess. Some accomplished athletes we consider heroes because they have overcome significant obstacles to achieve their goals. For example, Lance Armstrong was not the first Tour de France cycling champion from the U.S.; yet he was the first to overcome a life-threatening illness to win the race. Other accomplished athletes we consider heroes because they give back to the society which lionizes them. As Mohammed Ali fought not just for boxing titles but also for racial equality, so baseball hero Mark McGuire fights now for disadvantaged children, while basketball hero Magic Johnson fights for AIDS research and awareness. Yet, do the character traits and resulting charitable efforts of sports heroes reflect similar traits and efforts among our society at large? No; they simply reveal that we admire these traits and efforts in other people, and wish we could emulate them—but for our own personal failings.

Next consider the military hero, who gains heroic stature by way of courage in battle, or by otherwise facing certain defeat and emerging victorious. Former presidential hopeful John McCain, whom even his political opponents laud as a war hero for having not only endured years of torture as a prisoner of war but also for continuing to serve his country afterward. Do his patriotism and mettle reveal our society's true character? Certainly not. They reveal only that we admire his courage, fortitude, and strength.

On the other hand, consider a third type of hero: the champion of social causes who inspires and incites society to meaningful political and social change. Such luminaries as India's Mahatma Gandhi, America's Martin Luther King, South Africa's Nelson Mandela, and Poland's Lech Lawesa come immediately to mind. This unique brand of hero does reflect, and indeed must reflect, the character of the hero's society. After all, it is the function of the social champion to call attention to the character of society, which having viewed its reflection in the hero is incited to act bravely—in accordance with its collective character.

In sum, I agree with the speaker's claim only with respect to champions of society's social causes. Otherwise, what society deems heroic reflects instead a basic, and universal, human need for paragons—to whom we can refer as metaphors for the sorts of virtues that for lack of character we cannot ourselves reflect.

Issue:
Do people's appearance and behavior reveal **society's ideas and values**?

This statement generalizes unfairly that the way people look, dress, and act reveals their attitudes and their society's values. In my view, while in certain respects the habits and customs of a people are accurate indicators of their attitudes and values, in other respects they are not.

Turning first to the way people look and dress, certain aspects of the outward appearance of a culture's people do inform us of their ideas, attitudes, and values. A society whose members tend to be obese might place a high value on indulgence and pleasure, and a low value on physical health. A general preference for ready-made, inexpensive clothing might indicate a preference for practicality or for saving rather than spending. And, a society whose members prefer to wear clothing that is traditional and distinct to that society is one that values tradition over modernization. In other respects, however, the way people look and dress is not a function of their attitudes and values but rather their climatic and work environment. In harsh climates people bundle up, while in hot, humid climates they go with few clothes. In developed nations people dress for indoor work and their skin appears pink and supple, while in agrarian cultures people dress for outdoor work and appear weather-beaten.

I turn next to the way people act. The habits, rituals and lifestyles of a culture often do provide accurate signals about its values. For instance, a society characterized by over-consumption is clearly one that values comfort and convenience over a healthy environment. And, a society whose members behave in a genteel, respectful, and courteous manner toward one another is one which values human dignity, while a society of people who act in a hateful manner toward others clearly places a low value on respect for others and on tolerance of other people's opinions and beliefs. In other respects, however, the way people behave can belie their attitudes and values. For instance, a society whose members tend to work long hours might appear to place a high value on work for its own sake, when in reality these work habits might be born of financial necessity for these people, who would prefer more leisure time if they could afford it.

Finally, the statement overlooks a crucial distinction between free societies and oppressed ones. Free societies, such as contemporary America, are characterized by a panoply of rituals, behaviors, and manners of dress among its members. Such diversity in appearances surely indicates a society that places a high value on individual freedoms and cultural diversity. Accordingly, it might seem that a society whose members share similar rituals, ways of dressing, and public behaviors places a low value on individual freedoms and cultural diversity. However, any student of modern Communism and Fascism would recognize cultural homogeneity as an imposition on society's members, who would happily display their preference for individuality and diversity but for their oppressors.

To sum up, while the statement has merit, it amounts to an unfair generalization. The way that people look, dress, and act is often bred of necessity, not of attitude or values. And in oppressed societies people's customs and habits belie their true attitudes and values in any event.

Answers That Respond Convincingly to Counterarguments or Contrary Evidence

Your notes on a particular Issue topic might suggest either strong agreement or strong disagreement with the statement at hand. If so, then by all means express a definite viewpoint in your essay. But consider acknowledging at least one apparent merit of the opposing position, and then responding to it by applying the sorts of rhetorical techniques covered in Part 1.

The sample essays in this section illustrate this approach. Each essay either accepts or rejects the statement at hand, providing persuasive reasons and/or examples in support of that position. Along the way, it also recognizes and then responds directly to at least one counterargument or counterexample.

Issue:
Does the study of history overemphasize "**the famous few**"?

The speaker claims that significant historical events and trends are made possible by groups of people rather than individuals, and that the study of history should emphasize the former instead of the latter. I tend to disagree with both aspects of this claim. To begin with, learning about key historical figures inspires us to achieve great things ourselves—far more so than learning about the contributions of groups of people. Moreover, history informs us that it is almost always a key individual who provides the necessary impetus for what otherwise might be a group effort, as discussed below.

Admittedly, at times distinct groups of people have played a more pivotal role than key individuals in important historical developments. For example, although history and art appreciation courses on the Middle Ages tend to focus on the artistic achievements of particular artists such as Fra Angelico, a Benedictine monk of that period, Western civilization owes its very existence not to a few famous painters but rather to a group of Benedictine nuns of that period. Just prior to and during the decline of the Roman Empire, many women fled to join Benedictine monasteries, bringing with them substantial dowries which they used to acquire artifacts, art works, and manuscripts. As a result, their monasteries became centers for the preservation of Western culture and knowledge which would otherwise have been lost forever with the fall of the Roman Empire.

However, equally influential was Johannes Gutenberg, whose invention of the printing press several centuries later rendered Western knowledge and culture accessible to every class of people throughout the known world. Admittedly, Gutenberg was not single-handedly responsible for the outcomes of his invention. Without the support of paper manufacturers, publishers, and distributors, and without a sufficient demand for printed books, Gutenberg would never have become one of "the famous few." However, I think any historian would agree that studying the groups of people who rode the wave of Gutenberg's invention is secondary in understanding history to learning about the root historical cause of that wave. Generally speaking, then, undue attention to the efforts and contributions of various groups tends to obscure the cause-and-effect relationships with which the study of history is chiefly concerned.

Gutenberg is just one example of a historical pattern in which it is individuals who have been ultimately responsible for the most significant developments in human history. Profound scientific inventions and discoveries of the past are nearly all attributable not to forgettable groups of people but to certain key individuals—for example, Copernicus, Newton, Edison, Einstein, Curie, and of course Gutenberg. Moreover, when it comes to seminal sociopolitical events, the speaker's claim finds even less support from the historical record. Admittedly, sweeping social changes and political reforms require the participation of large groups of people. However, I would be hard-pressed to identify any watershed sociopolitical event attributable to a leaderless group. History informs us that groups rally only when incited and inspired by key individuals.

The speaker might claim that important long-term sociological trends are often instigated not by key individuals but rather by the masses. I concede that gradual shifts in demography, in cultural traditions and mores, and in societal attitudes and values can carry just as significant an historical impact as the words and deeds of "the famous few." Yet, it seems that key individuals almost invariably provide the initial spark for those trends. For instance, prevailing attitudes about sexual morality stem from the ideas of key religious leaders; and a culture's prevailing values concerning human life are often rooted in the policies and prejudices of political leaders. The speaker might also point out that history's greatest architectural and engineering feats—such as the Taj Mahal and the Great Wall—came about only through the efforts of large groups of workers. Again, however, it was the famous few—monarchs in these cases—whose whims and egos were the driving force behind these accomplishments.

To sum up, with few historical exceptions, history is shaped by key individuals, not by nameless, faceless groups. It is the famous few that provide visions of the future, visions that groups then bring to fruition. Perhaps the speaker's claim will have more merit at the close of the next millennium—since politics and science are being conducted increasingly by consortiums and committees. Yet, today it behooves us to continue drawing inspiration from "the famous few," and to continue understanding history chiefly in terms of their influence.

Issue:
Pragmatic vs. idealistic behavior

I agree with the speaker insofar as that a practical, pragmatic approach toward our endeavors can help us survive in the short term. However, idealism is just as crucial— if not more so—for long-term success in any endeavor, whether it be in academics, business, or political and social reform.

When it comes to academics, students who we would consider pragmatic tend not to pursue an education for its own sake. Instead, they tend to cut whatever corners are needed to optimize their grade average and survive the current academic term. But, is this approach the only way to succeed academically? Certainly not. Students who earnestly pursue intellectual paths that truly interest them are more likely to come away with a meaningful and lasting education. In fact, a sense of mission about one's area of fascination is strong motivation to participate actively in class and to study earnestly, both of which contribute to better grades in that area. Thus, although the idealist-student might sacrifice a high overall grade average, the depth of knowledge, academic discipline, and sense of purpose the student gains will serve that student well later in life.

In considering the business world it might be more tempting to agree with the speaker; after all, isn't business fundamentally about pragmatism—that is, "getting the job done" and paying attention to the "bottom line"? Emphatically, no. Admittedly, the everyday machinations of business are very much about meeting mundane short-term goals: deadlines for production, sales quotas, profit margins, and so forth. Yet underpinning these activities is the vision of the company's chief executive—a vision that might extend far beyond mere profit maximization to the ways in which the firm can make a lasting and meaningful contribution to the community, to the broader economy, and to the society as a whole. Without a dream or vision—that is, without strong idealist leadership—a firm can easily be cast about in the sea of commerce without clear direction, threatening not only the firm's bottom line but also its very survival.

Finally, when it comes to the political arena, again at first blush it might appear that pragmatism is the best, if not the only, way to succeed. Most politicians seem driven by their interest in being elected and reelected—that is, in surviving—rather than by any sense of mission, or even obligation to their constituency or country. Diplomatic and legal maneuverings and negotiations often appear intended to meet the practical needs of the parties involved—minimizing costs, preserving options, and so forth. But, it is idealists—not pragmatists—who sway the masses, incite revolutions, and make political ideology reality. Consider idealists such as America's founders, Mahatma Gandhi, or Martin Luther King. Had these idealists concerned themselves with short-term survival and immediate needs rather than with their notions of an ideal society, the United States and India might still be British colonies, and African Americans might still be relegated to the backs of buses.

In short, the statement fails to recognize that idealism—keeping one's eye on an ultimate prize—is the surest path to long-term success in any endeavor. Meeting one's immediate needs, while arguably necessary for short-term survival, accomplishes little without a sense of mission, a vision, or a dream for the long term.

Issue:
Is history **relevant to our daily lives**?

The speaker alleges that studying history is valuable only insofar as it is relevant to our daily lives. I find this allegation to be specious. It wrongly suggests that history is not otherwise instructive and that its relevance to our everyday lives is limited. To the contrary, studying history provides inspiration, innumerable lessons for living, and useful value-clarification and perspective—all of which help us decide how to live our lives.

To begin with, learning about great human achievements of the past provides inspiration. For example, a student inspired by the courage and tenacity of history's great explorers might decide as a result to pursue a career in archeology, oceanography, or astronomy. This decision can, in turn, profoundly affect that student's everyday life—in school and beyond. Even for students not inclined to pursue these sorts of careers, studying historical examples of courage in the face of adversity can provide motivation to face their own personal fears in life. In short, learning about grand accomplishments of the past can help us get through the everyday business of living, whatever that business might be, by emboldening us and lifting our spirits.

In addition, mistakes of the past can teach us as a society how to avoid repeating those mistakes. For example, history can teach us the inappropriateness of addressing certain social issues, particularly moral ones, on a societal level. Attempts to legislate morality invariably fail, as aptly illustrated by the Prohibition experiment in the U.S. during the 1930s. Hopefully, as a society we can apply this lesson by adopting a more enlightened legislative approach toward such issues as free speech, criminalization of drug use, criminal justice, and equal rights under the law.

Studying human history can also help us understand and appreciate the mores, values, and ideals of past cultures. A heightened awareness of cultural evolution, in turn, helps us formulate informed and reflective values and ideals for ourselves. Based on these values and ideals, students can determine their authentic life path as well as how they should allot their time and interact with others on a day-to-day basis.

Finally, it might be tempting to imply from the speaker's allegation that studying history has little relevance even for the mundane chores that occupy so much of our time each day, and therefore is of little value. However, from history we learn not to take everyday activities and things for granted. By understanding the history of money and banking we can transform an otherwise routine trip to the bank into an enlightened experience, or a visit to the grocery store into an homage to the many inventors, scientists, engineers, and entrepreneurs of the past who have made such convenience possible today. And, we can fully appreciate our freedom to go about our daily lives largely as we choose only by understanding our political heritage. In short, appreciating history can serve to elevate our everyday chores to richer, more interesting, and more enjoyable experiences.

In sum, the speaker fails to recognize that in all our activities and decisions— from our grandest to our most rote—history can inspire, inform, guide, and nurture. In the final analysis, to study history is to gain the capacity to be more human—and I would be hard-pressed to imagine a worthier end.

Issue:
Defining ourselves by identifying **with social groups**

I strongly agree that we define ourselves primarily through our identification with social groups, as the speaker asserts. Admittedly, at certain stages of life people often appear to define themselves in other terms. Yet, in my view, during these stages the fundamental need to define one's self through association with social groups is merely masked or suspended.

Any developmental psychologist would agree that socialization with other children plays a critical role in any child's understanding and psychological development of self. At the day-care center or in the kindergarten class young children quickly learn that they want to play with the same toys at the same time or in the same way as some other children. They come to understand generally what they share in common with certain of their peers—in terms of appearance, behavior, likes and dislikes—and what they do not share in common with other peers or with older students and adults. In other words, these children begin to recognize that their identity inextricably involves their kinship with certain peers and alienation from other people.

As children progress to the social world of the playground and other after-school venues, their earlier recognition that they relate more closely to some people than to others evolves into a desire to form well-defined social groups, and to set these groups apart from others. Girls begin to congregate apart from boys; clubs and cliques are quickly formed—often with exclusive rituals, codes, and rules to further distinguish the group's members from other children. This apparent need to be a part of an exclusive group continues through high school, where students identify themselves in their yearbooks by the clubs to which they belonged. Even in college, students eagerly join clubs, fraternities, and sororities to establish their identity as members of social groups. In my observation, children are not taught by adults to behave in these ways; thus, this desire to identify oneself with an exclusive social group seems to spring from some innate psychological need to define one's self through one's personal associations.

However, as young adults take on the responsibilities of partnering, parenting, and working, they appear to define themselves less by their social affiliations and more by their marital status, parental status, and occupation. The last of these criteria seems particularly important for many adults today. When two adults meet for the first time, beyond initial pleasantries the initial question almost invariably is "What do you do for a living?" Yet, in my opinion this shift in focus from one's belonging to a social group to one's occupation is not a shift in how we prefer to define ourselves. Rather, it is born of economic necessity—we don't have the leisure time or financial independence to concern ourselves with purely social activities. I find quite telling the fact that when older people retire from the world of work an interest in identifying with social groups—whether they be bridge clubs, investment clubs, or country clubs—seems to reemerge. In short, humans seem possessed by an enduring need to be part of a distinct social group—a need that continues throughout life's journey.

In sum, I agree that people gain and maintain their sense of self primarily through their belonging to distinct social groups. Admittedly, there will always be loners who prefer not to belong, for whatever reasons; yet loners are the exception. Also, while many working adults might temporarily define themselves in terms of their work for practicality's sake, at bottom we humans are nothing if not social animals.

Issue:
Is the **absence of choice** a rare circumstance?

I strongly agree with the contention that absence of choice is a rare circumstance, primarily because this contention accords with common sense and our everyday experience as human beings. Besides, the reverse claim—that we do not have free choice—serves to undermine the notions of moral accountability and human equality, which are critical to the survival of any democratic society.

Our collective life experience is that we make choices and decisions every day— on a continual basis. Common sense dictates that humans have free will, and therefore the true absence of choice is very rare. The only possible exceptions would involve extreme and rare circumstances such as solitary imprisonment or a severe mental or physical deficiency—any of which might potentially strip a person of his or her ability to make conscious choices. Yet, even under these circumstances, a person still retains choices about voluntary bodily functions and movement. Thus, the complete absence of choice would seem to be possible only in a comatose state or in death.

People often claim that life's circumstances leave them with "no choice." One might feel trapped in a job or a marriage. Under financial duress a person might claim that he or she has "no choice" but to declare bankruptcy, take a demeaning job, or even lie or steal to obtain money. The fundamental problem with these sorts of claims is that the claimants are only considering those choices that are not viable or attractive. That is, people in situations such as these have an infinite number of choices; it's just that many of the choices are unappealing, even self-defeating. For example, almost every person who claims to be trapped in a job is simply choosing to retain a certain measure of financial security. The choice to forego this security is always available, although it might carry unpleasant consequences.

Besides, the contention that we are almost invariably free to choose is far more appealing from a socio-political standpoint than the opposite claim. A complete lack of choice implies that every person's fate is determined, and that we all lack free will. According to the philosophical school of "strict determinism," every event, including human actions and choices, that occurs is physically necessary given the laws of nature and events that preceded that event or choice. In other words, the "choices" that seem part of the essence of our being are actually beyond our control. Recent advances in molecular biology and genetics lend some credence to the determinists' position that as physical beings our actions are determined by physical forces beyond our control. New research suggests that these physical forces include our own individual genetic makeup.

However, the logical result of strict determinism and of the new "scientific determinism" is that we are not morally accountable for our actions and choices, even those that harm other individuals or society. Moreover, throughout history monarchs and dictators have embraced determinism, at least ostensibly, to bolster their claim that certain individuals are preordained to assume positions of authority or to rise to the top levels of the socioeconomic infrastructure. Finally, the notion of scientific determinism opens the door for genetic engineering, which poses a potential threat to equality in socioeconomic opportunity, and could lead to the development of a so-called "master race." Admittedly, these disturbing implications neither prove nor disprove the determinists' claims. Nevertheless, assuming that neither free will nor determinism has been proven to be the correct position, the former is to be preferred by any humanist and in any democratic society.

In sum, despite the fact that we all experience occasional feelings of being trapped and having no choice, the statement is fundamentally correct. I would concede that science might eventually disprove the very notion of free will. However, until that time I'll trust my strong intuition that free will is an essential part of our being as humans and, accordingly, that humans are responsible for their own choices and actions.

Issue:
The value of art vs. that of art **critic**

This statement asserts that art, not the art critic, provides something of lasting value to society. I strongly agree with the statement. Although the critic can help us understand and appreciate art, more often than not, critique is either counterproductive to achieving the objective of art or altogether irrelevant to that objective.

Those who diagree with the statement might point out the three ostensible functions of the art critic. First, critics can help us understand and interpret art; a critic who is familiar with a particular artist and his or her works might have certain insights about those works that the layperson would not. Secondly, a critic's evaluation of an artwork serves as a filter, which helps us determine which art is worth our time and attention. For example, a new novel by a best-selling author might nevertheless be an uninspired effort, and if the critic can call our attention to this fact we gain time to seek out more worthwhile literature to read. Thirdly, a critic can provide feedback for artists; and constructive criticism, if taken to heart, can result in better work.

However, reflecting on these three functions makes clear that the art critic actually offers very little to society. The first function is better accomplished by docents and teachers, who are more able to enhance a layperson's appreciation and understanding of art by providing an objective, educated interpretation of it. Besides, true appreciation of art occurs at the moment we encounter art; it is the emotional, even visceral impact that art has on our senses, spirits, and souls that is the real value of art. A critic can actually provide a disservice by distracting us from that experience.

The critic's second function—that of evaluator who filters out bad art from the worthwhile—is one that we must be very wary of. History supports this caution. In the role of judge, critics have failed us repeatedly. Consider, for example, Voltaire's rejection of Shakespeare as barbaric because he did not conform to neo-classical principles of unity. Or, consider the complete dismissal of Beethoven's music by the esteemed critics of his time. The art critic's judgment is limited by the narrow confines of old and established parameters for evaluation. Moreover, critical judgment is often misguided by the ego; thus, its value is questionable in any event.

I turn finally to the critic's third function: to provide useful feedback to artists. The value of this function is especially suspect. Any artist, or anyone who has studied art, would agree that true art is the product of the artist's authentic passion, a manifestation of the artist's unique creative impulse, and a creation of the artist's spirit. If art were shaped by the concern for integrating feedback from all criticism, it would become a viable craft, but at the same time would cease to be art.

In sum, none of the ostensible functions of the critic are of much value at all, let alone of lasting value, to society. On the other hand, the artist, through works of art, provides an invaluable and unique mirror of the culture of the time during which the work was produced—a mirror for the artist's contemporaries and for future generations to gaze into for insight and appreciation of history. The art critic in a subordinate role, more often than not, does a disservice to society by obscuring this mirror.

Issue:
Must we choose between **tradition and modernization**?

Must we choose between tradition and modernization, as the speaker contends? I agree that in certain cases the two are mutually exclusive. For the most part, however, modernization does not reject tradition; in fact, in many cases the former can and does embrace the latter.

Oftentimes, so-called "modernization" is actually an extension or new iteration of tradition, or a variation on it. This is especially true in language and in law. The modern English language, in spite of its many words that are unique to modern Western culture, is derived from, and builds upon, a variety of linguistic traditions—and ultimately from the ancient Greek and Latin languages. Were we to insist on rejecting traditional in favor of purely modern language, we would have essentially nothing to say. Perhaps an even more striking marriage of modernization and tradition is our system of laws in the U.S., which is deeply rooted in English common-law principles of equity and justice. Our system requires that new, so-called "modern" laws be consistent with, and in fact build upon, those principles.

In other areas modernization departs from tradition in some respects, while embracing it in others. In the visual arts, for example, "modern" designs, forms, and elements are based on certain timeless aesthetic ideals—such as symmetry, balance, and harmony. Modern art that violates these principles might hold ephemeral appeal due to its novelty and brashness, but its appeal lacks staying power. An even better example from the arts is modern rock-and-roll music, which upon first listening might seem to bear no resemblance to classical music traditions. Yet, both genres rely on the same twelve-note scale, the same notions of what harmonies are pleasing to the ear, the same forms, the same rhythmic meters, and even many of the same melodies.

I concede that in certain instances, tradition must yield entirely to the utilitarian needs of modem life. This is true especially when it comes to architectural traditions and the value of historic and archeological artifacts. A building of great historic value might be located in the only place available to a hospital desperately needing additional parking area. An old school that is a prime example of a certain architectural style might be so structurally unsafe that the only practicable way to remedy the problem would be to raze the building to make way for a modern, structurally sound one. And when it comes to bridges whose structural integrity is paramount to public safety, modernization often requires no less than replacement of the bridge altogether. However, in other such cases architecturally appropriate retrofits can solve structural problems without sacrificing history and tradition, and alternative locations for new buildings and bridges can be found in order to preserve tradition associated with our historic structures. Thus, even in architecture, tradition and modernization are not necessarily mutually exclusive options.

To sum up, in no area of human endeavor need modernization supplant, reject, or otherwise exclude tradition. In fact, in our modern structures, architecture and other art, and especially languages and law, tradition is embraced, not shunned.

Issue:
Should students be skeptical about **what they are taught**?

The speaker contends that students should be skeptical in their studies, and should not accept passively whatever they are taught. In my view, although undue skepticism might be counterproductive for a young child's education, I strongly agree with the speaker otherwise. If we were all to accept on blind faith all that we are taught, our society would never progress or evolve.

Skepticism is perhaps most important in the physical sciences. Passive acceptance of prevailing principles quells innovation, invention, and discovery. In fact, the very notion of scientific progress is predicated on rigorous scientific inquiry— in other words, skepticism. And history is replete with examples of students of science who challenged what they had been taught, thereby paving the way for scientific progress. For example, in challenging the notion that the Earth was in a fixed position at the center of the universe, Copernicus paved the way for the corroborating observations of Galileo a century later, and ultimately for Newton's principles of gravity upon which all modern science is based. The staggering cumulative impact of Copernicus' rejection of what he had been taught is proof enough of the value of skepticism.

The value of skepticism is not limited to the physical sciences, of course. In the fields of sociology and political science, students must think critically about the assumptions underlying the status quo; otherwise, oppression, tyranny, and prejudice go unchecked. Similarly, while students of the law must learn to appreciate timeless legal doctrines and principles, they must continually question the fairness and relevance of current laws. Otherwise, our laws would not evolve to reflect changing societal values and to address new legal issues arising from our ever-evolving technologies.

Even in the arts, students must challenge established styles and forms rather than learn to imitate them; otherwise, no genuinely new art would ever emerge. Bee-bop musicians such as Charlie Parker demonstrated through their wildly innovative harmonies and melodies their skepticism about established rules for harmony and melody. In the area of dance, Balanchine showed by way of his improvisational techniques his skepticism about established rules for choreography. And Germany's Bauhaus School of Architecture, to which modem architecture owes its existence, was rooted in skepticism about the proper objective, and resulting design, of public buildings.

Admittedly, undue skepticism might be counterproductive in educating young children. I am not an expert in developmental psychology; yet observation and common sense informs me that youngsters must first develop a foundation of experiential knowledge before they can begin to think critically about what they are learning. Even so, in my view no student, no matter how young, should be discouraged from asking "Why?" and "Why not?"

To sum up, skepticism is the very stuff that progress is made of, whether it be in science, sociology, politics, the law, or the arts. Therefore, skepticism should be encouraged at all but the most basic levels of education.

Issue:
Should **parents and communities** participate in education?

Should parents and communities participate in local education because education is too important to leave to professional educators, as the speaker asserts? It might be tempting to agree with the speaker, based on a parent's legal authority over, familiarity with, and interest in his or her own children. However, a far more compelling argument can be made that, except for major decisions such as choice of school, a child's education is best left to professional educators.

Communities of parents concerned about their children's education rely on three arguments for active parental and community participation in that process. The first argument, and the one expressed most often and vociferously, is that parents hold the ultimately legal authority to make key decisions about what and how their own children learn—including choice of curriculum and text books, pace and schedule for learning, and the extent to which their child should learn alongside other children. The second argument is that only a parent can truly know the unique needs of a child—including what educational choices are best suited for the child. The third argument is that parents are more motivated—by pride and ego—than any other person to take whatever measures are needed to ensure their children receive the best possible education.

Careful examination of these three arguments, however, reveals that they are specious at best. As for the first one, were we to allow parents the right to make all major decisions regarding the education of their children, many children would go with little or no education. In a perfect world parents would always make their children's education one of their highest priorities. Yet, in fact many parents do not. As for the second argument, parents are not necessarily best equipped to know what is best for their child when it comes to education. Although most parents might think they are sufficiently expert by virtue of having gone through formal education themselves, parents lack the specialized training to appreciate what pedagogical methods are most effective, what constitutes a balanced education, how developmental psychology affects a child's capacity for learning at different levels and at different stages of childhood. Professional educators, by virtue of their specialized training in these areas, are far better able to ensure that a child receives a balanced, properly paced education.

There are two additional compelling arguments against the speaker's contention. First, parents are too subjective to always know what is truly best for their children. For example, many parents try to overcome their own shortcomings and failed self-expectations vicariously through their children's accomplishments. Most of us have known parents who push their child to excel in certain areas—to the emotional and psychological detriment of the child. Secondly, if too many parties become involved in making decisions about day-to-day instruction, the end result might be infighting, legal battles, boycotts, and other protests, all of which impede the educational process; and the ultimate victims are the children themselves. Finally, in many jurisdictions parents now have the option of schooling their children at home, as long as certain state requirements are met. In my observation, home schooling allows parents who prefer it great control over a child's education, while allowing the professional educators to discharge their responsibilities as effectively as possible—unfettered by gadfly parents who constantly interfere and intervene.

In sum, while parents might seem better able and better motivated to make key decisions about their child's education, in many cases they are not. With the possible exceptions of responsible home-schoolers, a child's intellectual, social, and psychological development is at risk when communities of parents dominate the decision-making process involving education.

Issue:
Are all observations **subjective**?

The speaker claims that all observation is subjective—colored by desire and expectation. While it would be tempting to concede that we all see things differently, careful scrutiny of the speaker's claim reveals that it confuses observation with interpretation. In fact, in the end the speaker's claim relies entirely on the further claim that there is no such thing as truth and that we cannot truly know anything. While this notion might appeal to certain existentialists and epistemologists, it runs against the grain of all scientific discovery and knowledge gained over the last 500 years.

It would be tempting to afford the speaker's claim greater merit than it deserves. After all, our everyday experience as humans informs us that we often disagree about what we observe around us. We've all uttered and heard uttered many times the phase "That's not the way I see it!" Indeed, everyday observations—for example, about whether a football player was out of bounds, or about which car involved in an accident ran the red light—vary depending not only on one's spatial perspective but also on one's expectations or desires. If I'm rooting for one football team, or if the player is well-known for his ability to make great plays while barely staying in bounds, my desires or expectations might influence what I think I observe. Or if I am driving one of the cars in the accident, or if one car is a souped-up sports car, then my desires or expectations will in all likelihood color my perception of the accident's events.

However, these sorts of subjective "observations" are actually subjective "interpretations" of what we observe. Visitors to an art museum might disagree about the beauty of a particular work, or even about which color predominates in that work. In a court trial several jurors might view the same videotape evidence many times, yet some jurors might "observe" an incident of police brutality, while others "observe" the appropriate use of force to restrain a dangerous individual. Thus, when it comes to making judgments about what we observe and about remembering what we observe, each person's individual perspective, values, and even emotions help form these judgments and recollections. It is crucial to distinguish between interpretations such as these and observation, which is nothing more than a sensory experience. Given the same spatial perspective and sensory acuity and awareness, it seems to me that our observations would all be essentially in accord—that is, observation can be objective.

Lending credence to my position is Francis Bacon's scientific method, according to which we can know only that which we observe, and thus all truth must be based on empirical observation. This profoundly important principle serves to expose and strip away all subjective interpretation of observation, thereby revealing objective scientific truths. For example, up until Bacon's time the Earth was "observed" to lie at the center of the Universe, in accordance with the prevailing religious notion that man (humankind) was the center of God's creation. Applying Bacon's scientific method Galileo exposed the biased nature of this claim. Similarly, before Einstein time and space were assumed to be linear, in accordance with our "observation." Einstein's mathematical formulas suggested otherwise, and his theories have been proven empirically to be true. Thus, it was our subjective interpretation of time and space that led to our misguided notions about them. Einstein, like history's other most influential scientists, simply refused to accept conventional interpretations of what we all observe.

In sum, the speaker confuses observation with interpretation and recollection. It is how we make sense of what we observe, not observation itself, that is colored by our perspective, expectations, and desires. The gifted individuals who can set aside their subjectivity and delve deeper into empirical evidence, employing Bacon's scientific method, are the ones who reveal that observation not only can be objective but must be objective if we are to embrace the more fundamental notion that knowledge and truth exist.

Issue:
Media scrutiny of society's heroes

In general, I agree with the assertion that intense media scrutiny nearly always serves to diminish the reputation of society's would-be heroes, for the chief reason that it seems to be the nature of media to look for ways to demean public figures—whether heroic or not. Moreover, while in isolated cases our so-called heroes have vindicated themselves and restored their reputations diminished by the media, in my observation these are exceptional cases to the general rule that once slandered, the reputation of any public figure, hero or otherwise, is forever tarnished.

The chief reason why I generally agree with the statement has to do with the forces that motivate the media in the first place. The media generally consist of profit-seeking entities, whose chief objective is to maximize profits for their shareholders or other owners. Moreover, our corporate culture has sanctioned this objective by codifying it as a fiduciary obligation of any corporate executive. For better or worse, in our society media viewers, readers, and listeners find information about the misfortunes and misdeeds of others, especially heroic public figures, far more compelling than information about their virtues and accomplishments. In short, we love a good scandal. One need look no further than the newsstand, local television news broadcast, or talk show to find ample evidence that this is the case. Thus, in order to maximize profits the media are simply giving the public what they demand—scrutiny of heroic public figures that serves to diminish their reputation.

A second reason why I fundamentally agree with the statement is that, again for better or worse, intense media scrutiny raises a presumption, at least in the public's collective mind, that their hero is guilty of some sort of character flaw or misdeed. This presumption is understandable. After all, I think any demographic study would show that the vast majority of people relying on mainstream media for their information lack the sort of critical-thinking skills and objectivity to see beyond what the media feeds them, and to render a fair and fully informed judgment about a public figure—heroic or otherwise.

A third reason for my agreement with the statement has to do with the longer-term fallout from intense media scrutiny and the presumption discussed above. Once tarnished as a result of intense media scrutiny, a person's reputation is forever besmirched, regardless of the merits or motives of the scrutinizers. Those who disagree with this seemingly cynical viewpoint might cite cases in which public figures whose reputations had been tarnished were ultimately vindicated. For example, certain celebrities have successfully challenged rag sheets such as the National Enquirer in the courts, winning large damage awards for libel. Yet, in my observation these are exceptional cases; besides, a damage award is no indication that the public has expunged from its collective memory a perception that the fallen hero is guilty of the alleged character flaw or peccadillo.

In sum, the statement is fundamentally correct. As long as the media are motivated by profit, and as long as the public at large demands stories that serve to discredit, diminish, and destroy reputations, the media will continue to harm whichever unfortunate individuals become their cynosures. And the opportunity for vindication is little consolation in a society that seems to thrive, and even feed, on watching heroes being knocked off their pedestals.

Issue:
What avenues of intellectual inquiry best serve **the public good**?

Are people who make the greatest contributions to society those who pursue their personal intellectual interests, as the speaker asserts? Or are they the ones who focus instead on areas that are most likely to benefit society? I strongly agree with the speaker, for three reasons.

First of all, by human nature we are motivated to pursue activities in which we excel. To compel people to focus their intellectual interests only on certain areas would be to force many to waste their true talents. For example, imagine relegating today's preeminent astrophysicist Stephen Hawking to researching the effectiveness of affirmative-action legislation in reducing workplace discrimination. Admittedly, this example borders on hyperbole. Yet the aggregate effect of realistic cases would be to waste the intellectual talents of our world's scholars and researchers.

Secondly, it is unusual avenues of personal interest that most often lead to the greatest contributions to society. Intellectual and scientific inquiry that breaks no new ground amount to wasted time, talent, and other resources. History is laden with quirky claims of scholars and researchers that turned out stunningly significant—that the sun lies at the center of our universe, that time and space are relative concepts, that matter consists of discrete particles, that humans evolved from other life-forms, to name a few. One current area of unusual research is terraforming—creating biological life and a habitable atmosphere where none existed before. This unusual research area does not immediately address society's pressing social problems. Yet, in the longer term it might be necessary to colonize other planets in order to ensure the survival of the human race; and after all, what could be a more significant contribution to society than preventing its extinction?

Thirdly, to adopt a view that runs contrary to the speaker's position would be to sanction certain intellectual pursuits while proscribing others—which smacks of thought control and political oppression. It is dangerous to afford ultimate decision-making power about what intellectual pursuits are worthwhile to a handful of regulators, legislators, or elitists, since they bring to bear their own quirky notions about what is worthwhile, and since they are notoriously susceptible to influence-peddling, which renders them untrustworthy in any event. Besides, history informs us well of the danger inherent in setting official research priorities. A telling modern example involves the Soviet government's attempts during the 1920s to not only control the direction and the goals of its scientists' research but also to distort the outcome of that research—ostensibly for the greatest good of the greatest number of people. During the 1920s the Soviet government quashed certain areas of scientific inquiry, destroyed entire research facilities and libraries, and caused the sudden disappearance of many scientists who were viewed as threats to the state's authority. Not surprisingly, during this time period no significant scientific advances occurred under the auspices of the Soviet government.

Those who would oppose the speaker's assertion might argue that intellectual inquiry in certain areas, particularly the arts and humanities, amounts to little more than a personal quest for happiness or pleasure, and therefore is of little benefit to anyone but the inquirer. This specious argument overlooks the palpable benefits of cultivating the arts. It also ignores the fact that earnest study in the humanities affords us wisdom to know what is best for society, and helps us understand and approach societal problems more critically, creatively, and effectively. Thus, despite the lack of a tangible nexus between certain areas of intellectual inquiry and societal benefit, the nexus is there nonetheless.

In sum, I agree that society is best served when people are allowed unfettered freedom of intellectual inquiry and research, and use that freedom to pursue their own personal interests. Engaging one's individual talents in one's particular area of fascination is most likely to yield advances, discoveries, and a heightened aesthetic appreciation that serve to make the world a better and more interesting place in which to live.

Issue:
What influences how **students and scholars interpret** materials?

I strongly disagree that personality is the key to how a student or scholar interprets the material with which he or she works. Whether those materials be facts, events, data, or observations, in my view the key factor in their interpretation is a person's training and educational background.

Assuming that by personality the speaker embraces such personal attributes as individual temperament, disposition and general mood, and outlook, it seems to me that personality has little bearing on how students and scholars interpret the materials with which they work. Admittedly, whether an individual tends to be an optimist or a pessimist might have some bearing on interpretation. For instance, an archeology student with a generally sanguine outlook toward life might respond to a lengthy yet unsuccessful search for certain artifacts as discovery and progress—insofar as certain possibilities have been eliminated, bringing us closer to affirmative discoveries. In contrast, an archeology student with a generally pessimistic outlook might conclude that the same effort was in vain and that nothing has been learned or otherwise gained. Yet it strikes me that these reactions are emotional ones that have nothing to do with intellectual interpretation.

In sharp contrast, one's educational background and training can serve as a strong influence on how one interprets historical events involving human affairs, statistical data, and especially art. With respect to human affairs, consider the centuries-old imperialist policies of Great Britain. A student of political science might interpret British imperialism as a manifestation of that nation's desire for political power and domination over others. A student of economics might see it as a strategy to gain control over economic resources and distribution channels for goods. A sociology or anthropology student might see it as an assimilation of culture. And, a student of theology or religion might interpret the same phenomenon as an attempt, well intentioned or otherwise, to proselytize and to impose certain beliefs, rituals, and customs on others.

Educational training and background also affects how students and scholars interpret seemingly objective statistical data. It is crucial here to distinguish between numbers themselves, which are not subject to varying interpretations, from what the numbers signify—that is, what conclusions, prescriptions, or lessons we might come away with. Consider, for example, a hypothetical increase in the rate of juvenile crime in a particular city. Although the percent change itself might be subject to only one reasonable meaning, what the change signifies is open to various interpretations. A sociologist might interpret this data as an indication of deteriorating family unit or community. A student of public policy or government might see this statistic as an indication that current legislation fails to implement public policy as effectively as it could. And a student of law or criminal justice might interpret the same statistic as a sign of overburdened courts or juvenile-detention facilities.

Finally, when it comes to how students and scholars interpret art, training and educational background play an especially significant role. After all, while facts and figures are to some extent objective, the meaning of art is an inherently subjective, and highly personal, matter. A business student might interpret a series of art works as attempts by the artist to produce viable products for sale in the marketplace. However, a theology student might eschew such a cold and cynical interpretation, seeing instead an expression of praise, a celebration of life, a plea for grace, or a struggle to come to terms with mortality. Even art students and scholars can interpret the same art differently, depending on their training. A student of art history might see a particular work as the product of certain artistic influences, while a student of art theory, composition, and technique might view the same work as an attempt to combine color for visual impact, or as an experiment with certain brush-stroke techniques.

To sum up, I concede that as students and scholars our working "materials"— facts, data, objects, and events—are open to subjective interpretation in terms of what they teach us. However, what our materials teach us is a function of what we've already learned, and has little if anything to do with our personal basket of emotions and moods called "personality."

Issue:
Should education devote itself to **enriching** our personal lives?

Should educators focus equally on enriching students' personal lives and on job preparation, as the speaker contends? In my view, preparing students for the mundane aspects of work should be secondary to providing a broader education that equips students with historical and cultural perspective, as well as thoughtful and principled personal value systems and priorities. Paradoxically, it is through the liberal studies, which provide these forms of personal enrichment, that students can also best prepare for the world of work.

One reason why educators should emphasize personal enrichment over job preparation is that rote technical knowledge and skill do not help a student determine which goals in life are worthwhile and whether the means of attaining those goals are ethically or morally acceptable. Liberal studies such as philosophy, history, and comparative sociology enable students to develop thoughtful and consistent value systems and ethical standards, by which students can determine how they can best put their technical knowledge and skills to use in the working world. Thus, by nurturing the development of thoughtful personal value systems, educators actually help prepare students for their jobs and careers.

Another reason why educators should emphasize personal enrichment over job preparation is that specific knowledge and skills needed for jobs are changing more and more quickly. Thus it would be a waste of our education system to focus on specific knowledge and skills that will soon become obsolete—at the expense of providing a lasting and personally satisfying educational experience. It seems more appropriate today for employers to provide the training our workforce needs to perform their jobs, freeing up our educators to help enrich students' lives in ways that will serve them in any walk of life.

A third reason why educators should emphasize personally enriching course work—particularly anthropology, sociology, history, and political philosophy—is that these courses help students understand, appreciate, and respect other people and their viewpoints. As these students grow into working adults they will be better able to cooperate, compromise, understand various viewpoints, and appreciate the rights and duties of coworkers, supervisors, and subordinates. Rote technical knowledge and skill do little to help us get along with other people.

Admittedly, certain aspects of personal enrichment, especially spirituality and religion, should be left for parents and churches to provide; after all, by advocating teachings of any particular religion, public educators undermine our basic freedom of religion. Yet it is perfectly appropriate, and useful, to inform students about various religious beliefs, customs and institutions. Learning about different religions instills respect, tolerance, and understanding. Moreover, students grow to appreciate certain fundamental virtues, such as compassion, virtue, and humility, which all major religions share. Through this appreciation students grow into adults who can work well together toward mutually agreed-upon goals.

In sum, it is chiefly through the more personally enriching liberal studies that educators help students fully blossom into well-rounded adults and successful workers. There will always be a need to train people for specific jobs, of course. However, since knowledge is advancing so rapidly, employers and job-training programs are better equipped to provide this function, leaving formal educators free to provide a broader, more personally enriching education that will serve students throughout their lives and in any job or career.

Answers to Issue Statements That Make Sense Only to a Limited Extent

Many of the official GRE Issue statements are essentially "blanket statements"—broad, sweeping assertions that fail to account for certain considerations, distinctions, implications, or logical limits. This sort of assertion might strike you as too all-encompassing or extreme—in other words, as "going too far." Or it might seem myopic or shortsighted in that it fails to see the entire picture or a longer time frame.

In handling this type of statement, try to acknowledge *some* merit in the statement. One paragraph should suffice for this purpose. The lion's share of your response should involve your points of critique, just as in each of the sample essays here.

Issue:
The merits of a **national curriculum** for schools

The speaker would prefer a national curriculum for all children up until college instead of allowing schools in different regions the freedom to decide on their own curricula. I agree insofar as some common core curriculum would serve useful purposes for any nation. At the same time, however, individual states and communities should have some freedom to augment any such curriculum as they see fit; otherwise, a nation's educational system might defeat its own purposes in the long term.

A national core curriculum would be beneficial to a nation in a number of respects. First of all, by providing all children with fundamental skills and knowledge, a common core curriculum would help ensure that our children grow up to become reasonably informed, productive members of society. In addition, a common core curriculum would provide a predictable foundation upon which college administrators and faculty could more easily build curricula and select course materials for freshmen that are neither below nor above their level of educational experience. Finally, a core curriculum would ensure that all school children are taught core values upon which any democratic society depends to thrive, and even survive—values such as tolerance of others with different viewpoints, and respect for others.

However, a common curriculum that is also an exclusive one would pose certain problems, which might outweigh the benefits, noted above. First of all, on what basis would certain course work be included or excluded, and who would be the final decision-maker? In all likelihood these decisions would be in the hands of federal legislators and regulators, who are likely to have their own quirky notions of what should and should not be taught to children—notions that may or may not reflect those of most communities, schools, or parents. Besides, government officials are notoriously susceptible to influence-peddling by lobbyists who do not have the best interests of society's children in mind.

Secondly, an official, federally sanctioned curriculum would facilitate the dissemination of propaganda and other dogma—which because of its biased and one-sided nature undermines the very purpose of true education: to enlighten. I can easily foresee the banning of certain textbooks, programs, and Web sites that provide information and perspectives that the government might wish to suppress—as some sort of threat to its authority and power. Although this scenario might seem far-fetched, these sorts of concerns are being raised already at the state level.

Thirdly, the inflexible nature of a uniform national curriculum would preclude the inclusion of programs, courses, and materials that are primarily of regional or local significance. For example, California requires children at certain grade levels to learn about the history of particular ethnic groups who make up the state's diverse population. A national curriculum might not allow for this feature, and California's youngsters would be worse off as a result of their ignorance about the traditions, values, and cultural contributions of all the people whose citizenship they share.

Finally, it seems to me that imposing a uniform national curriculum would serve to undermine the authority of parents over their own children, to even a greater extent than uniform state laws currently do. Admittedly, laws requiring parents to ensure that their children receive an education that meets certain minimum standards are well-justified, for the reasons mentioned earlier. However, when such standards are imposed by the state rather than at the community level parents are left with far less power to participate meaningfully in the decision-making process. This problem would only be exacerbated were these decisions left exclusively to federal regulators.

In the final analysis, homogenization of elementary and secondary education would amount to a double-edged sword. While it would serve as an insurance policy against a future populated with illiterates and ignoramuses, at the same time it might serve to obliterate cultural diversity and tradition. The optimal federal approach, in my view, is a balanced one that imposes a basic curriculum yet leaves the rest up to each state— or better yet, to each community.

Issue:
The growing significance of the **video camera**

According to the speaker, the video recording is a more important means of documenting contemporary life than a written record because video recordings are more accurate and convincing. Although I agree that a video provides a more objective and accurate record of an event's spatial aspects, there is far more to document in life than what we see and hear. Thus, the speaker overstates the comparative significance of video as a documentary tool.

For the purpose of documenting temporal, spatial events and experiences, I agree that a video record is usually more accurate and more convincing than a written record. It is impossible for anyone, no matter how keen an observer and skilled a journalist, to recount in complete and objective detail such events as the winning touchdown at the Super Bowl, a Balanchine ballet, the Tournament of Roses Parade, or the scene at the intersection of Florence and Normandy streets during the 1992 Los Angeles riots. Yet these are important events in contemporary life—the sort of events we might put in a time capsule for the purpose of capturing our life and times at the turn of this millennium.

The growing documentary role of video is not limited to seminal events like those described above. Video surveillance cameras are objective witnesses with perfect memories. Thus, they can play a vital evidentiary role in legal proceedings—such as those involving robbery, drug trafficking, police misconduct, motor vehicle violations, and even malpractice in a hospital operating room. Indeed, whenever moving images are central to an event the video camera is superior to the written word. A written description of a hurricane, tornado, or volcanic eruption cannot convey its immediate power and awesome nature like a video record. A diary entry cannot "replay" that wedding reception, dance recital, or surprise birthday party as accurately or objectively as a video record. And a real-estate brochure cannot inform about the lighting, spaciousness, or general ambiance of a featured property nearly as effectively as a video.

Nonetheless, for certain other purposes written records are advantageous to and more appropriate than video records. For example, certain legal matters are best left to written documentation: video is of no practical use in documenting the terms of a complex contractual agreement, an incorporation, or the establishment of a trust. And video is of little use when it comes to documenting a person's subjective state of mind, impressions, or reflections of an event or experience. Indeed, to the extent that personal interpretation adds dimension and richness to the record, written documentation is actually more important than video.

Finally, a video record is of no use in documenting statistical or other quantitative information. Returning to the riot example mentioned earlier, imagine relying on a video to document the financial loss to store owners, the number of police and firefighters involved, and so forth. Complete and accurate video documentation of such information would require video cameras at every street corner and in every aisle of every store.

In sum, the speaker's claim overstates the importance of video records, at least to some extent. When it comes to capturing, storing, and recalling temporal, spatial events, video records are inherently more objective, accurate, and complete. However, what we view through a camera lens provides only one dimension of our life and times; written documentation will always be needed to quantify, demystify, and provide meaning to the world around us.

Issue:
Our duty to disobey **unjust laws**

According to this statement, each person has a duty to not only obey just laws but also disobey unjust ones. In my view this statement is too extreme, in two respects. First, it wrongly categorizes any law as either just or unjust; and secondly, it recommends an ineffective and potentially harmful means of legal reform.

First, whether a law is just or unjust is rarely a straightforward issue. The fairness of any law depends on one's personal value system. This is especially true when it comes to personal freedoms. Consider, for example, the controversial issue of abortion. Individuals with particular religious beliefs tend to view laws allowing mothers an abortion choice as unjust, while individuals with other value systems might view such laws as just.

The fairness of a law also depends on one's personal interest, or stake, in the legal issue at hand. After all, in a democratic society the chief function of laws is to strike a balance among competing interests. Consider, for example, a law that regulates the toxic effluents a certain factory can emit into a nearby river. Such laws are designed chiefly to protect public health. But complying with the regulation might be costly for the company; the factory might be forced to lay off employees or shut down altogether, or increase the price of its products to compensate for the cost of compliance. At stake are the respective interests of the company's owners, employees, and customers, as well as the opposing interests of the region's residents whose health and safety are impacted. In short, the fairness of the law is subjective, depending largely on how one's personal interests are affected by it.

The second fundamental problem with the statement is that disobeying unjust laws often has the opposite affect of what was intended or hoped for. Most anyone would argue, for instance, that our federal system of income taxation is unfair in one respect or another. Yet the end result of widespread disobedience, in this case tax evasion, is to perpetuate the system. Free-riders only compel the government to maintain tax rates at high levels in order to ensure adequate revenue for the various programs in its budget.

Yet another fundamental problem with the statement is that by justifying a violation of one sort of law we find ourselves on a slippery slope toward sanctioning all types of illegal behavior, including egregious criminal conduct. Returning to the abortion example mentioned above, a person strongly opposed to the freedom-of-choice position might maintain that the illegal blocking of access to an abortion clinic amounts to justifiable disobedience. However, it is a precariously short leap from this sort of civil disobedience to physical confrontations with clinic workers, then to the infliction of property damage, then to the bombing of the clinic and potential murder.

In sum, because the inherent function of our laws is to balance competing interests, reasonable people with different priorities will always disagree about the fairness of specific laws. Accordingly, radical action such as resistance or disobedience is rarely justified merely by one's subjective viewpoint or personal interests. And in any event, disobedience is never justifiable when the legal rights or safety of innocent people are jeopardized as a result.

Issue:
Historic buildings—preservation vs. practicality

The speaker asserts that wherever a practical, utilitarian need for new buildings arises this need should take precedence over our conflicting interest in preserving historic buildings as a record of our past. In my view, however, which interest should take precedence should be determined on a case-by-case basis—and should account not only for practical and historic considerations but also aesthetic ones.

In determining whether to raze an older building, planners should of course consider the community's current and anticipated utilitarian needs. For example, if an additional hospital is needed to adequately serve the health-care needs of a fast-growing community, this compelling interest might very well outweigh any interest in preserving a historic building that sits on the proposed site. Or if additional parking is needed to ensure the economic survival of a city's downtown district, this interest might take precedence over the historic value of an old structure that stands in the way of a parking structure. On the other hand, if the need is mainly for more office space, in some cases an architecturally appropriate add-on or annex to an older building might serve just as well as razing the old building to make way for a new one. Of course, an expensive retrofit might not be worthwhile if no amount of retrofitting would meet the need.

Competing with a community's utilitarian needs is an interest preserving the historical record. Again, the weight of this interest should be determined on a case-by-case basis. Perhaps an older building uniquely represents a bygone era, or once played a central role in the city's history as a municipal structure. Or perhaps the building once served as the home of a founding family or other significant historical figure, or as the location of an important historical event. Any of these scenarios might justify saving the building at the expense of the practical needs of the community. On the other hand, if several older buildings represent the same historical era just as effectively, or if the building's history is an unremarkable one, then the historic value of the building might pale in comparison to the value of a new structure that meets a compelling practical need.

Also competing with a community's utilitarian needs is the aesthetic and architectural value of the building itself—apart from historical events with which it might be associated. A building might be one of only a few that represents a certain architectural style. Or it might be especially beautiful, perhaps as a result of the craftsmanship and materials employed in its construction—which might be cost-prohibitive to replicate today. Even retrofitting the building to accommodate current needs might undermine its aesthetic as well as historic value, by altering its appearance and architectural integrity. Of course it is difficult to quantify aesthetic value and weigh it against utilitarian considerations. Yet planners should strive to account for aesthetic value nonetheless.

In sum, whether to raze an older building in order to construct a new one should never be determined indiscriminately. Instead, planners should make such decisions on a case-by-case basis, weighing the community's practical needs against the building's historic and aesthetic value.

Issue:
Investing in research which may have **controversial** results

I agree with the speaker's broad assertion that money spent on research is generally money well invested. However, the speaker unnecessarily extends this broad assertion to embrace research whose results are "controversial," while ignoring certain compelling reasons why some types of research might be unjustifiable. My points of contention with the speaker involve the fundamental objectives and nature of research, as discussed below.

I concede that the speaker is on the correct philosophical side of this issue. After all, research is the exploration of the unknown for true answers to our questions, and for lasting solutions to our enduring problems. Research is also the chief means by which we humans attempt to satisfy our insatiable appetite for knowledge, and our craving to understand ourselves and the world around us. Yet, in the very notion of research also lies my first point of contention with the speaker, who illogically presumes that we can know the results of research before we invest in it. To the contrary, if research is to be of any value it must explore uncharted and unpredictable territory. In fact, query whether research whose benefits are immediate and predictable can break any new ground, or whether it can be considered "research" at all.

While we must invest in research irrespective of whether the results might be controversial, at the same time we should be circumspect about research whose objectives are too vague and whose potential benefits are too speculative. After all, expensive research always carries significant opportunity costs—in terms of how the money might be spent toward addressing society's more immediate problems that do not require research. One apt illustration of this point involves the so-called "Star Wars" defense initiative, championed by the Reagan administration during the 1980s. In retrospect, this initiative was ill-conceived and largely a waste of taxpayer dollars; and few would dispute that the exorbitant amount of money devoted to the initiative could have gone a long way toward addressing pressing social problems of the day—by establishing after-school programs for delinquent latchkey kids, by enhancing AIDS awareness and education, and so forth. As it turns out, at the end of the Star Wars debacle we were left with rampant gang violence, an AIDS epidemic, and an unprecedented federal budget deficit.

The speaker's assertion is troubling in two other respects as well. First, no amount of research can completely solve the enduring problems of war, poverty, and violence, for the reason that they stem from certain aspects of human nature—such as aggression and greed. Although human genome research might eventually enable us to engineer away those undesirable aspects of our nature, in the meantime it is up to our economists, diplomats, social reformers, and jurists—not our research laboratories—to mitigate these problems. Secondly, for every new research breakthrough that helps reduce human suffering is another that serves primarily to add to that suffering. For example, while some might argue that physics researchers who harnessed the power of the atom have provided us with an alternative source of energy and invaluable "peace-keepers," this argument flies in the face of the hundreds of thousands of innocent people murdered and maimed by atomic blasts, and by nuclear meltdowns. And, in fulfilling the promise of "better living through chemistry" research has given us chemical weapons for human slaughter. In short, so-called "advances" that scientific research has brought about often amount to net losses for humanity.

In sum, the speaker's assertion that we should invest in research whose results are "controversial" begs the question, because we cannot know whether research will turn out controversial until we've invested in it. As for the speaker's broader assertion, I agree that money spent on research is generally a sound investment—because it is an investment in the advancement of human knowledge and in human imagination and spirit. Nevertheless, when we do research purely for its own sake—without aim or clear purpose—we risk squandering resources which could have been applied to relieve the immediate suffering of our dispirited, disadvantaged, and disenfranchised members of society. In the final analysis, given finite economic resources we are forced to strike a balance in how we allocate those resources among competing societal objectives.

Issue:
Does **television** render books obsolete?

The speaker contends that people learn just as much from watching television as by reading books, and therefore that reading books is not as important for learning as it once was. I strongly disagree. I concede that in a few respects television, including video, can be a more efficient and effective means of learning. In most respects, however, these newer media serve as poor substitutes for books when it comes to learning.

Admittedly, television holds certain advantages over books for imparting certain types of knowledge. For the purpose of documenting and conveying temporal, spatial events and experiences, film and video generally provide a more accurate and convincing record than a book or other written account. For example, it is impossible for anyone, no matter how keen an observer and skilled a journalist, to recount in complete and objective detail such events as a Balanchine ballet, or the scene at the intersection of Florence and Normandy streets during the 1992 Los Angeles riots. Besides, since the world is becoming an increasingly eventful place, with each passing day it becomes a more onerous task for journalists, authors, and book publishers to recount these events, and disseminate them in printed form. Producers of televised broadcasts and videos have an inherent advantage in this respect. Thus, the speaker's claim has some merit when it comes to arts education and to learning about modern and current events.

However, the speaker overlooks several respects in which books are inherently superior to television as a medium for learning. Watching television or a video is no indication that any significant learning is taking place; the comparatively passive nature of these media can render them ineffectual in the learning process. Also, books are far more portable than television sets. Moreover, books do not break, and they do not depend on electricity, batteries, or access to airwaves or cable connections—all of which may or may not be available in a given place. Finally, the effort required to read actively imparts a certain discipline that serves any person well throughout a lifetime of learning.

The speaker also ignores the decided tendency on the part of owners and managers of television media to filter information in order to appeal to the widest viewing audience, and thereby maximize profit. And casting the widest possible net seems to involve focusing on the sensational—that is, an appeal to our emotions and basic instincts rather than our intellect and reasonableness. The end result is that viewers do not receive complete, unfiltered, and balanced information, and therefore cannot rely on television to develop informed and intelligent opinions about important social and political issues.

Another compelling argument against the speaker's claim has to do with how well books and television serve their respective archival functions. Books readily enable readers to review and cross-reference material, while televised broadcasts do not. Even the selective review of videotape is far more trouble than it is worth, especially if a printed resource is also available. Moreover, the speaker's claim carries the implication that all printed works, fiction and non-fiction alike, not transferred to a medium capable of being televised, are less significant as a result. This implication serves to discredit the invaluable contributions of all the philosophers, scientists, poets, and others of the past, upon whose immense shoulders society stands today.

A final argument that books are made no less useful by television has to do with the experience of perusing the stacks in a library, or even a bookstore. Switching television channels, or even scanning a video library, simply cannot duplicate this experience. Why not? Browsing among books allows for serendipity—unexpectedly coming across an interesting and informative book while searching for something else, or for nothing in particular. Moreover, browsing through a library or bookstore is a pleasurable sensory experience for many people—an experience that the speaker would have us forego forever.

In sum, television and video can be more efficient than books as a means of staying abreast of current affairs, and for education in the arts that involve moving imagery. However, books facilitate learning in certain ways that television does not and cannot. In the final analysis, the optimal approach is to use both media side by side—television to keep us informed and to provide moving imagery, along with books to provide perspective and insight on that information and imagery.

Issue:
How does a culture **perpetuate** its prevailing ideas?

The speaker asserts that a culture perpetuates the ideas it favors while discrediting those it fears primarily through formal education. I agree that grade-school, and even high-school, education involves cultural indoctrination. However, I think the speaker misunderstands the role of higher education as well as overlooks other means by which a culture perpetuates or discredits certain ideas

I agree with the speaker with respect to formal grade-school and even high-school education—which to some extent amount to indoctrination with the values, ideas, and principles of mainstream society. In my observation, young students are not taught to question authority, to take issue with what they are taught, or to think critically for themselves. Yet, this indoctrination is actually desirable to an extent. Sole emphasis on rote learning of facts and figures is entirely appropriate for grade-school children, who have not yet gained the intellectual capacity and real-world experience to move up to higher, more complex levels of thinking. Nevertheless, the degree to which our grade schools and high schools emphasize indoctrination should not be overstated. After all, cultural mores, values, and biases have little to do with education in the natural sciences, mathematics, and specific language skills such as reading and writing.

Although the speaker's assertion has some merit when it comes to the education of young people, I find it erroneous when it comes to higher education. The mission of our colleges and universities is to afford students cultural perspective and a capacity for understanding opposing viewpoints, and to encourage and nurture the skills of critical analysis and skepticism—not to indoctrinate students with certain ideas while quashing others. Admittedly, colleges and universities are bureaucracies and therefore not immune to political influence over what is taught and what is not. Thus, to some extent a college's curriculum is vulnerable to wealthy and otherwise influential benefactors, trustees, and government agencies—who by advancing the prevailing cultural agenda serve to diminish a college's effectiveness in carrying out its true mission. Yet, my intuition is that such influences are minor ones, especially in public university systems.

The speaker's assertion is also problematic in that it ignores two significant other means by which our culture perpetuates ideas it favors and discredits ideas it fears. One such means is our system of laws, by which legislators and jurists formulate and then impose so-called "public policy." Legislation and judicial decisions carry the weight of law and the threat of punishment for those who deviate from that law. As a result, they are highly effective means of forcing on us official notions of what is good for society and for quashing ideas that are deemed threatening to the social fabric, and to the safety and security of the government and the governed. A second such means is the mainstream media. By mirroring the culture's prevailing ideas and values, broadcast and print media serve to perpetuate them. It is important to distinguish here between mainstream media—such as broadcast television—and alternative media such as documentary films and non-commercial Web sites, whose typical aims are to call into question the status quo, expose the hypocrisy and unfair bias behind mainstream ideas, and bring to light ideas that the powers-that-be most fear. Yet, the influence of alternative media pales in comparison to that of mainstream media.

In sum, the speaker's assertion is not without merit when it comes to the role of grade schools and high schools. However, the speaker over-generalizes about what students are taught—especially at colleges and universities. Moreover, the speaker's assertion ignores other effective ways in which mainstream culture perpetuates its agenda.

Issue:
Should schools teach students to **explore their own emotions**?

The speaker asserts that educational systems should place less emphasis on reason and logical thinking and more emphasis on the exploration of emotions. While I concede that in certain fields students are well served by nurturing their emotions and feelings, in most academic disciplines it is by cultivating intellect rather than emotions that students master their discipline and, in turn, gain a capacity to contribute to the well-being of society.

I agree with the speaker insofar as undue emphasis on reason and logical thinking can have a chilling effect on the arts. After all, artistic ideas and inspiration spring not from logic but from emotions and feelings such as joy, sadness, hope, and love. And, the true measure of artistic accomplishment lies not in technical proficiency but rather in a work's impact on the emotions and spirit. Nevertheless, even in the arts, students must learn theories and techniques, which they then apply to their craft. And, creative writing requires the cognitive ability to understand how language is used and how to communicate ideas. Besides, creative ability is itself partly a function of intellect; that is, creative expression is a marriage of one's cognitive abilities and the expression of one's feelings and emotions.

Aside from its utility in the arts, however, the exploration of emotions has little place in educational systems. The physical sciences and mathematics are purely products of reason and logic. Even in the so-called "soft" sciences, emotion should play no part. Consider, for example, the study of history, political science, or public policy, each of which is largely the study of how the concepts of fairness, equity, and justice work themselves out. It is tempting to think that students can best understand and learn to apply these concepts by tapping feelings such as compassion, empathy, sympathy, and indignation. Yet fairness, equity, and justice have little to do with feelings, and everything to do with reason. After all, emotions are subjective things. On the other hand, reason is objective and therefore facilitates communication, consensus, and peaceful compromise.

Indeed, on a systemic scale undue emphasis on the exploration of our emotions can have deleterious societal consequences. Emotions invite irrationality in thought and action, the dangers of which are all too evident in contemporary America. For example, when it comes to the war on drugs, free speech and religion, abortion issues, and sexual choices, public policy today seems to simply mirror the voters' fears and prejudices. Yet common sense dictates that social ills are best solved by identifying cause-and-effect relationships—in other words, through critical thinking. The proliferation of shouting-match talk shows fueled by irrationality and emotion gone amuck is further evidence that our culture lends too much credence to our emotions and not enough to our minds. A culture that sanctions irrationality and unfettered venting of emotion is vulnerable to decline. Indeed, exploiting emotions while suppressing reason is how demagogues gain and hold power, and how humanity's most horrific atrocities have come to pass. In contrast, reason and better judgment are effective deterrents to incivility, despotism, and war.

In sum, emotions can serve as important catalysts for academic accomplishment in the arts. Otherwise, however, students, and ultimately society, are better off by learning to temper their emotions while nurturing judgment, tolerance, fairness, and understanding—all of which are products of reason and critical thinking.

Issue:
Setting **research priorities**

Should researchers focus on areas that are likely to result in the greatest benefit to the most people, as the speaker suggests? I agree insofar as areas of research certain to result in immediate and significant benefits for society should continue to be a priority. Yet, strictly followed, the speaker's recommendation would have a harmful chilling effect on research and new knowledge. This is particularly true in the physical sciences, as discussed below.

Admittedly, scientific research whose societal benefits are immediate, predictable, and profound should continue to be a high priority. For example, biotechnology research is proven to help cure and prevent diseases; advances in medical technology allow for safer, less invasive diagnosis and treatment; advances in genetics help prevent birth defects; advances in engineering and chemistry improve the structural integrity of our buildings, roads, bridges, and vehicles; information technology enables education; and communication technology facilitates global peace and participation in the democratic process. To demote any of these research areas to a lower priority would be patently foolhardy, considering their proven benefits to so many people. However, this is not to say that research whose benefits are less immediate or clear should be given lower priority. For three reasons, all avenues of scientific research should be afforded equal priority.

First of all, if we strictly follow the speaker's suggestion, who would decide which areas of research are more worthwhile than others? Researchers cannot be left to decide. Given a choice, they will pursue their own special areas of interest, and it is highly unlikely that all researchers could reach a fully informed consensus as to what areas are most likely to help the most people. Nor can these decisions be left to regulators and legislators, who would bring to bear their own quirky notions about what is worthwhile, and whose susceptibility to influence peddlers renders them untrustworthy in any event.

A telling example of the inherent danger of setting "official" research priorities involves the Soviet government's attempts during the 1920s to not only control the direction and the goals of its scientists' research but also to distort the outcome of that research—ostensibly for the greatest good of the greatest number of people. During the 1920s, the Soviet government quashed certain areas of scientific inquiry, destroyed entire research facilities and libraries, and caused the sudden disappearance of many scientists who were viewed as threats to the state's authority. Not surprisingly, during this time period no significant scientific advances occurred under the auspices of the Soviet government.

Secondly, to compel all researchers to focus only on certain areas would be to force many to waste their true talents. For example, imagine relegating today's preeminent astrophysicist Stephen Hawking to research the effectiveness of behavioral modification techniques in the reform of violent criminals. Admittedly, this example borders on hyperbole. Yet the aggregate effect of realistic cases would be to waste the intellectual talents of our world's researchers. Moreover, lacking genuine interest or motivation a researcher would be unlikely to contribute meaningfully to his or her "assigned" field.

Thirdly, it is difficult to predict which research avenues will ultimately lead to the greatest contributions to society. Research areas whose benefits are certain often break little new ground, and in the long term so-called "cutting-edge" research whose potential benefits are unknown often prove most useful to society. One current example involves terraforming—creating biological life and a habitable atmosphere where none existed before. This unusual research area does not immediately address society's pressing social problems. Yet, in the longer term, it might be necessary to colonize other planets in order to ensure the survival of the human race; and after all, what could be a more significant contribution to society than preventing its extinction?

In sum, when it comes to setting priorities for research, at least in the sciences, the speaker goes too far by implying that research whose benefits are unknown are not worth pursuing. After all, any research worth doing delves into the unknown. In the final analysis, the only objective of research should be to discover truths, whatever they might be—not to implement social policy.

Issue:
Studying the past to help us live **in the present**

The speaker claims that since so much in today's world is new and complex the past provides little guidance for living in the present. I agree with this assertion insofar as history offers few foolproof panaceas for living today. However, I disagree with the speaker's claim that today's world is so unique that the past is irrelevant. One good example that supports my dual position is the way society has dealt with its pressing social problems over time.

Admittedly, history has helped us learn the appropriateness of addressing certain social issues, particularly moral ones, on a societal level. Attempts to legislate morality invariably fail, as illustrated by Prohibition in the 1930s and, more recently, failed federal legislation to regulate access to adult material via the Internet. We are slowly learning this lesson, as the recent trend toward legalization of marijuana for medicinal purposes and the recognition of equal rights for same-sex partners both demonstrate.

However, the only firm lesson from history about social ills is that they are here to stay. Crime and violence, for example, have troubled almost every society. All manner of reform, prevention, and punishment have been tried. Today, the trend appears to be away from reform toward a "tough-on-crime" approach. Is this because history makes clear that punishment is the most effective means of eliminating crime? No; rather, the trend merely reflects our current mores, attitudes, and political climate.

Another example involves how we deal with the mentally ill segment of the population. History reveals that neither quarantine, treatment, nor accommodation solves the problem, only that each approach comes with its own trade-offs. Also undermining the assertion that history helps us to solve social problems is the fact that, despite the civil-rights efforts of Martin Luther King and his progenies, the cultural gap today between African Americans and white Americans seems to be widening. It seems that racial prejudice is a timeless phenomenon.

To sum up, in terms of how to live together as a society I agree that studying the past is of some value; for example, it helps us appreciate the futility of legislating morality. However, history's primary sociological lesson seems to be that today's social problems are as old as society itself, and that there are no panaceas or prescriptions for solving these problems—only alternate ways of coping with them.

Issue:
Will **computer connections** make tourism obsolete?

The speaker asserts that television and computer connectivity will soon render tourism obsolete. I agree that these technologies might eventually serve to reduce travel for certain purposes other than tourism. However, I strongly disagree that tourism will become obsolete, or that it will even decline, as a result.

As for the claim that television will render tourism obsolete, we already have sufficient empirical evidence that this will simply not happen. For nearly a half-century we have been peering through our television sets at other countries and cultures; yet tourism is as popular today as ever. In fact, tourism has been increasing sharply during the last decade, which has seen the advent of television channels catering exclusively to our interest in other cultures and countries. The more reasonable conclusion is that television has actually served to spark our interest in visiting other places.

It is somewhat more tempting to accept the speaker's further claim that computer connectivity will render tourism obsolete. However, the speaker unfairly assumes that the purpose of tourism is simply to obtain information about other people and places. Were this the case, I would entirely agree that the current information explosion spells the demise of tourism. But, tourism is not primarily about gathering information. Instead, it is about sensory experience—seeing and hearing firsthand, even touching and smelling. Could anyone honestly claim that seeing a picture or even an enhanced 3-D movie of the Swiss Alps serves as a suitable substitute for riding a touring motorcycle along narrow roads traversing those mountains? Surely not. The physical world is laden with a host of such delights that we humans are compelled to experience firsthand—as tourists.

Moreover, in my view tourism will continue to thrive for the same reason that people still go out for dinner or to the movies: we all need to "get away" from our familiar routines and surroundings from time to time. Will computer connectivity alter this basic need? Certainly not. In short, tourism is a manifestation of a basic human need for variety and for exploration. This basic need is why humans have come to inhabit every corner of the earth, and will just as surely inhabit other planets of the solar system.

In fact, computer connectivity might actually provide a boon for tourism. The costs of travel and accommodations are likely to decrease due to Internet price competition. Even more significantly, to the extent that the Internet enhances communication among the world's denizens, our level of comfort and trust when it comes to dealing with people from other cultures will only increase. As a result, many people who previously would not have felt safe or secure traveling to strange lands will soon venture abroad with a new sense of confidence.

Admittedly, travel for purposes other than tourism might eventually decline, as the business world becomes increasingly dependent on the Internet. Products that can be reduced to digital "bits and bites" can now be shipped anywhere in the world without any human travel. And the volume of business-related trips will surely decline in the future, as teleconferencing becomes more readily available. To the extent that business travelers "play tourist" during business trips, tourism will decline as a result. Yet it would be absurd to claim that these phenomena alone will render tourism obsolete.

In sum, while business travel might decline as a result of global connectivity, tourism is likely to increase as a result. Global connectivity, especially the Internet, can only pique our curiosity about other peoples, cultures, and places. Tourism helps satisfy that curiosity, as well as satisfying a fundamental human need to experience new things first-hand and to explore the world.

Issue:
From whom do our **leading voices come**?

I agree with the statement insofar as our leading voices tend to come from people whose ideas depart from the status quo. However, I do not agree that what motivates these iconoclasts is a mere desire to be different; in my view they are driven primarily by their personal convictions. Supporting examples abound in all areas of human endeavor—including politics, the arts, and the physical sciences.

When it comes to political power, I would admit that a deep-seated psychological need to be noticed or to be different sometimes lies at the heart of a person's drive to political power and fame. For instance, some astute presidential historians have described Clinton as a man motivated more by a desire to be great than to accomplish great things. And many psychologists attribute Napoleon's and Mussolini's insatiable lust for power to a so-called "short-man complex"—a need to be noticed and admired in spite of one's small physical stature.

Nevertheless, for every leading political voice driven to new ideas by a desire to be noticed or to be different, one can cite many other political leaders clearly driven instead by the courage of their convictions. Iconoclasts Mahatma Gandhi and Martin

Luther King, for example, secured prominent places in history by challenging the status quo through civil disobedience. Yet, no reasonable person could doubt that it was the conviction of their ideas that drove these two leaders to their respective places.

Turning to the arts, mavericks such as Dali, Picasso, and Warhol, who departed from established rules of composition, ultimately emerge as the leading artists. And our most influential popular musicians are the ones who are flagrantly "different." Consider, for example, jazz pioneers Thelonius Monk and Miles Davis, who broke all the harmonic rules, or folk musician-poet Bob Dylan, who established a new standard for lyricism. Were all these leading voices driven simply by a desire to be different? Perhaps; but my intuition is that creative urges are born not of ego but rather of some intensely personal commitment to an aesthetic ideal.

As for the physical sciences, innovation and progress can only result from challenging conventional theories—that is, the status quo. Newton and Einstein, for example, both refused to blindly accept what were perceived at their time as certain rules of physics. As a result, both men redefined those rules. Yet it would be patently absurd to assert that these two scientists were driven by a mere desire to conjure up "different" theories than those of their contemporaries or predecessors. Surely it was a conviction that their theories were better that drove these geniuses to their places in history.

To sum up, when one examines history's leading voices it does appear that they typically bring to the world something radically different than the status quo. Yet, in most cases, this sort of iconoclasm is a byproduct of personal conviction, not iconoclasm for its own sake.

Issue:
Rituals and ceremonies and cultural identity

The speaker asserts that rituals and ceremonies are needed for any culture or group of people to retain a strong sense of identity. I agree that one purpose of ritual and ceremony is to preserve cultural identity, at least in modern times. However, this is not their sole purpose; nor are ritual and ceremony the only means of preserving cultural identity.

I agree with the speaker insofar as one purpose of ritual and ceremony in today's world is to preserve cultural identity. Native American tribes, for example, cling tenaciously to their traditional ceremonies and rituals, which typically tell a story about tribal heritage. The reason for maintaining these rituals and customs lies largely in the tribes' 500-year struggle against assimilation, even extinction, at the hands of European intruders. An outward display of traditional customs and distinct heritage is needed to put the world on notice that each tribe is a distinct and autonomous people, with its own heritage, values, and ideas. Otherwise, the tribe risks total assimilation and loss of identity.

The lack of meaningful ritual and ceremony in homogenous mainstream America underscores this point. Other than a few gratuitous ceremonies such as weddings and funerals, we maintain no common rituals to set us apart from other cultures. The reason for this is that as a whole America has little cultural identity of its own anymore. Instead, it has become a patchwork quilt of many subcultures, such as Native Americans, Hasidic Jews, Amish, and urban African Americans—each of which resort to some outward demonstration of its distinctiveness in order to establish and maintain a unique cultural identity.

Nevertheless, preserving cultural identify cannot be the only purpose of ritual and ceremony. Otherwise, how would one explain why isolated cultures that don't need to distinguish themselves to preserve their identity nevertheless engage in their own distinct rituals and ceremonies? In fact, the initial purpose of ritual and ceremony is rooted not in cultural identity but rather superstition and spiritual belief. The original purpose of a ritual might have been to frighten away evil spirits, to bring about weather conditions favorable to bountiful harvests, or to entreat the gods for a successful hunt or for victory in battle. Even today some primitive cultures engage in rituals primarily for such reasons.

Nor are ritual and ceremony the only means of preserving cultural identity. For example, our Amish culture demonstrates its distinctiveness through dress and lifestyle. Hasidic Jews set themselves apart by their dress, vocational choices, and dietary habits. And African Americans distinguish themselves today by their manner of speech and gesture. Of course, these subcultures have their own distinct ways of cerebrating events such as weddings, coming of age, and so forth. Yet ritual and ceremony are not the primary means by which these subcultures maintain their identity.

In sum, to prevent total cultural assimilation into our modern-day homogenous soup, a subculture with a unique and proud heritage must maintain an outward display of that heritage—by way of ritual and ceremony. Nevertheless, ritual and ceremony serve a spiritual function as well—one that has little to do with preventing cultural assimilation. Moreover, rituals and ceremonies are not the only means of preserving cultural identity.

Issue:
Society's duty to identify children with **special talents**

I agree that we should attempt to identify and cultivate our children's talents. However, in my view the statement goes too far, by suggesting that selected children receive special attention. If followed to the letter, this suggestion carries certain social, psychological, and human-rights implications that might turn out to be more harmful than beneficial—not just to children but to the entire society.

At first blush the statement appears compelling. Although I am not a student of developmental psychology, my understanding is that unless certain innate talents are nurtured and cultivated during early childhood those talents can remain forever dormant; and both the child and the society stand to lose as a result. After all, how can a child who is musically gifted ever see those gifts come to fruition without access to a musical instrument? Or, how can a child who has a gift for linguistics ever learn a foreign language without at least some exposure to it? Thus I agree with the statement insofar as any society that values its own future well-being must be attentive to its children's talents.

Beyond this concession, however, I disagree with the statement because it seems to recommend that certain children receive special attention at the expense of other children—a recommendation that I find troubling in three respects. First, this policy would require that a society of parents make choices that they surely will never agree upon to begin with—for example, how and on what basis each child's talents should be determined, and what sorts of talents are most worth society's time, attention, and resources. While society's parents would never reach a reasonable consensus on these issues, it would be irresponsible to leave these choices to a handful of legislators and bureaucrats. After all, they are unlikely to have the best interests of our children in mind, and their choices would be tainted by their own quirky, biased, and otherwise wrongheaded notions of what constitutes worthwhile talent. Thus the unanswerable question becomes: Who is to make these choices to begin with?

Secondly, a public policy whereby some children receive preferential treatment carries dangerous sociological implications. The sort of selectivity that the statement recommends might tend to split society into two factions: talented elitists and all others. In my view any democratic society should abhor a policy that breeds or exacerbates socioeconomic disparities.

Thirdly, in suggesting that it is in society's best interest to identify especially talented children, the statement assumes that talented children are the ones who are most likely to contribute greatly to the society as adults. I find this assumption somewhat dubious, for I see no reason why a talented child, having received the benefit of special attention, might nevertheless be unmotivated to ply those talents in useful ways as an adult. In fact, in my observation many talented people who misuse their talents—in ways that harm the very society that helped nurture those talents.

Finally, the statement ignores the psychological damage that a preferential policy might inflict on all children. While children selected for special treatment grow to deem themselves superior, those left out feel that they a worth less as a result. I think any astute child psychologist would warn that both types of cases portend psychological trouble later in life. In my view we should favor policies that affirm the self-worth of every child, regardless of his or her talents—or lack thereof. Otherwise, we will quickly devolve into a society of people who cheapen their own humanity.

In the final analysis, when we help our children identify and develop their talents we are all better off. But if we help only some children to develop only some talents, I fear that on balance we will all be worse off.

Issue:
Are **most important discoveries** and creations accidental?

The speaker contends that most important discoveries and creations are accidental—that they come about when we are seeking answers to other questions. I concede that this contention finds considerable support from important discoveries of the past. However, the contention overstates the role of accident, or serendipity, when it comes to modern-day discoveries—and when it comes to creations.

Turning first to discoveries, I agree that discovery often occurs when we unexpectedly happen upon something in our quest for something else—such as an answer to an unrelated question or a solution to an unrelated problem. A variety of geographical, scientific, and anthropological discoveries aptly illustrate this point. In search of a trade route to the West Indies Columbus discovered instead an inhabited continent unknown to Europeans; and during the course of an unrelated experiment Fleming accidentally discovered penicillin. In search of answers to questions about marine organisms, oceanographers often happen upon previously undiscovered, and important, archeological artifacts and geological phenomena; conversely, in their quest to understand the earth's structure and history geologists often stumble upon important human artifacts.

In light of the foregoing examples, "intentional discovery" might seem an oxymoron; yet in fact it is not. Many important discoveries are anticipated and sought out purposefully. For instance, in their efforts to find new celestial bodies astronomers using increasingly powerful telescopes do indeed find them. Biochemists often discover important new vaccines and other biological and chemical agents for the curing, preventing, and treating of diseases not by stumbling upon them in search of something else but rather through methodical search for these discoveries. In fact, in today's world discovery is becoming increasingly an anticipated result of careful planning and methodical research, for the reason that scientific advancement now requires significant resources that only large corporations and governments possess. These entities are accountable to their shareholders and constituents, who demand clear strategies and objectives so that they can see a return on their investments.

Turning next to how our creations typically come about, in marked contrast to discoveries, creations are by nature products of their creators' purposeful designs. Consider humankind's key creations, such as the printing press, the internal combustion engine, and semi-conductor technology. Each of these inventions sprung quite intentionally from the inventor's imagination and objectives. It is crucial to distinguish here between a creation and the spin-offs from that creation, which the original creator may or may not foresee. For instance, the engineers at a handful of universities who originally created the ARPAnet as a means to transfer data amongst themselves certainly intended to create that network for that purpose. What these engineers did not intend to create, however, was what would eventually grow to become the infrastructure for mass media and communications, and even commerce. Yet the

ARPAnet itself was no accident, nor are the many creations that it spawned, such as the World Wide Web and the countless creations that the Web has in turned spawned.

In sum, the speaker has overlooked a crucial distinction between the nature of discovery and the nature of creation. Although serendipity has always played a key role in many important discoveries, at least up until now, purposeful intent is necessarily the key to human creation.

Issue:
The chief benefit of **the study of history**

I concede that basic human nature has not changed over recorded history, and that coming to appreciate this fact by studying history can be beneficial in how we live as a society. However, I disagree with the statement in two respects. First, in other ways there are marked differences between people of different time periods, and learning about those differences can be just as beneficial. Second, studying history carries other equally important benefits as well.

I agree with the statement insofar as through the earnest study of human history we learn that basic human nature—our desires and motives, as well as our fears and foibles—has remained constant over recorded time. And through this realization we can benefit as a society in dealing more effectively with our enduring social problems. History teaches us, for example, that it is a mistake to attempt to legislate morality, because humans by nature resist having their moral choices forced upon them. History also teaches us that our major social ills are here to stay, because they spring from human nature. For instance, crime and violence have troubled almost every society; all manner of reform, prevention, and punishment have been tried with only partial success. Today, the trend appears to be away from reform toward a "tough-on-crime" approach, to no avail.

However beneficial it might be to appreciate the unchanging nature of humankind, it is equally beneficial to understand and appreciate significant differences between peoples of different time periods—in terms of cultural mores, customs, values, and ideals. For example, the ways in which societies have treated women, ethnic minorities, animals, and the environment have continually evolved over the course of human history. Society's attitudes toward artistic expression, literature, and scientific and intellectual inquiry are also in a continual state of evolution. And, perhaps the most significant sort of cultural evolution involves spiritual beliefs, which have always spun themselves out, albeit uneasily, through clashes between established traditions and more enlightened viewpoints. A heightened awareness of all these aspects of cultural evolution help us formulate informed, reflective, and enlightened values and ideals for ourselves; and our society clearly benefits as a result.

Another problem with the statement is that it undervalues other, equally important benefits of studying history. Learning about the courage and tenacity of history's great explorers, leaders, and other achievers inspires us to similar accomplishments, or at least to face own fears as we travel through life. Learning about the mistakes of past societies helps us avoid repeating them. For instance, the world is slowly coming to learn by studying history that political states whose authority stems from suppression of individual freedoms invariably fall of their own oppressive weight. And, learning about one's cultural heritage, or roots, fosters a healthy sense of self and cultivates an interest in preserving art, literature, and other cultural artifacts—all of which serve to enrich society.

To sum up, history informs us that basic human nature has not changed, and this history lesson can help us understand and be more tolerant of one another, as well as develop compassionate responses to the problems and failings of others. Yet, history has other lessons to offer us as well. It helps us formulate informed values and ideals for ourselves, inspires us to great achievements, points out mistakes to avoid, and helps us appreciate our cultural heritage.

Issue:
Our tendency to look for similarities between **different things**

Do people too often look for similarities between things, regardless of whether it is helpful or harmful to do so, and not often enough evaluate things on their own individual merits? The speaker believes so. I agree to an extent, especially when it comes to making determinations about people. However, the speaker overlooks a fundamental and compelling reason why people must always try to find similarities between things.

I agree with the speaker insofar as insisting on finding similarities between things can often result in unfair, and sometimes harmful, comparisons. By focusing on the similarities among all big cities, for example, we overlook the distinctive character, architecture, ethnic diversity, and culture of each one. Without evaluating an individual company on its own merits before buying stock in that company, an investor runs the risk of choosing a poor performer in an otherwise attractive product sector or geographic region. And schools tend to group students according to their performance on general intelligence tests and academic exams. By doing so, schools overlook more specific forms of intelligence which should be identified and nurtured on a more individualized basis so that each student can fulfill his or her potential.

As the final example above illustrates, we should be especially careful when looking for similarities between people. We humans have a tendency to draw arbitrary conclusions about one another based on gender, race, and superficial characteristics. Each individual should be evaluated instead on the basis of his or her own merit—in terms of character, accomplishment, and so forth. Otherwise, we run the risk of unfair bias and even prejudice, which manifest themselves in various forms of discrimination and oppression. Yet prejudice can result from looking too hard for differences as well, while overlooking the things that all people share. Thus while partly correct, the speaker's assertion doesn't go far enough—to account for the potential harm in drawing false distinctions between types of people.

Yet, in another sense the speaker goes too far—by overlooking a fundamental, even philosophical, reason why we should always look for similarities between things. Specifically, it is the only way humans can truly learn anything and communicate with one another. Any astute developmental psychologist, epistemologist, or even parent would agree that we come to understand each new thing we encounter by comparing it to something with which we are already familiar. For example, if a child first associates the concept of blue with the sky's color, then the next blue thing the child encounters—a ball, for instance—the child recognizes as blue only by way of its similarity to the sky. Furthermore, without this association and a label for the concept of blue the child cannot possibly convey the concept to another person. Thus looking for similarities between things is how we make sense of our world, as well as communicate with one another.

To sum up, I agree that finding false similarities and drawing false analogies can be harmful, especially when reaching conclusions about people. Nevertheless, from a philosophical and linguistic point of view, humans must look for similarities between things in order to learn and to communicate.

Issue:
Praising **positive actions** and ignoring negative ones

The speaker suggests that the most effective way to teach others is to praise positive actions while ignoring negative ones. In my view, this statement is too extreme. It overlooks circumstances under which praise might be inappropriate, as well as ignoring the beneficial value of constructive criticism, and sometimes even punishment.

The recommendation that parents, teachers, and employers praise positive actions is generally good advice. For young children positive reinforcement is critical in the development of healthy self-esteem and self-confidence. For students appropriate positive feedback serves as a motivating force, which spurs them on to greater academic achievement. For employees, appropriately administered praise enhances productivity and employee loyalty, and makes for a more congenial and pleasant work environment overall.

While recommending praise for positive actions is fundamentally sound advice, this advice should carry with it certain caveats. First, some employees and older students might find excessive praise to be patronizing or paternalistic. Secondly, some individuals need and respond more appropriately to praise than others; those administering the praise should be sensitive to the individual's need for positive reinforcement in the first place. Thirdly, praise should be administered fairly and evenhandedly. By issuing more praise to one student than to others, a teacher might cause one recipient to be labeled by classmates as teacher's pet, even if the praise is well deserved or badly needed. If the result is to alienate other students, then the praise might not be justified. Similarly, at the workplace a supervisor must be careful to issue praise fairly and evenhandedly, or risk accusations of undue favoritism, or even discrimination.

As for ignoring negative actions, I agree that minor peccadilloes can, and in many cases should, be overlooked. Mistakes and other negative actions are often part of the natural learning process. Young children are naturally curious, and parents should not scold their children for every broken plate or precocious act. Otherwise, children do not develop a healthy sense of wonder and curiosity, and will not learn what they must in order to make their own way in the world. Teachers should avoid rebuking or punishing students for faulty reasoning, incorrect responses to questions, and so forth. Otherwise, students might stop trying to learn altogether. And employees who know they are being monitored closely for any sign of errant behavior are likely to be less productive, more resentful of their supervisors, and less loyal to their employers.

At the same time, some measure of constructive criticism and critique, and sometimes even punishment, is appropriate. Parents must not turn a blind eye to their child's behavior if it jeopardizes the child's physical safety or the safety of others. Teachers should not ignore behavior that unduly disrupts the learning process; and of course teachers should correct and critique students' class work, homework and tests as needed to help the students learn from their mistakes and avoid repeating them. Finally, employers must not permit employee behavior that amounts to harassment or that otherwise undermines the overall productivity at the workplace. Acquiescence in these sorts of behaviors only serves to sanction them.

To sum up, the speaker's dual recommendation is too extreme. Both praise and criticism serve useful purposes in promoting a child's development, a student's education, and an employee's loyalty and productivity. Yet both must be appropriately and evenhandedly administered; otherwise, they might serve instead to defeat these purposes.

Answers to Issue Statements That Contain Dual Claims or Raise More Than One Issue

The same Issue statement might actually consist of dual assertions, or it might raise two or three related but distinct issues, one of which might be a so-called threshold issue that is best addressed before the main issue. But don't expect an Issue statement to advertise itself as this type; you may need to read a statement carefully to determine whether you can break it down this way.

To handle this sort of Issue statement, first sort out the assertions or issues for the reader, then evaluate each one in turn. The sample essays in this section exemplify this approach.

Issue:
Government's duty to preserve **cultural traditions**

The speaker's claim is actually threefold: (1) ensuring the survival of large cities and, in turn, that of cultural traditions, is a proper function of government; (2) government support is needed for our large cities and cultural traditions to survive and thrive; and (3) cultural traditions are preserved and generated primarily in our large cities. I strongly disagree with all three claims.

First of all, subsidizing cultural traditions is not a proper role of government. Admittedly, certain objectives, such as public health and safety, are so essential to the survival of large cities and of nations that government has a duty to ensure that they are met. However, these objectives should not extend tenuously to preserving cultural traditions. Moreover, government cannot possibly play an evenhanded role as cultural patron. Inadequate resources call for restrictions, priorities, and choices. It is unconscionable to relegate normative decisions as to which cities or cultural traditions are more deserving, valuable, or needy to a few legislators, whose notions about culture might be misguided or unrepresentative of those of the general populace. Also, legislators are all too likely to make choices in favor of the cultural agendas of their home towns and states, or of lobbyists with the most money and influence.

Secondly, subsidizing cultural traditions is not a necessary role of government. A lack of private funding might justify an exception. However, culture—by which I chiefly mean the fine arts—has always depended primarily on the patronage of private individuals and businesses, and not on the government. The Medici's, a powerful banking family of Renaissance Italy, supported artists Michelangelo and Raphael. During the twentieth century the primary source of cultural support were private foundations established by industrial magnates Carnegie, Mellon, Rockefeller, and Getty.

And tomorrow cultural support will come from our new technology and media moguls—including the likes of Ted Turner and Bill Gates. In short, philanthropy is alive and well today, and so government need not intervene to ensure that our cultural traditions are preserved and promoted.

Finally, and perhaps most importantly, the speaker unfairly suggests that large cities serve as the primary breeding ground and sanctuaries for a nation's cultural traditions. Today a nation's distinct cultural traditions—its folk art, crafts, traditional songs, customs and ceremonies—burgeon instead in small towns and rural regions. Admittedly, our cities do serve as our centers for "high art"; big cities are where we deposit, display, and boast the world's preeminent art, architecture, and music. But big-city culture has little to do anymore with one nation's distinct cultural traditions. After all, modern cities are essentially multicultural stew pots; accordingly, by assisting large cities a government is actually helping to create a global culture as well to subsidize the traditions of other nations' cultures.

In the final analysis, government cannot philosophically justify assisting large cities for the purpose of either promoting or preserving the nation's cultural traditions; nor is government assistance necessary toward these ends. Moreover, assisting large cities would have little bearing on our distinct cultural traditions, which abide elsewhere.

Issue:
Should students learn concepts before they **memorize facts**?

The speaker makes a threshold claim that students who learn only facts learn very little, then concludes that students should always learn about concepts, ideas, and trends before they memorize facts. While I wholeheartedly agree with the threshold claim, the conclusion unfairly generalizes about the learning process. In fact, following the speaker's advice would actually impede the learning of concepts and ideas, as well as impeding the development of insightful and useful new ones.

Turning first to the speaker's threshold claim, I strongly agree that if we learn only facts we learn very little. Consider the task of memorizing the periodic table of elements, which any student can memorize without any knowledge of chemistry, or that the table relates to chemistry. Rote memorization of the table amounts to a bit of mental exercise—an opportunity to practice memorization techniques and perhaps learn some new ones. Otherwise, the student has learned very little about chemical elements, or about anything for that matter.

As for the speaker's ultimate claim, I concede that postponing the memorization of facts until after one learns ideas and concepts holds certain advantages. With a conceptual framework already in place, a student is better able to understand the meaning of a fact and to appreciate its significance. As a result, the student is more likely to memorize the fact to begin with, and less likely to forget it as time passes. Moreover, in my observation students whose first goal is to memorize facts tend to stop there—for whatever reason. It seems that by focusing on facts first students risk equating the learning process with the assimilation of trivia; in turn, students risk learning nothing of much use in solving real-world problems.

Conceding that students must learn ideas and concepts, as well as facts relating to them, in order to learn anything meaningful, I nevertheless disagree that the former should always precede the latter—for three reasons. In the first place, I see no reason why memorizing a fact cannot precede learning about its meaning and significance—as long as the student does not stop at rote memorization. Consider once again our hypothetical chemistry student. The speaker might advise this student to first learn about the historical trends leading to the discovery of the elements, or to learn about the concepts of altering chemical compounds to achieve certain reactions—before studying the periodic table. Having no familiarity with the basic vocabulary of chemistry, which includes the information in the periodic table, this student would come away from the first two lessons bewildered and confused in other words, having learned little.

In the second place, the speaker misunderstands the process by which we learn ideas and concepts, and by which we develop new ones. Consider, for example, how economics students learn about the relationship between supply and demand, and the resulting concept of market equilibrium, and of surplus and shortage. Learning about the dynamics of supply and demand involves (1) entertaining a theory, and perhaps even formulating a new one; (2) testing hypothetical scenarios against the theory; and (3) examining real-world facts for the purpose of confirming, refuting, modifying, or qualifying the theory. But which step should come first? The speaker would have us follow steps 1 through 3 in that order. Yet, theories, concepts, and ideas rarely materialize out of thin air; they generally emerge from empirical observations— i.e., facts. Thus, the speaker's notion about how we should learn concepts and ideas gets the learning process backward.

In the third place, strict adherence to the speaker's advice would surely lead to ill-conceived ideas, concepts, and theories. Why? An idea or concept conjured up without the benefit of data amounts to little more than the conjurer's hopes and desires. Accordingly, conjurers will tend to seek out facts that support their prejudices and opinions, and overlook or avoid facts that refute them. One telling example involves theories about the center of the universe. Understandably, we ego-driven humans would prefer that the universe revolve around us. Early theories presumed so for this reason, and facts that ran contrary to this ego-driven theory were ignored, while observers of these facts were scorned and even vilified. In short, students who strictly follow the speaker's prescription are unlikely to contribute significantly to the advancement of knowledge.

To sum up, in a vacuum facts are meaningless, and only by filling that vacuum with ideas and concepts can students learn, by gaining useful perspectives and insights about facts. Yet, since facts are the very stuff from which ideas, concepts, and trends spring, without some facts students cannot learn much of anything. In the final analysis, then, students should learn facts right along with concepts, ideas, and trends.

Issue:
The role of **nonmainstream areas** of inquiry

This statement actually consists of two claims: (1) that non-mainstream areas of inquiry are vital in satisfying human needs, and (2) that these areas are therefore vital to society. I concede that astrology, fortune-telling, and psychic and paranormal pursuits respond to certain basic human needs. However, in my view the potential harm they can inflict on their participants and on society far outweighs their psychological benefits.

Admittedly, these non-mainstream areas of inquiry address certain human needs, which mainstream science and other areas of intellectual inquiry inherently cannot. One such need involves our common experience as humans that we freely make our own choices and decisions in life and therefore carry some responsibility for their consequences. Faced with infinite choices, we experience uncertainty, insecurity, and confusion; and we feel remorse, regret, and guilt when in retrospect our choices turn out be poor ones. Understandably, to prevent these bad feelings many people try to shift the burden of making difficult choices and decisions to some nebulous authority outside themselves—by relying on the stars or on a stack of tarot cards for guidance.

Two other such needs have to do with our awareness that we are mortal. This awareness brings a certain measure of pain that most people try to relieve by searching for evidence of an afterlife. Absent empirical proof that life extends beyond the grave, many people attempt to contact or otherwise connect with the so-called "other side" through paranormal and psychic pursuits. Another natural response to the prospect of being separated from our loved ones by death is to search for a deeper connection with others here on Earth and elsewhere, in the present as well as the past. This response manifests itself in people's enduring fascination with the paranormal search for extraterrestrial life, with so-called "past life" regression and "channeling," and the like.

While the sorts of pursuits that the speaker lists might be "vital" insofar as they help some people feel better about themselves and about their choices and circumstances, query whether these pursuits are otherwise useful to any individual or society. In the first place, because these pursuits are not rooted in reason, they are favorite pastimes of charlatans and others who seek to prey on dupes driven by the aforementioned psychological needs. And the dupes have no recourse. After all, it is impossible to assess the credibility of a tarot card that tells us how to proceed in life— simply because we cannot know where the paths not taken would have led. Similarly, we cannot evaluate claims about the afterlife because these claims inherently defy empirical proof—or disproof.

In the second place, without any sure way to evaluate the legitimacy of these avenues of inquiry, participants become vulnerable to self-deception, false hopes, fantastic ideas, and even delusions. In turn, so-called "insights" gained from these pursuits can too easily serve as convenient excuses for irrational and unreasonable actions that harm others. On a personal level, stubborn adherence to irrational beliefs in the face of reason and empirical evidence can lead to self-righteous arrogance, intolerance, anti-social behavior, and even hatred. Moreover, on a societal level these traits have led all too often to holy wars, and to such other atrocities as genocide and mass persecution.

In sum, I concede that the non-mainstream pursuits that the speaker lists are legitimate insofar as they afford many people psychological solace in life. However, when such pursuits serve as substitutes for reason and logic, and for honest intellectual inquiry, participants begin to distrust intellect as an impediment to enlightenment. In doing so, they risk making ill-conceived choices for themselves and unfair judgments about others—a risk that in my view outweighs the psychological rewards of those pursuits.

Issue:
The **concept of individual responsibility**

I fundamentally agree with the speaker's first contention, for unless we embrace the concept of "individual responsibility" our notions of moral accountability and human equality, both crucial to the survival of any democratic society, will whither. However, I strongly disagree with the second contention—that our individual actions are determined largely by external forces. Although this claim is not entirely without support, it runs contrary to common sense and everyday human experience.

The primary reason that individual responsibility is a necessary fiction is that a society where individuals are not held accountable for their actions and choices is a lawless one, devoid of any order whatsoever. Admittedly, under some circumstances a society of laws should carve out exceptions to the rule of individual responsibility—for example, for the hopeless psychotic who has no control over his or her thoughts or actions. Yet to extend forgiveness much further would be to endanger the social order upon which any civil and democratic society depends.

A correlative argument for individual responsibility involves the fact that lawless, or anarchist, states give way to despotic rule by strong individuals who seize power. History informs us that monarchs and dictators often justify their authority by claiming that they are preordained to assume it—and that as a result they are not morally responsible for their oppressive actions. Thus, any person abhorring despotism must embrace the concept of individual responsibility.

As for the speaker's second claim, it flies in the face of our everyday experiences in making choices and decisions. Although people often claim that life's circumstances have "forced" them to take certain actions, we all have an infinite number of choices; it's just that many of our choices are unappealing, even self-defeating. Thus, the complete absence of free will would seem to be possible only in the case of severe psychosis, coma, or death.

Admittedly, the speaker's second contention finds support from "strict determinist" philosophers, who maintain that every event, including human actions and choices, is physically necessary, given the laws of nature. Recent advances in molecular biology and genetics lend some credence to this position, by suggesting that these determining physical forces include our own individual genetic makeup. But, the notion of scientific determinism opens the door for genetic engineering, which might threaten equality in socioeconomic opportunity, and even precipitate the development of a "master race." Besides, since neither free will nor determinism has been proven to be the correct position, the former is to be preferred by any humanist and in any democratic society.

In sum, without the notion of individual responsibility a civilized, democratic society would soon devolve into an anarchist state, vulnerable to despotic rule. Yet, this notion is more than a mere fiction. The idea that our actions spring primarily from our free will accords with common sense and everyday experience. I concede that science might eventually vindicate the speaker and show that our actions are largely determined by forces beyond our conscious control. Until that time, however, I'll trust my intuition that we humans should be, and in fact are, responsible for our own choices and actions.

Issue:
Ads portraying people we want to "**be like**"

The speaker asserts that the many ads that make consumers want to "be like" the person portrayed in the ad are effective not only in selling products but also in helping consumers feel better about themselves. This assertion actually consists of two claims: that this advertising technique is used effectively in selling many products, and that consumers who succumb to this technique actually feel better about themselves as a result. While I agree with the first claim, I strongly disagree with the second one.

Turning first to the statement's threshold claim, do many ads actually use this technique to sell products in the first place? Consider ads like the wildly popular Budweiser commercial featuring talking frogs. There's nothing in that ad to emulate; its purpose is merely to call attention to itself. Notwithstanding this type of ad, in my observation the majority of ads provide some sort of model that most consumers in the target market would want to emulate, or "be like." While some ads actually portray people who are the opposite of what the viewer would want to "be like," these ads invariably convey the explicit message that to avoid being like the person in the ad the consumer must buy the advertised product. As for whether the many, many ads portraying models are effective in selling products, I am not privy to the sort of statistical information required to answer this question with complete certainty. However, my intuition is that this technique does help sell products; otherwise, advertisers would not use it so persistently.

Turning next to the statement's ultimate claim that these ads are effective because they help people who buy the advertised products feel better about themselves, I find this claim to be specious. Consumers lured by the hope of "being like" the person in an ad might experience some initial measure of satisfaction in the form of an ego boost. We have all experienced a certain optimism immediately after acquiring something we've wanted—a good feeling that we're one step closer to becoming who we want to be. However, in my experience this sense of optimism is ephemeral, invariably giving way to disappointment that the purchase did not live up to its implicit promise.

One informative example of this false hope involves the dizzying array of diet aids, skin creams, and fitness machines available today. The people in ads for these products are youthful, fit, and attractive—what we all want to "be like." And the ads are effective in selling these products; today's health-and-beauty market feeds a multibillion dollar industry. But the end result for the consumer is an unhealthy preoccupation with physical appearance and youth, which often leads to low self-esteem, eating disorders, injuries from over-exercise, and so forth. And these problems are sure signs of consumers who feel worse, not better, about themselves as a result of having relied on the false hope that they will "be like" the model in the ad.

Another informative example involves products that pander to our desire for socioeconomic status. Ads for luxury cars and upscale clothing typically portray people with lucrative careers living in exclusive neighborhoods. Yet, I would wager that no person whose lifestyle actually resembles these portrayals could honestly claim that purchasing certain consumer products contributed one iota to his or her socioeconomic success. The end result for the consumer is envy of others that can afford even more expensive possessions, and ultimately low self-esteem based on feelings of socioeconomic inadequacy.

In sum, while ads portraying people we want to "be like" are undoubtedly effective in selling products, they are equally ineffective in helping consumers feel better about themselves. In fact, the result is a sense of false hope, leading ultimately to disappointment and a sense of failure and inadequacy—in other words, feeling worse about ourselves.

Issue:
Have we learned how to **raise children** who can **better society**?

I find the speaker's dual claim to be specious on both counts. The claim that society's destiny hinges on how children are socialized, while appealing in some respects, is an over-statement at best. And the claim that we have not yet learned how to raise children who can better society is poorly supported by empirical evidence.

Consider first the speaker's assertion that society's destiny depends on how children are socialized. I concede that unless a child is allowed sufficient opportunities for healthy interaction with peers, that child is likely to grow into an ineffectual, perhaps even an anti-social, adult. To witness healthy socialization in action, one need look no further than the school playground, where children learn to negotiate, cooperate, and assert themselves in a respectful manner, and where they learn about the harmful results of bullying and other anti-social behavior. These lessons help children grow up to be good citizens and effective leaders, as well as tolerant and respectful members of society.

However, socialization is only one factor influencing the extent to which an individual will ultimately contribute to a better society. And in my observation it is not the most important one. Consider certain prominent leaders who have contributed profoundly to a better society. Mahatma Gandhi's contributions sprang primarily from the courage of his inner convictions, in spite of his proper socialization among genteel Indian society and, as a law student, among British society. Martin Luther King's contribution was primarily the result of his strong religious upbringing, which had more to do with parental influence than with socialization. An even more remarkable modern example was Theodore Roosevelt, whose social and physical development were both stunted by life-threatening physical infirmities during his childhood. In spite of his isolation, odd manner and aloofness throughout his early life, Roosevelt ascended to a social-activist presidency by means of his will to overcome physical infirmities, his voracious appetite for knowledge, and his raw intellect.

Consider next the speaker's claim that we have not yet learned how to raise children who can better society. If we define a "better" society as one characterized by greater tolerance of differing viewpoints and people who are different from ourselves, greater respect for individual rights, and greater cooperation across cultural and national boundaries, then the children of the most recent half-century are creating a better society. The most recent quarter-century has seen an increasing sensitivity in our society toward ensuring public health by policing the food and drug industries and by protecting our natural environment. We're becoming more sensitive to, and respectful of, the rights of women, various ethnic and racial groups, homosexuals, and mentally- and physically-challenged individuals. The re-emergence of political third parties with decidedly libertarian ideals demonstrates an increasing concern for individual freedoms. And there is ample evidence of increasing international cooperation. The former Soviet Union and the U.S. have worked collaboratively in space research and exploration since the 1970s; peace-keeping missions are now largely multinational efforts; and nations are now tackling public health problems collaboratively through joint research programs. In short, the speaker's second claim flies in the face of the empirical evidence, as I see it.

In sum, when it comes to whether a child grows up to contribute to a better society, the key determinant is not socialization but rather some other factor—such as a seminal childhood event, parental influence, raw intelligence, or personal conviction. And, while reasonable people with differing political and social viewpoints might disagree about what makes for a "better" society, in my observation our society is steadily evolving into a more civilized, respectful, and tolerant one. In the final analysis, then, I fundamentally disagree with both aspects of the speaker's dual claim.

Issue:
Can a person be committed to an idea yet be **critical of it**?

The speaker claims that people who are the most firmly committed to an idea or policy are the same people who are most critical of that idea or policy. While I find this claim paradoxical on its face, the paradox is explainable, and the explanation is well supported empirically. Nevertheless, the claim is an unfair generalization in that it fails to account for other empirical evidence serving to discredit it.

A threshold problem with the speaker's claim is that its internal logic is questionable. At first impression it would seem that firm commitment to an idea or policy necessarily requires the utmost confidence in it, and yet one cannot have a great deal of confidence in an idea or policy if one recognizes its flaws, drawbacks, or other problems. Thus, commitment and criticism would seem to be mutually exclusive. But are they? One possible explanation for the paradox is that individuals most firmly committed to an idea or policy are often the same people who are most knowledgeable on the subject, and therefore are in the best position to understand and appreciate the problems with the idea or policy.

Lending credence to this explanation for the paradoxical nature of the speaker's claim are the many historical cases of uneasy marriages between commitment to and criticism of the same idea or policy. For example, Edward Teller, the so-called "father of the atom bomb," was firmly committed to America's policy of gaining military superiority over the Japanese and the Germans; yet at the same time he attempted fervently to dissuade the U.S. military from employing his technology for destruction, while becoming the most visible advocate for various peaceful and productive applications of atomic energy. Another example is George Washington, who was quoted as saying that all the world's denizens "should abhor war wherever they may find it." Yet this was the same military general who played a key role in the Revolutionary War between Britain and the States. A third example was Einstein, who while committed to the mathematical soundness of his theories about relativity could not reconcile them with the equally compelling quantum theory that emerged later in Einstein's life. In fact, Einstein spent the last twenty years of his life criticizing his own theories and struggling to determine how to reconcile them with newer theories.

In the face of historical examples supporting the speaker's claim are innumerable influential individuals who were zealously committed to certain ideas and policies but who were not critical of them, at least not outwardly. Could anyone honestly claim, for instance, that Elizabeth Stanton and Susan B. Anthony, who in the late nineteenth century paved the way for the women's rights movement by way of their fervent advocacy, were at the same time highly critical or suspicious of the notion that women deserve equal rights under the law? Also, would it not be absurd to claim that Mahatma Gandhi and Martin Luther King, history's two leading advocates of civil disobedience as a means to social reform, had serious doubts about the ideals to which they were so demonstrably committed? Finally, consider the two ideologues and revolutionaries Lenin and Mussolini. Is it even plausible that their demonstrated commitment to their own Communist and Fascist policies, respectively, belied some deep personal suspicion about the merits of these policies? To my knowledge, no private writing of any of these historical figures lends any support to the claim that these leaders were particularly critical of their own ideas or policies.

To sum up, while at first glance a deep commitment to and incisive criticism of the same idea or policy would seem mutually exclusive, it appears they are not. Thus the speaker's claim has some merit. Nevertheless, for every historical case supporting the speaker's claim are many others serving to refute it. In the final analysis, then, the correctness of the speaker's assertion must be determined on a case-by-case basis.

Issue:
The effects of high-speed **communications media**

Do high-speed means of communication, particularly television and computers, tend to prevent meaningful and thoughtful communication, as the speaker suggests? Although ample empirical evidence suggests so with respect to television, the answer is far less clear when it comes to communication via computers.

Few would argue that since its inception broadcast television has greatly enhanced communication to the masses. The circulation of even the most widely read newspapers pales compared to the number of viewers of popular television news programs. Yet traditional television is a one-way communications medium, affording viewers no opportunity to engage those so-called "talking heads" in dialogue or respond. Of course, there is nothing inherent about television that prevents us from meaningful and thoughtful communication with each other. In fact, in television's early days it was a fairly common occurrence for a family to gather around the television together for their favorite show, then afterward discuss among themselves what they had seen and heard. Yet, over time television has proven itself to serve primarily as a baby-sitter for busy parents, and as an means of escape for those who wish to avoid communicating with the people around them. Moreover, in the pursuit of profit, network executives have determined over time that the most effective uses of the medium are for fast-paced entertainment and advertising—whose messages are neither thoughtful nor meaningful.

Do computers offer greater promise for thoughtful and reflective communication than television? Emphatically, yes. After all, media such as e-mail and the Web are interactive by design. And the opportunity for two-way communication enhances the chances of meaningful and thoughtful communication. Yet their potential begs the question: Do these media in fact serve those ends? It is tempting to hasten that the answer is "yes" with respect to e-mail; after are, we've all heard stories about how e-mail has facilitated reunions of families and old friends, and new long-distance friendships and romances. Moreover, it would seem that two-way written communication requires far more thought and reflection than verbal conversation. Nevertheless, e-mail is often used to avoid face-to-face encounters, and in practice is used as a means of distributing quick memos. Thus, on balance it appears that e-mail serves as an impediment, not an aide, to thoughtful and reflective communication.

With respect to Web-based communication, the myriad of educational sites, interactive and otherwise, is strong evidence that the Web tends to enhance, rather than prevent, meaningful communication. Distance-learning courses made possible by the Web lend further credence to this assertion. Nonetheless, by all accounts it appears that the Web will ultimately devolve into a mass medium for entertainment and for e-commerce, just like traditional television. Meaningful personal interactivity is already yielding to advertising, requests for product information, buy-sell orders, and titillating adult-oriented content.

Thus, on balance these high-speed electronic media do indeed tend to prevent rather than facilitate meaningful and thoughtful communication. In the final analysis, any mass medium carries the potential for uplifting us, enlightening us, and helping us to communicate with and understand one another. However, by all accounts, television has not fulfilled that potential; and whether the Web will serve us any better is ultimately up to us as a society.

Issue:
Will humans always be **superior to machines**?

This statement actually consists of a series of three related claims: (1) machines are tools of human minds; (2) human minds will always be superior to machines; and (3) it is because machines are human tools that human minds will always be superior to machines. While I concede the first claim, whether I agree with the other two claims depends partly on how one defines "superiority," and partly on how willing one is to humble oneself to the unknown future scenarios.

The statement is clearly accurate insofar as machines are tools of human minds. After all, would any machine even exist unless a human being invented it? Of course not. Moreover, I would be hard-pressed to think of any machine that cannot be described as a tool. Even machines designed to entertain or amuse us—for example, toy robots, cars and video games, and novelty items—are in fact tools, which their inventors and promoters use for engaging in commerce and the business of entertainment and amusement. And, the claim that a machine can be an end in itself, without purpose or utilitarian function for humans whatsoever, is dubious at best, since I cannot conjure up even a single example of any such machine. Thus, when we develop any sort of machine we always have some sort of end in mind—a purpose for that machine.

As for the statement's second claim, in certain respects machines are superior. We have devised machines that perform number crunching and other rote cerebral tasks with greater accuracy and speed than human minds ever could. In fact, it is because we can devise machines that are superior in these respects that we devise them—as our tools—to begin with. However, if one defines superiority not in terms of competence in performing rote tasks but rather in other ways, human minds are superior. Machines have no capacity for independent thought, for making judgments based on normative considerations, or for developing emotional responses to intellectual problems.

Up until now, the notion of human-made machines that develop the ability to think on their own, and to develop so-called "emotional intelligence," has been pure fiction. Besides, even in fiction we humans ultimately prevail over such machines—as in the cases of Frankenstein's monster and Hal, the computer in 2001:A Space Odyssey. Yet it seems presumptuous to assert with confidence that humans will always maintain their superior status over their machines. Recent advances in biotechnology, particularly in the area of human genome research, suggest that within the twenty-first century we'll witness machines that can learn to think on their own, to repair and nurture themselves, to experience visceral sensations, and so forth. In other words, machines will soon exhibit the traits to which we humans attribute our own superiority.

In sum, because we devise machines in order that they may serve us, it is fair to characterize machines as "tools of human minds." And insofar as humans have the unique capacity for independent thought, subjective judgment, and emotional response, it also seems fair to claim superiority over our machines. Besides, should we ever become so clever a species as to devise machines that can truly think for themselves and look out for their own well-being, then query whether these machines of the future would be "machines" anymore.

Issue:
Are people free to **choose a career**?

The speaker believes that economic and other pragmatic concerns are what drive people's career decisions, and that very few people are free to choose their careers based on their talents and interests. I tend to disagree; although practical considerations often play a significant role in occupational trends, ultimately the driving forces behind people's career decisions are individual interest and ability.

At first glance the balance of empirical evidence would seem to lend considerable credence to the speaker's claim. The most popular fields of study for students today are the computer sciences—fields characterized by a relative glut of job opportunities. Graduates with degrees in liberal arts often abandon their chosen fields because they cannot find employment, and reenter school in search of more "practical" careers. Even people who have already achieved success in their chosen field are often forced to abandon them due to pragmatic concerns. For example, many talented and creative people from the entertainment industry find themselves looking for other, less satisfying, kinds of work when they turn 40 years of age because industry executives prefer younger artists who are "tuned in" to the younger demographic group that purchases entertainment products.

However, upon further reflection it becomes clear that the relationship between career-seekers and the supply of careers is an interdependent one, and therefore it is unfair to generalize about which one drives the other. Consider, for example, the two mainstream fields of computer science and law. In the computer industry it might appear that supply clearly drives job interest—and understandably so, given the highly lucrative financial rewards. But, would our legions of talented programmers, engineers, scientists, and technicians really pursue their careers without a genuine fascination, a passion, or at least an interest in those areas? I think not.

Conversely, consider the field of law, in which it would appear that demand drives the job market, rather than vice versa. The number of applications to law schools soared during the civil rights movement of the 1960s, and again in the 1980s during the run of the popular television series L.A. Law. More recently, the number of students pursuing paralegal and criminal justice careers spiked during and immediately after the O.J. Simpson trial. Query, though, whether these aspiring lawyers and paralegals would have been sufficiently motivated had the supply of jobs and the financial rewards not already been waiting for them upon graduation.

Another compelling argument against the speaker's claim has to do with the myriad of ways in which people earn their living. Admittedly, the job market is largely clustered around certain mainstream industries and types of work. Nevertheless, if one peers beyond these mainstream occupational areas it becomes evident that many, many people do honor their true interests and talents—in spite of where most job openings lie and regardless of their financial rewards. Creative people seem to have a knack for creating their own unique vocational niche—whether it be in the visual or the performing arts; many animal lovers create work which allows them to express that love. Caregivers and nurturers manage to find work teaching, socializing, counseling, and healing others. And people bitten by the travel bug generally have little trouble finding satisfying careers in the travel industry.

In sum, the speaker's threshold claim that it is strictly the pragmatic concerns of job availability and financial compensation that drive people's career decisions oversimplifies both why and how people make career choices. Besides, the speaker's final claim that people are not free to choose their work violates my intuition. In the final analysis, people are ultimately free to choose their work; it's just that they often choose to betray their true talents and interests for the sake of practical, economic considerations.

Issue:
Should colleges allow students to **make their own decisions**?

The speaker asserts that people prefer following directions to making their own decisions, and therefore colleges should make as many decisions as possible for their students. In my view, the speaker's threshold and ultimate claims are both specious. It might appear that people often prefer others to make decisions for them, and that colleges know what's best for their students. However, upon further reflection it becomes evident that following the speaker's advice would on balance do disservice to students and to society.

As for the speaker's threshold claim, I concede that under certain circumstances people prefer to take direction from others. For instance, when members of a football team heed their coach's directions, they are preferring not to make their own calls. Moreover, many people are natural followers who know that they function best when other people make decisions for them. Nevertheless, I find this threshold claim internally illogical. Yielding voluntarily to the direction of others for the purpose of serving one's own interests—such as winning the game or obtaining a useful college degree—is itself an expression of one's free preference to decide what is best for oneself. Accordingly, I find the speaker's threshold claim suspect.

I turn next to the speaker's ultimate claim that colleges should make as many decisions as possible for their students. I agree that when it comes to particular tasks in which college professors are more experienced and knowledgeable, following their directions is to be preferred, for failing to do so can result in costly mistakes. For instance, chemistry students must strictly follow proper laboratory procedures—or risk tainting experimental results, damaging equipment, or wasting their lab partners' time. Language students must follow the pedagogical lead of their teachers, or risk coming away without the linguistic foundation needed to master their new language. And, students who are free to disregard homework assignments find themselves unable to follow class discussions, let alone participate meaningfully in them.

However, when it comes to decisions about major and minor fields of study, curriculum choices, and other broad decisions, for the most part students themselves—and not college administrators—should be the final decision-makers. Admittedly, a college that requires exposure to a breadth of academic disciplines ensures that its graduates will be uniformly well rounded. And students are generally well-served in the long term as a result. Nevertheless, I think it is a mistake to take too many curriculum choices away from students. If they are not free to choose course work that most interests them, students are likely to be unmotivated in their studies. Moreover, these students will not have learned to assume responsibility for the consequences of their own decisions. Thus a curriculum which includes certain core requirements along with a broad array of electives provides an optimal balance of discipline and choice for most students.

The speaker might retort that many college students respond to freedom of choice regarding curriculum by enrolling in as few courses as possible, in courses that are most enjoyable, and in courses whose instructors are lenient graders. Yet, students who misuse their freedom in these ways will ultimately fall by the wayside, freeing up our educational resources for more committed students who are more likely to contribute meaningfully to society later in life. Besides, by allowing students to experience the consequences of their youthful misjudgments colleges can teach students life lessons that are just as valuable, if not more so, than the lessons taught in the classroom.

In sum, my intuition is that by nature people prefer autonomy, and reach their full potential, only if they steer their own ship. When colleges take away too much of that autonomy in the name of quality assurance, they breed legions of graduates incapable of handling their incipient autonomy responsibly. In the final analysis, while some curriculum guidelines might be appropriate in the interest of ensuring a breadth of educational experience, on balance a policy of student choice is to be preferred.

Issue:
Does conformity stifle **creativity and energy**?

This statement about the impact of conformity on individual energy and creativity actually involves two distinct issues. In my view, the extent to which conformity stifles a person's energy depends primarily on the temperament of each individual, as well as on the goals toward which the person's energy is directed. However, I am in full agreement that conformity stifles creativity; indeed, in my view the two phenomena are mutually exclusive.

Whether conformity stifles individual energy depends on the individual person involved. Some people are conformists by nature. By this I mean that they function best in an environment where their role is clearly defined and where teamwork is key in meeting group objectives. For conformists individual energy comes from sharing a common purpose, or mission, with a group that must work in lock-step fashion to achieve that mission. In the military and in team sports, for example, the group's common mission is clearly understood, and group members conform to the same dress code, drill regimen, and so forth. And rather than quelling energy, this conformity breeds camaraderie, as well as enthusiasm and even fervor for winning the battle or the game. Besides, nonconforming behavior in these environments only serves to undermine success; if game plans or battle strategies were left to each individual team member, the results would clearly be disastrous.

Conformists find enhanced energy in certain corners of the business world as well, particularly in traditional service industries such as finance, accounting, insurance, legal services, and health care. In these businesses it is not the iconoclasts who revel and thrive but rather those who can work most effectively within the constraints of established practices, policies, and regulations. Of course, a clever idea for structuring a deal, or a creative legal maneuver, might play a role in winning smaller battles along the way. But such tactics are those of conformists who are playing by the same ground rules as their peers.

In sharp contrast, other people are nonconformists by nature. These people are motivated more often by the personal satisfaction that comes with creativity, invention, and innovation. For these people a highly structured, bureaucratic environment only serves to quell motivation and energy. Artists and musicians typically find such environments stifling, even noxious. Entrepreneurial business people who thrive on innovation and differentiation are often driven to self-employment because they feel stifled and frustrated, even offended, by a bureaucracy which requires conformity.

As for whether conformity stifles individual creativity, one need only look around at the individuals whom we consider highly creative to conclude that this is indeed the case. Our most creative people are highly eccentric in their personal appearance, lifestyle, and so forth. In fact, they seem to eschew any sort of established norms and mores. Bee-bop music pioneer Thelonius Monk was renowned for his eccentric manner of speech, dress, and behavior. Even as a young student, Frank Lloyd Wright took to carrying a cane and wearing a top hat and a cape. And who could argue that musicians Prince and Michael Jackson, two of the most creative forces in popular music, are nothing if not nonconforming in every way. Besides, by definition creativity requires nonconformity. In other words, any creative act is necessarily in nonconformance with what already exists.

To sum up, conformists find their energy by conforming, nonconformists by not conforming. And creativity is the exclusive domain of the nonconformist.

Answers to Issue Statements That Can Be Interpreted in More Than One Way

Your viewpoint on an Issue topic might depend on how an important word or phrase in the Issue statement is defined or interpreted. If so, by all means bring this problem to the reader's attention. Then either present a viewpoint based on your interpretation or evaluate the statement according to different interpretations, each one in turn.

A problem of definition or interpretation might be merely a threshold or side issue to be raised either before or after the main issue. Or the problem might be central in evaluating the Issue statement, in which case it is perfectly appropriate to devote at least one entire paragraph to each possible definition or interpretation. You'll find illustrations of both variations among the sample essays in this section.

Issue:

Does it require **effort and courage** to make things simple?

Whether making things simple requires greater effort and courage than making them bigger and more complex depends on the sort of effort and courage. Indisputably, the many complex technological marvels that are part-and-parcel of our lives today are the result of the extraordinary cumulative efforts of our engineers, entrepreneurs, and others. And, such achievements always call for the courage to risk failing in a large way. Yet, humans seem naturally driven to make things bigger and more complex; thus, refraining from doing so, or reversing this natural process, takes considerable effort and courage of a different sort, as discussed below.

The statement brings immediately to mind the ever-growing and increasingly complex digital world. Today's high-tech firms seem compelled to boldly go to whatever effort is required to devise increasingly complex products, for the ostensible purpose of staying ahead of their competitors. Yet, the sort of effort and courage to which the statement refers is a different one—bred of vision, imagination, and a willingness to forego near-term profits for the prospect of making lasting contributions. Surely, a number of entrepreneurs and engineers today are mustering that courage, and are making the effort to create far simpler, yet more elegant, technologies and applications, which will truly make our lives simpler—in sharp contrast to what computer technology has delivered to us so far.

Lending even more credence to the statement is the so-called "big government" phenomenon. Human societies have a natural tendency to create unwieldy bureaucracies, a fitting example of which is the U.S. tax-law system. The Internal Revenue Code and its accompanying Treasury Regulations have grown so voluminous and complex that many certified accountants and tax attorneys admit that they cannot begin to understand it all. Admittedly, this system has grown only through considerable effort on the part of all three branches of the federal government, not to mention the efforts of many special-interest groups. Yet, therein lies the statement's credibility. It requires great effort and courage on the part of a legislator to risk alienating special interest groups, thereby risking reelection prospects, by standing on principle for a simpler tax system that is less costly to administer and better serves the interests of most taxpayers.

Adding further credibility to the statement is the tendency of most people to complicate their personal lives—a tendency that seems especially strong in today's age of technology and consumerism. The greater our mobility, the greater our number of destinations each day; the more time-saving gadgets we use, the more activities we try to pack into our day; and with readier access to information we try to assimilate more of it each day. I am hard-pressed to think of one person who has ever exclaimed to me how much effort and courage it has taken to complicate his or her life in these respects. In contrast, a certain self-restraint and courage of conviction are both required to eschew modern conveniences, to simplify one's daily schedule, and to establish and adhere to a simple plan for the use of one's time and money.

In sum, whether we are building computer networks, government agencies, or personal lifestyles, great effort and courage are required to make things simple, or to keep them that way. Moreover, because humans naturally tend to make things big and complex, it arguably requires more effort and courage to move in the opposite direction. In the final analysis, making things simple—or keeping them that way—takes a brand of effort born of reflection and restraint rather than sheer exertion, and a courageous character and conviction rather than unbridled ambition.

Issue:
Ethical and moral standards and successful leadership

Whether successful leadership requires that a leader follow high ethical and moral standards is a complex issue—one that is fraught with the problems of defining ethics, morality, and successful leadership in the first place. In addressing the issue it is helpful to consider in turn three distinct forms of leadership: business, political, and social-spiritual.

In the business realm, successful leadership is generally defined as that which achieves the goal of profit maximization for a firm's shareholders or other owners. Moreover, the prevailing view in Western corporate culture is that by maximizing profits a business leader fulfills his or her highest moral or ethical obligation. Many disagree, however, that these two obligations are the same. Some detractors claim, for example, that business leaders have a duty to do no intentional harm to their customers or to the society in which they operate—for example, by providing safe products and by implementing pollution control measures. Other detractors go further—to impose on business leaders an affirmative obligation to protect consumers, preserve the natural environment, promote education, and otherwise take steps to help alleviate society's problems.

Whether our most successful business leaders are the ones who embrace these additional obligations depends, of course, on one's own definition of business success. In my observation, as business leaders become subject to closer scrutiny by the media and by social activists, business leaders will maximize profits in the long term only by taking reasonable steps to minimize the social and environmental harm their businesses cause. This observation also accords with my personal view of a business leader's ethical and moral obligation.

In the political realm the issue is no less complex. Definitions of successful political leadership and of ethical or moral leadership are tied up in the means a leader uses to wield his or her power and to obtain that power in the first place. One useful approach is to draw a distinction between personal morality and public morality. In my observation, personal morality is unrelated to effective political leadership. Modern politics is replete with examples of what most people would consider personal ethical failings: the marital indiscretions of President Kennedy, for instance. Yet few would agree that these personal moral choices adversely affected his ability to lead.

In contrast, public morality and successful leadership are more closely connected. Consider the many leaders, such as Stalin and Hitler, whom most people would agree were egregious violators of public morality. Ultimately, such leaders forfeit their leadership as a result of the immoral means by which they obtained or wielded their power. Or consider less egregious examples such as President Nixon, whose contempt for the very legal system that afforded him his leadership led to his forfeiture of it. It seems that in the short term unethical public behavior might serve a political leader's interest in preserving his or her power; yet in the long term such behavior invariably results in that leader's downfall—that is, in failure.

One must also consider a third type of leadership: social-spiritual. Consider notable figures such as Gandhi and Martin Luther King, whom few would disagree were eminently successful in leading others to practice the high ethical and moral standards which they advocated. However, I would be hard-pressed to name one successful social or spiritual leader whose leadership was predicated on the advocacy of patently unethical or immoral behavior. The reason for this is simple: high standards for one's own public morality are prerequisites for successful social-spiritual leadership.

In sum, history informs us that effective political and social-spiritual leadership requires adherence to high standards of public morality. However, when it comes to business leadership the relationship is less clear—successful business leaders must strike a balance between achieving profit maximization and fulfilling their broader obligation to the society, which comes with the burden of such leadership.

Issue:
Recognizing the **limits of our knowledge**

Does recognizing the limits of our knowledge and understanding serve us equally well as acquiring new facts and information, as the speaker asserts? While our everyday experience might lend credence to this assertion, further reflection reveals its fundamental inconsistency with our Western view of how we acquire knowledge. Nevertheless, a careful and thoughtful definition of knowledge can serve to reconcile the two.

On the one hand, the speaker's assertion accords with the everyday experience of working professionals. For example, the sort of "book" knowledge that medical, law, and business students acquire, no matter how extensive, is of little use unless these students also learn to accept the uncertainties and risks inherent in professional practice and in the business world. Any successful doctor, lawyer, or entrepreneur would undoubtedly agree that new precedents and challenges in their fields compel them to acknowledge the limitations of their knowledge, and that learning to accommodate these limitations is just as important in their professional success as knowledge itself.

Moreover, the additional knowledge we gain by collecting more information often diminishes—sometimes to the point where marginal gains turn to marginal losses. Consider, for instance, the collection of financial-investment information. No amount of knowledge can eliminate the uncertainty and risk inherent in financial investing. Also, information overload can result in confusion, which in turn can diminish one's ability to assimilate information and apply it usefully. Thus, by recognizing the limits of their knowledge, and by accounting for those limits when making decisions, investment advisers can more effectively serve their clients.

On the other hand, the speaker's assertion seems self-contradictory, for how can we know the limits of our knowledge until we've thoroughly tested those limits through exhaustive empirical observation—that is, by acquiring facts and information. For example, it would be tempting to concede that we can never understand the basic forces that govern all matter in the universe. Yet due to increasingly precise and extensive fact-finding efforts of scientists, we might now be within striking distance of understanding the key laws by which all physical matter behaves. Put another way, the speaker's assertion flies in the face of the scientific method, whose fundamental tenet is that we humans can truly know only that which we observe. Thus Francis Bacon, who first formulated the method, might assert that the speaker is fundamentally incorrect.

How can we reconcile our experience in everyday endeavors with the basic assumption underlying the scientific method? Perhaps the answer lies in a distinction between two types of knowledge—one that amounts to a mere collection of observations (i.e., facts and information), the other that is deeper and includes a realization of principles and truths underlying those observations. At this deeper level "knowledge" equals "understanding": how we interpret, make sense of, and find meaning in the information we collect by way of observation.

In the final analysis, evaluating the speaker's assertion requires that we define "knowledge," which in turn requires that we address complex epistemological issues best left to philosophers and theologians. Yet perhaps this is the speaker's point: that we can never truly know either ourselves or the world, and that by recognizing this limitation we set ourselves free to accomplish what no amount of mere information could ever permit.

Issue:
Historians as **storytellers**

Are all historians essentially storytellers, for the reasons that the speaker cites? In asserting that we can never know the past directly, the speaker implies that we truly "know" only what we experience first-hand. Granting this premise, I agree that it is the proper and necessary role of historians to "construct" history by interpreting evidence. Nevertheless, the speaker's characterization of this role as "storytelling" carries certain unfair implications, which should be addressed.

One reason why I agree with the speaker's fundamental claim lies in the distinction between the role of historian and the roles of archivist and journalist. By "archivist" I refer generally to any person whose task is to document and preserve evidence of past events. And by "journalist" I mean any person whose task is to record, by writing, film, or some other media, factual events as they occur—for the purpose of creating evidence of those events. It is not the proper function of either the journalist or the archivist to tell a story. Rather, it is their function to provide evidence to the historian, who then pieces together the evidence to construct history, as the speaker suggests. In other words, unless we grant to the historian a license to "construct" history by interpreting evidence, we relegate the historian to the role of mere archivist or journalist.

Another reason why I agree with the speaker's characterization of the historian's proper function is that our understanding of history is richer and fuller as a result. By granting the historian license to interpret evidence—to "construct" history—we allow for differing viewpoints among historians. Based on the same essential evidence, two historians might disagree about such things as the contributing causes of a certain event, the extent of influence or impact of one event on subsequent events, the reasons and motives for the words and actions of important persons in history, and so forth. The inexorable result of disagreement, debate, and divergent interpretations among historians is a fuller and more incisive understanding of history.

However, we should be careful not to confuse this license to interpret history, which is needed for any historian to contribute meaningfully to our understanding of it, with artistic license. The latter should be reserved for dramatists, novelists, and poets. It is one thing to attempt to explain historical evidence; it is quite another to invent evidence for the sake of creating a more interesting story or to bolster one's own point of view. A recently released biography of Ronald Reagan demonstrates that the line that historians should not cross is a fine one indeed. Reagan's biographer invented a fictional character who provided commentary as a witness to key episodes during Reagan's life. Many critics charge that the biographer overstepped his bounds as historian; the biographer claims, however, that the accounts in the biography were otherwise entirely factual, and that the fictional narrator was merely a literary device to aid the reader in understanding and appreciating the historical Reagan.

In sum, I strongly agree that the historian's proper function is to assemble evidence into plausible constructs of history, and that an element of interpretation and even creativity is properly involved in doing so. And if the speaker wishes to call these constructs "story-telling," that's fine. This does not mean, however, that historians can or should abandon scholarship for the sake of an interesting story.

Issue:
Has technology failed to help **humanity** progress?

Have technological innovations of the last century failed to bring about true progress for humanity, as the statement contends? Although I agree that technology cannot ultimately prevent us from harming one another, the statement fails to account for the significant positive impact that the modern-industrial and computer revolutions have had on the quality of life—at least in the developed world.

I agree with the statement insofar as there is no technological solution to the enduring problems of war, poverty, and violence, for the reason that they stem from certain aspects of human nature—such as aggression and greed. Although future advances in biochemistry might enable us to "engineer away" those undesirable aspects, in the meantime it is up to our economists, diplomats, social reformers, and jurists—not our scientists and engineers—to mitigate these problems.

Admittedly, many technological developments during the last century have helped reduce human suffering. Consider, for instance, technology that enables computers to map Earth's geographical features from outer space. This technology allows us to locate lands that can be cultivated for feeding malnourished people in third-world countries. And, few would disagree that humanity is the beneficiary of the myriad of twentieth-century innovations in medicine and medical technology—from prostheses and organ transplants to vaccines and lasers.

Yet, for every technological innovation helping to reduce human suffering is another that has served primarily to add to it. For example, while some might argue that nuclear weapons serve as invaluable "peace-keepers," this argument flies in the face of the hundreds of thousands of innocent people murdered and maimed by atomic blasts. More recently, the increasing use of chemical weapons for human slaughter points out that so-called "advances" in biochemistry can amount to net losses for humanity.

Notwithstanding technology's limitations in preventing war, poverty, and violence, twentieth-century technological innovation has enhanced the overall standard of living and comfort level of developed nations. The advent of steel production and assembly-line manufacturing created countless jobs, stimulated economic growth, and supplied a plethora of innovative conveniences. More recently, computers have helped free up our time by performing repetitive tasks; have aided in the design of safer and more attractive bridges, buildings, and vehicles; and have made possible universal access to information.

Of course, such progress has not come without costs. One harmful byproduct of industrial progress is environmental pollution and its threat to public health. Another is the alienation of assembly-line workers from their work. And, the Internet breeds information overload and steals our time and attention away from family, community, and coworkers. Nevertheless, on balance both the modern-industrial and computer revolutions have improved our standard of living and comfort level; and both constitute progress by any measure.

In sum, enduring problems such as war, poverty, and violence ultimately spring from human nature, which no technological innovation short of genetic engineering can alter. Thus, the statement is correct in this respect. However, if we define "progress" more narrowly—in terms of economic standard of living and comfort level—recent technological innovations have indeed brought about clear progress for humanity.

Issue127
Are facts "**stubborn things**," or can we alter them?

Can we alter facts according to our wishes or inclinations? If by "facts" the speaker means such phenomena as political, economic, social, or legal status quo, then I concede that we can alter facts. The reason for this is that such systems are abstract constructs of our inclinations, wishes, and passions to begin with. Otherwise, I strongly agree with the speaker that we cannot alter facts. When it comes to certain aspects of our personal lives, and to historical events and scientific truths, no measure of desire or even passion can change external reality.

On an individual level, we all engage in futile attempts to alter facts—by pretending that certain things are not the way they are because they are inconsistent with our wishes or personal interests. Psychologists refer to this psychological defensive mechanism, which seems to be part of human nature, as "denial." Consider curious pastimes such as mind reading, psychic healing, rituals that purportedly impart immortality, and other such endeavors, which seems to transcend all cultures and periods of human history. Understandably, we would all like to have the ability to alter the physical world, including ourselves, as we see fit, or even to live forever by means of the sheer force of our will. Yet, not one iota of scientific evidence lends support to the claim that any human being has ever had any such ability.

Nor can we alter facts by virtue of our inclinations or passions when it comes to history. Admittedly, no person can truly know any particular past that the person did not experience firsthand. In this sense history is a construct, created for us by reporters, archivists, and historians. Historical facts are therefore susceptible to interpretation, characterization, and of course errors in commission and omission. This is not to say, however, that historical facts can be altered by our inventing versions that suit our inclinations or wishes. In short, a historical event is not rendered any less factual by either our ignorance or characterization of it.

Similarly, when it comes to science our wishes and desires ultimately yield to the stubbornness of facts—by which I mean empirical scientific evidence and the laws and principles of the physical world. Admittedly, in many cases it is difficult to distinguish between scientific "fact" and mere "theory." History is replete with examples of what were considered at one time to be facts, but later disproved as incorrect theories. Yet it is telling that many such obsolete theories were based on the subjective inclinations, desires, and wishes of theorists and of the societies in which the theorists lived. For example, the notions of an Earth-centered universe and of linear time and space were both influenced by religious notions—that is, by human wishes and passions. As our factual knowledge increased such theories ultimately give way.

In sum, I agree that facts are indeed "stubborn things." Understandably, all humans are guilty of ignoring, overlooking, and misunderstanding facts—at least to some extent. After all, human passion, desire, and individual bias and perspective are powerful influences when it comes to what we believe to be true and factual. Moreover, the statement carries deep epistemological implications regarding the nature of knowledge and truth, which I cannot begin to adequately address here. Nevertheless, on a less abstract level the speaker is correct that neither inclination, desire, nor passion, no matter how fervent, can alter that which is past or beyond our physical control.

Issue:
The **surest indicator of a great nation**

Does a nation's greatness lie in the general welfare of its people rather than in the achievements of its artists, rulers, and scientists, as the speaker claims? I find this claim problematic in two respects. First, it fails to define "general welfare." Second, it assumes that the sorts of achievements that the speaker cites have little to do with a nation's general welfare—when in fact they have everything to do with it.

At first blush the speaker's claim might appear to have considerable merit. After all, the overriding imperative for any democratic state is to enhance the general welfare of its citizenry. Yet the speaker fails to provide a clear litmus test for measuring that welfare. When we speak of "promoting the general welfare," the following aims come to mind: public health and safety, security against military invasions, individual autonomy and freedom, cultural richness, and overall comfort—that is, a high standard of living. Curiously, it is our scientists, artists, and political leaders—or so-called "rulers"—who by way of their achievements bring these aims into fruition. Thus, in order to determine what makes a nation great it is necessary to examine the different sorts of individual achievements that ostensibly promote these aims.

Few would disagree that many scientific achievements serve to enhance a nation's general welfare. Advances in the health sciences have enhanced our physical wellbeing, comfort, and life span. Advances in technology have enabled us to travel to more places, communicate with more people from different walks of life, and learn about the world from our desktops. Advances in physics and engineering make our abodes and other buildings safer, and enable us to travel to more places, and to travel to more distant places, with greater safety and speed. Artistic achievement is also needed to make a nation a better place for humans overall. Art provides inspiration, lifts the human spirit, and incites our creativity and imagination, all of which spur us on to greater accomplishments and help us appreciate our own humanity. Yet the achievements of scientists and artists, while integral, do not suffice to ensure the welfare of a nation's citizens. In order to survive, let alone be great, a nation must be able to defend its borders and to live peaceably with other nations. Thus, the military and diplomatic accomplishments of a nation's leaders provide an integral contribution to the general welfare of any nation's populace.

Notwithstanding the evidence that, in the aggregate, individual achievements of the sorts listed above are what promote a nation's general welfare, we should be careful not to hastily assume that a nation is necessarily great merely by virtue of the achievements of individual citizens. Once having secured the safety and security of its citizens, political rulers must not exploit or oppress those citizens. Also, the populace must embrace and learn to appreciate artistic accomplishment, and to use rather than misuse or abuse scientific knowledge. Of particular concern are the many ways in which scientific achievements have served to diminish our quality of life, thereby impeding the general welfare. It is through scientific "achievements" that chemicals in our food, water, and air increase the incidence and variety of cancers; that our very existence as a species is jeopardized by the threat of nuclear warfare; and that greenhouse gases which deplete our ozone layer and heat the Earth's atmosphere threaten civilization itself.

In sum, in asserting that general welfare—and neither the scientific, artistic, nor political achievements of individuals—provides the yardstick for measuring a nation's greatness, the speaker misses the point that general welfare is the end product of individual achievements. Besides, achievements of artists, scientists, and political leaders generally benefit people the world over and not just one nation.

Issue:
Is loyalty always a **positive force**?

Is loyalty all too often a destructive force, rather than a virtue, as the speaker contends? To answer this question it is crucial to draw a distinction between loyalty as an abstract concept and its application. Apart from its consequences, loyalty is clearly a virtue that all humans should strive to develop. Loyalty is part of a universal ethos that we commonly refer to as the golden rule: Do unto others as you would have others do unto you. However, whether loyalty in its application amounts to virtue depends on its extent and its object.

First consider the ways in which loyalty, if exercised in proper measure and direction, can be a positive force. Relationships between spouses and other exclusive pairs require some degree of trust in order to endure; and loyalty is part-and-parcel of that trust. Similarly, employment relationships depend on some measure of mutual loyalty, without which job attrition would run so rampant that society's economic productivity would virtually come to a halt. And, without some mutual loyalty between a sovereign state and its citizenry there can be no security or safety from either revolt or invasion. The world would quickly devolve into anarchy or into a despotic state ordered by brute force.

On the other hand, misguided or overextended loyalty can amount to a divisive and even destructive force. In school, undue loyalty to popular social cliques often leads to insulting and abusive language or behavior toward students outside these cliques. Undue loyalty amongst friends can turn them into an antisocial, even warring, gang of miscreants. And, undue loyalty to a spouse or other partner can lead to acquiescence in abusive treatment by that partner, and abuse of oneself by continuing to be loyal despite the abuse.

Misguided loyalty can also occur between people and their institutions. Undue loyalty to college alma maters often leads to job discrimination—for example, when a job candidate with the same alma mater as that of the person making the hiring decision is chosen over a more qualified candidate from a different school. Loyalty to one's employer can also become a destructive force, if it leads to deceptive business practices and disregard for regulations designed to protect public health and safety. By way of undue loyalty to their employers, employees sometimes harm themselves as well. Specifically, many employees fail to advance their own careers by moving on to another place of work, or type of work altogether, because of a misplaced sense of loyalty to one company. Finally, and perhaps foremost in terms of destructive potential, is misguided loyalty to one's country or political leaders. History shows all too well that crossing the fine line between patriotism and irrational jingoism can lead to such atrocities as persecution, genocide, and war.

To sum up, without loyalty there can be no basis for trust between two people, or between people and their institutions. A world devoid of loyalty would be a paranoid, if not anarchical, one. Nevertheless, loyalty must be tempered by other virtues, such as fairness, tolerance, and respect for other people and for oneself. Otherwise, I agree that it can serve to divide, damage, and even destroy.

Issue:
The comparative value of artistic and **scientific accomplishments**

I find the speaker's claim that a civilization's value lies more in its artistic accomplishments than its scientific ones to be problematic insofar as the speaker fails to adequately define the term "value." Nonetheless, assuming that by "value" the speaker means the extent to which an accomplishment enhances and improves the quality of our lives as humans, on balance I agree with the claim.

A threshold problem with the speaker's claim is that the comparative value of art and science lies largely in the eye of the individual beholder. A person who is more emotional, or who has heightened aesthetic sensibilities, will tend to agree with the speaker. On the other hand, a person who is more analytical or cognitive by nature might tend to disagree. Thus the speaker's claim seems an unfair generalization, which ignores its own vulnerability to subjectivity.

Aside from the highly subjective nature of the claim, if the value of a civilization's accomplishments is determined by the civilization itself, then the speaker's claim begs the question. If a civilization chooses to concern itself primarily with science, as our modern Western civilization does, then by definition scientific accomplishments must be of greater value to the civilization than artistic accomplishments. Of course, the reverse would be true for any culture that stresses artistic accomplishment over scientific inquiry.

Assuming that by "value" the speaker means the extent to which later civilizations depend on earlier artistic and scientific accomplishments, I strongly disagree with the speaker's claim. We speak of scientific accomplishments in terms of "progress" and "setback," or "advances" and "retreat." The reason for this is clear enough. With few historical exceptions great scientific accomplishments build on prior ones. Even where new discoveries disprove old theories, scientists would not be challenged and incited in the first place without the benefit of their predecessor's efforts. In sharp contrast, artistic accomplishment has little to do with either advances or retreats. Art is time-less—independent of prior art. Artists draw inspiration not from other art but from the world around them, the essence of which artists attempt to capture and convey. In short, if the value of an accomplishment lies simply in the extent to which subsequent accomplishments depend on it, then the speaker's claim is fundamentally wrong.

However, if by "value" the speaker means something more—the extent to which a scientific or an artistic accomplishment makes the world a better place for humans overall—then the speaker's claim has far more merit. Although it would be tempting to embrace the popular notion that better living is achieved primarily through science, on balance I disagree with this notion. Admittedly, advances in the health sciences serve to enhance our physical well-being, our comfort, and our life span. However, in a myriad of other respects scientific accomplishments have diminished our quality of life.

After all, it is through scientific accomplishment that chemicals in our food, water, and air increase the incidence and variety of cancers; that our very existence as a species is jeopardized by the threat of nuclear warfare; and that greenhouse gases which deplete our ozone layer and heat the Earth threaten civilization itself.

In sharp contrast, no great artistic accomplishment has brought about war, disease or any threat to the quality of life for any civilization. To the contrary, great art only serves to lift the human spirit in the face of the so-called "progress" that scientific accomplishments bring about. Therefore, on balance I agree with the speaker that the value of a civilization—in the long term—lies more in its artistic than scientific accomplishments.

Answers That Reject an Issue Statement Because It Defies Sense or Logic

Many of the Issue statements in the official topic pool don't entirely make sense if you think about them carefully. For example, a statement itself might reveal that it misunderstands the issue or misses the point. (Missing the point is also referred to as "begging the question.") Or it might imply that two choices are mutually exclusive, when in reality they probably aren't. Or it might fail to recognize a paradox: two seemingly contradictory or conflicting ideas, policies, or goals that in reality are consistent.

Each sample essay in this section discusses one of these types of problems. Note that the essay may raise the problem as either the main issue or a side issue.

Issue:
The value and **function of science** and art

The speaker maintains that the function of art is to "upset" while the function of science is to "reassure," and that it is in these functions that the value of each lies. In my view, the speaker unfairly generalizes about the function and value of art, while completely missing the point about the function and value of science.

Consider first the intent and effect of art. In many cases artists set about to reassure, not to upset. Consider the frescos of Fra Angelico and others monks and nuns of the late medieval period, who sought primarily through their representations of the Madonna and Child to reassure and be reassured about the messages of Christian redemption and salvation. Or consider the paintings of impressionist and realist painters of the late nineteenth century. Despite the sharp contrast in the techniques employed by these two schools, in both genres we find soothing, genteel, pastoral themes and images— certainly nothing to upset the viewer.

In other cases, artists set about to upset. For example, the painters and sculptors of the Renaissance period, like the artists who preceded them, approached their art as a form of worship. Yet Renaissance art focuses on other Christian images and themes—

especially those involving the crucifixion and apocalyptic notions of judgment and damnation—which are clearly "upsetting" and disconcerting, and clearly not reassuring. Or consider the works of two important twentieth-century artists; few would argue that the surrealistic images by Salvador Dali or the jarring, splashy murals by abstract painter Jackson Pollock serve to "upset," or at the very least disquiet, the viewer on a visceral level.

When it comes to the function and value of science, in my view the speaker's assertion is simply wrongheaded. The final objective of science, in my view, is to discover truths about our world, our universe, and ourselves. Sometimes these discoveries serve to reassure, and other times they serve to upset. For example, many would consider reassuring the various laws and principles of physics which provide unifying explanations for what we observe in the physical world. These principles provide a reassuring sense of order, even simplicity, to an otherwise mysterious and perplexing world.

On the other hand, many scientific discoveries have clearly "upset" conventional notions about the physical world and the universe. The notions of a sun-centered universe, that humans evolved from lower primate forms, and that time is relative to space and motion are all disquieting notions to anyone whose belief system depends on contrary assumptions. And more recently, researchers have discovered that many behavioral traits are functions of individual neurological brain structure, determined at birth. This notion has "upset" many professionals in fields such as behavioral psychology, criminology, mental health, and law, whose work is predicated on the notion that undesirable human behavior can be changed—through various means of reform and behavior modification.

In sum, the speaker over-generalizes when it comes to the function and value of art and science—both of which serve in some cases to reassure and in other cases to upset. In any event, the speaker misstates the true function and value of science, which is to discover truths, whether reassuring or upsetting.

Issue:
The impact of acquiring **more knowledge**

Does knowledge render things more comprehensible, or more complex and mysterious? In my view the acquisition of knowledge brings about all three at the same time. This paradoxical result is aptly explained and illustrated by a number of advances in our scientific knowledge.

Consider, for example, the sonar system on which blind bats rely to navigate and especially to seek prey. Researchers have learned that this system is startlingly sophisticated. By emitting audible sounds, then processing the returning echoes, a bat can determine in a nanosecond not only how far away its moving prey is but also the prey's speed, direction, size and even specie! This knowledge acquired helps explain, of course, how bats navigate and survive. Yet at the same time this knowledge points out the incredible complexity of the auditory and brain functions of certain animals, even of mere humans, and creates a certain mystery and wonder about how such systems ever evolved organically.

Or consider our knowledge of the universe. Advances in telescope and space-exploration technology seem to corroborate the theory of a continually expanding universe that began at the very beginning of time with a "big bang." On one level this knowledge, assuming it qualifies as such, helps us comprehend our place in the universe and our ultimate destiny. Yet on the other hand it adds yet another chapter to the mystery about what existed before time and the universe.

Or consider the area of atomic physics. The naked human eye perceives very little, of course, of the complexity of matter. To our distant ancestors the physical world appeared simple—seemingly comprehensible by means of sight and touch. Then by way of scientific knowledge we learned that all matter is comprised of atoms, which are further comprised of protons, neutrons, and electrons. Then we discovered an even more basic unit of matter called the quark. And now a new so-called "string" theory posits the existence of an even more fundamental, and universal, unit of matter. On the one hand, these discoveries have rendered things more comprehensible, by explaining and reconciling empirical observations of how matter behaves. The string theory also reconciles the discrepancy between the quantum and wave theories of physics. On the other hand, each discovery has in turn revealed that matter is more complex than previously thought. In fact, the string theory, which is theoretically sound, calls for seven more dimensions—in addition to the three we already know about! I'm hard-pressed to imagine anything more complex or mysterious.

In sum, the statement overlooks a paradox about knowledge acquired, at least when it comes to understanding the physical world. When through knowledge a thing becomes more comprehensible and explainable we realize at the same time that it is more complex and mysterious than previously thought.

Issue:
Is it a mistake **to theorize** without data?

Is it a "grave mistake" to theorize without data, as the speaker contends? I agree insofar as to theorize before collecting sufficient data is to risk tainting the process of collecting and interpreting further data. However, in a sense the speaker begs the question, by overlooking the fact that every theory requires some data to begin with. Moreover, the claim unfairly ignores equally grave consequences of waiting to theorize until we obtain too much data.

In one important respect I agree with the speaker's contention. A theory conjured up without the benefit of data amounts to little more that the theorist's hopes and desires—what he or she wants to be true and not be true. Accordingly, this theorist will tend to seek out evidence that supports the theory, and overlook or avoid evidence that refutes it. One telling historical example involves theories about the center of the Universe. Understandably, we ego-driven humans would prefer that the universe revolve around us. Early theories presumed so for this reason, and subsequent observations that ran contrary to this ego-driven theory were ignored, while the observers were scorned and even vilified.

By theorizing before collecting data the theorist also runs that risk of interpreting that data in a manner which makes it appear to lend more credence to the theory than it actually does. Consider the theory that the Earth is flat. Any person with a clear view of the horizon must agree in all honesty that the evidence does not support the theory. Yet prior to Newtonian physics the notion of a spherical Earth was so unsettling to people that they interpreted the arc-shaped horizon as evidence of a convex, yet nevertheless "flattish," Earth.

Despite the merits of the speaker's claim, I find it problematic in two crucial respects. First, common sense informs me that it is impossible to theorize in the first place without at least some data. How can theorizing without data be dangerous, as the speaker contends, if it is not even possible? While a theory based purely on fantasy might ultimately be born out by empirical observation, it is equally possible that it won't. Thus without prior data a theory is not worth our time or attention. Secondly, the speaker's claim overlooks the inverse problem: the danger of continuing to acquire data without venturing a theory based on that data. To postpone theorizing until all the data is in might be to postpone it forever. The danger lies in the reasons we theorize and test our theories: to solve society's problems and to make the world a better place to live. Unless we act timely based on our data we render ourselves impotent. For example, governments tend to respond to urgent social problems by establishing agencies to collect data and think tanks to theorize about causes and solutions. These agencies and think tanks serve no purpose unless they admit that they will never have all the data and that no theory is foolproof, and unless timely action is taken based on the best theory currently available—before the problem overwhelms us.

To sum up, I agree with the speaker insofar as a theory based on no data is not a theory but mere whimsy and fancy, and insofar as by theorizing first we tend to distort the extent to which data collected thereafter supports our own theory. Nevertheless, we put ourselves in equal peril by mistaking data for knowledge and progress, which require us not only to theorize but also to act upon our theories with some useful end in mind.

Issue:
Politics—pursuing ideals vs. pursuing **a reasonable consensus**

Is the proper goal of politics to pursue not an ideal but rather a reasonable consensus, as the speaker maintains? I concede that pursuing consensus is to be preferred over pursuing illegitimate ideals. Otherwise, I find the speaker's position troubling. It ignores the fact that a political ideal might be consensus itself, or require some measure of consensus, and it flies in the face of the nature or politics and of human nature.

The primary reason for my disagreement with the speaker's position is that reasonable consensus and a political ideal need not be mutually exclusive. In the first place, if one adopts the view that the ultimate goal of public politics should be to achieve the ideal of peace among nations, then attaining a reasonable consensus among nations on issues germane to world peace would be, in essence, to achieve this ideal— at least tentatively. In the second place, in order to gain the opportunity to pursue their ideals politicians must build some measure of consensus along the way. Politics is a business born not only of idealism but also of pragmatism. In order to be effective a politician must gain and hold onto political power, which in turn requires some degree of pandering and compromising to build a consensus of support for the politician's agendas. Modern politics is replete with ideal-promoters who refused to find common ground upon which most people can agree, thereby never affording themselves the chance to pursue their ideals in a way that might make a difference.

Another reason why I tend to disagree with the speaker's position is that it flies in the face of human nature and the nature of politics. History informs us that, for better or worse, it is human nature to disagree, and to dominate or be dominated. The harsh truth is that achieving consensus is just as illusory as other ideals that politicians typically espouse. Moreover, politics inherently involves a tug-of-war between conflicting interests. Those inclined to achieve complete consensus are not true political animals. True politicians thrive instead on conflict and on advocating certain agendas while fighting to quash others. Thus to assert the politics should strive for consensus is to deny the nature of politics and of politicians.

A third problem with the speaker's position is that it begs the question: What are the proper ideals for politicians? They have little to do with consensus, and everything to do with justice and fairness. It is idealists—not consensus seekers—who sway the masses, incite revolutions, and make political ideology reality. Consider idealists such as America's founders, or Mahatma Gandhi, or Martin Luther King. Had these idealists concerned themselves with consensus building rather than with their notions of an ideal society, the United States and India might still be British colonies, and African Americans might still be relegated to the backs of buses. This is not to say that pursuing idealism is necessarily preferable to pursuing consensus. After all, legitimate ideals require a certain measure of morality—that is, they must further humanity's best interests. Consider the many idealists, such as Stalin and Hitler, who most people would agree were egregious violators of human rights. Ultimately such leaders forfeit their leadership as a result of their illegitimate ideals and means of pursuing those ideals.

Finally, lacking idealism a political leader will tend to seek compromise and reasonable consensus for its own sake. It seems that pure pragmatism breeds a sort of unprincipled self-serving that unfortunately pervades contemporary politics. Most politicians seem driven today by their interest in being elected and reelected—that is, in short-term survival—rather than by any sense of mission, or even obligation to their constituency or country. All too often, diplomatic and legal maneuverings and negotiations are intended to meet the practical needs of the parties involved: minimizing costs, preserving options, and so forth. Idealists are better able to steer clear of short-term thinking, near-sighted goals, and self-serving maneuverings.

In sum, the speaker's call for consensus is ill conceived. It ignores the fact that consensus is a necessary means to achieving political ideals, if not part-and-parcel of those ideals. Moreover, politicians are not by nature consensus seekers, nor are humans by nature inclined to consensus. In the final analysis, the statement is wrongheaded; what politics is about, and should be about, is the pursuit of ideals that accord with the shared interests of all humanity.

Issue:
Should educators provide students with **a set of ideas** or with job preparation?

Should educators teach values or focus instead on preparing students for jobs? In my view the two are not mutually exclusive. It is by helping students develop their own principles for living, as well as by instilling in them certain fundamental values, that educators best prepare young people for the world of work.

One reason for my viewpoint is that rote learning of facts, figures, and technical skills does not help us determine which goals are worthwhile and whether the means of attaining those goals are ethically or morally acceptable. In other words, strong values and ethical standards are needed to determine how we can best put our rote knowledge to use in the working world. Thus, by helping students develop a thoughtful, principled value system educators actually help prepare students for jobs.

Another reason for my viewpoint lies in the fact that technology-driven industries account for an ever-increasing portion of our jobs. As advances in technology continue to accelerate, specific knowledge and skills needed for jobs will change more and more quickly. Thus it would be a waste of our education system to focus on specific knowledge and job skills that might soon become obsolete—at the expense of teaching values. It seems more appropriate today for employers to provide the training our workforce needs to perform their jobs, freeing up our educators to help students develop guiding principles for their careers.

Besides helping students develop their own thoughtful value systems, educators should instill in students certain basic values upon which any democratic society depends; otherwise, our freedom to choose our own jobs and careers might not survive in the long term. These values include principles of fairness and equity upon which our system of laws is based, as well as the values of tolerance and respect when it comes to the viewpoints of others. It seems to me that these basic values can best by instilled at an early age in a classroom setting, where young students can work out their value systems as they interact with their peers. Moreover, as students grow into working adults, practicing the basic values of fairness and respect they learned as students serves them well in their jobs. At the workplace these values manifest themselves in a worker's ability to cooperate, compromise, understand various viewpoints, and appreciate the rights and duties of coworkers, supervisors, and subordinates. This ability cannot help but serve any worker's career goals, as well as enhancing overall workplace productivity.

Admittedly, values and behavioral standards specific to certain religions are best left to parents and churches. After all, by advocating the values and teachings of any particular religion public educators undermine our basic freedom of religion. However, by exposing students to various religious beliefs, educators promote the values of respect and tolerance when it comes to the viewpoints of others. Besides, in my observation certain fundamental values—such as compassion, virtue, and humility— are common to all major religions. By appreciating certain fundamental values that we should all hold in common, students are more likely to grow into adults who can work together at the workplace toward mutually agreed-upon goals.

In sum, only when educators help students develop their own principles for living, and when they instill certain fundamental values, do young people grow into successful working adults. Although there will always be a need to train people for specific jobs, in our technological society where knowledge advances so rapidly, employers and job training programs are better equipped to provide this function— leaving formal educators to equip students with a moral compass and ballast to prevent them from being tossed about aimlessly in a turbulent vocational sea.

Issue:
Do **worthy** ends justify **any means**?

The speaker asserts that if a goal is worthy then any means of attaining that goal is justifiable. In my view this extreme position misses the point entirely. Whether certain means are justifiable in reaching a goal must be determined on a case-by-case basis, by weighing the benefits of attaining the goal against the costs, or harm, that might accrue along the way. This applies equally to individual goals and to societal goals.

Consider the goal of completing a marathon-running race. If I need to reduce my working hours to train for the race, thereby jeopardizing my job, or if I run a high risk of incurring a permanent injury by training enough to prepare adequately for the event, then perhaps my goal is not worth attaining. Yet if I am a physically challenged person with the goal of completing a highly publicized marathon, risking financial hardship or long-term injury might be worthwhile, not only for my own personal satisfaction but also for the inspiration that attaining the goal would provide many others.

Or consider the goal of providing basic food and shelter for an innocent child. Anyone would agree that this goal is highly worthy—considered apart from the means used to achieve it. But what if those means involve stealing from others? Or what if they involve employing the child in a sweatshop at the expense of educating the child? Clearly, determining the worthiness of such goals requires that we confront moral dilemmas, which we each solve individually—based on our own conscience, value system, and notions of fairness and equity.

On a societal level we determine the worthiness of our goals in much the same way—by weighing competing interests. For instance, any thoughtful person would agree that reducing air and water pollution is a worthy societal goal; dean air and water reduce the burden on our health-care resources and improves the quality of life for everyone in society. Yet to attain this goal would we be justified in forcing entire industries out of business, thereby running the risk of economic paralysis and widespread unemployment? Or consider America's intervention in Iraq's invasion of Kuwait. Did our dual interest in a continuing flow of oil to the West and in deterring a potential threat against the security of the world justify our committing resources that could have been used instead for domestic social-welfare programs—or a myriad of other productive purposes? Both issues underscore the fact that the worthiness of a societal goal cannot be considered apart from the means and adverse consequences of attaining that goal.

In sum, the speaker begs the question. The worthiness of any goal, whether it be personal or societal, can be determined only by weighing the benefits of achieving the goal against its costs—to us as well as others.

Issue:
Must art be widely understood **to have merit**?

The speaker's assertion that art must be widely understood to have merit is wrongheaded. The speaker misunderstands the final objective of art, which has little to do with cognitive "understanding."

First consider the musical art form. The fact that the listener must "understand" the composer's artistic expression without the benefit of words or visual images forces us to ask: "What is there to understand in the first place?" Of course, the listener can always struggle to appreciate how the musical piece employs various harmonic, melodic, and rhythmic principles. Yet it would be absurd to assert that the objective of music is to challenge the listener's knowledge of music theory. In fact, listening to music is simply an encounter—an experience to be accepted at face value for its aural impact on our spirit and our emotions.

Next consider the art forms of painting and sculpture. In the context of these art forms, the speaker seems to suggest that if we cannot all understand what the work is supposed to represent, then we should dismiss the work as worthless. Again, however, the speaker misses the point of art. Only by provoking and challenging us, and inciting our emotions, imagination, and wonder do paintings and sculpture hold merit. Put another way, if the test for meritorious art were its ability to be clearly understood by every observer, then our most valuable art would simply imitate the mundane physical world around us. A Polaroid picture taken by a monkey would be considered great art, while the abstract works of Pollock and Picasso would be worth no more than the salvage value of the materials used to create them.

Finally, consider art forms such as poetry, song, and prose, where the use of language is part-and-parcel of the art. It is easy to assume that where words are involved they must be strung together in understandable phrases in order for the art to have any merit. Moreover, if the writer-artist resorts exclusively to obscure words that people simply do not know, then the art can convey nothing beyond the alliterative or onomatopoeic impact that the words might have when uttered aloud. However, in poetry and song the writer-artist often uses words as imagery—to conjure up feelings and evoke visceral reactions in the reader or listener. In these cases stanzas and verses need not be "understood" to have merit, as much as they need be experienced for the images and emotions they evoke.

When it comes to prose, admittedly the writer-artist must use words to convey cognitive ideas—for example, to help the reader follow the plot of a novel. In these cases the art must truly be "understood" on a linguistic and cognitive level; otherwise it is mere gibberish—without merit except perhaps as a doorstop. Nevertheless, the final objective even of literature is to move the reader emotionally and spiritually— not simply to inform. Thus, even though a reader might understand the twists and turns of a novel's plot intellectually, what's the point if the reader has come away unaffected in emotion or spirit?

In the final analysis, whether art must be understood by most people, or by any person, in order for it to have merit begs the question. To "understand" art a person need only have eyes to see or ears to hear, and a soul to feel.

PART THREE
Answers to the Real GRE Argument Questions

Part 3 contains sample responses to more than 100 official GRE Argument questions, grouped into various categories. As you study the responses here in Part 3, keep in mind:

- These essays were not composed under timed conditions. Moreover, they were fine-tuned to make them better models for you to study. So don't be concerned if your essays aren't as polished, or as lengthy, as these. Be realistic about what *you* can produce in 30 minutes.

- In the first paragraph of each essay the corresponding Argument has been recapitulated, for your reference. Keep in mind, however, that the readers do not expect you, nor do they want you, to restate the Argument in your essay. Keep your introductory paragraph brief, like the one on page 26.

- These essays are intended to provide you with substantive, organizational, and style ideas for composing your Argument essay; they are *not* for copying word-for-word. Be forewarned: GRE readers will be on the lookout for plagiarism.

How to Match Our Essays to the Topics in the Official Pool

Preceding each essay here in Part 3 is a brief description of the topic at hand; this description will help you match the two. For additional help in matching each essay here in Part 3 to its corresponding topic, you can search the official pool's electronic file for our corresponding key phrase. **We've highlighted key phrases in bold.**

Answers to Arguments That Draw Questionable Analogies

This section contains sample essay responses to several Argument statements from the official GRE essay pool. Each of these Argument statements relies partly on a questionable analogy between two persons, places, or things. Before you read the essays here, be sure to review the discussion about this type of reasoning problem on pages 27–28.

> **NOTE:** Each essay addresses other major reasoning problems as well, but it is included only in this section of Part 3.

Argument:
Enhancing property values at **Deerhaven Acres**

In this letter, a committee of Deerhaven Acres homeowners recommends that in order to enhance Deerhaven property values homeowners should follow certain restrictions concerning their homes' exterior appearance. To support this recommendation the committee points out that in the seven years since Brookville adopted similar restrictions property values there have risen. This argument rests on a series of unsubstantiated assumptions, and it is therefore unpersuasive as it stands.

A threshold assumption upon which the recommendation relies is that Brookville homeowners implemented Brookville's restrictions in the first place. The letter fails to substantiate this crucial assumption. If these restrictions were not implemented, then any change in Brookville's property values cannot be attributed to them. Accordingly, the committee cannot draw any firm conclusion about what effect similar restrictions would have on Deerhaven property values.

Even assuming that Brookville homeowners implemented these restrictions, the committee relies on the additional assumption that this course of action was responsible for the increase in Brookville property values. However, it is entirely possible that one or more other factors were instead responsible for the increase, especially since a considerable period of time has passed since Brookville adopted its restrictions. Property values are a function of supply and demand. Perhaps the demand for housing in the area has increased due to an influx of major employers. Or, perhaps the supply of housing has decreased. Either scenario would provide an alternative explanation for the increase in property values.

Even assuming that Brookville's rising property values are attributable to the implementation of these restrictions, the committee fails to consider possible differences between Brookville and Deerhaven that might help to bring about a different result for Deerhaven. For instance, potential Deerhaven homebuyers might be less interested in a home's exterior appearance than Brookville homebuyers. For that matter, perhaps Deerhaven homebuyers would find consistent exterior appearance a distasteful feature—

in which case adopting these restrictions might actually tend to decrease Deerhaven property values. Without accounting for these and other possible dissimilarities, the committee cannot assume that what resulted in rising property values in Brookville would bring about the same result in Deerhaven.

In conclusion, to persuade me that Deerhaven should adopt the proposed restrictions the committee must supply clear evidence that the implementation of Brookville's restrictions, and not some other factor, was responsible for the rise in Brookville's property values. The committee must also provide evidence that other factors affecting home prices in the two areas are otherwise essentially the same.

Argument:
A lottery for **Impecunia**

In this editorial, the author concludes that by establishing a lottery, the state of Impecunia could use the profits from it to improve the state's education and public health programs. To support this conclusion the author points out that the neighboring state of Lucria established a lottery two years ago, and today Lucria spends more per pupil and treats more people through its health programs than Impecunia does. The editorial also cites a study showing that the average Impecunia resident now spends $50 per year on gambling. In several respects, however, the evidence lends little credible support for the argument.

First of all, the fact that Lucria now spends more than Impecunia per pupil, in itself, lends no support to the argument. Perhaps Lucria has always placed a high priority on education; or perhaps Lucria has always had more funds than Impecunia to spend on its programs, including education. Lacking clearer evidence that Lucria's lottery successfully raised revenues that were then used to increase the amount spent per pupil, the author cannot expect us to take seriously the claim that by establishing a similar lottery Impecunia would improve its education programs.

Similarly, the fact that Lucria's health programs treat more people than Impecunia's programs lends no support to the argument. Perhaps Lucria's population is greater than Impecunia's; or perhaps its residents are older, on average, than Impecunia's residents, and therefore require a greater measure of health care. Without considering and ruling out these and other possible explanations for the distinction cited, the author cannot justifiably conclude that Lucria's lottery was responsible for improved health care in that state or that a similar lottery in Impecunia would carry a similar result.

Moreover, the argument unfairly assumes that the lottery in Lucria has been profitable. The author provides no evidence that this is the case. It is entirely possible that the money used for education and health care in Lucria comes from sources other than the lottery. Without accounting for this possibility, the author cannot justify the conclusion that a lottery in Impecunia would be successful.

Finally, the fact that Impecunia's residents spend $50 per capita on gambling each year lends little support to the argument. Admittedly, this statistic amounts to some evidence of interest among Impecunia's residents in gambling, and therefore potential interest in a lottery. However, this evidence in itself does not suffice to prove that the lottery will in fact be popular. Perhaps Impecunia residents have no more discretionary income to participate in a lottery after spending $50 on other forms of gambling. Or perhaps Impecunia residents typically travel elsewhere to gamble as part of their vacations, and they would not otherwise be interested in gambling. In short, without more convincing evidence of both an ability and a willingness on the part of Impecunia's residents to participate in a lottery the author cannot convince me that the lottery will be profitable.

In conclusion, the editorial has not convinced me that a lottery would be profitable and would serve to improve Impecunia's education and health programs. To better evaluate the argument I would need more information comparing Lucria's level of health care and education expenditures before and after the lottery was established. To strengthen the argument, the author must provide clear evidence that Lucria's lottery was profitable and that these profits contributed to improved education and health care in Lucria. The author must also provide clearer evidence of the willingness and ability of Impecunia residents to participate broadly in a lottery.

Argument:
A new golf course and resort hotel for **Hopewell**

In this memo, Hopewell's mayor recommends that in order to stimulate the town's economy and boost tax revenues Hopewell should build a new golf course and resort hotel, just as the town of Ocean View did two years ago. To support this recommendation the mayor points out that in Ocean View during the last two years tourism has increased, new businesses have opened, and tax revenues have increased by 30%. I find the mayor's argument unconvincing in several important respects.

First of all, it is possible that the mayor has confused cause with effect respecting the recent developments in Ocean View. Perhaps Ocean View's construction of a new golf course and hotel was a response to previous increases in tourism and business development—increases that have simply continued during the most recent two years. Since the mayor has failed to account for this possibility, the claim that Hopewell would boost its economy by also constructing a golf course and hotel is completely unwarranted.

Secondly, the mayor fails to account for other possible causes of the trends in Ocean View during the last two years. The increase in tourism might have been due to improving economic conditions nationwide or to unusually pleasant weather in the region. The new businesses that have opened in Ocean View might have opened there irrespective of the new golf course and hotel. And, the 30% increase in tax revenues might have been the result of an increase in tax rates, or the addition of a new type of municipal tax. Without ruling out these and other alternative explanations for the three recent trends in Ocean View, the mayor cannot reasonably infer based on those trends that Hopewell's economy would benefit by following Ocean View's example.

Thirdly, even if the recent trends in Ocean View are attributable to the construction of the new golf course and hotel there, the mayor assumes too hastily that the golf course and hotel will continue to benefit that town's overall economy. The mayor has not accounted for the possibility that increased tourism will begin to drive residents away during tourist season, or that new business development will result in the town's losing its appeal as a place to visit or to live. Unless the mayor can convince me that these scenarios are unlikely I cannot accept the mayor's recommendation that Hopewell follow Ocean View's example.

Finally, the mayor's argument rests on the unsubstantiated assumption that Hopewell and Ocean View are sufficiently alike in ways that might affect the economic impact of a new golf course and hotel. Hopewell might lack the sort of natural environment that would attract more tourists and new businesses to the town—regardless of its new golf course and hotel. For that matter, perhaps Hopewell already contains several resort hotels and golf courses that are not utilized to their capacity. If so, building yet another golf course and hotel might amount to a misallocation of the town's resources—and actually harm the town's overall economy.

In sum, the mayor's recommendation is not well supported. To bolster it, the mayor must provide better evidence that Ocean View's new golf course and hotel—and not some other phenomenon—has been responsible for boosting Ocean View's economy during the last two years. To better assess the recommendation I would need to know why Ocean View decided to construct its new golf course and hotel in the first place—specifically, what events prior to construction might have prompted that decision. I would also need to thoroughly compare Hopewell with Ocean View—especially in terms of their appeal to tourists and businesses—to determine whether the same course of action that appears to have boosted Ocean View's economy would also boost Hopewell's economy.

Argument:
Aircraft maintenance and **airline** profits

In this memorandum, Get-Away Airline's personnel director asserts that Get-Away mechanics should enroll in the Quality Care Seminar on proper maintenance procedures in order to increase customer satisfaction and, in turn, profits. The director reasons that because the performance of auto-racing mechanics improves after the seminar, so will that of Get-Away's mechanics. The director's argument relies on a number of dubious assumptions and is therefore unconvincing.

First of all, the argument unfairly assumes that because the performance of auto-racing mechanics improves after the seminar so will the performance of aircraft mechanics. Common sense tells me that, even though aircraft and auto mechanics serve similar functions, aircraft repair and maintenance is far more involved than car repair and maintenance. Thus, a seminar that improves the performance of auto mechanics will not necessarily improve that of aircraft mechanics.

Secondly, the argument assumes that the performance of Get-Away mechanics is subject to improvement. However, it is entirely possible that their performance level is already very high and that the seminar will afford little or no improvement. Perhaps Get-Away's mechanics have already attended a similar seminar, or perhaps they meet higher standards than the ones imposed on auto-racing mechanics.

Thirdly, the argument concludes from the mere fact that the performance of auto-racing mechanics improved after the seminar that the seminar was responsible for this improvement. However, it is possible that some other factor, such as improved diagnostic technology or more stringent inspection requirements, was the reason for the improved performance. Without ruling out these and other such possibilities, I cannot accept the memo's final conclusion that enrolling in the seminar will improve the performance of Get-Away's mechanics as well.

Finally, the argument concludes without adequate evidence that improved performance on the part of Get-Away's mechanics will result in greater customer satisfaction and therefore greater profits for Get-Away. Admittedly, if a low performance level results in accidents, customer satisfaction and profits will in all probability decrease. Otherwise, however, improved mechanic performance will in all likelihood have no bearing on customer satisfaction; in other words, customers are unlikely to be aware of the level of performance of an aircraft's mechanics unless accidents occur.

In conclusion, the argument is unconvincing as it stands. To strengthen it, the director must provide more convincing evidence that the performance of Get-Away's mechanics will actually improve as a result of the seminar—perhaps by pointing out other airlines whose mechanics benefited from the seminar. The director must also show a strong causal nexus between improved mechanic performance and profit. In order to better evaluate the argument, I would need more information about the cost of the seminar compared to its expected benefits, and about what factors other than the seminar might have been responsible for the improved performance of auto-racing mechanics.

Argument:
Blaming the mayor for problems with **River Bridge**

This editorial concludes that Mayor Durant's approval of the River Bridge construction twenty years ago was the cause of current traffic and deterioration problems at the bridge. To support this conclusion, the editorial points out that a nearby bridge is not experiencing similar problems. However, the editorial relies on a number of doubtful assumptions and is therefore unconvincing.

First of all, since the bridge is 20 years old, it is unfair to assign blame for recent traffic problems and deterioration to Durant or to anyone else involved in the initial bridge-building project. Given this time span, it seems reasonable that these problems are due to ordinary wear and tear rather than to a design defect. Moreover, it is entirely possible that unforeseen developments during the last twenty years are partly responsible for the deterioration and traffic problems. For example, perhaps growth in the area's population, and therefore increased bridge traffic, has been greater than could have been anticipated twenty years ago.

Secondly, the editorial concludes without adequate evidence that if Durant had approved a wider and better-designed bridge none of the current problems would have occurred. This amounts to fallacious reasoning. Just because a bridge that Durant approved has experienced certain problems, one cannot reasonably conclude that without that particular bridge the same problems would not have occurred.

Thirdly, the editorial relies primarily on an analogy between River Bridge and Derby Bridge, yet it provides no evidence that the two bridges are similar in ways that are relevant to the argument. Even assuming weather conditions are generally the same at both locations, a variety of other factors might explain why the River Bridge problems have not occurred at the Derby Bridge. Perhaps relatively few people traverse the Derby Bridge; or perhaps the Derby Bridge is relatively new; or perhaps the comparatively long span of the Derby Bridge places less structural stress on any given point. In short, without ruling out other factors that might explain why similar problems have not occurred at the Derby Bridge this argument by analogy is untenable.

Finally, the argument assumes that mere approval of the proposed bridge is tantamount to causation of traffic and deterioration problems. But the editorial fails to indicate why Durant approved the bridge in the first place. It is quite possible, for example, that it was the only feasible plan, and that Durant had no choice. Moreover, common sense tells me that deterioration and traffic problems are consequences of poor planning and engineering, and therefore more likely caused by negligence of engineers and planners than by politicians.

In conclusion, the editorial is unconvincing as it stands. To strengthen the argument, the editorial's author must provide evidence that conditions that might have contributed to the bridge's deterioration and to traffic problems were reasonably foreseeable 20 years ago, and that some other feasible bridge design would have avoided the current problems. In order to better evaluate the argument, we would need more information about what choices Durant had at the time, as well as more information about the age of the Derby Bridge and about how heavily that bridge is used compared to the River Bridge.

Argument:
How to **save money on electricity**

This argument recommends that all citizens of Claria should run fans, as well as air conditioners, for the purpose of saving money on electricity. To support this recommendation, the argument's proponent points out that Claria citizens who run only fans incur higher electric costs than those who run only air conditioners, and those who run both incur the lowest electric costs among the three groups. However, the argument depends on certain dubious assumptions about climate, electric costs, and the cited statistics. As a result, the recommendation is ill conceived.

First, the argument relies on the assumption that climatic conditions are similar throughout all regions of Claria. Yet this is probably not the case, especially since the passage explicitly characterizes Claria as vast and widely diverse geographically. It is entirely possible that only fans are used in certain regions because the climate in these regions is comparatively cold year-round, and that electric heating costs are so high that they result in the highest overall electric costs in the country. If this is the case, implementing the proponent's suggestion would result in higher electric costs for citizens in these regions. Or perhaps people who run both fans and air conditioners live in regions where there is less need for artificial cooling. This would explain why total electric costs in these regions are comparatively low. If this is the case, then implementing the proponent's suggestion might still result in higher electric costs for citizens in other regions.

Secondly, the recommendation depends on the assumption that the cost of electricity is the same for all three groups. However, it is possible that people who use both fans and air conditioners incur the lowest total electric costs among the three groups simply because these people pay the least per unit of electricity. The fact that Claria is geographically diverse lends support to this notion: people who use both fans and air conditioners are likely to live in the same climatic region, and people in the same region are more likely to be subject to the same electricity usage rates.

Thirdly, the argument provides insufficient information about the study on which it relies. If the results were based on only one warm season then the argument would be less persuasive than if the results were based on more than one warm season; in other words, the larger the statistical sample the more reliable the results.

In conclusion, the recommendation for using both cooling methods is dubious at best. To bolster it, the argument's proponent must show that climatic conditions are similar in all regions. The proponent must also show that rates charged for electricity are similar in all regions. Finally, in order to better evaluate the extent to which the cited study supports the recommendation we would need more statistical information about the study's time span.

Argument:
Attracting new faculty to **Pierce University**

In this letter, a department chairperson at Pierce University recommends that Pierce offer jobs to spouses of new faculty in order to attract the most gifted teachers and researchers. To support this recommendation, the chairperson cites certain Bronston University studies, which concluded that in small towns male as well as female faculty are happier when their spouses are employed in the same geographic area. However, the chairperson's argument relies on certain unsubstantiated assumptions about the similarity between Pierce faculty and the faculty involved in the Bronston study, and about how the most gifted teachers and researchers choose among jobs in the first place.

A threshold problem with the argument involves the Bronston studies themselves. The letter provides no information about the faculty in the study—specifically, whether they were representative of college faculty in general, and of potential Pierce faculty in particular. For example, if the study involved only Bronston faculty, then it would be less reliable than if it involved Pierce faculty as well. In any case, the smaller and more biased the survey's sample, the less reliable it is for the purpose of drawing any conclusions about how Pierce might attract new faculty.

Secondly, the argument relies on the assumption that faculty whose spouses work for the same employer are just as happy as faculty whose spouses work for other employers. However, since the letter fails to substantiate this assumption it is entirely possible that the spouses involved in the Bronston study and who worked in the same geographic area attribute their happiness to the fact that they work for different employers. If so, then the chairperson's recommendation that Pierce try to entice gifted teachers and researchers by offering jobs to their spouses as well would seem ill advised.

Thirdly, the argument assumes that jobs for faculty spouses at Pierce would contribute to the happiness of Pierce faculty to at least as great an extent as the jobs in the geographical areas where the study's subjects resided. However, the letter provides no evidence to substantiate this assumption. Thus it is entirely possible that jobs in the areas where the study's faculty resided are higher-paying, offer better benefits, or otherwise contribute to the happiness of employees' spouses—college faculty— more so than a typical staff position at Pierce. In fact, the letter suggests that this might be the case. By admitting that Pierce job offers are not ideal, the letter implies that faculty candidates and their spouses might find a more attractive dual-employment package elsewhere.

Finally, the argument assumes that gifted teachers and researchers consider employment for spouses a key factor in choosing among job offers. However, the letter provides no evidence that this is the case. In fact, it is entirely possible that the faculty in the Bronston study are not exceptional teachers and researchers and therefore do not have as many job options as the kind of faculty Pierce hopes to attract. If this is the case, Pierce cannot justifiably expect the most exceptional teachers to accept positions at Pierce just because Pierce provides employment to faculty spouses.

In conclusion, the letter is unpersuasive as it stands. To strengthen the argument, the chairperson must show that jobs for spouses of faculty involved in the Bronston study are no more attractive than non-faculty jobs at Pierce. The chairperson must also provide clear evidence that the most gifted teachers and researchers find the sort of benefit that this letter proposes to be significantly attractive in choosing among job offers. Finally, to better assess the argument we would need more information about the faculty involved in the Bronston studies, so that we can determine the study's relevance to Pierce, as well as its statistical reliability.

Argument:
Small **nonprofit hospitals** vs. large for-profit hospitals

This newspaper story concludes that the small, nonprofit hospital in Saluda provides more efficient, better-quality care than the for-profit hospital in Megaville. To justify this conclusion the author cites the following comparisons between the Saluda hospital and the Megaville hospital: At the Saluda hospital the average length of a patient's stay is shorter, the cure rate and employee-patient ratio are both higher, and the number of complaints from patients is lower. However, careful consideration of these facts reveals that they fail to justify the author's conclusion.

In the first place, the author unfairly assumes that a shorter hospital stay indicates a quicker recovery and therefore better care. It is equally possible that the Saluda hospital simply cannot afford to keep patients as long as it should to ensure proper care and recovery. Perhaps the hospital sends patients home prematurely for the purpose of freeing up beds for other patients. Since the author has failed to rule out other possible explanations for this shorter average stay, I remain unconvinced based on this evidence that the Saluda hospital provides better care than Megaville's hospital.

In the second place, the mere fact that the rate of cure at the Saluda hospital is higher than at Megaville's hospital proves nothing about the quality of care at either hospital. It is entirely possible that more Saluda patients suffer from curable problems than Megaville patients do. Without considering this possibility the author cannot justifiably rely on cure rates to draw any conclusions about comparative quality of care.

In the third place, a higher employee-patient ratio at Saluda is weak evidence of either better care or greater efficiency. Common sense informs me that it is the competence of each employee, not the number of employees, that determines overall quality of care. Besides, it is entirely possible that the comparatively large staff at Saluda is the result of organizational inefficiency, and that a smaller staff of more effective, better-managed people would provide better care.

Finally, the mere fact that the Saluda hospital receives fewer patient complaints than Megaville's hospital proves nothing about either efficiency or quality of care. Even though the number of complaints is smaller, the percentage of patients complaining might be higher. Also, Megaville's staff might openly encourage patient feedback while Saluda's does not. This scenario accords with my observation that for-profit organizations are generally more concerned with customer satisfaction than nonprofit organizations are.

In sum, the facts that the story cites amount to weak evidence that the Saluda hospital provides more efficient, better-quality care than Megaville's hospital. To strengthen the argument, the author must provide clear evidence that at the Saluda hospital patients are released earlier because they have received better care—rather than for some other reason. To better assess the argument, I would need to compare the percentage of Megaville's hospital patients who suffer from curable problems with the percentage of Saluda patients who suffer from similar problems. Also, I would need more information from each hospital about complaint procedures and the percentage of patients who lodge complaints.

Argument:
Peanuts as a replacement for sugar crops

This letter concludes that to increase farm revenue this country's farmers should replace their sugar crops with peanuts. To support this assertion, the letter's author claims that demand for sugar is sure to decline due to a growing awareness of the health hazards of eating too much sugar. The author also cites the fact that in the nearby country of Palin increased peanut production has resulted in increased revenue for farmers. However, the author's argument relies on several poor assumptions and is therefore unpersuasive as it stands.

A threshold problem with the letter involves the new research that the author cites to support his conclusion. The author fails to indicate whether consumers are in fact aware of the new research about the harmful effects of eating too much sugar, or whether consumers eat too much sugar in the first place. If consumers are unaware of the research or if they do not currently eat too much sugar, then this research lends no support to the author's assertion that sugar consumption is likely to decline as a result of the new research.

Secondly, the argument unjustifiably assumes that growing consumer awareness of sugar's health hazards will cause consumers to not only decrease sugar consumption but also increase peanut consumption. Common sense informs me otherwise, especially considering the addictive quality of sugar. In fact, the author provides explicitly that peanuts are low in sugar, suggesting that peanuts are a poor substitute for sugar.

Thirdly, the author's claim that farm revenues will increase should farmers replace sugar crops with peanuts relies on certain dubious economic assumptions. One such assumption is that the market price of peanuts will be sufficiently high to compensate for lost revenue from current sugar sales. Another is that the supply of peanuts will suffice to provide farmers with sufficient revenue. Absent evidence comparing the market price of sugar to that of peanuts, as well as evidence about the capacity of this country's farms to grow peanut crops, it is impossible to assess the author's assertion that replacing sugar crops with peanuts will increase farm revenues.

Finally, the author's reliance on the fact that peanut-farming revenues in neighboring Palin have increased is problematic in two respects. First, the analogy depends on the assumption that dietary tastes of consumers in both countries are similar. However, it is entirely possible that consumer demand for peanuts in Palin would be higher than that in this country in any event. This would explain why, in Palin, demand has met increased production, and therefore why Palin's peanut-farming revenues have increased. The analogy also depends on the assumption that environmental conditions in both countries equally support peanut crops. If they do not, then the author cannot justifiably rely on the profitability of Palin's peanut farms to conclude that peanut farms in the author's country would be just as profitable.

In conclusion, the argument is unconvincing as it stands. To strengthen it, the author must demonstrate that this country's consumers will in fact decrease their sugar consumption as a result of their growing awareness of its health risks. The author must also provide clear evidence that the demand for peanuts and the revenue from peanut production in this country are likely to match the current demand for sugar and farm revenue from sugar production, respectively. To better evaluate the argument we would need to compare the two countries' climatic and soil conditions; we would also need to compare consumer tastes in Palin with consumer tastes in the author's country.

Argument:
Increasing factory efficiency by using **robots**

This editorial concludes that using robots for factory work would improve factory efficiency. To justify this conclusion the editorial's author cites the fact that robots have been used effectively in many space missions. Also, the author claims that the use of robots in factories would (1) reduce absenteeism because robots never get sick, (2) improve output because robots do not make errors, and (3) improve factory-worker morale because these workers could be reassigned to less boring jobs. However, the author's argument is problematic in several critical respects.

To begin with, the argument depends on the hasty assumption that the kinds of tasks robots perform in space are similar to the ones they would perform in factories, and that there are no differences between the two environments that would render robots less effective in factory jobs than in space missions. Perhaps the effectiveness of robots in space missions is due largely to the weightless environment of space. Or perhaps the average space-mission robot performs less work than a typical factory robot would be required to perform. In either case, the fact that robots are effective in space would amount to scant support for the author's argument.

As for the author's claim that the use of robots would decrease absenteeism, although robots clearly do not get sick, in all likelihood factory robots would break down from time to time—which is tantamount to absenteeism. Without accounting for this likelihood the author cannot rely on this claim to conclude that the use of robots would improve overall factory efficiency.

Also questionable is the author's claim that the use of robots would increase factory output because robots do not make errors. Unless the author can provide clear evidence that human errors result in a lower rate of factory output, and not just a lower quality of product, I cannot be convinced that using robots would in fact increase the rate of output.

Two final problems involve the author's claim that using robots would improve the morale of factory workers, thereby improving factory efficiency. First, the author provides no assurances that if factory workers are reassigned to other types of jobs their morale would improve as a result. Although the new jobs might be less boring, these jobs might pose other problems that would adversely affect worker morale.

Secondly, even if the morale of the workers improves as a result of reassignment, overall factory efficiency will not necessarily improve as a result. These workers might be ill suited for their new jobs and thus be extremely ineffective in them.

In sum, the editorial relies on a potentially weak analogy as well as on a series of unwarranted claims. To strengthen the argument that the use of robots would improve factory efficiency, the editorial's author must at the very least provide clear evidence that factory robots would perform the same types of tasks, and just as well, as the tasks robots have performed in space missions. To better assess the strength of each of the author's three unwarranted claims, respectively, I would need to know: (1) the expected downtime—i.e., absenteeism—for factory robots; (2) the extent to which human error decreases the rate of factory output; and (3) the extent to which human factory workers would be happy and effective in the new jobs to which they would be assigned.

Argument:
Funding public schools in **Blue City** and **Parson City**

This argument concludes that Parson City residents value public-school education more highly than Blue City residents do. To justify this conclusion the argument points out that in both cities the majority of funds for public schools comes from taxes, and that Blue City budgets only half as much money per year for its public schools as Parson City, even though the population in both cities is about the same. The argument relies on a series of unsubstantiated assumptions, which considered together render the argument wholly unconvincing.

One such assumption is that the total budget for the two cities is about the same. It is entirely possible that Blue City's total budget is no more than half that of Parson City. If so, then the fact that Blue City budgets only half as much as Parson City for its public schools would suggest at least the same degree of care about public-school education among Blue City's residents as among Parson City's residents.

Even if Parson City devotes a greater percentage of its budget each year for its schools, the argument relies on the additional assumption that this percentage is a reliable indicator of the value a city's residents place on public-school education. Yet it is entirely possible, for example, that Blue City's schools are already well funded, or that Blue City has some other extremely urgent problem that requires additional funding despite a high level of concern among its residents about its public schools. Absent evidence that the two cities' various needs are similar, any comparison between the level of concern about public schools among residents in the two cities based simply on funds spent for public schools is dubious at best.

A third assumption upon which the argument rests is that the percentage of residents who attend public schools is about the same in both cities. The argument indicates only that the total population of the two cities is about the same. If a comparatively small percentage of Blue City residents attend public schools, then the comparatively small amount of money Blue City devotes to those schools might be well justified despite an equal level of concern about the quality of public-school education among residents in the two cities.

Finally, although the argument states that in both cities "the majority" of money spent on public schools comes from taxes, perhaps the actual percentage is smaller in Blue City than in Parson City, and other such funds come from residents' donations, earmarked for public education. Compliance with tax laws is scant evidence of taxpayer support of public-school education, while voluntary giving is strong evidence. Thus, it is possible that Blue City residents donate more money per capita for public-school education than Parson City residents do. If so, this fact would seriously weaken the argument that Blue City residents place a comparatively low value on public-school education.

In sum, the argument is unpersuasive as it stands. To strengthen it, the argument's proponent must provide clear evidence that the percentage of the budget allotted to public schools, as well as the percentage of money spent on public schools and derived from taxes, is about the same in both cities. To better assess the argument I would need to compare the neediness of Blue City's public schools with that of Parson's public schools. I would also need more information about other urgent financial needs in each city and about the other sources of the money applied toward public-school education in each city.

Argument:
Advertising **Eco-Power** tools and appliances

In this memo, Eco-Power's sales manager recommends that the company switch from print ads to ads with catchy songs in order to reverse its declining profits. To support this recommendation the memo cites the fact that most high-school students easily recognize tunes used to advertise leading soft drinks and fast-food restaurants. However, the argument is unconvincing in light of several problems.

A threshold problem with the argument is that the author assumes that the current ad strategy is the cause of Eco-Power's declining profits. The author provides no evidence that this is the case. It is entirely possible that other factors are responsible for the decline. Perhaps the demand for all tools and home appliances generally has slowed, or perhaps Eco-Power's management or pricing policies are to blame. Without ruling out such possibilities, the author cannot persuade me that switching ad strategies would reverse Eco-Power's declining profits.

Another problem with the argument involves the memo's reliance on the high rate of tune recognition among teenagers. For two reasons, this evidence lends little credible support for the recommended strategy. First, even if Eco-Power were to achieve a high rate of tune recognition among teenagers, this demographic group is not the same group that purchases tools and home appliances. Secondly, even assuming Eco-Power can achieve a high tune recognition rate among its target demographic group, this fact alone is no guarantee that these consumers would be more likely to buy Eco-Power products as a result of recognizing the company's tunes.

A third problem with the argument is that it assumes that the increased sales due to a high tune-recognition rate would outweigh the costs of achieving this rate. However, a tune can be communicated only via such media as radio and television; real-world experience informs us that these advertising media are more costly than print media. Although leading soft-drink and fast-food companies can well afford the costs of producing effective tunes and of ensuring that these tunes are heard again and again by many, many consumers, Eco-Power might lack the resources to ensure the sort of tune recognition that these other companies have achieved. Unless the sales manager can convince us that the proposed ad strategy will be cost effective, his conclusion that this strategy will result in increased profits for Eco-Power is untenable.

In conclusion, the sales manager has not provided a convincing argument for the proposed ad strategy. To strengthen the argument the manager must show that the current ad strategy is in fact the cause of Eco-Power's declining profits. The manager must also provide strong evidence that the people who buy the kinds of tools Eco-Power sells would hear the company's tunes frequently enough to immediately associate the tune with the company, and that this association would cause these listeners to buy Eco-Power products. Finally, to better evaluate the argument we would need a detailed cost-benefit analysis of the proposed ad strategy.

Argument:
A change in programming format for **KNOW radio station**

This memo recommends that KNOW radio station shift from rock-and-roll (R&R) music programming to all-news programming. To support this recommendation the manager points out that the number of KNOW listeners is decreasing while the number of older people in KNOW's listening area is increasing. The manager also points out that area sales of music recordings are in decline, and a recent survey suggests that local residents are becoming better informed about politics. Finally, the manager cites the success of all-news stations in nearby cities. Careful scrutiny of the manager's argument reveals several unproven assumptions, which render it unconvincing.

First, the manager unfairly assumes that the decline in the number of KNOW listeners is attributable to the station's current format. Perhaps the decline is due instead to KNOW's specific mix of R&R music, or to transmission problems at the station. Without ruling out these and other feasible reasons for the decline, the manager cannot convince me that changing the format would reverse the trend.

Secondly, the manager's assumption that older people favor all-news programming is unsupported. Perhaps KNOW listeners are dedicated R&R fans who will continue to prefer this type of programming as they grow older. Or perhaps as KNOW's regular audience ages it will prefer a mix of R&R and news programming—rather than one format to the total exclusion of the other. Besides, the number of young people in the listening area might be increasing as well. In short, the mere fact that the number of older people in KNOW's listening area is increasing suggests nothing about KNOW's best programming strategy.

Thirdly, a decrease in local music recording sales is scant evidence that KNOW should eschew music in favor of an all-news format. Although overall music sales are in decline, perhaps sales of R&R recordings are actually increasing while sales of all other types of music recordings are decreasing. For that matter, perhaps people who buy music recordings are generally not the same people who listen to music on the radio. Either scenario, if true, would seriously undermine the manager's contention that KNOW should discontinue R&R programming.

Fourth, it is unfair to conclude from one survey suggesting that local residents are becoming better informed about politics that they are becoming less interested in listening to R&R music, or that they are becoming more interested in listening to news. After all, news embraces many topics in addition to politics. Besides, there is no reason why people interested in politics cannot also be interested in listening to R&R music. Moreover, a single survey taken just prior to an election is poor evidence that local residents' piqued interest in politics is sustainable.

Finally, it is unwarranted to infer from the success of all-news stations in nearby cities that KNOW will also succeed by following the same format. Those stations might owe their success to their powerful transmitters, popular newscasters, or other factors. Besides, the very success of these stations suggests that the area's radio listeners might favor those well-established news providers over the fledgling all-news KNOW.

In sum, the manager's evidence accomplishes little toward supporting the manager's argument for the proposed format shift. To further bolster the argument the manager must provide better evidence, perhaps by way of a reliable survey, that people within KNOW's listening area are becoming more interested in news and less interested in R&R music—or any other kind of music. The manager must also show that an all-news format would be more popular than a mixed format of music and news, and that a significant number of people would prefer KNOW's all-news programming over that of other stations in the listening area.

Answers to Arguments That Rely on Doubtful Cause-and-Effect Relationships

This section contains sample essay responses to several Argument statements from the official GRE essay pool. Each of these Argument statements relies partly on at least one doubtful cause-and-effect relationship. Before you read these essays, be sure to review the discussion about this type of reasoning problem, on pages 28–29.

> **NOTE:** Each essay addresses other major reasoning problems as well, but it is included only in this section of Part 3.

Argument:
Which **real estate firm** is better?

The author of this argument claims that Adams Realty is superior to Fitch Realty. To support this claim the author cites certain statistics about the number and working hours of the firms' agents, and the number and sales prices of homes sold by the two firms. The author also cites anecdotal evidence involving her own experience with Fitch and Adams. Close scrutiny of this evidence reveals that it lends little credible support for the author's assertion.

The author bases her claim partly on the fact that Adams has more agents than Fitch and that many of Fitch's agents work only part-time. However, the author provides no evidence that the quality of a real estate firm is directly proportional to the number of its agents or the number of hours per week that its agents work. Lacking such evidence, it is equally possible that a smaller firm is more effective than a larger one, and that a part-time agent is more effective than a full-time agent. Besides, the author does not provide any information about how many Adams agents work part-time.

To further support her claim the author cites the fact that Adams sold more properties last year than Fitch. However, the author overlooks the possibility that last year's sales volume amounted to an aberration, and that in most other years Adams has actually sold fewer properties than Fitch. Moreover, the disparity in sales volume can readily be explained by factors other than the comparative quality of the two firms. Perhaps Adams serves a denser geographic area, or an area where turnover in home-ownership is higher for reasons unrelated to Adams' effectiveness. Or perhaps sales volume is higher at Adams simply because it employs more agents, and each Adams agent actually sells fewer homes on average than each Fitch agent does. Without ruling out such alternative explanations for the disparity in sales volume, the author cannot defend the conclusion that based on this evidence Adams is superior to Fitch.

In further support of her claim, the author points out that the average sales price of a home sold by Adams is greater than the average price of a home sold by Fitch. However, this evidence shows only that the homes that Adams sells are more valuable on average than the ones that Fitch sells, not that Adams is more effective in selling homes than Fitch. Moreover, it is possible that a few relatively high-priced or low-priced properties skewed these averages, rendering any conclusions about the comparative quality of the two firms based on these averages unfair.

For additional support, the author points out that it took Fitch Realty considerably longer to sell one of the author's homes than it took Adams Realty to sell another one of her homes ten years earlier. However, this disparity is explainable by other plausible factors, such as changing economic conditions during that ten-year period, or a difference in the desirability of the two properties. Without establishing that all other factors affecting the speed of a sale were essentially the same for the two homes, the author cannot rely on this limited anecdotal evidence to support her claim.

In conclusion, the author's evidence lends little credible support to her claim. To persuade me that Adams is better than Fitch, the author would need to provide clear evidence that individual Adams agents are more effective in selling homes than individual Fitch agents, and that the disparity in home sales and sales price is attributable to that difference. Finally, to better evaluate the author's claim we would need more information comparing the percentage of agents working part-time at Fitch versus Adams. We would also need more information about the comparative attractiveness of the author's two homes, and the extent to which the residential real estate market changed during the decade between the sale of these two homes.

Argument:
Grade inflation at **Omega University**

In this memo Omega University's dean points out that Omega graduates are less successful in getting jobs than Alpha University graduates, despite the fact that during the past 15 years the overall grade average of Omega students has risen by 30%. The dean also points out that during the past 15 years Omega has encouraged its students, by way of a particular procedure, to evaluate the effectiveness of their professors. The dean reasons that this procedure explains the grade-average increase, which, in turn, has created a perception among employers that Omega graduates are less qualified for jobs. On the basis of this line of reasoning the dean concludes that to enable Omega graduates to find better jobs Omega must terminate its professor-evaluation procedure. This argument contains several logical flaws, which render it unconvincing.

A threshold problem with the argument involves the voluntary nature of the evaluation procedure. The dean provides no evidence about the number or percentage of Omega students who participate in the procedure. Lacking such evidence it is entirely possible that those numbers are insignificant, in which case terminating the procedure is unlikely to have any effect on the grade average of Omega students or their success in getting jobs after graduation.

The argument also assumes unfairly that the grade-average increase is the result of the evaluation procedure—rather than some other phenomenon. The dean ignores a host of other possible explanations for the increase—such as a trend at Omega toward higher admission standards, or higher quality instruction or facilities. Without ruling out all other possible explanations for the grade-average increase, the dean cannot convince me that by terminating the evaluation procedure Omega would curb its perceived grade inflation—let alone help its graduates get jobs.

Even if the evaluation procedure has resulted in grade inflation at Omega, the dean's claim that grade inflation explains why Omega graduates are less successful than Alpha graduates in getting jobs is unjustified. The dean overlooks a myriad of other possible reasons for Omega's comparatively poor job-placement record. Perhaps Omega's career services are inadequate; or perhaps Omega's curriculum does not prepare students for the job market as effectively as Alpha's. In short, without accounting for other factors that might contribute to Omega graduates' comparative lack of success in getting jobs, the dean cannot justify the claim that if Omega curbs its grade inflation employers will be more likely to hire Omega graduates.

Finally, even if the dean can substantiate all of the foregoing assumptions, the dean's assertion that Omega must terminate its evaluation procedure to enable its graduates to find better jobs is still unwarranted, in two respects. First, the dean ignores other possible ways by which Omega can increase its job-placement record—for example, by improving its public relations or career-counseling services. Second, the dean unfairly equates "more" jobs with "better" jobs. In other words, even if more Omega graduates are able to find jobs as a result of the dean's recommended course of action, the kinds of jobs Omega graduates find would not necessarily be better ones.

In sum, the dean's argument is unpersuasive as it stands. To strengthen it the dean must provide better evidence that the increase in grade average is attributable to Omega's professor-evaluation procedure, and that the end result is a perception on the part of employers that Omega graduates are less qualified for jobs than Alpha graduates. To better assess the argument I would need to analyze 15-year trends in (1) the percentage of Omega students participating in the evaluation procedure, (2) Omega's admission standards and quality of education, and (3) Omega's emphasis on job training and career preparation. I would also need to know what other means are available to Omega for enabling its graduates to find better jobs.

Argument:
The demand for **alpaca overcoats**

In this memo the vice president of Sartorian, a clothing manufacturer, argues that by resuming production of alpaca (wool) overcoats, after discontinuing production of these coats five years ago due to an unreliable alpaca supply, Sartorian would increase its profits. To support this argument the vice president points out that Sartorian now has a new fabric supplier, and reasons that since Sartorian's chief competitor has discontinued making these coats there must be pent-up consumer demand for them, which Sartorian would fill. The vice president also reasons that, since overall clothing prices have risen in each of the last five years, consumers will be willing to pay higher prices for Sartorian's alpaca coats. I find the argument specious in several respects.

To begin with, the argument relies on the assumption that the new fabric supplier will be a reliable supplier of alpaca. Yet the memo provides no substantiating evidence for this assumption. Perhaps the supply problems Sartorian experienced years earlier were attributable not to its supplier at the time but rather to factors beyond any supplier's control and that might render the alpaca supply unreliable today as well. Besides, without evidence to the contrary, it is entirely possible that Sartorian's new supplier will turn out to be unreliable and to be blameworthy for that unreliability.

Even if the new supplier turns out to be reliable, the memo assumes too hastily, on the basis of a competitor's discontinuing alpaca coat production, that consumer demand for alpaca coats made by Sartorian is now pent-up. Perhaps that competitor stopped making alpaca coats due to diminishing consumer demand for them. Or, perhaps other clothing manufacturers are now beginning to fill the market void by producing similar coats. Either of these scenarios, if true, would cast serious doubt on the vice president's claim that there is now pent-up alpaca coat demand from which Sartorian would profit.

Even if the vice president can substantiate the two foregoing assumptions, the argument relies on the additional assumption that consumers will be willing to pay whatever price Sartorian requires to turn a profit on its alpaca coat sales. Yet, perhaps Sartorian's costs for alpaca wool will be so high as to preclude any profit from alpaca coat sales. Also, the fact that clothing prices have been steadily increasing for five years suggests that consumers might have less disposable income for purchasing items such as alpaca coats, especially if consumers' income has not kept pace with escalating prices. Thus, without stronger evidence that consumers would be both willing and able to pay high prices for Sartorian's alpaca coats the vice president cannot convince me that the proposed course of action would be a profitable one.

Finally, even if Sartorian would turn a profit from the sale of its alpaca coats, the memo's claim that the company's overall profits would increase thereby is unwarranted. Sartorian's overall profitability is a function of revenue and expenses relating to all of Sartorian's products. Since the memo provides no evidence that Sartorian will continue to be profitable in other respects, I simply cannot take the vice president's argument seriously.

In sum, the argument is unpersuasive as it stands. To bolster it, the vice president must provide assurances that the new supplier will be a reliable and affordable alpaca supplier, and that consumers will be able and willing to pay whatever prices Sartorian requires in order to turn a profit from selling its alpaca coats. To better assess the argument I would need to know whether consumers are demanding alpaca coats anymore, and if so whether new competitors entering the alpaca coat market would thwart Sartorian's efforts to profit from any pent-up demand for these coats. I would also need detailed financial projections for Sartorian to determine the likelihood that it will continue to be profitable overall, aside from its predicted profitability from alpaca coat sales.

Argument:
Improving a school district's **music education programs**

In this memo the chairperson of the Saluda school board recommends hiring Schade, Steel City High's music director for the past five years, to plan and direct the school district's general music-education programs. To support this recommendation, the chairperson points out that over the past five years Steel's band has won three regional awards and that the school's facilities and instruments have improved markedly. However, close scrutiny of this evidence reveals that it lends little support for the recommendation.

First of all, the chairperson unfairly assumes that the three band awards were attributable to Schade's abilities and efforts. Lacking evidence to confirm this assumption, it is entirely possible that Schade was not the school's band instructor when the band won these awards. Or, perhaps the band won all three awards early in Schade's tenure, and his predecessor is to be credited. For that matter, perhaps it was the improved quality of the band's musical instruments that should be credited for the awards. After all, the chairperson provides no evidence that Schade was actually responsible for this improvement. Without considering and ruling out other possible reasons why the band won the awards the chairperson cannot convince me of Schade's abilities or, in turn, that he should be appointed to the district job.

Even if Schade is to be credited for the band's awards, it is possible that the skills that Schade possesses and that resulted in the band's winning these awards are not the same skills required for the district position. For example, perhaps Schade's music-conducting ability or his ability to motivate individual students was responsible for the band's award-winning performances. If so, then the fact that Steel's band won these awards would amount to scant evidence at best that Schade would make an effective administrator for the district.

Next, the chairperson unfairly assumes that improvements in the school's music facilities and instruments are attributable to Schade's efforts. If they are, then I would agree that Schade might possess valuable administrative skills that would serve the district well. Yet, just because these improvements occurred during Schade's tenure it is unreasonable to assume that Schade is to be credited for them. It is entirely possible that the improvements were the result of another administrator's efforts, or even the efforts of parents. Without showing clearly that Schade, and not some other person, was responsible for the improvements, the chairperson cannot convince me that Schade possesses the administrative abilities needed for the district job.

Finally, in recommending Schade for the job the chairperson fails to consider other possible job candidates. Even if all the evidence shows that Schade is well qualified, perhaps one or more other individuals would be even more suitable for the job. Without addressing this possibility the chairperson cannot convince me that the district should hire Schade.

In conclusion, the argument is unpersuasive as it stands. To convince me that Schade would be effective in the new job, the chairperson must provide clear evidence that the band's awards and especially the improvements cited are attributable to Schade's abilities and efforts, and that these abilities would translate directly to those required for the district position. Finally, to better evaluate the argument, I would need to compare Schade's qualifications with those of other possible job candidates.

Argument:
The link between **iron in the diet** and heart disease

In this argument, the author cites a study correlating the amount of iron in a person's diet with the person's risk of heart disease. The author also cites a well-established correlation between diets that include large amounts of red meat, which is high in iron, and the incidence of heart disease. The author concludes that the correlation observed in the study is a function of the correlation between red meat and heart disease. This argument suffers from a series of poor assumptions, which render it wholly unpersuasive as it stands.

To begin with, the author provides no evidence that the study's results are statistically reliable. In order to establish a strong correlation between dietary iron and heart disease, the study's sample must be sufficient in size and representative of the overall population of heart-disease victims. Lacking evidence of a sufficiently representative sample, the author cannot justifiably rely on the study to draw any conclusion whatsoever.

Even assuming that the study is statistically reliable, a direct correlation between a high-iron diet and heart disease does not necessarily prove that the former causes the latter. While a high correlation is strong evidence of a causal relationship, in itself it is not sufficient. The author must also account for all other possible factors leading to heart disease, such as genetic propensity, amount of exercise, and so forth. Lacking evidence that the heart-disease sufferers whom the study observed were similar in all such respects, the author cannot justifiably conclude that a high-iron diet is the primary cause, or even a contributing cause, of heart disease.

Similarly, a correlation between a diet that includes large amounts of red meat and heart disease does not necessarily infer a causal relationship. Lacking evidence to the contrary, it is possible that red-meat eaters are comparatively likely to incur heart disease due to factors that have nothing to do with the amount of red meat in their diet. Perhaps red-meat eaters are the same people who generally overeat, and it is obesity rather the consumption of red meat specifically that causes heart attacks. The author must consider and eliminate this and other possible reasons why red-meat eaters are more likely than other people to suffer from heart disease. Otherwise, I cannot accept the author's implicit claim that eating red meat is any more likely to cause heart disease than eating other foods.

Even assuming that a high-iron diet, including a diet high in red meat, promotes heart disease, the author cannot reasonably conclude that this causal relationship fully explains the study's results. The author overlooks the possibility that other foods are also high in iron, and that the study's participants ate these other foods as well as, or instead of, red meat. Without accounting for this possibility the author cannot convincingly conclude from the study that red meat is the chief cause of heart disease.

In conclusion, the argument unfairly assumes that correlation is tantamount to causation. To strengthen the argument, the author must provide clear evidence that a high-iron diet contributes to heart disease. The author must also provide clear evidence that people who eat red meat are more likely to incur heart disease because of the amount of red meat in their diet, rather than some other factor. To better evaluate the reliability of the study upon which the author's conclusion depends, I would need more information about the size and makeup of the study's sample. I would also need to know whether other foods are also high in iron and, if so, which high-iron foods the study's participants ate on a regular basis.

Argument:
Yosemite's amphibian decline

The author of this letter concludes that a worldwide decline in the number of amphibians is an indication, or result, of global air and water pollution. To support this assertion the author first notes a decline in amphibians in Yosemite Park between 1915 and 1992, and acknowledges that trout, which eat amphibian eggs, were introduced there in 1925. But, the author then claims that the introduction of trout cannot be the reason for the decline in Yosemite because the introduction of trout in Yosemite does not explain the worldwide decline. I find this argument logically unconvincing in three critical respects.

First, the author fails to provide any evidence to refute the strong inference that the amphibian decline in Yosemite was indeed caused by trout. Because the author provides no affirmative evidence that pollution—or some other phenomenon—was instead the reason for the decline, the author's broad assertion that a worldwide decline in amphibians indicates global pollution is entirely unconvincing.

Secondly, even if I were to concede that the introduction of trout was not the cause of Yosemite's amphibian decline, the author provides no evidence that the decline was caused by pollution—rather than some other phenomenon. Perhaps some other environmental factor was instead the cause. Without ruling out all other possible explanations the author cannot convince me that pollution is the cause of the worldwide amphibian decline—or even the decline in Yosemite alone.

Thirdly, even if I were to concede that pollution caused Yosemite's amphibian decline, this single sample is insufficient to draw any general conclusion about the reason for a worldwide amphibian decline. It is entirely possible that the cause-and-effect relationships in Yosemite are not typical of the world in general. Without additional samples from diverse geographic locations, I cannot accept the author's sweeping generalization about the decline of amphibians and global pollution.

In sum, the scant evidence the author cites proves nothing about the reason for the general decline of amphibians worldwide; in fact, this evidence only serves to refute the author's own argument. To strengthen the argument the author should examine all changes occurring in Yosemite between 1915 and 1992 and show that air and water pollution have at least contributed to the park's amphibian decline. In any event, the author must provide data about amphibian population changes and pollution at diverse geographical locations; and this data must show a strong inverse correlation between levels of air and water pollution and amphibian populations worldwide.

Argument:
Improving **learning and memory**

This argument concludes that certain compounds should be administered to students with poor memory and concentration to improve their performance in school. The argument cites an experiment involving rats in which the same compounds prevented the enzyme PEP from breaking down chemicals involved in learning and memory. The argument suffers from several flaws, which render it unconvincing.

A threshold problem with the argument is that it assumes that what improves memory and learning in rats will also improve memory and learning in humans. Although this is entirely possible, the argument provides no evidence to support this assumption. Without such evidence the argument can be rejected out of hand.

A second problem involves the fact that PEP increasingly breaks down the chemicals needed for learning and memory as humans age—as the argument points out. Yet the argument seems to claim that inhibiting PEP will be effective in improving learning and memory in young people. (The argument refers to students' "parents," implying that proposed human subjects are young people rather than adults.) Thus, the effectiveness of the compounds is likely to be far less significant than it would be for older people.

A third problem with the argument is that it assumes that learning and memory are the only significant factors affecting performance in school. Common sense and experience tells us this is not the case, and that a variety of other factors, such as motivation and natural ability, also play major roles. Thus, the compounds might very well turn out to be largely ineffective.

A final problem with the argument is that it asserts that the compounds will improve concentration, yet it makes no claim that the same compounds improved concentration in rats—only that they improved the rats' learning and memory. Thus, the argument's conclusion is indefensible to this extent.

In sum, the argument is weak on several grounds. To strengthen it, the argument's proponent must provide clear evidence that the same compounds that improved learning and memory in rats will do so in young humans. Moreover, the argument's proponent must show that poor academic performance is due primarily to learning and memory problems, rather than to poor concentration, motivation, or other factors.

Argument:
Vitamin D, calcium, and bone mass in older people

This argument concludes that elderly people should take twice the recommended dosage of vitamin D and calcium in order to minimize loss of bone mass, and therefore the risk of bone fractures. To support this conclusion, the argument's proponent cites a 3-year study involving a group of French female nursing home residents in their eighties. After three years of weight training, along with taking the indicated dosages of vitamin D and calcium, these women as a group were observed to suffer far fewer hip fractures than is average for their age. This argument suffers from several critical flaws and is therefore unconvincing.

First and foremost, the argument assumes unfairly that the additional vitamin D and calcium, rather than the weight training, were responsible for the lower-than-average incidence of hip fractures among this group of women. It is entirely possible that the weight training, not the supplements, was responsible for preserving bone mass. Also, weight training is known to improve muscular strength, coordination, and flexibility, which in turn might reduce the likelihood of accidental falls and other injuries. Thus, the weight training could also have been responsible in this respect.

The argument also overlooks many other possible explanations for the comparatively low incidence of hip fractures among this group of women. For example, perhaps these women were more physically fit than average to begin with. Or perhaps the nursing homes where the group resided provided special safeguards against accidental injuries that are not ordinarily available for most elderly people. Or perhaps French people are less susceptible to bone loss than other people are—due perhaps to cultural dietary habits or genetic predisposition. For that matter, perhaps women are genetically less disposed to lose bone mass than men are. Any of these scenarios, if true, would undermine the conclusion that the lower incidence of hip fractures was attributable to the additional vitamin D and calcium.

Finally, even if we accept that taking twice the recommended dosages of vitamin D and calcium significantly reduces the risk of bone fractures for older people, the argument ignores the possibility that some other dosage—perhaps three times the recommended dosage—would reduce the risk of bone fractures even more. Without ruling out this possibility, the argument's proponent cannot justifiably conclude that twice the recommended dosage provides the optimal reduction of risk.

In sum, this is a weak argument. To strengthen it, the argument's proponent must consider and eliminate all other possible explanations for the comparatively low incidence of hip fractures among this group of women. The proponent must also provide evidence that this group of women are representative of older people generally in ways that might affect the incidence of hip fractures—aside from their vitamin D and calcium intake. To better assess the argument, I would need more information about other means of preventing bone loss in older adults, and whether such other means are more or less effective than taking twice the recommended dosage of vitamin D and calcium.

Argument:
International **cover stories** and magazine sales

In this memo, the publisher of the magazine Newsbeat claims that to maximize sales the magazine should decrease its emphasis on international news and refrain from displaying such stories on its covers. To support this conclusion the publisher points out that the magazine's poorest-selling issues during the last three years have been those with cover stories about international events, and that during this same period the number of international cover stories appearing in other news magazines has decreased. On several grounds, this evidence lends little credible support for the memo's conclusion.

First of all, the fact that the magazine's poorest-selling issues were the ones with international cover stories might be explained by a variety of factors. Perhaps international events themselves were not as interesting during those periods. If so, it might be a mistake to refrain from emphasizing international events when those events are interesting enough to stimulate sales. Or perhaps the news magazine business is seasonal, or cyclical, and those particular issues would have sold more poorly regardless of the cover story. In short, without ruling out other possible explanations for the relatively poor sales of those particular issues the publisher cannot justifiably conclude that international cover stories were the cause of the relatively poor sales.

Secondly, the memo fails to indicate whether other magazines experienced an increase or a decrease in sales by reducing their emphasis on international news. It is possible, for instance, that the other magazines experienced declining sales even for issues focusing only on domestic news. If so, then the publisher's recommendation would make little sense. On the other hand, if other magazines experienced the same correlation between cover story and sales volume, this fact would lend considerable support to the publisher's conclusion that international cover stories were responsible for poor sales.

Thirdly, the memo cites increasing costs of maintaining international news bureaus as an additional reason to de-emphasize international news. While this fact does lend support to the publisher's suggestion, the publisher overlooks the possibility that if other news magazines de-emphasize international coverage due to increasing bureau costs, Newsbeat might turn out to be the only magazine covering international news, which in turn might actually stimulate sales. It would be hasty to implement the publisher's suggestion without acknowledging and exploring this possible scenario.

In conclusion, the memo is unconvincing as it stands. To strengthen the argument, the publisher must show that it was the international covers of Newsbeat, and not some other factor, that were responsible for the relatively poor sales of issues with those covers. To better assess the publisher's recommendation that Newsbeat should de-emphasize international news, we would need to know what changes in sales volume other news magazines experienced by de-emphasizing international news. We would also need more information about the impact that increasing bureau costs will have on magazines presently competing with Newsbeat in the area of international news.

Argument:
Driver's education at **Centerville High**

This letter recommends mandatory driver's education courses at Centerville High School. The author bases this recommendation on three facts: during the last two years several Centerville car accidents have involved teenage drivers; Centerville parents are too busy to teach driving to their children; and the two private driver-education courses in the area are expensive. As discussed below, the argument suffers from several critical flaws and is therefore unpersuasive.

First of all, the letter fails to indicate who or what caused the car accidents to which the letter refers. If Centerville High School students caused the accidents, and if those accidents would have been avoided had these students enrolled in the high school's driving course, then the argument would have merit. However, it is equally likely that the other drivers were at fault, or that no driver was at fault. Moreover, it is entirely possible that the teenage drivers had in fact taken the high school's driving course, or that they were not local high school students in the first place. The author must rule out all these possibilities in order to conclude confidently that a school-sponsored mandatory driving course would have prevented these accidents.

Secondly, whether the fact that several car accidents the last two years involved teenage drivers suggests a need for a mandatory driving course depends partly on the comparative accident rate during earlier years. It is entirely possible, for instance, that the rate of accidents involving teenagers has been steadily declining, and that this decline is due to the availability of the two private driving courses. Without ruling out this possibility, the letter's conclusion is not defensible.

The argument is problematic in certain other respects as well. It assumes that a mandatory school-sponsored course would be effective, yet it provides no evidence to support this assumption. Similarly, the argument fails to substantiate its assumption that a significant percentage of Centerville's parents cannot afford private driving instruction for their teenage children. Absent substantiating evidence for either of these necessary assumptions, I cannot be convinced that Centerville should establish the proposed driving course.

In conclusion, the letter's author fails to adequately support the recommendation for a school-sponsored mandatory driving course. To strengthen the argument, the author must provide clear evidence that Centerville High School students caused the accidents in question, and that a mandatory driving course would have prevented them. To better evaluate the argument, I would need more information about the affordability of the two private driving courses and about the effectiveness of a mandatory school-sponsored course compared to that of the two private courses.

Argument:
Mammal extinction in the **Kaliko** Islands

In this argument the speaker concludes that humans could not have been a factor in the extinction of large mammal species in the Kaliko islands 3,000 years ago. To justify this conclusion, the speaker points out that no evidence exists that humans hunted or had other significant contact with these mammals. The speaker also points out that while archeologists have found bones of discarded fish in the islands, they have not found any discarded mammal bones there. For three reasons, this evidence lends little credibility to the speaker's argument.

First, the argument concludes too hastily that humans could not have had any significant contact with these mammals. In relying on the lack of physical evidence such as bones, the speaker overlooks the possibility that humans exported mammals—particularly their bones—during this time period. Without ruling out this alternative explanation for the disappearance of these species from the islands, the speaker cannot justify the conclusion that humans were not a factor in their extinction from the islands.

Secondly, the argument relies on the assumption that without significant contact with these other species humans could not have been a factor in their extinction. But the speaker provides no evidence that this is the case. Moreover, perhaps humans drove these other species away from their natural habitat not by significant contact but merely by intruding on their territory. Or perhaps humans consumed the plants and animals on which these species relied for their subsistence. Either scenario would explain how humans could have been a factor in the extinction of these species despite a lack of significant contact.

Thirdly, the speaker assumes that the bones of fish that archeologists have found discarded on the island were discarded by humans, and not by some other large mammal. However, the speaker provides no evidence to substantiate this assumption. Given other possible explanations for these discarded fish bones, this evidence in itself lends little credible support to the speaker's theory about the extinction of large species of mammals.

In conclusion, the argument is unconvincing as it stands. To strengthen it, the speaker must rule out the possibility that humans exported the bones of these other species. To better evaluate the argument, we would need more information about the diet of humans and of the now-extinct mammals during that time period; particularly, we would need to know whether those other mammals also fed on the fish whose discarded bones have been found on the islands.

Argument:
A new president for the **Fancy Toy Company**

In this memo, a manager at Fancy Toy Company recommends replacing Pat Salvo, the company's current president, with Rosa Winnings, who is currently president of Starlight Jewelry. To support this recommendation the manager points out that Fancy's profits have declined during the last three quarters under Pat's leadership, while Starlight's profits have been increasing dramatically. The manager's argument is unconvincing for several reasons.

First, the manager's recommendation relies partly on the assumption that Pat was the cause of Fancy Toy's declining profits. However, this need not be the case. Perhaps the toy business is seasonal, and the coming quarter is always the most profitable one. Or perhaps the cost of materials or labor have increased, and Pat has had no control over these increases. Without taking into account such possibilities, the manager simply cannot reasonably conclude that Pat is responsible for Fancy's declining profits, and that replacing Pat will therefore enhance Fancy's profits.

Similarly, the manager's recommendation assumes that it is Rosa who has been primarily responsible for Starlight's profitability. However, the manager provides no evidence to affirm this assumption. It is entirely possible that all jewelry businesses have prospered recently, regardless of the abilities of the managers. Or perhaps the costs of precious metals and other materials have declined in recent years, thereby leading to increased profits for Starlight. Moreover, perhaps Rosa has only served as president of Starlight for a short while, and it was her predecessor who is to credit for Starlight's profitability. Without taking into account these possibilities, the manager cannot defend the conclusion that it is Rosa who is responsible for Starlight's increasing profitability.

Finally, the manager's recommendation to replace Pat with Rosa rests on the poor assumption that the two businesses are sufficiently similar that Rosa's experience and skill in one business will transfer to the other. Even if Starlight's increasing profitability is attributable to Rosa's leadership, she might nevertheless be unsuccessful leading a toy company, depending on how much experience in the toy business is required to successfully lead such a company.

In conclusion, the argument is unconvincing as it stands. To strengthen it the manager must show that Pat, and not some other factor beyond Pat's control, is responsible for Fancy's declining profits. Similarly, the manager must show that it is Rosa who is primarily responsible for Starlight's profitability, and that Rosa's abilities will transfer to the toy business. In order to better evaluate the argument, we would need more information about how long Pat and Rosa have served as presidents of their respective companies, and what their long-term record is for leading their respective companies to profitability.

Argument:
Patriot car company's marketing strategy

In this memo, the president of Patriot car manufacturing argues that in order to increase its market share Patriot should (1) discontinue its older models, which look "old-fashioned" and have not been selling well, (2) begin manufacturing sporty models, and (3) hire Youth Advertising agency, which has successfully promoted the country's leading soft drink. To justify this recommendation the president points out that many regions report a rapid increase in the number of newly licensed drivers. However, this argument relies on several dubious assumptions, and is therefore unpersuasive.

To begin with, the president's argument relies on certain unproven assumptions about the reports of a sharp increase in the number of newly licensed drivers. First, the argument assumes that the reports are accurate, and that these regions account for a statistically significant portion of Patriot's potential buyers. Secondly, the president overlooks the possibility that in other regions that number is actually declining, so that there is no net increase at all.

Even assuming that the reports are accurate and the regions cited are representative of the overall territory in which Patriot cars are marketed, the president concludes too hastily that newly licensed drivers will tend to favor new cars over used ones, and to favor Patriot's sporty new cars over other manufacturers' new vehicles. The president ignores the likelihood that the vast majority of new drivers are teenagers who cannot afford new sports cars, or new cars of any kind. Even teenagers who can afford new sports cars might prefer other manufacturers' cars—perhaps due to Patriot's old-fashioned image. Lacking evidence that new drivers who buy cars will tend to buy

Patriot sports cars, the president cannot convince me that the recommended course of action will increase Patriot's market share.

Finally, the fact that Youth has successfully promoted the country's leading soft drink amounts to scant evidence that Youth would also be successful in promoting Patriot cars.

Marketers that are effective in one industry are not necessarily effective in another. Besides, the president unfairly assumes that Patriot's current advertising agency is partly responsible for Patriot's relatively small market share. Perhaps some other factor—such as poor management, distribution, or pricing decisions—is the true reason for Patriot's market-share problem. Moreover, perhaps Youth would be less effective than Patriot's current ad agency. Thus, switching to Youth will not necessarily improve Patriot's market share—and might even result in a decline in that share.

In sum, the president's recommendation is weak. To strengthen it the president must show that the reports are a reliable indicator of the overall change in the number of newly licensed drivers. The president must also provide clear evidence—perhaps by way of a reliable survey—that a sufficient percentage and number of new drivers who are able and willing to buy new cars will choose Patriot's sports cars over other manufacturers' cars, so that Patriot's overall market share will increase. To better assess the recommendation that Patriot switch to Youth, I would need to know the extent to which Patriot's current ad strategy is responsible for Patriot's market-share problems; then I would need to know Youth's experience and success record in the car industry—relative to that of Patriot's current agency as well as other available agencies.

Argument:
Water rationing and economic growth

In this letter, a Grandview City business leader concludes that in order to promote economic health the city must abolish the water-rationing rules it implemented during last year's drought. To support this conclusion the letter's author points out that since the city implemented these rules industrial growth in the area has declined. However, this argument contains several logical problems, which render it unconvincing as it stands.

First of all, the argument relies on two threshold assumptions: that people who use the city's water have complied with the rules, and that area industry is subject to the rules in the first place. Yet the author supplies no evidence to substantiate either assumption. In other words, if area industries have not in fact been rationing water, the author's conclusion that water rationing is a contributing cause of the recent decline in industry growth would be indefensible.

A second problem with the argument is that it overlooks other possible explanations for the decline in industry growth. Perhaps the decline is the result of a general economic recession that has also impacted businesses in areas not subject to water rationing. Or perhaps local or state regulations unrelated to water rationing are instead responsible for the slowdown. Without accounting for such possibilities, the author cannot justify the conclusion that the water rationing is the cause of the slowdown.

A third problem with the argument is that it unjustifiably assumes that stopping water rationing would help reverse the decline in industry growth. It is entirely possible that this course of action would actually exacerbate the decline. Specifically, perhaps the lack of water has been the primary factor in the slowdown. If so, and if the rationing stops, water might become even more scarce depending on current drought conditions, in which case the slowdown would worsen.

In conclusion, the argument is unconvincing as it stands. To strengthen it the business leader must provide strong evidence that no other factors were responsible for the slowdown in industry growth, and that industry has complied with the rules in the first place. Finally, to better evaluate the argument we would need more information about current water availability in the area, so that we can assess how stopping water rationing would affect this availability.

Argument:
Solano's music education programs

This letter concludes that Solano school district should discontinue its music programs altogether. To justify this conclusion the author points out that only 20% of Solano's students enroll in music classes and that few Solano students pursue music as a major course of study in college. The author also points out that in nearby Rutherford student grades increased the year after that district discontinued music education. This argument is problematic in several critical respects.

A threshold problem with the argument is that it relies on certain implicit assumptions about the value of music education. Specifically, the author assumes that any education program is valuable only to the extent that it enhances overall grades and only if students choose to pursue that course of study in college. Such normative assumptions are dubious at best; common sense tells me that the chief value of music education, like that of art or physical education, lies in its contribution to the full development of a child, not in its influence on grades or choice of career. Without addressing this issue, the author's conclusion can be dismissed out of hand.

Another problem with the argument involves the implicit claim that only 20% of Solano students enroll in music courses because they are uninterested in music. This claim assumes that students have a choice in what courses they take in the first place; yet we are not informed that this is the case. It also unfairly assumes that no other factor influences students' decisions about whether to enroll in music courses. Perhaps Solano's current music teachers are unpopular; or perhaps the district lacks sufficient funds to meet current demand for music courses or to provide adequate facilities and instruments for more students. Since the author has not ruled out these other possible explanations for the low enrollment rate, the author's implicit claim that Solano students are not interested in music is doubtful at best.

Yet another problem with the argument involves the implicit claim that music education is not worthwhile because few Solano students pursue music as a college major. This claim assumes that all Solano students pursuing a career in music attend college in the first place; yet this is not necessarily the case. The claim also assumes that Solano students are properly advised about choosing their college major; yet it is entirely possible that Solano's high school advisers dissuade students from pursuing music. Since the author fails to rule out these possibilities, the fact that few Solano students pursue music in college lends little credible support for the author's conclusion.

A final problem with the argument involves Rutherford's increase in its students' grades the year after that district discontinued music programs. This increase might be attributable to numerous factors. Perhaps that year Rutherford received substantial funding to enhance its after-school tutoring program; or perhaps it hired more effective teachers that year. Or perhaps the outgoing graduating class one year was less bright overall than the incoming freshman class the next year. Any of these scenarios, if true, would discredit the author's assertion that music education contributes to lower academic grades. Besides, the author cites an increase during only one year—an insufficiently small range to draw any reliable general conclusion.

In sum, the author's argument for discontinuing music education is weak. To strengthen the argument the author must show that the cited statistics about Solano students reflect their lack of interest in music rather than some other phenomenon, and that the increase in Rutherford's grades was the result of its discontinuing music education.

Answers to Arguments That Assume All Group Members Share the Same Attributes

This section contains sample essay responses to several Argument statements from the official GRE essay pool. Each of these Argument statements relies partly on one of two unwarranted assumptions:

1. Group characteristics apply to all individual group members.
2. Characteristics of a certain member apply to the group as a whole.

Before you read these essays, be sure to review the discussion about this type of reasoning problem on pages 29–30.

> **NOTE:** Each essay addresses other major reasoning problems as well, but it is included only in this section of Part 3.

Argument:
Hiring new **law school graduates**

This article concludes that despite the relatively high salaries at Megalopolis' large law firms, these firms must begin offering more benefits and incentives to new law-school graduates, while requiring them to work fewer hours, in order to reverse a three-year 15% decline in the number of graduates going to work for these firms. To justify this conclusion the article's author notes that during the last three years the number of new law-school graduates going to work for small firms has risen. The author also cites a survey at one leading law school in which most first-year students indicated that job satisfaction was more important than salary. I find this argument logically unconvincing in several respects.

First of all, the 15% decline that the author cites is not necessarily due to the vocational preferences of new law-school graduates. It is entirely possible that the number of new graduates preferring to work for large firms has not declined, but that during the last three years Megalopolis' large firms have had fewer and fewer job openings for these graduates. Since the article fails to account for this alternative explanation for the 15% decline, the article's author cannot make any sound recommendations to law firms based on that decline.

As for the survey that the article cites, the vocational goals of first-year law students do not necessarily reflect those of graduating students; after all, a law student's vocational goals can change over a three-year period. Moreover, the goals of students at one law school do not necessarily reflect those of the overall pool of graduates that might seek employment with Megalopolis law firms. In fact, given that the school whose students participated in the survey was a "leading" school, it is entirely possible that the vast majority of the school's graduates may choose among offers from many large firms in many cities. If so, this fact would further undermine the survey's relevance in prescribing any course of action for Megalopolis' law firms.

Finally, the author falsely equates the proposed tangible incentives with job satisfaction, which is an intangible reward based on the nature of one's work. Moreover, enhanced job benefits can be tantamount to an enhanced salary, and shorter working hours amount to a higher hourly wage. Thus if new law-school graduates seeking jobs in Megalopolis are less interested in monetary rewards than in job satisfaction, then the proposed incentives are not likely to entice these graduates.

In sum, the argument is logically flawed and therefore unconvincing as it stands. To strengthen it the author must either modify the proposal to provide incentives for those seeking job satisfaction over monetary rewards, or provide better evidence that new law school graduates seeking jobs in Megalopolis would find the proposed incentives enticing.

Argument:
Mesa Foods: a profitable investment?

This Omni, Inc. memorandum recommends that Omni buy snack-food manufacturer Mesa Foods and aggressively promote its brand of salsa nationwide. To support this recommendation the memo relies on the exceptional profitability of Mesa's salsa during the last three years, along with the fact that Mesa's overall profits were up last year. However, the recommendation relies on a series of unsubstantiated assumptions, which render it unconvincing as it stands.

First of all, the memo indicates that Omni is interested in selling to 14-to-25-year-olds. Accordingly, the argument rests on the assumption that Mesa's snack foods appeal to this age group. Yet, we are not informed what types of snack foods Mesa manufactures, aside from its salsa. It is entirely possible that Mesa's foods, including its salsa, appeal primarily to other age groups. If this is the case, the recommended acquisition would not serve Omni's goal.

Secondly, the argument rests on the assumption that in the region where Mesa's products are sold the preferences of consumers between the ages of 14 and 25 typify nationwide preferences among this age group. If this is not the case, then it is entirely possible that Omni would not sell enough Mesa snack foods, including its salsa, to earn a profit from its Mesa operation. Thus, without more marketing information about the snack-food tastes of 14-to-25-year-olds nationwide it is difficult to assess the merit of the memo's recommendation.

Even if the memo's author can substantiate the foregoing assumptions, the author overlooks the possibility that last year's 20% increase in Mesa's profits was an aberration, and that in most other years Mesa has not been profitable. Also, the 20% increase might have been due entirely to sales of Mesa's salsa, and aside from the profit from salsa sales Mesa's profitability is actually declining. If either is the case, and if Mesa's salsa does not turn out to be popular among 14-to-25-year-olds across the nation, then Omni is unlikely to profit from the recommended course of action.

In conclusion, the recommendation is not well supported. To convince me that the Mesa Foods acquisition would be profitable Omni would need to provide clear statistical evidence that Mesa's snack foods, and its salsa in particular, would appeal to 14-to-25-year-olds nationwide. To better evaluate the recommendation, I would need more information about Mesa's profitability over a longer time period, and about the extent to which Mesa's salsa accounts for any such profitability.

Argument:
Green Thumb Gardening Center

In this memo, the owner of Green Thumb Gardening Center (GT) concludes that GT could increase its profits by expanding its stock of vegetable seeds. The owner cites a national survey showing growing dissatisfaction with supermarket vegetables, and points out that a certain gardening magazine has sold out at one local newsstand three months in a row. I find the owner's argument weak, for three reasons.

First, by relying on the national survey to support its conclusion the argument depends on the assumption that the level of satisfaction locally with store-bought groceries reflects national levels. Yet the owner provides no evidence to support this assumption. It is possible that residents of this town are quite satisfied with these vegetables. Without eliminating this possibility, the owner cannot rely on the national survey to conclude that this town's residents would be interested in buying vegetable seeds from GT.

Secondly, by relying on the survey the argument assumes that consumers who are dissatisfied with store-bought groceries are likely to grow their own vegetables instead. However, the owner fails to provide any evidence to support this assumption. Perhaps consumers are continuing to buy vegetables from grocery stores despite their dissatisfaction. Or perhaps this dissatisfaction is leading consumers to buy their vegetables from special produce markets and vegetable stands instead of supermarkets. Since the owner has failed to consider and rule out these possibilities, the owner's assertion that this town's dissatisfied consumers would be eager to buy vegetable seeds from GT to grow their own vegetables cannot be taken seriously.

Thirdly, the mere fact that a certain gardening magazine has recently sold out at one newsstand in this town is scant evidence that the town's residents would be eager to buy vegetable seeds from GT. Perhaps three months ago this newsstand decreased the number of copies it stocks; or perhaps the magazine does not even concern itself with vegetable gardening; or perhaps the only reason for this apparent increase in sales is that other newsstands in town have stopped stocking the magazine. Given these possible scenarios, the fact that one newsstand has sold every copy of the last three monthly issues proves nothing about local trends in vegetable gardening.

In conclusion, the owner's argument is unpersuasive. To strengthen it the owner must provide more convincing evidence that consumers in this town are actually becoming less satisfied with supermarket vegetables, and that as a result they are buying fewer such vegetables. To better evaluate the argument we would need more information about alternative sources of vegetables for local consumers—for example, the number and quality of produce stands. We would also need to know why the newsstand's copies of the gardening magazine sold out.

Argument:
A seafood restaurant for **Bay City**

This argument's conclusion is that a new Bay City restaurant specializing in seafood would be both popular and profitable. To justify this conclusion the argument points out that seafood consumption in Bay City's restaurants has risen by 30% during the last five years. Also, the argument points out that most Bay City families are two-income families, and cites a national survey showing that two-income families eat out more often and express more concern about eating healthily than they did ten years ago. I find the argument unpersuasive, for several reasons.

First, a 30% increase in seafood consumption at Bay City restaurants does not necessarily indicate a sufficient demand for a new Bay City restaurant serving seafood dishes only. Although a 30% increase seems significant, the actual level of consumption might nevertheless be very low. This scenario is quite possible, especially considering that there are currently no seafood restaurants in Bay City. Lacking evidence that a significant number of the city's restaurant patrons are ordering seafood, the argument's conclusion that a new seafood restaurant would be popular and profitable is unjustified.

Secondly, even if current demand would otherwise support an increase in the availability of seafood at Bay City's restaurants, the argument unfairly assumes that Bay City's restaurant patrons who order seafood would frequent the new restaurant. Perhaps the vast majority of these patrons would remain loyal to their favorite restaurant. Thus, lacking evidence that these patrons would be willing to try the new restaurant the argument's claim that a new seafood restaurant would be popular is dubious.

Thirdly, the nationwide study showing clear trends among two-income families toward dining out and eating healthily does not necessarily apply to Bay City. It is quite possible that Bay City's two-income families do not follow these general trends. For that matter, in Bay City the trend might be just the opposite. Thus, the nationwide trends that the argument cites amount to scant evidence that Bay City residents in particular would frequent a new seafood restaurant in their city.

Fourth, even if most of Bay City's families are following the nationwide trends indicated above, it is unreasonable to infer that these families will necessarily patronize a new seafood restaurant in Bay City. For all we know Bay City might boast a variety of health-oriented restaurants that do not specialize in seafood. For that matter, perhaps Bay City's existing restaurants are responding to the trends by providing more healthful dishes. Moreover, perhaps either or both of these trends will soon reverse themselves— at least in Bay City—for whatever reason. Any of these scenarios, if true, would cast considerable doubt on the argument's conclusion that a new seafood restaurant in Bay City would be popular and profitable.

Finally, even if Bay City families flock to the new seafood restaurant, the restaurant would not necessarily be profitable as a result. Profitability is a function of both revenue and expense. Thus, it is entirely possible that the restaurant's costs of obtaining high quality, healthful seafood, or of promoting the new restaurant, might render it unprofitable despite its popularity. Without weighing revenue against expenses the argument's conclusion is premature at best.

In sum, the argument is unpersuasive as it stands. To bolster it the argument's author must show—perhaps by way of a reliable citywide study—that the demand among restaurant patrons for seafood is sufficient to support a new seafood restaurant, and that a sufficient number of people who order fish at Bay City restaurants will be able and willing to at least try the new restaurant. The author would also bolster the argument by providing reliable evidence that Bay City reflects the nationwide trends cited, and that these trends will continue in the foreseeable future—in Bay City. Finally, to better assess the argument I would need detailed cost and revenue estimates for a new Bay City seafood restaurant—to determine the likelihood that even a popular such restaurant would turn a profit.

Argument:
Monroetown's election between **Brown** and **Greene**

The author of this editorial concludes that most Monroetown residents favor Greene's proposal to raise taxes in order to improve education over Brown's proposal to cut taxes, even though incumbent Brown defeated Greene by way of a 52% majority vote in a recent mayoral election. To support this conclusion the author points out a nationwide tendency to reelect incumbent candidates regardless of their positions. The author also points out that a survey taken after the election showed that most Monroetown residents oppose Brown's proposal. As the following discussion shows, the author's argument is not well supported by the evidence.

First of all, the author unfairly assumes that the nationwide tendency applies specifically to Monroetown residents. Lacking evidence that Monroetown voters reflect this general tendency, it is entirely possible that Monroetown residents vote strictly according to their position on the issues. For that matter, it is possible that Monroetown voters tend strongly to vote against incumbents, in which case the author's claim that Monroetown residents oppose Brown's proposal would more flagrantly fly in the face of the election results.

Secondly, the author fails to indicate when the statistics showing this nationwide tendency were collected. The longer the time period between the collection of these statistics and the election, the greater the possibility that the tendency has changed over this time span, and the less justifiable the author's reliance on these statistics to support the claim that Monroetown residents oppose Brown's proposal.

Thirdly, the author fails to indicate how much time passed between the Brown-Greene election and the survey showing that most Monroetown residents oppose her proposal. If the survey was conducted immediately after the election, then the fact that the election results conflict with the survey results would cast considerable doubt on the reliability of either to indicate what proposals Monroetown residents truly support. However, if the survey occurred long after the election, then the conflict can readily be explained by changing opinions and demographics over time. In either case, it is impossible to weigh the evidence without more specific information about percentages. The larger the percentage of Monroetown residents participating in the election, the greater the extent to which the election results would cast doubt on the survey results. By the same token, the larger the percentage of Monroetown residents shown by the survey to oppose Brown's proposal the more clearly this evidence would support the author's argument.

Finally, the argument suffers from "either-or" reasoning. Based on the fact that Monroetown residents are opposed to Brown's proposed tax cut, the author unfairly concludes that they must be in favor of Greene's proposal. However, the author overlooks the possibility that Monroetown residents are not in favor of either proposal.

In sum, the author's argument that Monroetown residents oppose Brown's proposal and are in favor of the proposals set forth by Greene is unconvincing. To strengthen the argument the author must provide clear evidence that Monroetown residents voted contrary to their own positions on the issues when they reelected Brown. To better evaluate the argument I would need to know how much time passed between the collection of the statistics showing the national tendency cited by the author and the election. I would also need to know how much time passed between the election and the survey showing that Monroetown residents oppose Brown's proposal. Finally, I would need to know what portion of Monroetown's residents voted in the election, and what portion of these residents were shown by the survey to oppose Brown's policies.

Argument:
Dickens Academy's interpersonal-skills seminars

This Dickens Academy ad claims that any company wanting to improve customer relations will benefit from enrolling its employees in Dickens' one-day seminars. To support this claim the ad cites Mega-Publishing's improved sales after its new employees attended Dickens' seminar as an indication of improved customer relations. As it stands the ad rests on a series of dubious assumptions, and is therefore unconvincing.

In the first place, the ad relies on the unsubstantiated assumption that the Mega employees attending the seminar are positioned to influence Mega's sales and its customer relations. Perhaps these new employees were hired for production, editorial, or personnel positions that have nothing to do with customer relations and that have only an indirect and negligible impact on sales. Without providing evidence that these new employees directly influence Mega's customer relations and sales, I cannot accept the argument that the Dickens seminar was responsible for any of Mega's sales or customer-relations improvements subsequent to the seminar.

Even if Mega's seminar attendees are involved in sales and customer relations, the ad unfairly assumes that the improvement in Mega's sales must be attributable to the seminar. Perhaps the improvement in sales was the result of increasing product demand, new pricing policies, decreased competition, or any one of a myriad of other possible developments. For that matter, perhaps Mega's new employees as a group already possessed exceptional interpersonal skills, and therefore Mega's sales and customer relations would have improved during the ensuing months regardless of the seminar. Since the ad fails to consider and rule out these and other alternative explanations for the improvements at Mega, I find the ad's claim that the Dickens seminar should receive credit unconvincing.

Even if the Dickens seminar was responsible for improved sales and customer relations at Mega, the ad's claim that all other businesses would benefit similarly from a Dickens seminar is unjustified. It is entirely possible that the techniques and skills that participants in Dickens' seminars learn are effective for the kind of business in which Mega engages, but not for other types of businesses. Although it is possible that Dickens' training methods would be equally effective for other types of businesses, since Dickens has not provided evidence that this is the case I remain unconvinced by the ad's claim.

In sum, this ad fails to provide key evidence needed to support its claim. To strengthen that claim Dickens must show that Mega's seminar attendees—and not other employees or other occurrences—were indeed responsible for the subsequent improvement in sales, and that customer relations also improved as a result of their attending the seminar. Dickens must also provide additional success stories—about other types of businesses—to convince me that Dickens' training methods will work for any business.

Argument:
The health benefits of **Venadial**

In this memo, the sales director of Healthy-and-Good food company recommends obtaining the exclusive right to sell the new margarine Venadial internationally in order to increase company profits substantially and quickly. To support this recommendation the director points out that, in a recent study, participants who consumed Venadial daily experienced a decrease in their cholesterol level and in their risk of heart attack. The director also points out that in Alta, the only country where Venadial is currently produced, this margarine is extremely popular among consumers. This argument contains several critical flaws, which render it unpersuasive.

First of all, the memo lacks sufficient information about how the study was conducted to determine what conclusions, if any, can be drawn from it. Unless all other conditions potentially affecting cholesterol level and heart attack risk remained constant during the study, and unless the study included a statistically significant number of participants, any conclusions from the study are simply unreliable. Moreover, the memo fails to indicate whether the study also included a distinct group of participants who did not consume Venadial daily. If it did, then the comparison of cholesterol levels and heart attacks between the two groups would help us to assess the strength of the memo's claims about the health benefits of Venadial.

Secondly, the memo unfairly assumes that since Venadial is popular in Alta it will also be popular in other countries. Consumer tastes in foods like margarine, as well as concerns about health matters such as cholesterol level, vary widely from country to country. It is quite possible that consumers in Alta enjoy the taste of Venadial more than other consumers would, or that consumers in Alta are more concerned than the average person about cholesterol level and heart attacks. Since the memo provides no evidence that tastes and health concerns of Alta consumers are representative of those of people generally, the sales director's conclusion that Venadial will be popular elsewhere is unjustifiable, at least based on the memo.

Thirdly, even if Venadial is shown conclusively to carry the touted health benefits and to be popular worldwide, Healthy-and-Good will not necessarily earn a substantial profit by acquiring international rights to sell Venadial. The memo provides no information about the costs involved in manufacturing and distributing Venadial— only that it is derived from pine-tree resin and has been produced only in Alta. Perhaps Venadial can be derived only from certain pine trees located in Alta and surrounding regions. If so, then the costs of procuring Venadial might prevent the company from earning a profit. In short, without more information about supply, demand, and production costs, it is impossible to determine whether the company can earn a profit from acquiring international rights to sell Venadial.

In sum, the memo's recommendation is not well supported. Before I can accept it, the sales director must supply dearer evidence that (1) Venadial contributes to lower cholesterol level and decreased heart-attack risk, (2) consumers outside of Alta would prefer Venadial over alternative products, and (3) the revenue from sales of Venadial would significantly outweigh the costs of producing and distributing the product.

Argument:
A speed-reading course for **Acme Publishing**

In this argument, the personnel director of Acme Publishing claims that Acme would benefit greatly from improved employee productivity if every employee takes the 3-week Easy-Read seminar at a cost of $500 per employee. To support this claim the director points out that many other companies have claimed to benefit from the seminar, that one student was able to read a long report very quickly afterward, and that another student saw his career advance significantly during the year after the seminar. However, close scrutiny of the evidence reveals that it accomplishes little toward supporting the director's claim, as discussed below.

First of all, the mere fact that many other companies benefited greatly from the course does not necessarily mean that Acme will benefit similarly from it. Perhaps the type of reading on which the course focuses is not the type in which Acme Publishing employees often engage at work. Moreover, since Acme is a publishing company its employees are likely to be excellent readers already, and therefore might stand to gain far less from the course than employees of other types of companies.

Secondly, the two individual success stories the argument cites amount to scant evidence at best of the course's effectiveness. Moreover, the director unfairly assumes that their accomplishments can be attributed to the course. Perhaps both individuals were outstanding readers before taking the course, and gained nothing from it. Regarding the individual whose career advanced after taking the course, any one of a myriad of other factors might explain that advancement. And the individual who was able to read a long report very quickly after the course did not necessarily absorb a great deal of the material.

Thirdly, the director assumes without warrant that the benefits of the course will outweigh its costs. While all of Acme's employees take the 3-week course, Acme's productivity might decline significantly. This decline, along with the substantial fee for the course, might very well outweigh the course's benefits. Without a complete cost-benefit analysis, it is unfair to conclude that Acme would benefit greatly should all its employees take the course.

In sum, the director's evidence does not warrant his conclusion. To support his recommendation he must first provide evidence that employees with similar reading skills as those that Acme employees possess have benefited significantly from the course; a survey of other publishing companies might be useful for this purpose. To better assess the argument I would need more information about the extent to which the course would disrupt Acme's operations. Specific information that would be useful would include the proximity of the seminar to Acme, the hours involved, and the percentage of Acme employees enrolled simultaneously.

Argument:
Organized sports for **Parkville**'s children

This letter concludes that Parkville should not allow children under age nine to participate in organized competitive sports. To support this conclusion, the author points out the increasing number of children nationwide who become injured during athletic competitions. The author also cites the fact that in some big cities children report undue pressure from coaches and parents to win, and that long practice sessions take time away from a child's academic pursuits. However, the author's argument relies on a series of unsubstantiated assumptions, and is therefore unpersuasive as it stands.

One problem with the argument is that it assumes that the nationwide statistics about the incidence of sports injuries among youngsters applies equally to Parkville's children. Yet this might not be the case, for a variety of possible reasons. Perhaps Parkville maintains more stringent safety standards than the national norm; or perhaps children's sporting events in Parkville are better supervised by adults, or supervised by more adults. Without ruling out such possibilities, the author cannot justifiably conclude that Parkville has a sports-injury problem to begin with.

A second problem with the argument is that it unjustifiably assumes that in Parkville parents and coaches unduly pressure youngsters to win organized athletic competitions. The only evidence the author provides to substantiate this assumption are the reports from "big city" children. We are not informed whether Parkville is a big city. Perhaps people who live in big cities are generally more competitive than other people. If so, and if Parkville is not a big city, then the author cannot justifiably rely on these reports to conclude that the proposed course of action is necessary.

A third problem with the argument is that it unfairly assumes that children do not benefit academically from participating in competitive sports. It is entirely possible that such sports provide children with the sort of break from academics that helps them to be more productive academically. It is also possible that the competitive drive that these sports might instill in young children carries over to their academics and spurs them on to perform well in school. Without considering such potential academic benefits, the author cannot reasonably conclude that for young children the disadvantages of participating in athletic competition outweigh the benefits.

In conclusion, the argument is unconvincing as it stands. To better evaluate the argument we would need more information about the incidence of sports injuries among young children in Parkville. To strengthen the argument the author must demonstrate that Parkville's parents and coaches exert the kind of pressure on their children reported by "big city" children and, if so, that this pressure in fact contributes to the sort of problems with which the author is concerned.

Argument:
The ozone layer and the **salamander** population

In this argument the speaker claims that increased ultraviolet radiation due to thinning of the earth's ozone layer is responsible for the significant decline in the number of salamanders who lay their eggs in mountain lakes, and that this thinning will cause population declines in other species. To justify these claims the speaker points out that salamander eggs lack a protective shell and thus their tissues are highly susceptible to radiation damage, then reasons that the increased radiation must damage these eggs and prevent them from hatching. The argument is problematic in several critical respects, which render it unconvincing.

To begin with, the argument assumes that the salamander population is in fact declining, yet this assumption is not born out by the mere fact that the number of salamanders laying eggs in mountain lakes is declining. It is entirely possible that in other locations the salamander population is increasing. For that matter, perhaps the number of eggs a salamander lays in a mountain lake is increasing on average. Either scenario, if true, would seriously call into question any prediction about population changes for salamanders or for other species.

Even if the total salamander population is declining, an inverse correlation between ultraviolet radiation and salamander population does not suffice in itself to prove that the former causes the latter. The speaker must account for the possibility that the number of eggs salamanders lay is declining in all areas—regardless of the amount of radiation reaching the surface. The speaker must also eliminate all other reasonable explanations for the decline. For example, if the population of species that prey on salamanders or eat their eggs is increasing, this would explain the population decline and therefore undermine the speaker's entire argument.

Even assuming that the total salamander population is declining as a result of increasing radiation, the speaker cannot reasonably infer that other species are equally vulnerable to a population decline as a result. Perhaps the absence of a shell, combined with its mountain-lake location, renders a salamander egg more vulnerable to ultraviolet radiation than any other type of egg. If so, this fact would cast considerable doubt on the speaker's prediction for other species.

Finally, the speaker's grave prediction relies on the assumption that the ozone-thinning process will not reverse in the future. Although this assumption might be born out, on the other hand it might not. Without providing some assurance that the ozone layer will at least continue to be as thin as it is now, the speaker cannot convince me that other species will experience a population decline as a result of radiation damage to eggs.

In sum, the speaker's argument depends on a series of doubtful assumptions, and is therefore weak. To strengthen it the speaker must supply better evidence that the total salamander population is declining, and must rule out all other possible explanations for that decline. The speaker must also provide clear evidence that the current level of radiation reaching the surface is as potentially damaging to the eggs of other species, and must account for why other species have not already experienced a declining population. Finally, to better assess the argument I would need a reliable prognosis for the earth's ozone layer.

Argument:
Boosting **Armchair Video**'s profits

In this memo, the owner of Armchair Video concludes that in order to boost sagging profits Armchair's stores should eliminate evening operating hours and should stock only movies that are less than 2 years old. To support this conclusion the owner points out that since Armchair's downtown Marston store implemented these changes, very few customers have complained. The owner's argument relies on several unsubstantiated assumptions, and is therefore unconvincing as it stands.

In the first place, implicit in the argument is the assumption that no other means of boosting profits is available to Armchair. While the owner has explicitly ruled out the option of raising its rental rates, the owner ignores other means, such as selling videos, or renting and selling compact discs, candy, and so forth. Without considering such alternatives, the owner cannot justifiably conclude that the proposed changes are the only ways Armchair can boost its profits.

A second problem with the argument is that it assumes that the proposed changes would in fact enhance profits. It is entirely possible that the lost revenue from reducing store hours would outweigh the savings in reduced operating costs. Perhaps Armchair customers are attracted to the stores' wide selection and variety of movies, and that Armchair would lose their patronage should it reduce its inventory. Moreover, common sense informs me that video rental stores do most of their business during evening hours, and therefore that the proposed action would actually result in a further decline in profits.

Two additional problems involve the downtown Marston store. First, the owner implicitly assumes that the store has increased its profits as a result of eliminating evening operating hours and stocking only newer movies. Yet the owner provides no evidence to support this assumption. One cannot infer from the mere fact that the store's patrons have not complained that the store's business, and in turn profits, have increased as a result of these changes.

A second problem with Marston is that the owner assumes this store is representative of Armchair outlets generally. It is entirely possible that, due to its downtown location, the Marston store attracts a daytime clientele more interested in new movies, whereas other outlets depend on an evening clientele with different or more diverse tastes in movies. Or perhaps downtown Marston lacks competing video stores or movie theaters, whereas Armchair's other stores are located in areas with many competitors. Without accounting for such possibilities, the owner cannot convince me that the profits of other Armchair outlets would increase by following Marston's example.

In conclusion, the argument is unconvincing as it stands. To strengthen it the owner must provide strong evidence that the cost savings of the proposed course of action would outweigh any loss in revenue, and that no other viable means of boosting its profits is available to Armchair. To better evaluate the argument we would need information enabling us to compare the Marston store's clientele and competition with that of other Armchair stores. We would also need more information about Marston's profitability before and after it implemented the new policies.

Argument:
How to increase profitability at **ABC Cereal Company**

This ABC Cereal Company memo concludes that to increase its profitability ABC must lower both the sugar content and price of its Better Bran (BB) cereal. To justify this conclusion the memo cites the fact that sales of BB have declined in recent years. The memo attributes this decline to a concern among most consumers about the amount of sugar in their cereals, and to the 5% increase in the price of BB during each of the last three years. The memo is unconvincing for several reasons.

First, the mere fact that most consumers are concerned about sugar in cereal amounts to scant evidence that the decline in BB sales is due to that concern. The level of concern, or the amount of sugar in BB, might not be sufficiently high to cause consumers to stop buying BB cereal on either basis. Moreover, unless the level of concern has grown during recent years I cannot take seriously the claim that declining BB sales in recent years is due to that concern—rather than to some other event or trend.

Secondly, assuming that the 5% price increases have contributed to the decline in BB sales, it would be premature to conclude that profits from BB sales have also declined as a result. Perhaps the additional revenue from the price increases more than offset the decline in revenue due to the diminishing number of units sold. Thus, ABC cannot convince me on the basis of the price increases and the sales decline that lowering BB's price would serve to improve ABC's overall profitability.

Thirdly, the memo's recommendation rests on the dubious assumption that the proposed actions are the only two means of increasing ABC's overall profitability. In all likelihood, ABC's profits are a function not only of how many boxes of BB it sells but also of its costs and its revenue from other products. Perhaps ABC can improve its profits by other means—such as expanding its cereal line, marketing BB to health-conscious consumers and raising the price of BB, or cutting costs in other areas. For that matter, if other cereal companies raise their prices, consumers might begin to consider BB a bargain at its current price—or perhaps even at a somewhat higher price. In short, since the memo has not ruled out all other possible scenarios that might serve to improve ABC's overall profitability I simply cannot take the memo's recommendation seriously.

Finally, even in the unlikely event that one of the two proposed changes is necessary to increase ABC's overall profitability, the memo's assertion that both changes are necessary might nevertheless be unwarranted. Perhaps only one of the two changes will suffice. Since the memo ignores this possibility the strength of its recommendation remains questionable at best.

In sum, ABC might be ill advised to follow the memo's advice. To strengthen the argument that ABC must lower BB's price and sugar content to improve profitability, ABC's planners must provide clear evidence that consumer concern about sugar in cereals is the primary reason for declining BB sales, and that this decline has diminished BB's profitability. To better assess ABC's claim that the proposed course of action is necessary to improve ABC's profitability, I would need to know what other alternatives, if any, are available to ABC for cutting costs and for increasing revenue.

Argument:
Finding new jobs for laid-off **XYZ company** employees

This XYZ company memo recommends that XYZ continue to use Delany instead of Walsh as its personnel service for helping laid-off XYZ employees find new jobs. To support this recommendation the memo points out that 8 years ago, when XYZ was using Walsh, only half of XYZ's laid-off workers found new jobs within a year. The memo also points out that last year XYZ employees using Delany's services found jobs much more quickly than those who did not, and that the average Delany client found a job in six months, compared to nine months for the average Walsh client. The memo also mentions that Delany has more branch offices and a larger staff than Walsh. I find the memo's argument unconvincing for several reasons.

To begin with, Walsh's prior rate of placing laid-off XYZ employees is not necessarily a reliable indicator of what that rate would be now. Perhaps the placement rate 8 years ago was due to a general economic downturn or some other factor beyond Walsh's control. For that matter, perhaps the rate was relatively high among all placement services during that time period. In short, without ruling out other possible reasons for Walsh's ostensibly low placement rate 8 years ago, and without convincing me that this rate was low to begin with, the memo's author cannot convince me on the basis of XYZ's past experience with Walsh that XYZ should favor Delany over Walsh.

The memo also makes two hasty assumptions about the benefits of Delany's services last year. One such assumption is that these services were in fact responsible for helping the laid-off XYZ employees who used those services find jobs more quickly. It is entirely possible that the comparative success of this group was due instead to their other aggressive job-seeking efforts, which might even have included using Walsh's services—in addition to Delany's. Also, the memo unfairly equates the speed with which one finds a job with job-seeking success. Common sense informs me that the effectiveness of a job search depends not only on how quickly one finds a job, but also on compensation, benefits, location, and type of work.

Furthermore, the difference in the two firms' overall placement time last year does not necessarily indicate that Delany would be the better choice to serve XYZ's laid-off employees. These employees might have particular skills or needs that are not representative of the two firms' clients in general. Besides, a single year's placement statistics hardly suffices to draw any firm conclusions. Last year might have been exceptional—perhaps due to some unusual event that is unlikely to reoccur, such as a major employer's move to an area that Delany serves, or out of an area that Walsh serves.

Finally, the fact that Delany has more branch offices and a larger staff than Walsh proves nothing in itself about which firm would be more effective in finding jobs for laid-off XYZ employees. Perhaps these employees generally look for jobs in geographic areas or industries outside of Delany's domain. Or perhaps the number of Delany staff members per office is actually lower than at Walsh. Either scenario, if true, would cast serious doubt on the memo's conclusion that XYZ should favor Delany over Walsh.

In sum, as it stands the recommendation is not well supported. To bolster it the memo's author must provide better evidence—perhaps from XYZ's records—that Delany's services have consistently helped laid-off XYZ employees find jobs. Instead of attempting to convince me that Walsh provided a disservice to XYZ 8 years ago, the author should provide better evidence that Walsh's services would be inferior to Delany's in the foreseeable future. Accordingly, to better assess the recommendation it would be helpful to compare the number of staff members per office at the two firms, and the level of experience of those staff members. It would also be useful to know what sorts of skills laid-off XYZ employees possess, and which firm, Delany or Walsh, serves industries and areas with more openings for people with those skills.

Argument:
Cheating at **Groveton College**

In this editorial, the author concludes that colleges should adopt an honor code for detecting academic cheating. To support this conclusion the author points out that the first year after switching from a monitoring system to an honor system the annual number of reported cheating incidents at Groveton College decreased from 30 to 21, and that five years later the number was only 14. The author also cites a survey in which most students indicated they would be less likely to cheat under an honor system than if they are closely monitored. This argument is unconvincing for several reasons.

First and foremost, the argument relies on the assumptions that Groveton students are just as capable of detecting cheating as faculty monitors, and that these students are just as likely to report cheating whenever they observe it. However, without evidence to substantiate these assumptions one cannot reasonably conclude that the honor code has in fact resulted in a decline in the incidence of cheating at Groveton. Besides, common sense tells me that these assumptions are dubious at best; an impartial faculty observer is more likely to detect and report cheating than a preoccupied student under peer pressure not to report cheating among classmates.

The argument also assumes that during the five-year period all other conditions possibly affecting the reported incidence of cheating at Groveton remained unchanged. Such conditions include the number of Groveton students and the overall integrity of the student body. After five years it is entirely possible that these conditions have changed, and that the reported decrease in cheating is attributable to one or more such changes. Thus, without ruling out such alternative explanations for the reported decrease, the author cannot convince me that the honor code has in fact contributed to a decline in the incidence of cheating at Groveton.

The author's recommendation that other colleges follow Groveton's example depends on the additional assumption that Groveton is typical in ways relevant to the incidence of cheating. However, this is not necessarily the case. For instance, perhaps Groveton students are more or less likely to report cheating, or to cheat under an honor system, than typical college students. Lacking evidence that Groveton students are typical in these respects, the argument is indefensible.

Finally, the survey that the author cites might be unreliable in any of three respects. First, the author fails to assure us that the survey's respondents are representative of all college students. Second, the survey results depend on the honesty and integrity of the respondents. Third, hypothetical predictions about one's future behavior are inherently less reliable than reports of proven behavior. Lacking evidence that the survey is reliable, the author cannot reasonably rely on the survey in recommending that other colleges adopt an honor code.

In conclusion, to persuade me that other colleges should adopt an honor code in order to reduce cheating, the author must supply clear evidence that cheating at Groveton in fact decreased after the honor code was instituted there, and that it is this code that was responsible for the decrease. Finally, to better assess the usefulness of the survey I would need specific information about the survey's sampling methodology.

Answers to Arguments Based On Dubious Statistical Reports or Surveys

This section contains sample essay responses to several Argument statements from the official GRE essay pool. Each of these Argument statements relies partly on one of the following:

1. A potentially unrepresentative statistical sample

2. A potentially unreliable poll, survey, study, or report

Before you read these essays, be sure to review the discussion about these two types of reasoning problems on pages 31–33.

> **NOTE:** Each essay addresses other major reasoning problems as well, but it is included only in this section of Part 3.

Argument:
The recycling habits of **West Egg**'s residents

In this memo West Egg's mayor reasons that West Egg's residents are now strongly committed to recycling, and projects that the city's landfill will not be filled to capacity until considerably later than anticipated two years ago. To support this projection the mayor cites (1) a twofold increase in aluminum and paper recycling by West Egg residents over the last two years, (2) an impending twofold increase in charges for trash pickup, and (3) a recent survey in which 90% of respondents indicated that they intend to do more recycling in the future. For several reasons, I am not convinced that the mayor's projection is accurate.

To begin with, in all likelihood aluminum and paper account for only some of the materials West Egg's residents can recycle. Perhaps recycling of other recyclable materials—such as plastic and glass—has declined to the point that the total amount of recycled materials has also declined. If so, then the mayor could hardly justify the claim that West Egg's residents are becoming more committed to recycling.

Another problem with the argument is that an increase in the amount of recycled materials does not necessarily indicate a decrease in the total amount of trash deposited in the city's landfill. Admittedly, if West Egg residents previously disposed of certain recyclable materials that they now recycle instead, then this shift from disposal to recycling would serve to reduce the amount of trash going to the landfill. However, the mayor provides no evidence of such a shift.

Moreover, the argument overlooks the strong possibility that the recycling habits of West Egg residents are not the only factor affecting how quickly the landfill will reach capacity. Other such factors might include population and demographic shifts, the habits of people from outside West Egg whose trash also feeds the landfill, and the availability of alternative disposal methods such as burning. Thus, regardless of the recycling efforts of West Egg residents the landfill might nevertheless reach full capacity by the date originally forecast.

Yet another problem with the argument involves the mayor's implicit claim that increased charges for trash pickup will serve to slow the rate at which the landfill is reaching capacity. This claim relies on the unlikely assumption that West Egg residents have the option of recycling—or disposing in some other way—much of what they would otherwise send to the landfill. However, it is likely these residents have no practical choice but to send some refuse to the landfill. The greater the amount, the less likely higher trash charges would have any effect on how quickly the landfill reaches capacity.

Finally, the mayor provides no evidence that the survey's respondents are representative of the overall group of people whose trash goes to the city's landfill. Lacking such evidence, it is entirely possible that people inclined to recycle were more willing to respond to the survey than other people were. In short, without better evidence that the survey is statistically reliable the mayor cannot rely on it to draw any firm conclusions about the overall recycling commitment of West Egg residents—let alone about how quickly the landfill will reach capacity.

In sum, the mayor's projection is simply not credible, at least based on the memo. Rather than relying solely on questionable recycling statistics, the mayor should provide direct evidence that the amount of trash going to the landfill is declining and that this trend will not reverse itself anytime soon. To better assess the accuracy of the mayor's projection it would be useful to know who besides West Egg residents contributes trash to the landfill, and whether the amount of trash those people contribute is declining or is likely to decline in the near future.

Argument:
Investing in **Old Dairy** stock

This excerpt from an investment newsletter cites a recent study in which 80% of respondents indicated a desire to reduce their consumption of high-fat and high-cholesterol foods, then points out that food stores are well stocked with low-fat food products. Based on this evidence the newsletter predicts a significant decline in sales and profits for Old Dairy (OD), a producer of dairy products high in fat and cholesterol, and advises investors not to own OD stock. I find this advice specious, on several grounds.

First, the excerpt fails to assure me that the survey results accurately reflect the desires of most consumers, or that the results accurately predict consumer behavior. Without evidence that the respondents' desires are representative of those of the overall population where OD products are sold, it is hasty to draw any conclusions about future food buying habits from the survey. Moreover, common sense informs me that consumers do not necessarily make food-purchase decisions in strict accordance with their expressed desires. Thus, as it stands the statistic that the newsletter cites amounts to scant evidence that OD sales and profits will decline in the future.

Secondly, the fact that low-fat foods are in abundant supply in food stores does not necessarily indicate an increasing demand for low-fat dairy products or a diminishing demand for high-fat dairy products. Absent evidence to the contrary, it is quite possible that consumers are buying other types of low-fat foods but are still demanding high fat in their dairy products. For that matter, it is entirely possible that food stores are well stocked with low-fat foods because actual demand has not met the demand anticipated by the stores.

Thirdly, even assuming an indisputable consumer trend toward purchasing more low-fat dairy products and fewer high-fat dairy products, the newsletter concludes too hastily that OD profits will decline as a result. OD can always raise the price of its dairy products to offset declining sales, and given a sufficient demand OD might still turn a profit, despite the general consumer trend. Besides, profit is a function of not just revenue but also expenses. Perhaps OD expenses will decline by a greater amount than its revenue; if so, then OD profits will increase despite falling revenues.

In sum, without additional information prudent investors should refrain from following the newsletter's advice. To better assess the soundness of this advice it would be helpful to know the following: (1) the demographic profile of the survey's respondents; (2) the extent to which consumer desires regarding food intake accord with their subsequent behavior; (3) the extent of OD loyalty among its regular retail customers who might continue to prefer OD products over low-fat products even at higher prices; and (4) the extent to which OD might be able to reduce expenses to offset any revenue loss resulting from diminishing sales of OD products.

Argument:
Breakfast for students in the **Mylar school district**

In this memo, the superintendent of the Mylar school district concludes that by providing breakfast to all its students the district would reduce tardiness and absenteeism as well as improve the overall academic performance of its students. To support this conclusion the superintendent points out that during a 6-month trial program involving 100 students ranging in age from 5 to 12, these students were less likely to be tardy or absent than other students. The superintendent also cites the well-known fact that eating healthful breakfasts on a regular basis improves academic performance. The superintendent's argument is problematic in several respects, rendering the argument unconvincing as it stands.

The argument's chief problem is that it relies on numerous unsubstantiated assumptions about the 6-month study. One such assumption is that the participants' regular and punctual attendance was attributable to the fact that breakfasts were provided. Yet logic and common sense inform me that the results might have been due instead to one or more other factors. Perhaps these particular students were compelled to show up punctually and regularly for some other reason. Perhaps the 100 participants were comparatively reliable and disciplined children who are less likely in any event to be late for school. Or perhaps the participants are relatively healthy and therefore less likely to be absent from school than the average student. Moreover, it is uncertain whether the program's participants even ate the breakfasts that the trial program provided. In short, without considering and ruling out alternative explanations for the study's results, the superintendent cannot justifiably conclude that the results are due to the fact that breakfasts were provided to participating students.

Even if the participants' punctual and regular attendance was due to the breakfasts provided to them, the statistical reliability of the trial program's results is questionable. The number of participants, 100, might constitute an insufficiently small sample to draw any reliable conclusions about how district students 5-12 years of age would behave under similar conditions—as a group. The larger this group compared to the sample of 100 participants, the less reliable the study's results. Also, the sample might be unrepresentative of district students as a group. For example, perhaps the 100 participants happened to be children who eat small dinners and are therefore hungry for breakfast.

Even if the 100 participants are statistically representative of district students who are 5-12 years of age, one cannot infer that older, secondary school students would behave similarly under similar conditions. Yet by concluding that the district should implement the program for its secondary-school students as well, the superintendent seems to assume without supporting evidence that this is the case. In short, lacking assurances that the 100 participants are statistically representative of all district students, the superintendent cannot draw any reliable conclusions based on the study.

Aside from the problems involving the 6-month study, the superintendent's conclusion that the overall academic performance of district students would improve under the proposed program is unwarranted. By relying on the fact that eating healthful breakfasts on a regular basis improves academic performance, the superintendent assumes that the district's breakfasts would be healthful and that students would eat them on a regular basis. Yet no evidence is offered to substantiate these crucial assumptions. It is entirely possible that the district's breakfasts would not be sufficiently healthful, or that district students would not eat these breakfasts regularly. In fact, the superintendent has not shown either that the trial program's participants or that the broader population of district students would eat healthful breakfasts, or any breakfast at all, under any circumstances.

In conclusion, the superintendent's argument is specious. To bolster it she must provide clear evidence that the 100 participants in the trial program actually attended school regularly and punctually because of the breakfasts provided, and that these 100 students are statistically representative not only of other 5-12 year-olds but of older students as well—as a group. Finally, to better evaluate the claim that the program would improve academic performance I would need more information about the healthfulness of the breakfasts provided under the proposed program.

Argument:
Rates of **charitable** donations

In this argument the author cites a poll showing that the amount of charitable donations increased last year, but that the increase to educational institutions was far less than to either religious or environmental groups. Based on this evidence the author concludes that more people are willing and able to make charitable donations, but that education is not a priority for most people. The author also concludes that the discrepancy among donation rates is the result of a general perception that educational institutions are in less need of money than other institutions are. This argument depends on several unsubstantiated assumptions and is therefore unpersuasive as it stands.

First of all, the author's conclusions about people's willingness to donate to the three types of charities listed depend on the assumption that the poll results are statistically reliable. Yet, the author offers no evidence to substantiate this assumption. The author must show that the 200 charitable organizations polled constitute a sufficiently large sample of religious, environmental, and educational charities, and that this sample is representative of all such charities. Otherwise, the author cannot confidently draw any general conclusions about the willingness of people to donate to these three types of institutions, or about general perceptions regarding the needs of any such institutions.

Similarly, the author's sweeping claim that "more people are willing and able to give money to charities" depends on the assumption that the poll results are sufficiently representative of charitable giving in general. Yet, the author offers no evidence to substantiate this assumption. The author must show that the 25% total increase in the rate of donations to the three types of institutions polled is representative of the increase in donations to all types of charities. The author must also show that the total number of donors actually increased last year; as it stands the argument leaves open the possibility that the total number of donors decreased last year while the average amount given by each donor increased. Absent evidence to support these assumptions, the author's broad conclusion that "more people are willing and able" to make charitable donations is dubious at best.

Additionally, the author provides no evidence whatsoever for the claim that educational institutions are perceived as less needy than other institutions, or that this perception explains the lower donation rate to educational institutions. Lacking such evidence, there are many other possible explanations for the discrepancy in donation rates. Perhaps people's perception is that educational institutions are more likely than the other types to squander or misuse donated money; or perhaps most donors are simply more interested in advocating religions or environmental protection than in subsidizing education. For that matter, perhaps among all charitable organizations educational institutions ranked third last year in terms of gifts received—bettered only by religious and environmental charities. Such evidence would serve to undermine the author's claim that funding for education is "not a priority for most people."

In conclusion, the argument is indefensible as it stands. To strengthen it the author must assure me that the poll results accurately reflect donation rates not only to all religious, environmental, and educational institutions but also to the broader group of all charitable institutions. The author must also provide clear evidence for the claimed perception about the need of educational institutions and that this perception, and not some other factor, explains the comparatively low donation rate to these institutions.

Argument:
Violent **teenage crime** and television programming

This editorial concludes that increasingly violent television programming during prime time in the country of Alta is responsible for the steady increase in violent crime among Alta's teenagers. To support this conclusion the editorial cites various statistical studies about violence on television. However, this evidence provides little credible support for the editorial's conclusion.

To begin with, the editorial observes a correlation between violence on television and violent teenage crime, then concludes that the former is the cause of the latter. However, the editorial fails to rule out other possible explanations for the rise in violent crime among teenagers. For example, since the 1950s it is entirely possible that Alta has seen a large growth in its population, or a deterioration of its juvenile justice system or economy. Any of these factors, or other social, political or economic factors, might lead to an increase in violent crime among teenagers. Without ruling out all other such factors it is unfair to conclude that television programs are responsible for this increase.

Next, the editorial cites studies showing that young children exposed to violent images are more likely to behave violently in the home. This evidence would support the editorial's conclusion only if teenagers and younger children react similarly to television. However, common sense tells me that young children are more likely than teenagers to mimic observed behavior. Moreover, the editorial fails to provide any evidence that this sort of mimicry ultimately develops into violent criminal behavior.

The editorial then cites the Observer survey in which "90% of the respondents were parents" who would prefer less violent television programming during prime time. However, the editorial fails to provide any information about the survey population; therefore it is impossible to determine whether the survey results apply generally to the Alta population. In addition, we are not informed how many parents were surveyed but did not respond. The greater this number, the less reliable the survey. Thus, as it stands the Observer study is statistically unreliable and lends no credible support to the editorial's conclusion.

Aside from the survey's statistical unreliability, in citing the survey the editorial assumes that parents' preferences about television programming have some bearing on whether their teenage children will commit violent crimes. However, the editorial provides no evidence to link one with the other. Moreover, the survey is relevant only to the extent that teenagers watch television during prime time. However, the editorial provides no evidence about this extent.

In conclusion, the editorial is unconvincing as it stands. To strengthen the argument, the editorial's author must rule out all other possible factors contributing to the rise in teenage violence. The author must also show that teenagers react to violent television images similarly to how younger children react to the same images, and that Alta teenagers watch a significant amount of television programming during prime time. In order to better evaluate the argument, we would need more information about the Observer survey population, and about the percentage of those surveyed who responded.

Argument:
Exercise and **longevity**

This editorial concludes that to maximize longevity people should engage in vigorous outdoor exercise on a daily basis. To support this conclusion the editorial cites a 20-year study of 500 middle-aged men in which, among subjects responding to an annual survey, those who followed this regimen lived longer, on average, than those who exercised mildly once or twice per week. A careful analysis of the study reveals several problems with the editorial's argument.

First of all, the excerpt provides no information about the number of respondents or their occupational or residential profiles. The fewer respondents, the less reliable the study's results. Also, the narrower the spectrum of occupations and geographic areas represented among respondents, the more likely that one of these two phenomena, rather than exercise, played the key role in the subjects' longevity. Moreover, once a subject dies it would be impossible for that subject to respond to the annual survey. Unless a sufficient number of subjects from diverse geographic areas and occupations responded accurately and on a regular basis, and unless accurate responses were made on behalf of deceased subjects, I simply cannot accept the editorial's conclusion.

Secondly, a 20-year time span might not be sufficient to gauge the longevity of the study's subjects; that is, until a significant number of subjects have died, it is impossible to determine with certainty the effect of exercise on the subjects' longevity as a group. Lacking information about how many deaths among the 500 subjects were reported by the end of the study, it is impossible to draw any reliable conclusion about the relationship between exercise and longevity.

Thirdly, the editorial fails to indicate how many or what percentage of the respondents engaged in vigorous outdoor exercise on a daily basis. Lacking this information, it is entirely possible that only a few subjects matched this profile and that those few subjects happened to live to an old age—due to some factor other than exercise habits. The longevity of a small number of respondents is scant evidence upon which to draw any broad conclusions about the effect of exercise on longevity.

Finally, even if we accept the reliability of the study as it relates to men, the study does not support the editorial's broad conclusion that doctors should recommend to all patients vigorous daily outdoor exercise. Since the study excluded women, it is entirely possible that a different exercise regime would maximize female longevity.

In sum, the evidence cited in this excerpt does not permit any reliable inference about the effect of exercise on longevity. To better assess the study's reliability I would need more information about the number of respondents and the number of deaths among them by the end of the 20-year period. I would also need information about the occupational and residential history of each respondent. To strengthen the argument the editorial should either limit its conclusion to men or provide evidence that its recommended exercise regimen also maximizes longevity for women.

Argument:
Garbage sites and the health of nearby residents

The Trash-Site Safety Council concludes here that there is no public-health reason to restrict the size of trash sites or their proximity to homes. The Council cites its recent statewide study involving five sites and 300 people; in the study the Council observed only a small correlation between the residents' proximity to a trash site and unexplained rashes, and only a "slightly higher incidence" of rashes among people living near larger sites. The study suffers from certain statistical and other problems, which render the Council's argument based upon it unpersuasive.

First, the Council has not convinced me that the five sites in the survey are representative of trash sites in general throughout the state—in terms of their impact on the health of nearby residents. Admittedly, the study was a "statewide" one. Nevertheless, it is entirely possible that the five sites studied are characterized by certain environmental conditions that are not typical of most sites in the state and that render nearby residents either more or less susceptible to rashes and other health problems.

Secondly, the 300 people in the study are not necessarily representative of the state's general population—in terms of their susceptibility to health problems. For example, perhaps nearly all of these people are adults, while most of the health problems associated with trash sites occur among children. Or perhaps preventative health-care programs in these particular communities are unusually effective in preventing health problems. In short, lacking evidence that these 300 people are typical in terms of their vulnerability to health problems the Council cannot convince me that no statewide trash-site regulations are needed.

Thirdly, the Council's conclusion that the five sites studied pose no serious health hazards to nearby residents seems premature. Common sense informs me that a serious health problem might become apparent only after a long period of exposure to the environmental cause of the problem. The Council fails to take into account the length of time these residents have been exposed to the conditions created by the trash sites; and in any event, one "recent" study amounts to scant evidence that the sites pose no significant long-term public-health hazards.

In sum, the Council's argument is unconvincing as it stands. To strengthen it the Council must provide better evidence that the environmental conditions at the five sites studied represent conditions at trash sites throughout the state, and that the 300 people studied are representative of state residents generally in terms of vulnerability to health problems. To better assess the argument I would need more information comparing the health of the 300 people studied before and after continual exposure to the environmental conditions associated with the trash sites. I would also need to know the length of the study to determine whether it adequately accounted for latent health problems.

Argument:
The reading habits of **Leeville citizens**

This argument concludes that in a certain study about reading habits Leeville citizens misrepresented their true reading habits. To justify this conclusion, the argument points out an apparent discrepancy between their representations and the results of a follow-up study showing that a different type of book is the one most frequently checked out from Leeville's public libraries. However, the argument fails to account for several other possible explanations for this apparent discrepancy.

First of all, the argument does not indicate how much time passed between the two studies. During a sufficiently long interim period the demographic makeup of Leeville might have changed, or the reading habits of the first study's respondents might have changed. In other words, the longer the time between studies the less reliable the conclusion that respondents in the first study misrepresented their reading habits.

Secondly, the argument fails to account for the possibility that the respondents in the first study constitute a different population than public library patrons. Admittedly, both groups are comprised of Leeville citizens. However, it is entirely possible that more highly educated citizens who frequent the University library rather than public libraries, or who purchase books rather than borrow them, are the ones who responded to the first study.

Thirdly, the argument fails to account for the possibility that literary classics, the book type that the first study's respondents indicated they preferred, are not readily available at Leeville's public libraries—or at least not as readily available as mystery novels. Experience informs me that this is likely, because mystery novels are in greater supply and are cheaper for libraries to acquire than literary classics. If this is the case, it provides an alternative explanation for the fact that more mystery novels than literary classics are checked out from Leeville's public libraries.

Finally, the reliability of the first study rests on its statistical integrity. The argument fails to indicate what portion of the people surveyed actually responded; the smaller this portion, the less reliable the results. Nor does the argument indicate how many people were surveyed, or whether the sample was representative of Leeville's general population. Again, the smaller the sample, the less reliable the results.

In conclusion, the assertion that respondents in the first study misrepresented their reading habits is untenable, in light of a variety of alternative explanations for the apparent discrepancy between the two studies. To strengthen the argument, its proponent must show that the respondents in the first study are representative of Leeville citizens generally, and that both groups are equally likely to check out books from Leeville's public libraries. To better evaluate the argument, we would need to know the length of time between the two studies, and whether any significant demographic changes occurred during this time. We would also need to know the availability of literary classics compared to mystery novels at Leeville's public libraries.

Argument:
Should **Grove College** adopt a coeducational policy?

In this memo, Grove College's administration recommends preserving its tradition of admitting only female students. The administration admits that most faculty members are in favor of a co-educational policy as a means of encouraging more students to apply to Grove. But the administration defends its recommendation by citing a student government survey in which 80% of student respondents and more than 50% of alumni respondents reported that they favor the status quo. The administration reasons that preserving the status quo would improve student morale and help ensure continued alumni donations to Grove. This argument is flawed in several critical respects.

First, the memo provides no evidence that the results of either of the two surveys are statistically reliable. For example, suppose newer students tend to be content with the all-female policy while students who have attended Grove for a longer time would prefer a co-educational policy. If a disproportionate number of the survey's respondents were newer students, then the survey results would distort the student body's opinion as a group. With respect to the alumni survey, perhaps fewer alumni who donate substantial sums to Grove responded to the survey than other alumni did. If so, then the survey results would distort the comparison between the total amount of future donations under the two scenarios. Besides, the memo provides no information about what percentage of Grove's students and alumni responded to the surveys; the lower the percentages, the less reliable the results of the surveys.

Secondly, the administration hastily assumes that Grove's alumni as a group would be less inclined to donate money merely if Grove begins admitting male students. This aspect of Grove's admission policy is only one of many factors that might affect alumni donations. For example, since Grove's faculty are generally in favor of changing the policy, perhaps the change would improve faculty morale and therefore the quality of instruction, in turn having a positive impact on alumni donations. And, if the particular alumni who are in a position to make the largest contributions recognize faculty morale as important, an increase in donations by these individuals might very well offset a decline in smaller donations by other alumni.

Finally, the administration's argument that student morale would improve under the status quo is logically unsound in two respects. First, the administration provides no reason why morale would improve, as opposed to remaining at its current level, if the status quo is simply maintained. Second, the administration cannot logically determine how the morale of the student body would be affected under a co-educational policy until it implements that policy and takes into account the morale of the new male students along with that of all female students.

In sum, the administration has failed to convince me that maintaining Grove's all-female policy would be more likely to improve student morale and help ensure continued alumni donations than moving to a co-educational policy. To better assess the argument I would need detailed information about the two surveys to determine whether the respondents as groups were representative of their respective populations. To bolster its recommendation the administration must provide better evidence— perhaps by way of a reliable alumni survey that takes into account respondents' financial status and history of donations—that prospective donor alumni would be strongly opposed to a co-educational policy and would be less inclined to donate money were Grove to implement such a policy.

Argument:
Sleep and **academic performance**

This letter concludes that the academic performance of local high school students would improve if the daily school schedule were to begin and end one hour later. To support this recommendation the letter's author cites two studies, one showing that adolescents generally do not get enough sleep, the other showing that many local high school students are dissatisfied with their academic performance. The recommendation relies on a series of unsubstantiated assumptions about the habits of high school students and about the studies themselves. As a result, the letter is not convincing.

First of all, the letter's recommendation depends on the doubtful assumption that by beginning classes one hour later students will sleep one hour longer each night. Experience tells us, however, that this will not necessarily be the case. Just as likely, students will adjust to the new schedule by falling asleep one hour later. Moreover, by staying up one hour later at night students might very well engage in the sort of late-night social or even delinquent activities that would disrupt their productivity at school.

Secondly, the letter's conclusion relies on the assumption that one additional hour of sleep would in fact result in improved academic performance. While this might be the case, the letter provides no evidence to substantiate this assumption. It is entirely possible that one hour of additional sleep would not suffice. Moreover, the letter provides no evidence that the students who are dissatisfied with their academic performance are also the ones who would benefit from the new schedule. It is entirely possible that these particular students already sleep longer than most other students, or that their academic performance is already optimal. Conversely, it is entirely possible that those students whose academic performance could stand the greatest improvement would be unmotivated to become better students regardless of how much they sleep each night.

A final problem with the argument involves the two studies themselves. The letter provides no information about how either study was conducted. Without knowing whether the sample of adolescents studied was representative of the overall high school population in the city, it is impossible to confidently apply the studies' results to that population. Moreover, we are not informed about the size of the sample in either study; the smaller the sample, the less reliable the study's conclusion.

In conclusion, this letter's recommendation for beginning and ending the high school day one hour later is not well justified. To strengthen the argument, the author must provide clear evidence that adjusting the schedule will in fact result in the students' sleeping longer each night, and that this additional sleep will in fact improve their academic performance. To better assess the author's recommendation, we would need more information about the sampling method used in the two studies.

Argument:
The effectiveness of **pain medication**

This argument concludes that the pain medication kappa opioids (KO) should be prescribed for women but not for men. To support this conclusion the speaker cites a recent study involving 28 men and 20 women who took KO when having wisdom teeth removed; according to these patients' reports, the women felt less pain than the men, and for the women the easing of pain lasted longer. The argument is flawed in several important respects.

One problem with the argument is that since the study involved only 48 people it is impossible to confidently draw any conclusions about the general population from it. Specifically, the argument overlooks other possible reasons why these particular women reported less pain than the men did. The women in the study might have a higher-than-average pain threshold; conversely, the men in the study might have a lower-than-average pain threshold. Or perhaps this group of women are less prone to complain about pain than this group of men—due to their unusually stoical nature or their experience with painful medical procedures.

Another problem with the argument is that it overlooks other factors that might have contributed to the amount of pain these patients experienced. Perhaps the women's wisdom teeth were not as impacted as the men's teeth generally, so that for the women the surgery was not as invasive and painful. Perhaps some of the women took other medications as well to help relieve the pain. For that matter, some of the men might have taken certain foods or medications that counteracted the effects of KO. In short, unless the experiment was conducted in a controlled environment in which all factors were the same for the men as for the women, it is impossible to draw any firm conclusions about the comparative effectiveness of KO for the two sexes.

Even if KO is more effective for women than for men, the argument's conclusion that men should take another pain medication instead is unwarranted. It is entirely possible that KO is still the most effective pain medication for men. Without comparing the effectiveness of KO to that of other pain medications, the speaker simply cannot justify his recommendation that men avoid KO.

In sum, the argument has not convinced me that men should take a medication other than KO for pain. To strengthen the argument the speaker must assure me that the men and women in the study are representative of men and women generally— in terms of their dental profile, experience in handling pain, and willingness to recognize and report pain. The speaker must also assure me that the study was performed in a controlled environment where all other factors possibly affecting pain remained constant. To better assess the argument I would need to know how effective KO is compared to other medications in reducing pain for men.

Argument:
Dentists who advertise

This argument contends that dentists' advertisements should target male patients and should focus on assuaging distress about the pain associated with dental work. To support this assertion the argument cites statistics showing that three times more men than women faint while visiting dentists. The argument suffers from several logical problems, and is therefore unpersuasive.

To begin with, the argument depends on the assumption that men who faint while visiting the dentist do so because they are distressed about the sorts of factors that the proposed advertising aims to address. Yet the argument provides no evidence clearly establishing this causal relationship. It is equally likely that other factors are instead responsible for the fact that more men than women faint at the dentist's office. Perhaps on average men suffer from more painful dental problems than women, explaining why more men than women faint at dental offices. Without ruling out this and other alternative explanations, the speaker cannot convince me that any advertising technique will reduce either distress or fainting among male patients.

Another problem with the argument is that the speaker provides no evidence that the proposed advertising techniques will have the intended effect. Perhaps fewer men than women notice dental advertisements. Or perhaps the proposed advertising techniques will have the opposite effect—by calling attention to the very sorts of images that cause distress and fainting. The speaker must address these possibilities and rule them out before we can accept the recommendation.

Finally, the speaker's recommendation relies on two unsubstantiated assumptions about the statistics that the speaker cites. The first is that the patients contributing to these statistics are representative of all dental patients. It is entirely possible, for instance, that a disproportionate number of male patients contributed to the statistics, rendering them biased and therefore unreliable. The second unsubstantiated assumption is that the number of patients contributing to these statistics is large enough to be statistically significant. Unless the speaker can substantiate this assumption, he cannot justifiably rely on these statistics to draw any general inferences about dental patients.

In conclusion, the argument cannot be taken seriously as it stands. To strengthen it, the speaker must show why men become distressed and faint during visits to their dentists, and that the proposed advertising techniques would in fact achieve their intended result. To better evaluate the argument we would need more information about the statistics that the argument cites—specifically, how many patients contributed to these statistics and whether these patients are representative of dental patients in general.

Argument:
Jobs for **Hooper**'s social science majors

This article concludes that in order to help its new social science graduates find permanent jobs Hooper University should enhance its reputation in this field by adding courses and hiring eminent faculty. To support this claim the letter points out that more physical science than social-science students find permanent jobs within a year after graduation. The letter also cites a survey in which the former group of graduates attributed their job finding success to the prestige of Hooper's physical-science department, while the latter group attributed their job-finding success to their own initiative. However, careful scrutiny of the argument reveals various statistical and other logical problems, which render it unconvincing.

To begin with, the survey that the argument cites is potentially problematic in three respects. First, we are not informed whether the survey's respondents were representative of the overall population of recent Hooper graduates in these two fields. The smaller the sample, the greater the possibility for biased results, and the less reliable the survey. Second, the survey reflects the graduates' subjective "beliefs" about why they obtained jobs; yet it is entirely possible these beliefs are not in accord with the true reason why they obtained jobs. Third, we are informed that the survey involved "recent" Hooper graduates; however, if the only graduates surveyed were those from last year's class, then the survey results would be less reliable than if the survey embraced a wider range of graduating classes. The smaller the range the less reliable any general conclusions drawn from the survey.

Even assuming the statistics that the letter cites are reliable, the letter's claim that the proposed course of action will achieve its intended result assumes a sufficient job market for social-science graduates. However, it is entirely possible that the number of jobs for physical-science graduates greatly exceeds the number of jobs for social-science graduates, and that this is the reason for the disparity in job-finding success between the two groups. In fact, real-world observation suggests that this is a reasonable explanation for the disparity. Moreover, the letter fails to account for the possibility that the latter group of graduates are less likely than the former group to be interested in immediate employment—electing instead to pursue graduate-level study. Without accounting for these possibilities, the letter's author cannot justifiably conclude that the proposed course of action will boost the employment rate of new social-science graduates.

A third problem with the argument is that it unfairly infers that the proposed course of action is the only means of achieving the desired result. The letter's author overlooks other possible means of ensuring that social-science students find immediate employment—such as co-op programs, job seminars, and so forth. Without ruling out alternative means of achieving the same goal, the author cannot convince me that the proposed course of action is needed.

In conclusion, as it stands the argument is unconvincing. To strengthen it the author must provide strong evidence that the survey's respondents were statistically representative of all recent Hooper graduates in these two fields of study. The author must also rule out all other possible explanations for the disparity between job-finding success between the two groups of Hooper graduates. Finally, to better evaluate the argument I would need more information about the portion of graduates in each field pursuing immediate employment, and what alternative means are available to help ensure that Hooper's new social-science graduates find permanent employment.

Argument:
Mira Vista College's job-placement record

This letter recommends that in order to improve its job-placement record Mira Vista College should offer more business and computer courses and should hire more job counselors. To support this recommendation the author points out that at Green Mountain College 90 percent of last year's graduates had job offers, but that only 70 percent of Mira Vista seniors who reported that they planned to seek employment had jobs within three months after graduation, and only half of these graduates were employed in their major fields of study. This argument is problematic in several critical respects.

First, the author assumes that Green Mountain's comparatively strong job-placement record is due to the fact that it provides more business courses and job counselors than Mira Vista, rather than some other factor. But this need not be the case. Perhaps Green Mountain students are exceptionally bright or resourceful to begin with. Or perhaps the quality of instruction and job counseling at Green Mountain is exceptionally high. Moreover, perhaps Green Mountain provides more business courses and job counselors than Mira Vista simply because Green Mountain is a larger school with more students; if so, then the comparative numbers are not likely to have any bearing on job-placement success. In short, without ruling out other possible explanations for the difference between job-placement rates, the author cannot reasonably conclude that additional business courses and job counselors would enhance Mira Vista's job-placement record.

Another problem with the argument is that the statistics comparing job-placement rates might be distorted in one or more respects. First, the author fails to indicate the percentage of Green Mountain graduates who find employment in their major fields of study. Without this information it is impossible to assess the comparative success of the two colleges in helping their recent graduates find such employment. Second, the author ignores the possibility that the time parameters defining the two schools' job-placement rates differ. Mira Vista's record was determined only three months after graduation. It is entirely possible that Green Mountain's record was based on a longer period of time, thereby distorting the comparative success of the schools in helping their recent graduates find jobs.

The cited statistics about Mira Vista's job-placement record might be unreliable in other respects as well. These statistics were based only on data from Mira Vista seniors who reported to the college's job-placement center. The author overlooks the possibility that only a small portion of Mira Vista seniors reported to begin with. The author also ignores the possibility that many of these reporting students later changed their minds about seeking employment or were offered jobs but turned them down.

Without ruling out these possible scenarios, the author cannot reasonably rely on these statistics to support the claim that Mira Vista's job-placement record is comparatively poor and thus could be improved by Mira Vista's emulating Green Mountain.

In conclusion, the argument is unconvincing as it stands. To strengthen it the author must show that additional business courses and job counselors would in fact improve Mira Vista's job-placement rate, and that the comparison between the job-placement rates at the two schools is fair. Finally, the author provides no evidence whatsoever to support his recommendation for providing more computer courses; to justify this claim the author must provide supporting evidence.

Answers to Arguments That Ignore Possible Changes Over Time

This section contains sample essay responses to several Argument statements from the official GRE essay pool. Each of these Argument statements relies partly on the unwarranted assumption that conditions or circumstances at the present time are not significantly different than at some other time, either past or future—at least in ways that are relevant to the Argument statement.

Before you read these essays, be sure to review the discussion about this type of reasoning problem on pages 33–34.

> **NOTE:** Each essay addresses other major reasoning problems as well, but it is included only in this section of Part 3.

Argument:
Speed limits in **Prunty County**

This editorial argues that a recent reduction in Prunty County's speed limit on its major roads, from 55 to 45 miles per hour (mph), has proven ineffective, and that the county should therefore restore its 55-mph speed limit and improve its roads. To support this argument the editorial's author points out that the accident rate has decreased only "slightly" since the speed limit was reduced. The author also points out that in nearby Butler County, which has maintained a 55-mph limit while widening and resurfacing its roads, the accident rate has decreased by 25% over the last 5 years. The editorial suffers from several problems, which render it unconvincing as it stands.

First of all, Prunty only "recently" reduced its speed limit, and only for "major" roads. Perhaps not enough time has passed to determine the effectiveness of this change in reducing the accident rate—especially if the new speed limit remains untested during a season of the year in which better driving conditions prevail. Additionally, the editorial refers only to the overall accident rate countywide. Perhaps the accident rate on the county's major roads has decreased while on minor roads not subject to the speed-limit reduction it has increased. Thus, lacking reliable evidence of the effectiveness of the new speed limit it is difficult to accept the conclusion that Prunty's safety effort has failed.

Secondly, the argument assumes that all other factors affecting highway accident rates have remained unchanged since the county lowered its speed limit. Yet the author fails to provide evidence to support this assumption. It is entirely possible that the lower speed limit does in fact serve to reduce the accident rate, while some other factor, such as unseasonably poor weather, reduced law enforcement measures, or even an influx of teenage drivers to the area, has served to increase the accident rate. Without considering and ruling out these and other factors that might have served to increase the accident rate since the speed limit was lowered, the author cannot justifiably conclude that this safety effort has failed.

Thirdly, the author unfairly implies that the higher speed limit in Butler County has not served to increase the incidence of road accidents in that county. It is entirely possible that the 55-mph speed limit actually serves to increase the accident rate on Butler's highways, but that other factors, such as stricter law enforcement measures or improved driver education, have served to decrease the accident rate to a greater extent. Without considering and ruling out these and other factors that might have served to decrease the accident rate in Butler County, the author cannot confidently recommend that Prunty County emulate Butler's speed-limit policy. Moreover, the cited statistic involves only "reported" accidents in Butler County. It is possible that an increasingly large percentage of accidents are going unreported in that county.

In conclusion, the editorial fails to convince me that Prunty County should emulate Butler County's road-safety measures. To strengthen the argument the author must account for all other factors that might influence the accident rate on roads in both counties. To better assess the impact of the new speed limit on road safety, I would need more statistical information about the accident rate on Prunty's major roads, collected over a longer time period. I would also need to know what percentage of road accidents in Butler County go unreported.

Argument:
Restricting moped rentals on **Balmer Island**

The author of this editorial recommends that to reduce accidents involving mopeds and pedestrians Balmer Island's city council should restrict moped rentals to 30 per day, down from 50, at each of the island's six rental outlets. To support this recommendation the author cites the fact that last year, when nearby Torseau Island's town council enforced similar measures, Torseau's rate of moped accidents fell by 50%. For several reasons, this evidence provides scant support for the author's recommendation.

To begin with, the author assumes that all other conditions in Balmer that might affect the rate of moped-pedestrian accidents will remain unchanged after the restrictions are enacted. However, with a restricted supply of rental mopeds people in Balmer might purchase mopeds instead. Also, the number of pedestrians might increase in the future; with more pedestrians, especially tourists, the risk of moped-pedestrian accidents would probably increase. For that matter, the number of rental outlets might increase to make up for the artificial supply restriction per outlet—a likely scenario assuming moped rental demand does not decline. Without considering and ruling out these and other possible changes that might contribute to a high incidence of moped-pedestrian accidents, the author cannot convince me that the proposed restrictions will necessarily have the desired effect.

Next, the author fails to consider other possible explanations for the 50% decline in Torseau's moped accident rate last year. Perhaps last year Torseau experienced unusually fair weather, during which moped accidents are less likely. Perhaps fewer tourists visited Torseau last year than during most years, thereby diminishing the demand for rental mopeds to below the allowed limits. Perhaps last year some of Torseau's moped rental outlets purchased new mopeds that are safer to drive. Or perhaps the restrictions were already in effect but were not enforced until last year. In any event, a decline in Torseau's moped accident rate during only one year is scarcely sufficient to draw any reliable conclusions about what might have caused the decline, or about what the accident rate will be in years ahead.

Additionally, in asserting that the same phenomenon that caused a 50% decline in moped accidents in Torseau would cause a similar decline in Balmer, the author relies on what might amount to an unfair analogy between Balmer and Torseau. Perhaps Balmer's ability to enforce moped-rental restrictions does not meet Torseau's ability; if not, then the mere enactment of similar restrictions in Balmer is no guarantee of a similar result. Or perhaps the demand for mopeds in Torseau is always greater than in Balmer. Specifically, if fewer than all available mopeds are currently rented per day from the average Balmer outlet, while in Torseau every available moped is rented each day, then the proposed restriction is likely to have less impact on the accident rate in Balmer than in Torseau.

Finally, the author provides no evidence that the same restrictions that served to reduce the incidence of all "moped accidents" by 50% would also serve to reduce the incidence of accidents involving "mopeds and pedestrians" by 50%. Lacking such evidence, it is entirely possible that the number of moped accidents not involving pedestrians decreased by a greater percentage, while the number of moped-pedestrian accidents decreased by a smaller percentage, or even increased. Since the author has not accounted for these possibilities, the editorial's recommendation cannot be taken seriously.

In conclusion, the recommendation is not well supported. To convince me that the proposed restriction would achieve the desired outcome, the author would have to assure me that no changes serving to increase Balmer's moped-pedestrian accident rate will occur in the foreseeable future. The author must also provide clear evidence that last year's decline in moped accidents in Torseau was attributable primarily to its moped rental restrictions rather than to one or more other factors. In order to better evaluate the recommendation, I would need more information comparing the supply of and demand for moped rentals on the two islands. I would also need to know the rate of moped-pedestrian accidents in Torseau both prior to and after the restrictions were enforced in Torseau.

Argument:
The market for new houses in **Steel City**

In this memo, the president of a new-home construction firm in Steel City concludes that the firm can increase its profits by focusing on building expensive homes, priced above $150,000, rather than lower-priced homes, and by hiring additional workers to increase the number of homes the firm can build. To support this recommendation the president cites the fact that Steel City's population has increased by more than 20% over the last five years and that family income in Steel City is rising much faster than the nationwide average. The president also points out that nationwide sales of homes priced above $150,000 are rising faster than sales of lower-priced homes. In several respects, this evidence provides little credible support for the president's recommendation.

First, by citing Steel City's population increase in order to argue for a step-up in home construction, the speaker relies on certain unsubstantiated demographic assumptions. One such assumption is that area demand for new housing will support additional home construction in the foreseeable future. Yet lacking firm evidence that this will be the case, it is entirely possible that the area's population will stabilize, or even decrease, and that the firm will have trouble selling its new homes at profitable levels. Another unfair demographic assumption is that Steel City residents will be interested in purchasing more expensive single-family homes. Perhaps the population increase has been and will continue to be the result of an influx of retired people who regardless of their income level are interested in smaller, less expensive homes and condominiums, or even rental housing.

Secondly, by citing Steel City's fast-rising family-income levels to support the recommendation, the speaker relies on other tenuous assumptions. One such assumption is that area residents interested in buying new homes can afford homes priced over $150,000. It is entirely possible that in Steel City family-income levels are rising rapidly primarily among current homeowners who would not be in the market for new homes in the foreseeable future, or among only a handful of the area's wealthiest residents. It is also possible that despite the rapid increase the average family income in Steel City is still low compared to national averages—too low to justify the president's recommendation to shift focus to more expensive homes.

Thirdly, even if this firm builds and can sell expensive homes according to the president's proposal, the firm's profits would not necessarily increase as a result. Hiring additional workers adds to the expense of building a home, and of course the cost of materials will no doubt increase with the value of the homes that are built. Furthermore, in all likelihood the firm would not be able to build a greater number of expensive homes than cheaper homes. Moreover, given the scant evidence that area residents could actually afford expensive homes, it is entirely possible that the firm would have trouble selling these homes quickly and at profitable price levels. In short, without a detailed cost-benefit analysis the president cannot convince me that the proposed course of action would increase this firm's profits.

In conclusion, the president's argument is unpersuasive. To strengthen it the president must convince me that in the foreseeable future Steel City residents will actually demand and be able to afford houses costing more than $150,000. To better evaluate the argument I would need more information about Steel City's demographic trends and about the income of area residents interested in buying new homes in the foreseeable future. I would also need a detailed analysis comparing the costs and revenues associated with the proposed course of action with the costs and revenues associated with the construction and sale of the firm's less expensive homes.

Argument:
The best location for **Viva-Tech**'s new plant

In this memo the president of Viva-Tech, a high-tech medical equipment firm, recommends closing its small assembly plants and centralizing its operations at one location—in the city of Grandview. To support this recommendation the president points out certain attractive demographic features, as well as the town's willingness to allow Viva-Tech to operate there without paying property taxes for the first three years. However, careful scrutiny of the evidence reveals that it provides little credible support for the president's recommendation.

To begin with, the fact that Grandview's adult population is larger than that of any other locale under consideration is scant evidence in itself that Grandview would be the best location for Viva-Tech. Perhaps Grandview's adult residents are not skilled to work in the medical equipment industry. Or perhaps a large portion of its residents are retired. Or perhaps virtually all of its residents are already employed in jobs that they would be unwilling or unable to leave to work at Viva-Tech. Without considering and eliminating these and other possible reasons why Viva-Tech might have difficulty finding enough suitable employees in Grandview, the president cannot rely on the fact that Grandview has a large adult population to bolster the recommendation.

Furthermore, the fact that the earnings of the average Grandview worker are comparatively low does not necessarily mean that Viva-Tech could minimize labor costs by employing Grandview residents, as the president suggests. It is entirely possible that this low average wage is attributable to a high percentage of jobs requiring low-level skills. This scenario would be particularly likely if a large portion of Grandview's workers are teenagers and college students. In fact, the low average wage in Grandview is further evidence that Grandview residents do not possess the sorts of high-tech skills that would command a higher wage and that Viva-Tech might require among its workforce.

A final problem with the argument involves Grandview's willingness to forego payment of property taxes for the first three years. Admittedly, this evidence lends some measure of support to the recommendation. However, the president ignores the possibility that other cities under consideration would be willing to make similar concessions, or provide other equally attractive financial incentives. The president also overlooks the expense of property taxes over the longer term. Lacking evidence to the contrary, it is entirely possible that Grandview's property-tax rates are otherwise comparatively high, and that in the longer term Viva-Tech's property-tax liability would be greater in Grandview than in other locales. Until the president accounts for these two possibilities, I cannot be persuaded that Grandview is the best location for Viva-Tech from a property-tax standpoint.

In the final analysis, the recommendation of Viva-Tech's president is not well supported. To strengthen it the president must provide detailed demographic evidence showing that a sufficient number of Grandview residents would be able and willing to work in Viva-Tech's high-tech environment. A proper evaluation of the recommendation requires more information about Grandview's property-tax rates vis-a-vis those of other locales under consideration, and about the willingness of these other municipalities to provide their own financial or tax incentives to Viva-Tech.

Argument:
Bargain Brand Cereal profits

In this memo the marketing director of Bargain Brand Cereal claims that the company will continue to make a profit from sales of its cereal, and therefore that the company should expand its bargain-priced product line to include other foods as well. To support these assertions, the memo points out that Bargain Brand is still earning a profit from its cereal sales, despite the fact that major competitors have lowered their cereal prices and plan to offer bargain-priced cereal brands. On several grounds, this evidence lends little credible support for the memo's conclusions.

First of all, the mere fact that Bargain Brand is still earning a profit from its cereal sales is not the key in determining whether its competitors are succeeding. The key instead is the extent to which Bargain Brand profits have diminished since other companies lowered their cereal prices. It is entirely possible that Bargain Brand has been less profitable since its competitors lowered their cereal prices, and that given a little more time these competitors will draw enough additional sales away from Bargain Brand to render it unprofitable. The fact that the other companies offer the "top brands" is strong evidence that these companies can survive a prolonged price war and ultimately prevail over Bargain Brand.

Secondly, the memo states that several major competitors plan to offer their own special bargain brands to compete directly with Bargain Brand. Yet the memo fails to account for this fact in concluding that Bargain Brand will continue to be profitable. In all likelihood, after the introduction of competing brands Bargain Brand's profits will diminish even further. Without providing evidence that this will not occur, the director cannot convincingly conclude that Bargain Brand will continue to profit from its cereal sales.

Thirdly, based on the fact that Bargain Brand continues to profit from cereal sales, the memo concludes that Bargain Brand should expand its product line to include other food products. Yet the memo provides no evidence that Bargain Brand is likely to be profitable in other markets. Common sense suggests the contrary—that Bargain Brand is unlikely to succeed in markets in which it has no previous experience or exposure. Without providing evidence as to how Bargain Brand would overcome natural barriers to entry into other markets, the director's conclusion is weak at best.

In conclusion, the memo is unpersuasive as it stands. To strengthen the argument, the director must show that Bargain Brand will continue to profit from cereal sales even after its major competitors introduce their own bargain brands. To better assess the director's conclusion that Bargain Brand should expand its line of bargain-priced foods, we would need more information about the extent of competition and other barriers to entry in those other markets.

Argument:
Employee compensation at **National Brush Company**

In this report, the president of National Brush Company (NBC) concludes that the best way to ensure that NBC will earn a profit next year is for the company to pay its workers according to the number of brushes they produce—rather than hourly. To support this conclusion, the president claims that the new policy will result in the production of more and better brushes, which in turn will allow NBC to reduce its staff size and operating hours, thereby cutting expenses. This argument is fraught with dubious assumptions, which render it entirely unconvincing.

First of all, the argument relies on the unsubstantiated assumption that the new policy will motivate workers to produce brushes more quickly. Whether this is the case will depend, of course, on the amount earned per brush and the rate at which workers can produce brushes. It will also depend on the extent to which NBC workers are content with their current income level. Lacking evidence that the new policy would result in the production of more brushes, the president cannot convince me that this policy would be an effective means to ensure a profit for NBC in the coming year.

Even if the new policy does motivate NBC workers to produce more brushes, the president's argument depends on the additional assumption that producing brushes more quickly can be accomplished without sacrificing quality. In fact, the president goes further by predicting an increase in quality. Yet, common sense informs me that, if the production process otherwise remains the same, quicker production is likely to reduce quality—and in any event certainly not increase it. And a decline in quality might serve to diminish the value of NBC's brushes in the marketplace. Thus, the ultimate result of the new policy might be to reduce NBC's revenue and, in turn, profits.

Even assuming that as the result of the new policy NBC's current workforce produces more brushes without sacrificing quality, reducing the size of the workforce and the number of operating hours would serve to offset those production gains. Admittedly, by keeping the most efficient employees NBC would minimize the extent of this offset. Nevertheless, the president provides no evidence that the result would be a net gain in production. Without any such evidence the president's argument that the new policy will help ensure profitability is highly suspect.

In sum, the president has failed to provide adequate evidence to support his claim that the new policy would serve to ensure a profit for NBC in the coming year. To strengthen the argument, NBC should conduct a survey or other study to demonstrate not only its workers' willingness to work more quickly but also their ability to maintain quality at a quicker pace. To better assess the argument I would need detailed financial projections comparing current payroll and other operating costs with projected costs under the new policy—in order to determine whether NBC is likely to be more profitable under the proposed scheme.

Argument:
Saving water at the **Sunnyside Towers**

In this letter, the owner of an apartment building concludes that low-flow showerheads should be installed in showers on all 20 floors of the building, for the purpose of saving money. To support this conclusion, the owner cites the fact that since installing low-flow heads in showers on the bottom five floors only a few tenants have complained about low water pressure, and that no other problems with showers have been reported. However, this evidence provides little credible support for the owner's argument, as discussed below.

In the first place, the argument depends on the assumption that installation of low-flow heads on the first five floors has resulted in lower water costs for the owner.

However, this need not be the case. It is equally possible that tenants on these floors compensate for lower flow by either taking longer showers or by opening their shower valves further than they would otherwise. It is also possible that water pressure, and therefore water usage, on the remaining floors has increased as a result. It is even possible that during the month since installation many of the tenants on the bottom five floors have been absent from the building, and this fact explains why few tenants have complained.

In the second place, the owner ignores possible indirect consequences of installing low-flow showerheads on all 20 floors—consequences that in turn might adversely affect the owner's net operating income. For example, the more low-flow installations the more likely that one or more tenants will become disgruntled and vacate as a result. In fact, the owner has admitted that at least a few tenants have complained about these new showerheads. High tenant turnover might very well serve to increase the owner's overall operating costs.

In the third place, in order to reasonably conclude that low-flow heads will reduce total water usage in the building the owner must assume that other water uses will remain constant in the future. However, this will not necessarily be the case. Perhaps the water supplier will raise rates, or perhaps current tenants will be replaced by other tenants who use more water. Without ruling out such possibilities the owner cannot justifiably conclude that his total water costs will decrease after installing low-flow heads in every shower.

In conclusion, the argument is unconvincing as it stands. To strengthen it the owner must provide clear evidence that the use of a low-flow showerhead in fact reduces total water usage. To better assess the argument we would need figures comparing water usage before and after installation. We would also need to know how many of the bottom five floors were occupied since the new heads were installed, and whether the tenants on these floors are likely to use more or less water than tenants on the upper floors.

Argument:
Have **Forsythe** citizens adopted healthier lifestyles?

In this argument, the speaker concludes that Forsythe citizens have adopted healthier lifestyles. To justify this conclusion the speaker cites a recent survey of Forsythe citizens suggesting that their eating habits now conform more closely to government nutritional recommendations than they did ten years ago. The speaker also points out that sales of kiran, a substance known to reduce cholesterol, have increased fourfold, while sales of sulia, which few of Forsythe's healthiest citizens eat regularly, have been declining. This argument is unpersuasive for several reasons.

First, the survey must be shown to be reliable before I can accept any conclusions based upon it. Specifically, the responses must be accurate, and the respondents must be statistically significant in number and representative of the overall Forsythe citizenry in terms of eating habits. Without evidence of the survey's reliability, it is impossible to draw any firm conclusions about the current dietary habits of Forsythe citizens based on the survey.

Second, the argument relies on the dubious assumption that following the government's nutrition recommendations promotes health to a greater extent than following any other nutrition regime. It is entirely possible that the dietary habits of Forsythe citizens were healthier ten years ago than they are now. Thus, without evidence to substantiate this assumption, the speaker cannot reasonably conclude that the diet of Forsythe's citizens has become more nutritious.

Third, the speaker assumes too hastily that increasing sales of products with kiran indicates healthier eating habits. Perhaps Forsythe citizens are eating these foods in amounts or at intervals that undermine the health benefits of kiran. Without ruling out this possibility the speaker cannot reasonably conclude with any confidence that increased kiran consumption has resulted in improved health for Forsythe's citizens.

Fourth, the mere fact that few of Forsythe's healthiest citizens eat sulia regularly does not mean that sulia is detrimental to health—as the speaker assumes. It is possible that sulia has no effect on health, or that it actually promotes health. Lacking firm evidence that sulia affects health adversely, and that healthy people avoid sulia for this reason, the speaker cannot justify any conclusions about the health of Forsythe's citizens from the mere fact that sulia sales are declining.

Finally, even if the dietary changes to which the speaker refers are healthful ones, the speaker overlooks the possibility that Forsythe citizens have been making other changes in their dietary or other habits that offset these healthful changes. Unless all other habits affecting health have remained unchanged, the speaker cannot justifiably conclude that the overall lifestyle of Forsythe's citizenry has become healthier.

In sum, the argument is unconvincing as it stands. To strengthen it the speaker must show that the survey accurately reflects the dietary habits of Forsythe's citizens, and that by following the government's nutritional recommendations more closely these citizens are in fact healthier. The speaker must also show that Forsythe's citizens have not made other dietary or other lifestyle changes that offset healthful changes. Finally, to better assess the argument I would need more information about the manner and extent to which Forsythe's citizens now consume kiran and about the healthfulness of sulia.

Argument:
The need for more **electric generating plants**

The author of this memo concludes that there is no need for an additional electric power plant in the area because total electricity demand in the area is not likely to increase in the future. To support this conclusion the author cites the availability of new energy-efficient appliances and systems for homes, and the eagerness of area homeowners to conserve energy. However, the argument relies on several doubtful assumptions, and is therefore unpersuasive as it stands.

First, the author's projection for flat or declining total demand for electricity ignores business and commercial electricity usage. It is entirely possible that area businesses will increase their use of electricity in the future and that total electricity consumption will actually increase despite flat or declining residential demand. The author's projection also ignores the possibility that the number of area residents will increase in the future, thereby resulting in an increase in electricity usage regardless of whether more efficient appliances are used in area homes. Without taking into account these possibilities, the author cannot persuade me that total demand for electricity will not increase in the future.

Secondly, the author's conclusion relies on the assumption that area residents will actually purchase and install the energy-saving appliances and systems the author describes. Admittedly, the author points out that homeowners are "eager to conserve energy." Nevertheless, these homeowners might not be able to afford these new systems and appliances. Moreover, the energy-efficient insulation that the author mentions might be available only for new home construction, or it might be a gas system. In either case, the mere availability of this system might have no effect on total electric usage in existing homes.

A final problem involves the assertion that no new electric power plants are needed because the three existing plants, which are 20 years old, have always been adequate for the area's electric needs. The author fails to account for the possibility that the old plants are themselves less energy efficient than a new plant using new technology would be, or that the old plants need to be replaced due to their age, or for some other reason. Besides, this assertion ignores the possible influx of residents or businesses in the future, thereby increasing the demand for electricity beyond what the three existing plants can meet.

In conclusion, the argument is unconvincing as it stands. To strengthen it the author must show that area residents can afford the new energy-efficient appliances and systems, and that area commercial demand for electricity will not increase significantly in the foreseeable future. In order to better evaluate the argument, we would need to know whether the new energy-efficient technologies are available to businesses as well, and whether area businesses plan to use them. We would also need more information about expected changes in the area's population, and about the condition and energy-efficiency of the three current electric power plants

Argument:
Megamart's leisure-activity product lines

In this memo, the vice president of Megamart concludes that Megamart should expand its line of products related to leisure activities. To support this claim the memo points out that for three years in a row the average household income nationwide has risen. However, close inspection of the argument reveals several logical problems, which render it unconvincing as it stands.

First of all, the claim relies on two threshold assumptions about rising income. One is that this trend will continue in the future; if it does not then the proposed course of action is unlikely to result in increased profits for Megamart. The other threshold assumption is that the cost of living is not also increasing at least at a commensurate rate. Yet it is entirely possible that living costs have risen to meet or even exceed the rise in income. If so, Megamart would in all likelihood sell fewer leisure products than otherwise.

Even assuming that discretionary income is rising and will continue to rise, the argument relies on the additional assumption that people will spend this discretionary income on leisure products. However, the memo provides no evidence to substantiate this assumption. Perhaps people are increasing their savings rather than spending their additional income. If so, this fact would significantly undermine the vice president's claim that demand for leisure products is increasing, and therefore that Megamart would benefit by offering more such products.

Yet another problem with the argument involves the reason why average income has risen in the first place. It is entirely possible that income has risen because people have been working more hours. If so, then in all likelihood people have less leisure time, in which case they will not spend more money on leisure products—simply because they have less time for leisure pursuits. Without addressing this issue, the vice president cannot convince me that Megamart should expand its line of leisure products.

In conclusion, the vice president's argument is unconvincing as it stands. To strengthen it the vice president must provide strong evidence that discretionary income is rising and will continue to rise. The vice president must also show that people will in fact choose to spend this income on leisure products, and that people have enough free time for leisure pursuits in the first place.

Argument:
Transopolis' urban renewal plan

The planning department for the city of Transopolis recommends, as part of its urban renewal plan, that the city convert a certain residential area for industrial use and relocate residents from that area to nearby unoccupied housing. To support this recommendation, the planners point out that ten years ago the city converted an area of substandard housing on the other side of town, near a freeway, for industrial use, and that afterward that area's crime rate declined while the city's overall property-tax revenue increased. I find the recommendation specious on several grounds.

To begin with, the recommendation relies on two poor assumptions about the effects of the freeway-area conversion. One such assumption is that the freeway-area conversion caused the decline in that area's crime rate. The mere fact that the conversion occurred before the decline does not suffice to prove that the conversion caused the decline. Perhaps the true cause was some unrelated development—such as a new city-wide "tough-on-crime" policy or improvements in police training. Another such assumption is that the increase in overall property-tax revenue indicates an increase in tax revenue from properties in the freeway area. Perhaps property-tax revenue from the converted properties remained the same, or even declined, after the conversion, and that the city's overall property-tax revenue increase was attributable to properties located elsewhere in the city. For that matter, perhaps the city raised its property-tax rates shortly after the conversion. In short, without ruling out alternative explanations for the developments that came after the freeway-area conversion, the planners cannot convince me that the conversion was responsible for those developments.

Even if the evidence turns out to substantiate the two foregoing assumptions, the recommendation further assumes that the proposed conversion would carry the same results as the freeway-area conversion. Yet key differences between the two areas might undermine the analogy. For example, perhaps the properties surrounding the ones converted in the freeway area were not residential. Common sense informs me that crimes such as burglary and robbery are less likely in areas where few people reside. Since at least some nearby housing is available for residents displaced by the proposed conversion, this conversion might not result in any significant decline in the area's crime rate. At the same time, unless unoccupied nearby housing can accommodate all displaced residents, the conversion might create a homelessness problem, thereby undermining the city's objectives.

Finally, the recommendation assumes that all conditions bearing on whether residential-to-industrial conversions would help renew Transopolis have remained unchanged over the past ten years—and will continue unchanged in the foreseeable future. Yet, perhaps Transopolis had more and better housing for displaced residents ten years ago than today. Or perhaps Transopolis would have more trouble finding occupants for additional industrial buildings today than it did ten years ago. Indeed, a myriad of factors—including the regional and national economy, demographic shifts, and political influences—might explain why an urban-renewal program that had a salutary impact on Transopolis' crime rate and property-tax revenues in the past might nevertheless not revitalize the city today, or in the future.

In sum, the planners' recommendation is largely unfounded. To bolster it they must provide clear evidence that the freeway-area conversion contributed to the decline in that area's crime rate and to the city's overall property-tax revenue increase. To better assess the argument I would need to know what other changes have occurred in the city that might explain those developments. Finally, to better assess the proposed plan's chances of success I would need to compare the circumstances surrounding the decline in the area slated for conversion with the decline in the freeway area prior to its conversion.

Argument:
Will business incentives help **Beauville**'s economy?

This article argues that the fastest way for Beauville to stimulate its economic development and reduce unemployment would be to provide the same kinds of tax and financial incentives for business as the incentives which the city of Dillton began providing 18 months ago. Dillton's incentives included a reduced corporate tax rate as well as relocation grants and favorable utility rates for businesses willing to relocate to Dillton. The article points out that during the last 18 months two manufacturing companies, which together now employ 300 people, relocated to Dillton. The argument is logically unconvincing in several respects.

To begin with, the argument depends on the assumption that the two businesses moving to Dillton did so because of Dillton's new incentives—rather than for some other reason. Yet lacking evidence to the contrary it is entirely possible that the two businesses were motivated primarily by Dillton's climate, labor pool, or some other factor. Without ruling out all other reasons why the two businesses might have relocated to Dillton, the argument that Beauville can entice businesses to move to Beauville by offering similar incentives is dubious at best.

Even if it was Dillton's new incentives that enticed the two manufacturers to Dillton, the argument relies on the further assumption that the two firms' relocating to Dillton in fact had a beneficial impact on the city's economy. Yet the only evidence the article offers to substantiate this assumption is that the two manufacturers now employ 300 people. Perhaps those 300 employees left other jobs in Dillton to go to work for those two firms; if so, then the incentives had no positive impact on Dillton's employment rate. Or perhaps other businesses have left Dillton during the last 18 months, taking even more job opportunities with them. For that matter, perhaps on average more businesses relocated to Dillton each year prior to Dillton's establishing the new incentives than afterward. In short, without more information about Dillton's economic conditions and employment level both before and after the incentives were established it is impossible to assess whether those incentives had a positive or negative impact—or any impact at all—on Dillton's overall economy.

Even if Dillton's new incentives did in fact serve to help Dillton's economy, the article unfairly assumes that similar incentives will carry a similar result for Beauville. It is entirely possible that the two cities differ in ways that would undermine the effectiveness of similar incentives for Beauville. For instance, perhaps Beauville's labor pool is smaller; or perhaps unemployed Beauville residents would be less willing or able to go to work if offered the chance. Without accounting for such differences any analogy between the two cities is premature, and any conclusion based on that analogy is unjustified.

Furthermore, the author's inference that incentives which were effective in the past will also be effective in the future rests on the poor assumption that during the last 18 months all conditions upon which their effectiveness depend have remained unchanged. Perhaps the general economy is expected to turn down. Or perhaps other cities have recently begun to provide similar incentives. Indeed, the fact that Dillton is already providing these incentives might actually portend failure for Beauville, which might need to devise even stronger incentives to convince businesses to move to Beauville rather than Dillton.

Finally, the article fails to consider any other course of action that might help Beauville attain the same economic goals. Perhaps by improving its schools or hospitals, or by reducing its crime rate, Beauville can just as quickly and effectively attract new businesses and achieve its economic objectives. In short, without weighing the proposal against alternatives, the article's claim that the proposed incentives are the "best" means of achieving Beauville's objectives is wholly unconvincing.

To sum up, the article has not convinced me that the proposed incentives would be the best way for Beauville to achieve its economic goals. To bolster the argument the article's author must provide clear evidence that Dillton's incentives—and not some other phenomenon—were in fact responsible for stimulating Dillton's economy during the last 18 months. To better assess the argument I would need to know what other conditions in Beauville that were not present in Dillton might dissuade businesses from moving to Beauville—despite the proposed incentives. I would also need to compare near-term economic forecasts with economic conditions during the last 18 months. Finally, I would need to consider the proposed incentives in light of alternative courses of action.

Answers to Arguments That Propose Unnecessary or Insufficient Preconditions

This section contains sample essay responses to several Argument statements from the official GRE essay pool. Each of these Argument statements relies partly on the unwarranted assumption that a certain course of action is necessary and/or sufficient to achieve a desired outcome or objective. Before you read these essays, be sure to review the discussion about this type of reasoning problem on pages 30–31.

> NOTE: Each essay addresses other major reasoning problems as well, but it is included only in this section of Part 3.

Argument:
Clearview's city-council election

This editorial recommends that Clearview residents vote to replace city-council member Frank Braun with Ann Green, a member of the Good Earth Coalition. To support this recommendation the editorial cites a significant increase during the last year in the number of Clearview factories and in the number of Clearview hospital patients treated for respiratory illnesses. On the basis of this evidence the author infers that the current council members are not protecting the city's environment and that electing Green will solve the city's environmental problems. This argument is logically flawed in several critical respects.

To begin with, the argument unfairly assumes that last year's increase in the number of factories was due to the city council's decisions—rather than to some other phenomenon—and that this increase poses environmental problems for Clearview. The editorial provides no evidence to substantiate these assumptions. Lacking such evidence it is entirely possible that the council actually opposed the increase but lacked adequate authority to prevent it, or that the new factories do not in fact harm Clearview's environment.

The argument also assumes unfairly that last year's increase in the number of patients reporting respiratory problems indicates worsening environmental problems in Clearview. Perhaps the actual incidence of such health problems has not increased, and the reported increase is due to increasing awareness among Clearview residents of respiratory problems. Even if the incidence of respiratory problems has in fact increased, the increase might be due to an influx of people with pre-existing such problems, or to more effective cigarette marketing. Since the editorial fails to rule out these and other possible explanations for the increase, I cannot accept any conclusions about Clearview's environment—let alone about who voters should elect to city council—based on last year's hospital records.

Even if the two cited increases do indicate a worsening of Clearview's environment due to the city council's decisions, the argument rests on the further assumption that Braun was a factor in those decisions. But, since the editorial provides no evidence to substantiate this assumption it is equally possible that Braun actually opposed the decisions that were responsible for these increases. Thus, without better evidence that Braun contributed to key decisions adversely effecting Clearview's environment, the editorial remains unconvincing.

Even assuming that Braun was at least partially responsible for the two increases, and that those increases indicate a worsening environment, the editorial provides no clear evidence that Green would be effective in reversing that trend—let alone more effective than Braun. The mere fact that Green is a member of the Good Earth Coalition hardly suffices to prove her willingness and ability to help solve Clearview's environmental problems, at least not without more information about that coalition and Green's involvement in it.

Finally, even if Green would in fact be more effective than Braun in solving Clearview's environmental problems, the author provides no firm evidence that electing Green is necessary to solve those problems, or that electing Green would suffice. Perhaps another candidate, or another course of action, would be more effective. Even if Green does everything in her power as city-council member to solve these problems, perhaps additional measures—such as replacing other council members, state legislators, or even the state's governor—would also be required in order to achieve Clearview's environmental objectives.

In sum, the editorial's author cannot justify his or her voting recommendation on the basis of the scant evidence provided in the editorial. To bolster the recommendation the author must provide better evidence that (1) Clearview has environmental problems to begin with, (2) Green would be more effective than either Braun or any other candidate in solving those problems, and (3) electing Green would suffice to solve those problems. To better assess the argument I would need to know the scope of the city council's authority respecting environmental decisions. I would also need to know Braun's voting record on environmental issues, Green's experience and position on those issues, and the voters' other choices—besides Green and Braun.

Argument:
Promoting the rock band **Double Rice**

The manager of the rock band Double Rice (DR) concludes that the band should hire the advertising agency Ad Lib to promote the band throughout the country. To justify this conclusion the manager cites Ad Lib's campaign to promote a recent DR concert at a large venue in Megalopolis. Tickets for this concert sold out in 12 minutes, whereas one year ago tickets for DR concerts at large venues rarely sold out in less than 24 hours—if at all. The manager reasons that the Megalopolis success must have been attributable to both Ad Lib's efforts and DR's popularity. The manager's argument is flawed in several critical respects.

To begin with, assuming that the Megalopolis success was in fact due to DR's popularity there, the manager overlooks the possibility that Ad Lib's campaign had nothing to do that popularity. Perhaps the band recently became overwhelmingly popular due to a new hit song or to a revival of the type of music DR plays. Either scenario, if true, would serve to undermine the manager's claim that Ad Lib's efforts are to be credited for the Megalopolis success.

The manager also overlooks the possibility that one or more factors other than Ad Lib's efforts or DR's popularity were instead responsible for the Megalopolis success. For instance, perhaps DR shared the bill at the concert with another band, whose appearance was the actual reason for the concert's success. If so, this fact would seriously weaken the manager's claim that the Megalopolis success is attributable to Ad Lib's efforts and to DR's popularity in Megalopolis—whether or not that popularity resulted from Ad Lib's campaign.

Even assuming that either DR's popularity or Ad Lib's campaign, or both, were responsible for the Megalopolis success, the manager's claim that this success can be repeated elsewhere might nevertheless be unwarranted. Megalopolis might not be representative of most cities in which DR plans to appear—in any one of various ways that would adversely impact ticket sales in other cities. For instance, perhaps DR hails from Megalopolis and has far more fans in Megalopolis than any other city. Or, perhaps the kind of ad campaign that is Ad Lib's specialty, although effective in Megalopolis, would not be effective in most cities.

Finally, in concluding that DR must hire Ad Lib in order to ensure similar success throughout the country, the manager assumes that Ad Lib's services are both necessary and sufficient for this purpose. Yet the manager has not provided any evidence to substantiate either assumption. Lacking such evidence, it is just as likely that some other ad agency would be equally or more effective. Even if Ad Lib's services are necessary to achieve the manager's goal, it is entirely possible that Ad Lib's services would not suffice to ensure similar success elsewhere—due to the sort of factors mentioned above that might have contributed to the Megalopolis success but would not come into play in other cities.

In sum, the manager has not convinced me that DR's interests would be well served if and only if it hires Ad Lib to promote the band throughout the country. To bolster the argument the manager must rule out all other possible reasons for the success of the Megalopolis concert, and must show that Ad Lib is capable of achieving similar success in other cities.

Argument:
A salary raise and promotion for **Professor Thomas**

In this report, an Elm City University committee recommends increasing Professor Thomas' salary and promoting her to Department Chairperson because of her effectiveness as a teacher and researcher. To support this recommendation the report points out that Thomas' classes are among the University's most popular and that last year the amount of grant money she attracted to the University exceeded her $50,000 salary. The committee argues further that unless the University implements its recommendation Thomas is likely to defect to another school. For several reasons, the evidence offered in support of the recommendation provides little credible support for it.

First, the recommendation relies on the assumption that the popularity of Thomas' classes is attributable to her effectiveness as a teacher. Yet this assumption overlooks other possible reasons for the popularity of these classes. Perhaps Thomas is a comparatively lenient grader, or perhaps the classes she teaches are requirements for every science student. Without considering and eliminating these and other possible alternative explanations for the popularity of Thomas' classes, the committee cannot convincingly conclude based on that popularity that Thomas is an effective teacher and therefore should be granted a raise and a promotion.

Secondly, the mere fact that the amount of grant money Thomas attracted to the University last year exceeded her salary proves nothing about either her teaching abilities or her research abilities. Perhaps last year was an aberration, and in other years Thomas did not attract much grant money. For that matter, perhaps many—or even most—other professors at the University attracted even more grant money than Thomas, relative to their salary levels. Under either scenario, Thomas would appear undeserving of the recommended raise and promotion—based on this particular criterion.

Thirdly, the report provides no evidence whatsoever regarding the likelihood that Thomas would leave the University if she is not granted the proposed raise and promotion. Lacking such evidence, it is entirely possible that Thomas is quite content in her current position and at her current salary level. Thus, the committee cannot justifiably rely on this claim to bolster its recommendation.

In conclusion, the committee's recommendation is ill founded. To strengthen it the committee must provide clear evidence that Thomas is in fact an effective teacher—perhaps by citing student or peer evaluations. The committee must also provide specific evidence of Thomas' research abilities—perhaps by listing scientific journals that have published the results of her work. Finally, to better evaluate the argument I would need more information about the degree to which Thomas is content in her current position and at her current salary, and whether any other University would be willing to offer her a more attractive employment package.

Argument:
Encouraging students to use school **libraries**

In this editorial the author claims that the town's students are reading less, and that by improving the atmosphere in the town's school libraries students would visit their school library more frequently and, in turn, would read more. To support these claims the author points out that the number of annual visits students make to their school library, on average, has decreased significantly in recent years. Specifically, the average seventh-grader paid five such visits last year, four of which were required for classes. Close inspection of the evidence reveals, however, that it lends little credible support for the proposed course of action.

First, the author unfairly assumes that since the number of library visits per student is declining the amount of reading on the part of students must also be declining. This poor assumption overlooks the possibility that students are doing more reading or checking out more reading materials during each library visit. It also ignores the possibility that more and more students are obtaining reading material elsewhere— for example, from public libraries or from the Internet. Without considering and ruling out these possibilities, the author cannot justifiably conclude that students are reading less merely because they are visiting their school library less often.

Secondly, the author assumes that the reason for the declining number of library visits is that the library is uncomfortable. Yet, the author offers no evidence to substantiate this assumption. Lacking such evidence, a variety of other factors might account for the decline. As noted above, perhaps students are becoming less dependent on the school library for obtaining reading material and information. Besides, lacking evidence to the contrary it is entirely possible that library atmosphere is completely insignificant to most students.

Thirdly, the author assumes that improving atmosphere and comfort is necessary to reverse the current trend. However, even if the surroundings go unchanged there might be other ways to attract students to their library. Perhaps increasing the number of computer terminals or the number of staff members would reverse the current trend. Or perhaps increasing the number of books and periodicals, or enhancing their variety, would be effective. In short, without ruling out all other possible means of achieving the desired results, the author cannot convince me that the proposed course of action is necessary.

Finally, the author assumes that improving the library's atmosphere would suffice to increase the frequency of student visits and the amount of reading on the part of students. Yet, the author offers no evidence that these improvements alone would suffice. In fact, a more comfortable library might actually discourage students from reading by creating a social rather than work atmosphere.

In sum, the recommendation is not well supported. To strengthen the argument the author must provide clear evidence that the school's students are in fact reading less and that if they visit the school library more frequently they will read more. The author must also provide evidence—perhaps by way of a student survey—that the library atmosphere is the chief determinant of the frequency with which students visit the library. Finally, to better evaluate the argument I would need to know what alternatives, if any, are available for increasing the frequency with which students visit their library, and for increasing the amount that students read.

Argument:
The prospects for **Whirlwind** video-game sales

This editorial concludes that a two-year decline in sales of Whirlwind's video games is about to reverse itself, and that sales will increase dramatically in the next few months. To justify this conclusion the editorial's author cites a recent survey in which video-game players indicated a preference for games with realistic graphics requiring state-of-the art computers. The editorial then points out that Whirlwind has just introduced several such games, along with an extensive advertising campaign aimed at people 10-25 years old—the demographic group most likely to play video games. I find this argument specious on several grounds.

First, the author provides no assurances that the survey on which the argument depends is statistically reliable. Unless the survey's respondents are representative of the overall population of video-game enthusiasts, the author cannot rely on it to predict the success of Whirlwind's new games. For all we know a significant percentage of the respondents were not 10-25 years of age; for that matter, perhaps the number of respondents was too low to ensure that they are typical of video-game enthusiasts in that age group.

Secondly, the argument relies on the assumption that the two-year decline in Whirlwind's sales is attributable to a problem that Whirlwind's introduction of its new games and ad campaign will solve. Yet it is entirely possible that the decline was due to factors such as imprudent pricing and distribution strategies or poor management, and that these problems have not been remedied. In fact, perhaps the same advertising agency that is promoting Whirlwind's new games also promoted Whirlwind's earlier games, and it was the agency's inability to attract interest among the key demographic group that caused the decline. Since the author has not clearly identified the cause of the decline, I cannot be convinced that Whirlwind's new strategy will reverse that decline at all—let alone dramatically.

Thirdly, even if the ad campaign successfully attracts many 10-25 year-olds to Whirlwind's new games, the argument rests on the further assumption that this result will suffice to cause the predicted sales increase during the next few months. Yet this need not be the case. Perhaps Whirlwind's new state-of-the-art games are prohibitively expensive for the key demographic group. Or perhaps Whirlwind's competitors are now introducing similar games at lower prices or with additional features that render them more attractive to video-game enthusiasts than Whirlwind's new games. Unless the author can rule out such possibilities, I simply cannot be swayed by the prediction that Whirlwind is about to experience a dramatic increase in sales.

Finally, even if the author can substantiate the foregoing assumptions, I remain unconvinced that the impending increase in sales will occur within the next few months. Perhaps video-game sales are highly seasonal and Whirlwind will need to wait longer than two months to see the dramatic increase it expects. If so, the author must modify the prediction accordingly.

In sum, the argument is unconvincing as it stands. To strengthen it the author must provide clear evidence that video-game enthusiasts 10-25 years of age would be interested in Whirlwind's new games, and that they could afford to buy them. To better assess the argument I would need to know (1) what caused the two-year sales to decline to begin with, and whether Whirlwind's new strategy eliminates that cause; (2) what competing products might serve to diminish sales of Whirlwind's new games during the next few months; and (3) when Whirlwind's introduction of its new games has occurred in relation to the peak video-game sales season, if any.

Argument:
The price of **oysters**

This argument points out that, ever since harmful bacteria were found in a few Gulf Coast oysters five years ago, California consumers have been willing to pay twice as much for northeastern Atlantic oysters as for Gulf oysters. The argument then notes that scientists have now developed a process for killing these bacteria. The argument concludes that once consumers become aware of this fact they will be willing to pay as much for these oysters as for Atlantic oysters, and that profits for Gulf oyster producers will thereby increase. The argument is flawed in three critical respects.

First, the argument assumes that the bacteria discovery is the reason for California consumers' unwillingness to pay as much for Gulf shrimp during the past five years. However, this is not necessarily so. Perhaps regional culinary tastes shifted during the last five years, and perhaps Atlantic oysters have a distinct taste, texture, size, or other quality that has made them more popular among California consumers. Since the argument fails to rule out this and other alternative explanations for the willingness of California consumers to pay more for Atlantic oysters, the argument's conclusion is unwarranted.

Secondly, the argument assumes too hastily that consumer awareness of the process that kills the bacteria will necessarily result in the behavior that the argument predicts. Perhaps after five years of favoring Atlantic oysters, consumer oyster tastes and habits have become so well entrenched that consumers will continue to favor Atlantic oysters and will happily pay a premium for them. Moreover, in my observation consumers often act unpredictably and irrationally, and therefore any prediction about consumer preferences is dubious at best. Besides, it is entirely possible that Gulf oyster producers will be unwilling to employ the new bacteria-killing process; if so, and if consumers are aware of this fact, then in all likelihood consumers will continue to favor Atlantic oysters.

Thirdly, even if consumers begin paying as much for Gulf oysters once they become aware of the bacteria-killing process, the argument's conclusion that Gulf oyster producers will enjoy increased profits as a result is unwarranted. Profit is a factor of not only revenue but also costs. It is entirely possible that the costs of employing this new process for killing bacteria, or other costs associated with producing Gulf oysters, will offset additional revenue. Besides, a myriad of other possible occurrences, such as unfavorable regional weather or economic conditions, might prevent the Gulf oyster producers from being as profitable in the foreseeable future as the argument predicts.

In sum, the argument is unpersuasive as it stands. To strengthen it the argument's proponent must consider and rule out all other possible explanations for the willingness of California consumers to pay a premium for Atlantic oysters, and must convince me that with consumer awareness of the bacteria-killing process Gulf oysters will become just as desirable as Atlantic oysters. To better assess the argument's claim that profits for Gulf oyster producers will increase as an end result, I would need to know whether Gulf oyster producers will incur the expenses involved in killing the bacteria and, if so, the extent to which these expenses will impinge on the producers' profits.

Argument:
Membership in **Oak City's Civic Club**

This letter recommends that membership in Oak City's Civic Club, the primary objective of which is to discuss local issues, be limited to local residents. To support this recommendation, the author claims that since only residents pay local taxes they are the only people who sufficiently understand local business and political issues. The author also cites the fact that in the last ten years very few non-residents of Oak City who work in Oak City have joined nearby Elm City's Civic Club, which is open to any person. The argument suffers from two critical flaws and is therefore unpersuasive as it stands.

To begin with, the letter fails to adequately support the claim that since only residents pay local taxes only they truly understand local business and political issues. Even given the dubious assumption that being a local taxpayer affords one an understanding of local business and political issues, it is fallacious to conclude that being a local taxpayer is a necessary condition for understanding these issues. Moreover, common sense tells me that local business people, residents or not, would probably be more intimately involved in many such issues than local residents who do not have business interests in the town. Having failed to address this distinct possibility, the letter is wholly unconvincing.

In further support of the recommendation, the letter cites the fact that nearby Elm City's Civic Club is open to any person, yet very few Oak City business people who are not residents have joined Elm City's club in the last ten years. But this fact alone lends no support to the recommendation. It is possible, for instance, that these business people have no connection with Elm City whatsoever, or that these business people have been members of Elm City's Civic Club for longer than ten years. The author must eliminate these possibilities in order to rely justifiably on this evidence for his or her recommendation.

In conclusion, the letter's author fails to adequately support the recommendation that Oak City Civic Club membership be restricted to local residents. To strengthen the argument, the author must provide clear evidence that non-residents who work in Oak City do not understand local issues as well as residents do. To better evaluate the argument, we would need more information about why non-resident business people in Oak City have not joined Elm City's Civic Club during the last ten years.

Argument:
Omega-3 **fatty acids** and depression

The author of this article asserts that people who live in the U.S. should increase their fish consumption in order to prevent depression. To support this assertion, the author cites the fact that our ancestors, who were less likely to experience depression than we are today, consumed more omega-3 fatty acids, which help prevent depression and are found in some fish and fish oils. The author also cites the fact that in modern societies where people eat more fish than we do the reported incidence of depression is comparatively low. However, the author's reasoning is problematic in several critical respects.

The first problem with the argument involves the comparatively low incidence of depression among our ancestors. The author assumes that no factor other than the ingestion of omega-3 is responsible for this lower incidence. However, it is entirely possible that environmental or other dietary factors are instead responsible for the lower incidence. For example, perhaps other substances common in the U.S. diet today, and which promote depression, were not part of our ancestors' diets.

Another problem with the argument involves the low incidence of depression reported among today's fish-eating societies. To reasonably infer a causal relationship between fish-eating and low rates of depression in these societies, two assumptions are required. The first is that the types of fish consumed in these societies in fact contain omega-3; however, the article provides no evidence that this is the case. The second assumption is that the reported incidence of depression accurately reflects the actual incidence. However, it is entirely possible that in those societies people generally do not report depression.

A third problem with the argument is that it assumes that omega-3 is only available in fish. However, the author provides no evidence to substantiate this crucial assumption.

Perhaps people can ingest omega-3 by taking fish oil capsules rather than eating fish. Or perhaps omega-3 is also found in other foods as well. In either case, the author cannot reasonably conclude that we must eat more fish to ingest omega-3 and thereby help prevent depression.

Finally, in concluding that people in the U.S. must ingest more omega-3 to prevent depression, the author infers that this is the only means of preventing depression. This reasoning is fallacious. There might be a myriad of alternative ways to prevent depression; moreover, experience and common sense informs me that this is indeed the case.

In conclusion, the argument is unconvincing as it stands. To strengthen it, the author must provide clear evidence that no other factors explain the comparatively low incidence of depression among our ancestors. The author must also show that in modern fish-eating societies people in fact ingest more omega-3 than people in the

U.S. do, and that the incidence of depression is in fact lower in those societies. To better evaluate the argument, we would need more information about alternative methods of preventing depression and alternative sources of omega-3.

Argument:
How to increase enrollment at **Foley College**

The dean of Foley College claims that by guaranteeing prospective students that they will obtain jobs immediately upon graduation Foley can increase its enrollment and more effectively compete against more prestigious schools. To support this assertion the dean claims that students who commit early to a course of study and are guaranteed eventual employment are more likely to complete that course work and will be better prepared for the future. On several grounds, however, the dean's argument is unconvincing.

First of all, the argument assumes that providing this guarantee will in fact result in increased enrollment. However, the dean provides no evidence that this will be the case. It is entirely possible that the sort of student attracted to Foley in the first place would not find such a guarantee a particularly enticing feature. In fact, since Foley is a liberal arts college its students are more likely to be interested in graduate-level study rather than immediate employment upon graduation.

Secondly, the dean provides no support for the claim that because of the proposed guarantee Foley students would be more likely to successfully complete the course work they choose as entering freshman. To the contrary, experience and common sense inform us that while in college students often change their minds about their best career direction. Accordingly, by requiring an early commitment to a course of study

Foley might be doing its students a disservice in terms of helping them select the course of study that they are most likely to complete successfully.

Thirdly, the dean provides no support for the final conclusion that the earlier a student's commitment to a course of study the better prepared the student will be for the future. It is entirely possible that exploring diverse options during the first year or two of college is a better way to prepare for one's future—by providing the sort of well-rounded education that one might need for career flexibility. Without addressing this issue the dean cannot justifiably conclude that the proposed guarantee will better prepare Foley students for the future.

In conclusion, the argument is unconvincing as it stands. To strengthen it the dean must provide statistical evidence that college students who commit early to a course of study or who are promised eventual employment in that field are more likely than other college students to succeed in college and in their careers. Finally, to better evaluate the argument, we would need more information about why prospective students apply to Foley in the first place.

Argument:
Reducing crime in the city of **Amburg**

Amburg's Chamber-of-Commerce president has recommended high-intensity lighting throughout Amburg as the best means of reducing crime and revitalizing city neighborhoods. In support of this recommendation the president points out that when Belleville took similar action vandalism declined there almost immediately. The president also points out that since Amburg's police began patrolling on bicycles the incidence of vandalism has remained unchanged. The president's argument is flawed in several critical respects.

First, the argument rests on the unsupported assumption that in Belleville the immediate decline in vandalism was attributable to the lighting—rather than to some other phenomenon—and that the lighting has continued to serve as an effective deterrent there. Perhaps around the same time the city added police units or more after-school youth programs. Moreover, perhaps since the initial decline vandals have grown accustomed to the lighting and are no longer deterred by it. Without ruling out other feasible explanations for the decline and showing that the decline was a lasting one, the president cannot reasonably conclude on the basis of Belleville's experience that the same course of action would serve Amburg's objectives.

Secondly, the president assumes too hastily that Amburg's bicycle patrol has been ineffective in deterring vandalism. Perhaps other factors—such as a demographic shift or worsening economic conditions—have served to increase vandalism while the bicycle patrol has offset that increase. Thus, without showing that all other conditions affecting the incidence of vandalism have remained unchanged since the police began its bicycle patrol the president cannot convincingly conclude that high-intensity lighting would be a more effective means of preventing vandalism.

Thirdly, the president falsely assumes that high-intensity lighting and bicycle patrolling are Amburg's only possible means of reducing crime. In all likelihood Amburg has a myriad of other choices—such as social programs and juvenile legal-system reforms, to name just a few. Moreover, undoubtedly vandalism is not the only type of crime in Amburg. Thus, unless the president can show that high-intensity lighting will deter other types of crime as well I cannot take seriously the president's conclusion that installing high-intensity lighting would be the best way for Amburg to reduce its overall crime rate.

Finally, even if high-intensity lighting would be Amburg's best means of reducing crime in its central business district, the president's further assertion that reducing crime would result in a revitalization of city neighborhoods is unwarranted. Perhaps the decline of Amburg's city neighborhoods is attributable not to the crime rate in Amburg's central business district but rather to other factors—such as the availability of more attractive housing in the suburbs. And if the neighborhoods in decline are not located within the central business district the president's argument is even weaker.

In sum, the recommendation is not well supported. To bolster it the president must show that Belleville's decline in vandalism is lasting and is attributable to the lighting. The president must also show that lighting would be more effective than any other means at Amburg's disposal to reduce not just vandalism but other crimes as well. To better assess the recommendation I would need to know whether Amburg's declining city neighborhoods are located within the central business district, and whether any other factors might have contributed to the decline.

Argument:
A job-opportunity program for **Waymarsh University**

In this memo, a Waymarsh University administrator recommends that in order to achieve its academic goals Waymarsh should adopt the same "job-op" program currently offered at Plateau Technical College. To support this recommendation, the administrator points out a high enrollment rate in the program at Plateau, high academic grades among Plateau students enrolled in the program compared to other Plateau students, and a high success rate among new Plateau graduates in finding jobs. The administrator's argument is unconvincing for several reasons.

First of all, the administrator does not inform us what Waymarsh's academic goals are. It is entirely possible that these goals have nothing to do with enrollment in job opportunity programs or in the job-placement rate for new graduates. Although Plateau's goals are likely to depend on its job-placement rate, perhaps Waymarsh's primary goal is to prepare its students for graduate-level study. Even if Waymarsh's goals involve job placement, there might be alternative means of accomplishing those goals. In short, without identifying Waymarsh's goals and ruling out other possible means of attaining them, the administrator cannot justifiably conclude that Waymarsh should adopt the job-op program.

Secondly, the fact that a high percentage of Plateau students enroll in Plateau's job-op program does not mean that a large portion of Waymarsh students will also enroll in the program. Plateau students might be far more concerned about obtaining employment immediately after graduation than Waymarsh students are. The fact that Plateau is a two-year technical college while Waymarsh is a university supports this assertion.

Thirdly, the fact that Plateau students enrolled in the job-op program attain higher grades than other Plateau students does not necessarily mean that the job-op program is responsible for this phenomenon. Perhaps only the brighter, more competitive Plateau students enroll in the job-op program in the first place. Without ruling out this possibility, the administrator cannot convincingly conclude that Waymarsh students who enroll in the job-op program are more likely to attain better grades or find jobs upon graduation. In fact, a job-op program might actually thwart Waymarsh's efforts, by encouraging enrollees to quit school and take jobs for which a four-year degree is not needed.

Finally, the administrator overlooks the possibility that the job-op program is oriented toward the needs of students at technical schools. A job-op program that successfully places technical students might not be as successful in placing graduates of four-year universities, because the types of jobs the two groups of graduates typically seek and would qualify for are quite different.

In conclusion, the argument is unconvincing as it stands. To strengthen it the administrator must show that one of Waymarsh's academic goals is to place its new graduates in jobs. The administrator must also show that this job-op program is equally successful in placing university graduates as it is in placing technical-school graduates. To better evaluate the argument we would need more information about the extent to which the job-op program is actually responsible for the successful job placement rate among Plateau's graduates.

Argument:
How to increase profitability at **ABC Cereal Company**

This ABC Cereal Company memo concludes that to increase its profitability ABC must lower both the sugar content and price of its Better Bran (BB) cereal. To justify this conclusion the memo cites the fact that sales of BB have declined in recent years. The memo attributes this decline to a concern among most consumers about the amount of sugar in their cereals, and to the 5% increase in the price of BB during each of the last three years. The memo is unconvincing for several reasons.

First, the mere fact that most consumers are concerned about sugar in cereal amounts to scant evidence that the decline in BB sales is due to that concern. The level of concern, or the amount of sugar in BB, might not be sufficiently high to cause consumers to stop buying BB cereal on either basis. Moreover, unless the level of concern has grown during recent years I cannot take seriously the claim that declining BB sales in recent years is due to that concern—rather than to some other event or trend.

Secondly, assuming that the 5% price increases have contributed to the decline in BB sales, it would be premature to conclude that profits from BB sales have also declined as a result. Perhaps the additional revenue from the price increases more than offset the decline in revenue due to the diminishing number of units sold. Thus, ABC cannot convince me on the basis of the price increases and the sales decline that lowering BB's price would serve to improve ABC's overall profitability.

Thirdly, the memo's recommendation rests on the dubious assumption that the proposed actions are the only two means of increasing ABC's overall profitability. In all likelihood, ABC's profits are a function not only of how many boxes of BB it sells but also of its costs and its revenue from other products. Perhaps ABC can improve its profits by other means—such as expanding its cereal line, marketing BB to health-conscious consumers and raising the price of BB, or cutting costs in other areas. For that matter, if other cereal companies raise their prices, consumers might begin to consider BB a bargain at its current price—or perhaps even at a somewhat higher price. In short, since the memo has not ruled out all other possible scenarios that might serve to improve ABC's overall profitability I simply cannot take the memo's recommendation seriously.

Finally, even in the unlikely event that one of the two proposed changes is necessary to increase ABC's overall profitability, the memo's assertion that both changes are necessary might nevertheless be unwarranted. Perhaps only one of the two changes will suffice. Since the memo ignores this possibility the strength of its recommendation remains questionable at best.

In sum, ABC might be ill advised to follow the memo's advice. To strengthen the argument that ABC must lower BB's price and sugar content to improve profitability, ABC's planners must provide clear evidence that consumer concern about sugar in cereals is the primary reason for declining BB sales, and that this decline has diminished BB's profitability. To better assess ABC's claim that the proposed course of action is necessary to improve ABC's profitability, I would need to know what other alternatives, if any, are available to ABC for cutting costs and for increasing revenue.

Argument:
Improving **Central Plaza**'s attractiveness

This editorial concludes that the city should ban skateboarding from its downtown Central Plaza in order to attract visitors to that area, to return the area to its "former glory," and to make it "a place where people can congregate for fun and relaxation." To justify this conclusion the editorial points out that skateboarders are nearly the only people one sees anymore at Central Plaza, and that the Plaza is littered and its property defaced. The editorial also points out that the majority of downtown merchants support the skateboarding ban. This argument is flawed in several critical respects.

First, the editorial's author falsely assumes that a ban on skateboarding is both necessary and sufficient to achieve the three stated objectives. Perhaps the city can achieve those objectives by other means as well—for example, by creating a new mall that incorporates an attractive new skateboard park. Even if banning skateboarders altogether is necessary to meet the city's goals, the author has not shown that this action by itself would suffice. Assuming that the Plaza's reputation is now tarnished, restoring that reputation and, in turn, enticing people back to the Plaza might require additional measures—such as removing litter and graffiti, promoting the Plaza to the public, or enticing popular restaurant or retail chains to the Plaza.

Secondly, the editorial assumes too hastily that the Plaza's decline is attributable to the skateboarders—rather than to some other phenomenon. Perhaps the Plaza's primary appeal in its glory days had to do with particular shops or eateries, which were eventually replaced by less appealing ones. Or perhaps the crime rate in surrounding areas has risen dramatically, for reasons unrelated to the skateboarders' presence at the Plaza. Without ruling out these and other alternative explanations for the Plaza's decline, the editorial's author cannot convince me that a skateboard ban would reverse that decline.

Thirdly, the editorial's author might be confusing cause with effect—by assuming that the skateboarders caused the abandonment of the Plaza, rather than vice versa. It is entirely possible that skateboarders did not frequent the Plaza until it was largely abandoned—and because it had been abandoned. In fact this scenario makes good sense, since skateboarding is most enjoyable where there are few pedestrians or motorists to get in the way.

Fourth, it is unreasonable to infer from the mere fact that most merchants favor the ban that the ban would be effective in achieving the city's objectives. Admittedly, perhaps these merchants would be more likely to help clean up the Plaza area and promote their businesses were the city to act in accordance with their preference. Yet lacking any supporting evidence the author cannot convince me of this. Thus, the survey amounts to scant evidence at best that the proposed ban would carry the intended result.

Finally, the author recommends a course of action that might actually defeat the city's objective of providing a fun and relaxing place for people to congregate. In my experience skateboarding contributes to an atmosphere of fun and relaxation, for adults and children alike, more so than many other types of ambiance. Without considering that continuing to allow skateboarding—or even encouraging this activity— might achieve the city's goal more effectively than banning the activity, the author cannot convincingly conclude that the ban would be in the city's best interests.

In sum, the argument is a specious one. To strengthen it, the editorial's author must provide clear evidence that skateboarding, and not some other factor, is responsible for the conditions marking the Plaza's decline. The author must also convince me that no alternative means of restoring the Plaza are available to the city, and that the proposed ban by itself would suffice to attract tourists and restore the Plaza to its former glory. Finally, to better assess the argument it would be useful to know the circumstances under which the downtown merchants would be willing to help the city achieve its objectives.

Argument:
The benefits of a **new expressway**

In this newsletter the author concludes that, in order to promote the economic health of the city's downtown area, voters should approve the construction of an expressway linking downtown to outlying suburbs. To support this conclusion the author claims that the expressway would alleviate shortages of stock and materials among downtown businesses and manufacturers, and would attract workers from elsewhere in the state. However, the argument relies on a series of unsubstantiated assumptions, which render it unconvincing.

The first problem with the argument involves the author's claim that the expressway would help prevent downtown merchants and manufacturers from experiencing shortages in stock and materials. This claim depends on three assumptions. One assumption is that such a problem exists in the first place. A second assumption is that the absence of an expressway is the cause of such shortages; yet common sense tells me that the availability of these commodities is probably the primary such factor. A third assumption is that stock and materials would be delivered primarily via the expressway. Yet it is entirely possible that these commodities are delivered directly to the downtown area by other means, such as rail or air transport. Without substantiating these assumptions the author cannot justifiably conclude that the expressway would help prevent shortages of stock and materials.

Another problem with the argument involves the author's dual claim that because of the new expressway workers from elsewhere in the state will be lured to work in this city's downtown area and at the same time will choose to live in the suburbs. The author provides no evidence that the existence of an expressway would suffice to entice people to work in this city's downtown area. Moreover, the author ignores the possibility that people who might want to work in the city's downtown area would generally prefer to live in that area as well. In this case, the expressway would be of no help in attracting qualified workers to this city's downtown area.

A third problem with the argument is that it unfairly assumes that the expressway will result in a net influx, rather than outflow, of workers to the downtown area. In fact, the expressway might make it easier for people who currently live and work downtown to commute to jobs in other areas or even relocate their businesses to outlying areas. Either scenario would serve to undermine the author's claim that the expressway would provide a boon to the downtown economy.

Finally, the argument rests on the assumption that funds used to build the expressway and to create jobs for construction workers cannot be applied to some other program instead—one that would be even more effective in promoting the health of the downtown economy. Without identifying and weighing such alternatives, the author cannot defend the conclusion that voters should approve the expressway project.

In conclusion, the argument is unconvincing as it stands. To strengthen it the author must provide strong evidence that the expressway would help alleviate shortages of supply and materials among downtown businesses and manufacturers. The author must also show that the expressway would in fact result in a net influx of workers who would change jobs because of the availability of the expressway. Finally, to better evaluate the argument we would need more information about possible alternatives to the proposal, and whether any such alternative would be more effective in promoting the health of the downtown economy.

Answers to Arguments That Demonstrate Other Reasoning Problems

The previous sections of Part 3 covered the most common GRE Argument flaws—the "meat and potatoes" of the Argument writing task. This final section of Part 3 addresses additional flaws that are somewhat less common but which you should be sure not to overlook:

A Failing to adequately *define* a certain word or phrase on which the argument relies

B Appealing to potentially *irrelevant* considerations

C Relying on a factual account or statement that is too *vague* to provide meaningful support to the argument

D Relying on *ambiguous* evidence, which could serve to either support or undermine the argument

E Drawing an *overly broad conclusion*—one that is too sweeping or all-encompassing, given the evidence at hand

F Committing an error in logic; for example, calling for a *false choice* between two alternatives, *begging the question* (circular reasoning or "missing the point"), or *equivocating* (making irreconcilable claims, drawing conflicting conclusions, or advocating for both of two mutually exclusive choices).

This section contains essay responses to 36 official GRE Arguments. Each of these arguments suffers from at least one of the reasoning problems listed above (A–F). In the essays, specific paragraphs are marked by letter according to the type of reasoning problem (**A**, **B**, **C**, **D**, **E**, or **F**) under discussion.

> **NOTE:** Each of the essays here appears only in this section. Keep in mind, however, that these essays also discuss reasoning problems of the types covered earlier in Part 3.

Argument:
The environmental impact of copper **mining**

The author of this newsletter excerpt concludes that if consumers refuse to buy products made with Consolidated Copper Company (CCC) copper the company will eventually abandon its mining plans in the nation of West Fredonia, thereby preventing pollution and an "environmental disaster" in that country. To justify this conclusion the author points out that CCC has recently bought more than a million square miles of land in West Fredonia, and that West Fredonia is home to several endangered animal species. I find this argument specious on several grounds.

First, the author provides no evidence that the West Fredonia land that CCC has acquired amounts to a significant portion of land inhabited by endangered animal species, or that CCC's land is inhabited by endangered animal species at all. Nor does the author provide clear evidence that CCC's mining activities are of the type that might cause pollution, the extinction of animal species, or any other environmental damage. Lacking such evidence the author simply cannot convince me that CCC must abandon its plans in order that such damage be prevented.

Ⓐ Secondly, even assuming CCC's planned mining activities in West Fredonia will cause pollution and will endanger several animal species, it is nevertheless impossible to assess the author's broader contention that CCC's activities will result in "environmental disaster," at least without an agreed-upon definition of that term. If by "environmental disaster" the author simply means some pollution and the extinction of several animal species, then the claim would have merit; otherwise, it would not. Absent either a clear definition of the term or clear evidence that CCC's activities would carry grave environmental consequences by any reasonable definition, the author's contention that CCC's activities will result in environmental disaster is simply unjustified.

Thirdly, the author's position that environmental disaster is "inevitable" absent the prescribed boycott precludes the possibility that other measures can be taken to prevent CCC from carrying out its plans, or to offset any harm that CCC causes should it carry out its plans. Yet the author fails to provide assurances that no other means of preventing the predicted disaster are available. Lacking such evidence the author cannot reasonably conclude that the proposed boycott is needed to prevent that disaster.

Finally, even if the prescribed boycott is needed to prevent pollution and environmental disaster in West Fredonia, the author assumes too hastily that the boycott will suffice for these purposes. Perhaps additional measures would be required as well. For instance, perhaps consumers would also need to boycott other companies that pollute West Fredonia's environment. In short, without any evidence that the recommended course of action will be enough to prevent the predicted problems, the author's conclusion remains dubious at best.

In sum, as it stands the argument is wholly unpersuasive. To bolster it the author must show that CCC's planned mining activities on its newly acquired land will pollute and will threaten endangered animal species. The author must also define "environmental disaster" and show that the inevitable results of CCC's activities, absent the proposed boycott, would meet that definition. To better assess the argument it would be useful to know what other means are available for preventing CCC from mining in West Fredonia or, in the alternative, for mitigating the environmental impact of those mining activities. Also useful would be any information about the likelihood that the boycott would be effective in accomplishing its intended objectives.

Argument:
Eating soy to prevent fatigue and depression

This argument concludes that North Americans should eat soy on a regular basis as a means of preventing fatigue and depression. The argument cites a recent study showing that North Americans suffer far greater from these problems than people in Asia do, that Asians eat soy regularly whereas North Americans do not, and that soy is known to possess disease-preventing properties. The argument relies on several doubtful assumptions, and is therefore unconvincing.

First, the argument assumes that depression and fatigue are just as readily diagnosed in Asia as in North America. However, it is entirely possible that Asians suffering from these problems do not complain about them or otherwise admit them. For that matter, perhaps Asian medical doctors view certain symptoms that North Americans would consider signs of fatigue and depression as signs of some other problem.

Secondly, the argument assumes that the difference in soy consumption is the only possible explanation for this disparity in the occurrence of fatigue and depression. Yet the argument fails to substantiate this assumption. Common sense informs me that any one of a myriad of other differences—environmental, dietary, and genetic—might explain why North Americans suffer from these problems to a greater extent than Asians do. Without considering and ruling out alternative reasons for this disparity, the argument's conclusion that soy is the key to the disparity is indefensible.

Thirdly, the argument unfairly infers from the fact that soy is known to possess disease-preventing properties that these properties help prevent fatigue and depression specifically. The argument supplies no evidence to substantiate this assumption. Moreover, whether fatigue and depression are appropriately classified as diseases in the first place is questionable.

A Finally, even if the properties in soy can be shown to prevent fatigue and depression, the argument unfairly assumes that eating soy is the only means of ingesting the key substances. It is entirely possible that these same properties are found in other forms, and therefore that North Americans need not increase soy consumption to help prevent fatigue and depression.

The key to GRE Argument flaws **A**–**F** *can be found on page 289.*

In sum, the argument is dubious at best. Before I can accept its conclusion, the argument's proponent must provide better evidence that people in Asia in fact suffer less from fatigue and depression than North Americans do. To better evaluate the argument I would need to know what kinds of diseases the properties of soy are known to help prevent, and whether they relate at all to fatigue and depression. I would also need to know what other foods contain the same properties as soy— to determine what alternatives, if any, are available for preventing fatigue and depression.

Argument:
Lavender as a cure for **insomnia**

The speaker concludes that the scent of lavender provides an effective short-term cure for insomnia. To support this conclusion the speaker cites a three-week experiment in which researchers monitored the apparent effects of lavender on 30 insomniacs, who slept on lavender-scented pillows each night of the experiment. The speaker's account of the experiment reveals several critical problems with it. Together, these problems serve to undermine the speaker's argument.

A A threshold problem involves the definition of insomnia. The speaker fails to define this critical term. If insomnia is defined as an inability to fall asleep, then how soundly or long a person sleeps, or how tired a person feels after sleep, is irrelevant to whether the person suffers from insomnia. In short, without a dear definition of insomnia it is impossible to assess the strength of the argument.

Another fundamental problem is that the speaker omits to inform us about the test subjects' sleep patterns just prior to the experiment. It is impossible to conclude with any confidence that the subjects benefited from sleeping on lavender-scented pillows without comparing how they slept with the pillows to how they sleep without them.

B Yet another problem involves the fact that subjects slept more soundly and awakened less tired the first week than the second, and that they used their regular sleep medication the first week but not the second. This evidence tends to show only that the subjects' other sleep medications were effective; it proves nothing about the effectiveness of lavender.

A fourth problem involves the speaker's account of the experiment's third week, during which the speaker reports only that the subjects slept longer and more soundly than in the previous two weeks. We are not informed whether the subjects took any medication during the third week. Assuming they did not, any one of a variety of factors other than the lavender-scented pillows might explain the third week's results. Perhaps the subjects were simply making up for sleep they lost the previous week—when they discontinued their regular medication. Or perhaps the subjects were finally becoming accustomed to the lavender-scented pillows, which actually disturbed sleep initially. In short, without ruling out other explanations for the third week's results, the speaker cannot confidently identify what caused the subjects to sleep longer and more soundly that week.

Two final problems with the argument involve the experimental process. The experiment's results are reliable only if all other factors that might affect sleep patterns remained constant during the three-week period, and if the number of experimental subjects is statistically significant. Without evidence of the experiment's methodological and statistical reliability, the speaker's conclusion is unjustifiable.

In conclusion, the argument is unconvincing as it stands. To strengthen the assertion that lavender-scented pillows provide a short-term cure for insomnia, the author must provide evidence that the test subjects' insomnia was worse just prior to the experiment than at the conclusion of the experiment, and that the number of subjects is statistically sufficient to warrant the conclusion. To better assess the argument, we would need a clear definition of insomnia, as well as more information about whether the researchers conducted the experiment in a controlled environment.

Argument:
Governor Riedeburg's candidacy

This letter concludes that Governor Riedeburg is the best-qualified candidate for the job of state governor. To justify this conclusion the letter points out various statewide trends since the governor was elected, and the fact that she has promised to keep big companies in the state, thereby providing jobs for any new residents. However, close scrutiny of the argument reveals various logical problems, which render it unconvincing.

One problem with the argument is that the letter's author might be assigning a false cause to these statewide trends. The author provides no evidence that Riedeburg's policies and actions as governor were indeed the reason for these developments. Without such evidence, it is equally possible that other factors are instead responsible for the trends. For instance, perhaps the crime rate has declined due to legislative or judicial action over which Riedeburg had no control. Perhaps the rise in the state's population is the result of sociological trends that have nothing to do with Riedeburg's policies as governor. Or perhaps people are moving to the state for other reasons, such as the state's climate. Moreover, the argument assumes that an increase in population is a positive development in the first place; yet it is entirely possible that the state's residents properly view this trend as a negative one. If so, and if Riedeburg's policies have contributed to this trend, then the author cannot reasonably conclude based on this evidence that Riedeburg is the best-qualified candidate.

Another problem with the argument involves Riedeburg's promise to keep big companies in the state, thereby providing jobs for any new residents. Assuming that Riedeburg keeps her promise in the first place, the author provides no evidence that these employers would be either willing or able to hire new residents. Perhaps these employers plan to curtail new hiring in any event; or perhaps they plan to hire new employees only among current state residents. Moreover, whether these employers are able to hire new employees depends on a variety of extrinsic economic factors over which Riedeburg might have no control. Without accounting for these possibilities, the

The key to GRE Argument flaws **Ⓐ**—**Ⓕ** *can be found on page 289.*

author cannot rely on Riedeburg's promise to conclude that she is the best-qualified candidate for the job of state governor.

A Finally, the author's conclusion that Riedeburg is "the best-qualified candidate" raises two problems in itself. First, regardless of Riedeburg's record as governor it is entirely possible that one or more other candidates are actually better qualified. Second, the letter fails to adequately define what makes a candidate for state governor qualified. Without indicating what the ideal qualifications would be and ruling out the possibility that another candidate better meets these qualifications, the author cannot make a convincing case that Riedeburg is the best-qualified candidate.

In conclusion, the argument is unpersuasive as it stands. To strengthen it the author must provide clear evidence that it was Riedeburg who was responsible for the currents trends, and that the current population trend is desirable in the first place. The author must also show that the state's major employers would be willing and able to hire new residents in the future. Finally, to better evaluate the argument we would need more information about what defines an ideal governor and how well other candidates meet that definition.

Argument:
How an **automobile manufacturing company** can thrive

In this memo, the manager of a car manufacturing company argues that the company must add a second plant in order to continue to thrive. To support this argument the manager points out that its existing plant can only produce 40 million cars, but that according to company projections 80 million people will want to buy the company's cars. The manager claims that the company can achieve its objective by operating the new plant on a part-time basis using workers from the existing plant on a rotational basis. To support this claim the manager points out that a certain airplane manufacturing company employed this strategy successfully five years ago. The manager's argument is problematic in several critical respects.

First of all, the manager assumes that no course of action other than the proposed one will ensure that the company continues to thrive; yet the manager fails to substantiate this assumption. Since demand is expected to be very high, perhaps the company can continue to thrive simply by raising the price of its cars. For that matter, perhaps the company can continue to thrive if it makes no changes at all. Without accounting for either possibility the manager cannot convince me that building a second plant is necessary.

Secondly, even if building a second plant is necessary for the company to continue to thrive, in itself this course of action might not suffice. After all, how can the manager reasonably expect that a second plant will produce as many cars as the existing one if it operates on only a part-time basis? And if the new plant borrows labor from the existing plant then production at the existing plant might decline.

Ⓐ Thus, unless the manager can convince me that the new plant will be far more efficient than the current plant I do not see any way that operating a new plant on a part-time basis can double the company's production.

Finally, the mere fact that one certain airplane manufacturer adopted a similar plan with some success is scant evidence that this car company will succeed if it follows the manager's plan. The memo provides no information about how many airplanes the airplane manufacturer produced. Nor does the memo identify what constituted "success" for the airplane manufacturer. Perhaps that company considered itself successful by producing only an additional 10% more airplanes, or by merely managing to avoid bankruptcy. In short, as it stands the anecdotal evidence about the airplane company is far too vague to lend meaningful support to the manager's argument.

In sum, the manager's plan seems ill conceived. To strengthen the argument that the company must add a second plant to continue to thrive, the manager must at the very least convince me that the company has no alternative means of achieving this objective. The manager should also provide evidence that operating a new plant on only a part-time basis would suffice to double production—perhaps by showing that the new plant would employ newer, more efficient equipment than the existing plant. To better assess the argument it would be useful to know what constituted "success" for the airplane manufacturer and, more specifically, the percentage by which that company increased production as a result of adding a second plant.

Argument:
Should the city of **Dalton** adopt a curfew for minors?

The author of this editorial argues that in order to reduce its rising crime rate the city of Dalton should establish a 10:00 p.m. curfew for minors under age 18. The author also claims that the curfew would control juvenile delinquency as well as prevent minors from becoming crime victims. To support these claims the author points out that Williamsville established a similar curfew four months ago, and that since then Williamsville's youth crime rate has dropped by 27% during curfew hours. The author also points out that in Williamsville's town square no crimes have been reported in the last four months, yet Williamsville residents had previously expressed particular outrage about the square's high crime rate. I find the editorial logically unconvincing in several respects.

To begin with, the author has failed to convince me that Williamsville's overall crime rate has declined, or that the curfew was responsible for any such decline. It is entirely possible that although that city's youth crime rate has declined, its adult crime rate has risen. If so, this fact would seriously call into question the author's claim that a similar curfew would reduce Dalton's overall crime rate. Even if Williamsville's overall crime rate has declined in the last four months, the decline is not necessarily attributable to the curfew. Perhaps Williamsville has also enhanced its police enforcement, or established social programs that help minors avoid delinquency. In short, without evidence that all other conditions that might affect Williamsville's crime rate have remained unchanged

The key to GRE Argument flaws **Ⓐ**–**Ⓕ** *can be found on page 289.*

during the last four months, the author's claim that the curfew is responsible for the drop in that city's crime rate is dubious at best.

Moreover, the evidence involving the town square does not adequately show that Williamsville's curfew has been effective in reducing its crime rate. The number of crimes reported in the square does not necessarily reflect the number actually committed there. Also, it is entirely possible that Williamsville's residents had already abandoned the town square at night by the time Williamsville established the curfew. If so, then the mere fact that no crimes in the square have been committed or reported recently proves nothing about the effectiveness of the curfew.

Even if Williamsville's curfew was responsible for a decline in that city's overall crime rate, the editorial's claim that a similar curfew would be effective in Dalton is unwarranted. Dalton might differ from Williamsville in ways that would undermine the curfew's effectiveness in Dalton. Or perhaps the percentage of crimes that are committed by adults is far greater in Dalton that in Williamsville. In either case, a curfew that is effective in reducing Williamsville's overall crime rate might be far less effective in reducing Dalton's.

Ⓐ Even assuming the proposed curfew would reduce Dalton's overall crime rate, the author unfairly infers that the curfew would also curb juvenile delinquency. The author's definition of juvenile delinquency might embrace additional behaviors— ones that don't amount to crimes. Besides, a reduction in the overall crime rate does not necessarily indicate a reduction in the youth crime rate.

The author's further inference that the curfew would protect minors from becoming crime victims is also unwarranted. This inference depends on the assumption that all crimes against youths occur during curfew hours. Yet common sense informs me that many such crimes occur during other hours. The inference also rests on the assumption that it is adults who are committing all crimes against youths. Yet the author fails to account for the possibility that some crimes against youths are committed by other youths.

In sum, the editorial relies on a series of dubious assumptions, which render it wholly unpersuasive. To bolster the editorial's claims the author must provide clear evidence that the curfew, and not some other phenomenon, was in fact responsible for a decline in Williamsville's youth crime rate. The author must also show that the curfew would have a similar effect in Dalton, and that the curfew would result in a decline in not just the youth crime rate but also the overall crime rate. To better assess the author's final two claims I would need to know how the author defines "juvenile delinquency," and what percentage of crimes against Dalton's youth are committed by other youths.

Argument:
Should Nature's Way open a store in **Plainsville**?

In this memo the vice president of Nature's Way (NW), a chain of stores selling health food and health-related products, recommends opening a store in Plainsville. To support this recommendation the vice president cites the following facts about Plainsville:

(1) sales of exercise shoes and clothing are at all-time highs; (2) the local health club is more popular than ever; and (3) the city's schoolchildren are required to participate in a fitness program. Close scrutiny of each of these facts, however, reveals that none of them lend credible support to the recommendation.

First, strong sales of exercise apparel do not necessarily indicate that Plainsville residents would be interested in NW's products, or that these residents are interested in exercising. Perhaps exercise apparel happens to be fashionable at the moment, or inexpensive compared to other types of clothing. For that matter, perhaps the stronger-than-usual sales are due to increasing sales to tourists. In short, without ruling out other possible reasons for the strong sales the vice president cannot convince me on the basis of them that Plainsville residents are exercising regularly, let alone that they would be interested in buying the sorts of food and other products that NW sells.

Secondly, even if exercise is more popular among Plainsville residents than ever before, the vice president assumes further that people who exercise regularly are also interested in buying health food and health-related products. Yet the memo contains no evidence to support this assumption. Lacking such evidence it is equally possible that aside from exercising Plainsville residents have little interest in leading a healthy lifestyle. In fact, perhaps as a result of regular exercise they believe they are sufficiently fit and healthy and do not need a healthy diet.

B Thirdly, the popularity of the local health club is little indication that NW will earn a profit from a store in Plainsville. Perhaps club members live in an area of Plainsville nowhere near feasible sites for a NW store. Or perhaps the club's primary appeal is as a singles meeting place, and that members actually have little interest in a healthy lifestyle. Besides, even if the club's members would patronize a NW store these members might be insufficient in number to ensure a profit for the store, especially considering that this health club is the only one in Plainsville.

Fourth, the fact that a certain fitness program is mandatory for Plainsville's schoolchildren accomplishes nothing toward bolstering the recommendation. Many years must pass before these children will be old enough to make buying decisions when it comes to food and health-related products. Their habits and interests might change radically over time. Besides, mandatory participation is no indication of genuine interest in health or fitness. Moreover, when these children grow older it is entirely possible that they will favor an unhealthy lifestyle—as a reaction to the healthful habits imposed upon them now.

Finally, even assuming that Plainsville residents are strongly interested in eating health foods and health-related products, the recommendation rests on two additional assumptions: (1) that this interest will continue in the foreseeable future, and (2) that

The key to GRE Argument flaws **A** – **F** *can be found on page 289.*

Plainsville residents will prefer NW over other merchants that sell similar products. Until the vice president substantiates both assumptions I remain unconvinced that a NW store in Plainsville would be profitable.

In sum, the recommendation relies on certain doubtful assumptions that render it unconvincing as it stands. To bolster the recommendation the vice president must provide clear evidence—perhaps by way of a local survey or study—that Plainsville residents who buy and wear exercise apparel, and especially the health club's members, do in fact exercise regularly, and that these exercisers are likely to buy health foods and health-related products at a NW store. To better assess the recommendation, I would need to know why Plainsville's health club is popular, and why Plainsville does not contain more health clubs. I would also need to know what competition NW might face in Plainsville.

Argument:
Walnut Grove's trash collection service

This letter recommends that Walnut Grove continue to contract with EZ Disposal, which has provided trash-collection services to Walnut Grove for ten years, rather than switching to ABC Waste. To justify this recommendation the letter's author notes that even though ABC's weekly fee is $500 less than EZ's, EZ collects twice per week whereas ABC would collect only once per week. The author also points out that, although both companies have the same number of trucks, EZ has ordered additional trucks. Finally, the author cites a recent survey in which 80% of respondents indicated that they were satisfied with EZ's service. I find this recommendation specious on several grounds.

Ⓑ First of all, the fact that EZ collects trash twice as often as ABC is significant only if the town would benefit from an additional collection each week. Yet the author provides no evidence that this is the case. For all we know, one collection per week suffices to dispose all of the town's trash. If so, then on the basis of frequency of collection it would make no sense to favor EZ's costlier service over ABC's less expensive one.

Ⓑ Secondly, the fact that EZ has ordered more trucks proves little in itself about which service would be the better choice for Walnut Grove. Perhaps EZ does not plan to use its new trucks for collecting Walnut Grove's trash. For that matter, perhaps EZ does not use its entire current fleet for this purpose, whereas ABC would. Besides, the author does not indicate when EZ will receive its new trucks; the later the delivery date, the less significant this factor should be in Walnut Grove's decision.

Thirdly, the mere fact that most respondents to a recent survey considered EZ's service satisfactory provides little support to the author's recommendation. The author fails to provide assurances that these respondents are representative of the overall population of people whose trash EZ collects. Moreover, even if that population is generally satisfied it is entirely possible that they would be even more satisfied with ABC's services.

In sum, the recommendation is not well supported. To bolster it the letter's author must provide specific evidence that Walnut Grove would benefit from an additional trash collection each week, and that the use of additional trucks would improve service to Walnut Grove. To better assess the strength of the recommendation I would need more information about the demographic profile of the survey's respondents. It would also be helpful to obtain opinions from municipalities and individuals that have some experience with both EZ and ABC.

Argument:
The effects of corporate **downsizing**

This editorial disagrees with a certain article's claim that as a result of widespread corporate downsizing many able workers have faced serious long-term economic hardship—due to their inability to find other suitable employment. To justify its disagreement with this claim the editorial cites the following three findings of a recent report: (1) There has been a net increase in the number of new jobs created since 1992, (2) many workers who lost their jobs have found other work, and (3) most newly created jobs are full-time positions in industries that tend to pay above-average wages. Careful scrutiny of these findings, however, reveals that they accomplish little toward refuting the article's claim.

B Regarding the first finding, the editorial overlooks the possibility that most of the newly created jobs since 1992 are not suitable for job seekers downsized by corporations. Perhaps the vast majority of these jobs involve food serving, clerical assistance, cleaning and maintenance, and other tasks requiring a low level of skill and experience. At the same time, perhaps most downsized job seekers are highly educated middle managers looking for the same type of work elsewhere. In short, lacking evidence that the newly created jobs match the skills, experience, and interests of the downsized corporate employees, the editorial's author cannot convincingly refute the article's claim.

C As for the second finding, the term "many" is far too vague to allow for any meaningful conclusions; if "many" amounts to an insignificant percentage of downsized employees, then the finding is of little use in refuting the article's claim. Moreover, the workers to whom this finding refers to are not necessarily downsized corporate employees. To the extent that they are not, this second finding is irrelevant in drawing any conclusions about the impact of corporate downsizing on downsized employees.

B The third finding would lend support to the author's position only under two assumptions: (1) that the newly created jobs in those high-paying industries are suitable for downsized corporate employees, and (2) that the new jobs are among the high-paying ones. Otherwise, downsized employees seeking jobs would be unlikely to regain their former economic status by applying for these newly created positions, whether or not these positions are full-time.

In sum, the author has not effectively refuted the article's claim that corporate downsizing has worked economic hardship on downsized corporate employees. To more effectively refute the claim the author should provide clear evidence that most of those job-seekers are able to fill the sorts of new jobs that have been created since 1992, and

The key to GRE Argument flaws **A** – **F** *can be found on page 289.*

that these new positions are suitable for those job-seekers given their work experience, areas of interest, and former salaries.

Argument:
Saving **Tria**'s beach sand and its tourist industry

This letter's author recommends charging fees for public access to Tria's beaches as an effective means of raising funds for the purpose of saving Tria's tourist industry. The author reasons that beach-access fees would reduce the number of beachgoers while providing revenue for replenishing beach sand needed to protect nearby buildings, thereby enhancing the area's attractiveness to tourists. To support this argument the author points out that beach sand was replenished on the nearby island of Batia, thereby reducing the risk of storm damage to buildings there. I find the argument unconvincing for several reasons.

First of all, the author makes certain dubious assumptions about the impact of beach-access fees. On the one hand, the author ignores the possibility that charging fees might deter so many tourists that Tria would be worse off overall. On the other hand, perhaps the vast majority of Tria's tourists and residents alike would happily pay for beach access, in which case Tria's beaches would continue to be no less crowded than they are now. Under either scenario, adopting the author's proposal might harm, rather than benefit, Tria's tourist industry in the long run.

Secondly, the mere fact that on nearby Batia replenishing beach sand has served to protect shoreline buildings is scant evidence that Tria would achieve its goals by following Batia's example. Perhaps the same course of action would be ineffective on Tria due to geological differences between the two islands. Or perhaps Batia is in a far better position than Tria financially to replenish its sand on a continual basis. In short, lacking evidence that conditions on the two islands are relevantly similar, the author cannot convince me on the basis of Batia's experience that the proposed course of action would be effective in attaining Tria's goals.

B Thirdly, even if replenishing Tria's beach sand is financially feasible and would protect nearby buildings, the author provides no evidence that Tria's tourist industry would be saved thereby. Perhaps Tria's tourist appeal has little to do with the beach and nearby buildings; for that matter, perhaps Tria's tourist appeal would be greater with fewer buildings along the coast. Since the author provides no firm evidence that replenishing sand and protecting nearby buildings would be more beneficial to Tria's tourist industry than allowing nature to take its course, I do not find the author's argument the least bit compelling.

Argument:
Replacing an **old town hall**

This editorial concludes that the town of Rockingham would save money by replacing its old town hall with a larger, more energy-efficient one. To support the argument the editorial's author cites the need for a larger building to comfortably accommodate employees, and the fact that the proposed building would cost less per cubic foot to heat and cool than the current building would. However, the editorial is unconvincing for several reasons.

First of all, even though it would cost less per cubic foot to heat and cool the new building, because the new building would be larger the total cooling and heating costs might actually be greater than they are now. Add to this possibility the initial cost of replacing the structure, and in all likelihood the new building would not save money for the town. Besides, the argument ignores other, potentially less expensive, means of reducing current heating and cooling costs—for example, retrofitting the building with a new climate control system.

B Secondly, the editorial relies partly on the fact that the current building cannot comfortably accommodate all the people who work in it. However, this fact in itself is irrelevant to whether the town would save money by replacing the building. Besides, the editorial ignores other, potentially less expensive, solutions to the current comfort problem—for example, adding an annex to the current structure.

F Thirdly, the editorial relies partly on the assertion that the town could generate income by renting out part of a larger new building. However, the author equivocates here—on the one hand claiming that a larger building is needed because the old one is too small to accommodate employees, while on the other hand proposing that the additional space not be used to solve this problem. The use of conflicting evidence to support the same conclusion renders the argument wholly unpersuasive.

In conclusion, the editorial is unconvincing as it stands. To strengthen the assertion that a new building would save the town money, the editorial's author must provide a detailed analysis comparing the cost of cooling and heating the current hall to the anticipated cost of cooling and heating the new hall. In this analysis, the author must factor in the initial cost of replacing the old hall, as well as the additional rental income that the larger hall might generate. Finally, the author must choose between two competing objectives: creating a more spacious environment for current employees or creating a larger hall for the purpose of generating rental income.

Argument:
Selecting a food service provider for an **employee cafeteria**

This memo recommends that Cedar Corporation replace its current food provider, Good-Taste, with Discount Foods. To support this recommendation, the memo's author cites Good-Taste's increasing fees, the fact that three Cedar employees refuse to eat in the cafeteria, and various features of Discount Foods. For several reasons, this evidence fails to provide adequate support for the recommendation.

The memo's reliance on the fact that three Cedar employees find eating in the company cafeteria "unbearable" presents two problems. First, the memo unfairly assumes that Good-Taste is responsible for these complaints. It is entirely possible that other conditions in the cafeteria are instead responsible. Second, the memo assumes

The key to GRE Argument flaws **A**—**F** *can be found on page 289.*

that complaints by only three Cedar employees constitutes a statistically significant number which warrants replacing Good-Taste with another food provider. However, the memo provides no evidence that this is the case.

B Another problem with the recommendation is that it relies partly on the fact that Good-Taste has been increasing its fees and is now the second-most-expensive food provider available to Cedar. Yet the recommendation is based on what food provider would best satisfy Cedar's employees, not what provider would reduce Cedar's costs.

In other words, this evidence is not directly relevant to the reasons for the author's recommendation. Even if expense were a legitimate factor, it is possible that Discount is even more expensive than Good-Taste.

Yet another problem with the recommendation is that it relies partly on the need to accommodate employees with special dietary needs. The memo provides no evidence that Good-Taste is any less capable than Discount of accommodating these employees. Rather, the memo merely provides that Discount offers "a varied menu of fish and poultry." Without a more detailed comparison between the offerings of the two companies, it is unfair to conclude that one would meet the needs of Cedar's employees better than the other would.

Finally, the recommendation relies partly on the fact that in one taste test the memo's author found Discount Foods to be "delicious." In all likelihood, however, the author's tastes do not represent the collective tastes of Cedar employees; accordingly, the author's report is patently insufficient to demonstrate that Cedar's employees would be more satisfied with Discount than with Good-Taste.

In conclusion, the letter's author fails to adequately support the recommendation that Cedar replace Good-Taste with Discount. To strengthen the argument, the author must provide clear evidence that Cedar employees are dissatisfied with Good-Taste's food and that they would be more satisfied with Discount's food. To better evaluate the argument, we would need more information comparing the two companies' menus to determine which is more varied and caters to those with special dietary needs.

Argument:
Outlook for **new hires** and layoffs

The speaker concludes that employees of major U.S. corporations should not fear that they will lose their jobs in the near future. To support this conclusion the speaker cites the fact that most companies expect to hire new employees next year, while fewer plan to lay off employees. The speaker also cites the current proliferation of job-finding resources. The argument is problematic in several critical respects.

First of all, the argument depends on the assumption that the total number of expected hires exceeds the total number of expected layoffs. However, we are not informed whether this is the case. It is possible that, although more companies expect to hire than lay off employees, the total number of employees expected to be laid off exceeds the total number expected to be hired. If true, this fact would serve to refute the speaker's conclusion that employees of major U.S. corporations should not expect to be laid off.

Secondly, the argument assumes that the companies that expect to hire next year are major U.S. corporations. However, it is entirely possible that these are the firms that expect layoffs, while it is smaller companies that expect to hire. Common sense tells me that this is a reasonable possibility, because the number of small companies greatly exceeds the number of large U.S. corporations. Moreover, even if it is the major U.S. corporations that expect to do most of the hiring next year, it is entirely possible that it is these same companies that expect to do most of the laying off. Again, common sense informs me that this is entirely possible—that these employers intend to replace many current employees or job positions with new ones.

Thirdly, the argument rests on the dubious assumption that all conditions relevant to a company's decision to hire or lay off employees will remain unchanged in the near future. While this might be the case, it is equally possible that unexpected changes in general economic conditions will result in more layoffs among major U.S. corporations next year than these firms now anticipate.

B Finally, the argument seems to rely partly on the proliferation of job-finding programs. While this fact might allay the worries of employees that they will not find new employment, it is irrelevant to whether these employees should expect to be laid off in the first place. In fact, it can even be argued that the proliferation of job-finding programs is evidence of increasing job attrition, and therefore evidence that these employees' fears are well founded.

In conclusion, the argument is unconvincing as it stands. To strengthen it the author must provide clear evidence that the number of expected hires exceeds the number of expected layoffs, and that major U.S. corporations are the companies planning to hire rather than to lay off employees.

Argument:
Reelecting members of the **town school board**

This editorial argues that the town's school board members are unconcerned about promoting high-quality arts education in local schools, and therefore should not be reelected. To support this argument the editorial's author points out that student participation in high-school drama programs has been declining steadily, and that the board recently refused to renew the high-school drama director's contract, despite the fact that he has written several award-winning plays. The author also cites the fact that $300,000 of the high school budget is allotted to athletic programs, and that the head football coach is the highest paid teacher. This argument is unpersuasive for a variety of reasons.

B First and foremost, the editorial indicates neither how long the current board members have occupied their board positions nor the scope of their authority. Perhaps they are new members and the facts that the editorial cites are attributable to events and decisions occurring before the current board members assumed their positions. If

The key to GRE Argument flaws **A**–**F** *can be found on page 289.*

so, and if the current board either has not had adequate opportunity or does not have adequate authority to reverse these developments, then any claim regarding their level of concern about arts education is unjustifiable—at least based on the evidence cited.

Even assuming adequate authority and tenure on the part of the current board members, they are not necessarily responsible for the declining student participation in drama programs. The decline might be due to some other factor. For instance, perhaps students generally dislike the current drama director. If so, then the board's refusal to renew his contract would indicate that the board is attempting to reverse the decline, and that the board is in fact concerned about facilitating arts education.

D As for the fact that $300,000 is devoted to athletic programs, the editorial does not indicate the school's total budget. It is entirely possible that $300,000 accounts for a small portion of that budget compared to the amount budgeted for the arts. If so, and if the current school board is at least partly responsible for the current budget, these facts would cast considerable doubt on the editorial's claim that the board is unconcerned about promoting arts education.

Admittedly, the fact that the head football coach is the highest paid teacher provides some support for the editorial's claim—assuming that the current board members are at least partially responsible for that salary. However, this fact in itself is insufficient to show that the board members are unconcerned about promoting arts education. Perhaps the football coach carries additional duties that warrant the high salary; in fact, perhaps he also teaches drama or music. Or perhaps his salary is high simply because he has been a teaching-staff member longer than nearly any other local school teacher.

D Finally, the editorial's claim overlooks the fact that local arts education embraces not just high-school drama but also drama programs at lower levels, and music, dance, and visual- and graphic-arts programs. Thus, even if the board's decisions indicate that they place a low priority on high-school drama education, it is entirely possible that the board is real-locating resources from that program to other arts programs. If so, then the editorial's claim is wrong, and the proper conclusion is that the board is actively concerned about promoting arts education as a whole in local schools.

In sum, the argument is unconvincing as it stands. To strengthen it the editorial's author must at the very least assure me that the current board members have been on the board long enough to have adequate opportunity to demonstrate their level of concern for arts education, and that they have the authority to do so. The author should also provide clear evidence that the decisions of these board members were responsible for the declining student participation in drama programs. To better assess the argument I would need to know the reason why the board has not renewed the current drama director's contract. I would also need to know what percentage of the high school's current budget is allocated not just to drama programs but to arts education generally, so that I could compare that percentage with the percentages allocated to other programs.

Argument:
How **Automate** can retain its best workers

In this memo the president of Automate, an automobile manufacturer, concludes that to retain its best employees Automate must offer them salaries equal to those that Sparks automobile manufacturing pays its employees. To justify this conclusion the president points out that Sparks has just moved into the state and is now advertising job openings with salaries twice as high as those Automate pays its assembly-line workers, and that some Automate employees have already defected to Sparks. As further support for the argument, the president notes that Sparks plans to build additional plants in the state and will need to staff those plants. I find the argument unconvincing on several grounds.

ⓒ First, the memo does not indicate what kinds of jobs Sparks is now advertising— the ones for which salaries are to be twice those paid to Automate's assembly-line workers. Those jobs might be top management positions or other jobs for which salaries are often significantly higher than those for assembly-line work. If so, this fact would serve to refute the president's assumption that Sparks is paying higher salaries than Automate for similar work.

Secondly, the president assumes that the reason why some Automate workers have defected to Sparks is that Sparks has offered them higher salaries. Yet, the president fails to provide evidence to substantiate this assumption. Lacking such evidence, those defectors might have gone to work for Sparks because the city where Sparks is located is a preferable place to live, or because Sparks offers other job incentives that Automate does not. And, if the defectors accepted jobs at Sparks before Sparks began offering higher salaries, then salary could not have been a factor in their decision to defect to Sparks. In short, until the president establishes a clear causal relationship between the advertised salaries and the defection of some Automate employees to Sparks, the president cannot reasonably conclude that Automate must increase its salaries in order to prevent additional employees from defecting to Sparks in the future.

Thirdly, even assuming that those defectors did leave Automate because Sparks offered higher salaries for similar work, the president's argument rests on the additional assumptions that the number of defectors is significant and that these defectors are valuable to Automate. Yet the president fails to substantiate either assumption. Perhaps only a very small percentage of Automate's worker's have defected; if so, the president's proposed salary increases might amount to an overreaction. Or, perhaps the defectors were among Automate's least valuable employees; for that matter, perhaps Automate's most valuable employees are the ones who are most loyal and would not leave Automate even if they were offered a higher salary elsewhere. Without substantiating both assumptions, the president cannot reasonably conclude that Automate must raise the salaries of its best workers in order to retain them.

Finally, the mere fact that Sparks plans to build additional new plants in the state amounts to scant evidence that Automate will continue to lose valuable employees unless it raises their salaries. Perhaps Sparks plans to staff those new plants with workers

The key to GRE Argument flaws **Ⓐ**–**Ⓕ** *can be found on page 289.*

from its other plants, or from other sources besides Automate. Or, perhaps Sparks is advertising high salaries now simply to gain a foothold into the state's labor market, and that once Sparks is established in the state it will offer lower salaries for new jobs. Besides, Sparks' plan to build additional plants might amount to sheer speculation, in which case the president's proposed salary increases would seem hasty.

In sum, the president's recommendation seems ill conceived, at least lacking additional supporting evidence. To bolster the argument the president must provide clear evidence that a significant percentage of Automate's valuable employees have defected to Sparks because Sparks offered them higher salaries for similar work—rather than for some other reason. The president must also provide better evidence that this is a trend that is likely to continue and to harm Automate's operations unless Automate boosts the salaries of its best employees to match the salaries Sparks would pay those employees

---

Argument:
Learning to read by listening to **books on tape**

This editorial concludes that the school board should invest in audiocassettes because listening to audiocassettes makes elementary students more eager to learn and to read. To support this conclusion the editorial cites studies showing the value of listening to someone else read. However, close scrutiny of this evidence and of the editorial's line of reasoning reveals that they provide little credible support for the editorial's conclusion.

To begin with, the argument claims that for a poor reader the isolation of reading will provide a general disincentive to do schoolwork. However, the author provides no evidence to support this claim. It is just as possible that a child who has difficulty reading might excel at other subjects that do not require much reading, such as mathematics or music. Besides, this argument assumes that learning to read must be an isolated activity. Experience informs us, however, that this is not the case, especially for elementary school students who typically learn to read in a group environment.

C The editorial goes on to cite studies which "attest to the value" of allowing students to hear books read allowed. However, as it stands this evidence is far too vague to support the editorial's conclusion; we are not informed whether the "value" relates specifically to reading skills. Common sense tells me that while audiocassettes can help any person learn facts and understand concepts, a skill such as reading can only be learned by practicing the skill itself.

Nor are we informed about the manner in which books were read aloud in the study; were they read directly by parents or were they recorded on audiocassettes? Absent additional information about the cited studies, these studies lend no credible support to the conclusion that audiocassettes will help elementary school students to read and to learn.

The editorial continues by claiming that listening to audiocassettes will make children better readers because when parents read aloud to their children these children become better readers. This argument by analogy is wholly unpersuasive. The latter allows for interaction between parent and child, while the former does not. The latter allows for the child to view written words as the parent reads—that is, to read—while the former does not. Besides, common sense and experience tell us that audiocassettes, which provide for passive listening, are likely to serve as crutches that dissuade children from active reading—instead of encouraging them to read.

In conclusion, the editorial is unconvincing as it stands. To strengthen the argument, the editorial's author must provide more compelling evidence that listening to audiocassettes will actually help and encourage elementary school students to read, not just to learn in general. In order to better evaluate the argument, we would need more information about whether the cited studies refer specifically to the value of audiocassettes and specifically to their value in terms of the reading and learning processes.

Argument:
Should **Happy Pancake House** serve margarine or butter?

In this argument the speaker recommends that, in order to save money, Happy Pancake House (HPH) should serve margarine instead of butter at all its restaurants. To support the argument, the speaker points out that HPH's Southwestern restaurants now serve margarine but not butter, and that only 2% of these restaurants' customers have complained about the change. The speaker also cites reports from many servers that a number of customers asking for butter have not complained when given margarine instead. This argument is unconvincing for several reasons.

First of all, the speaker does not indicate how long these restaurants have been refusing butter to customers. If the change is very recent, it is possible that insufficient data have been collected to draw any reliable conclusions. Lacking this information I cannot assess the reliability of the evidence for the purpose of showing that HPH customers in the Southwest are generally happy with the change.

Secondly, the speaker fails to indicate what portion of HPH customers order meals calling for either butter or margarine. Presumably, the vast majority of meals served at any pancake restaurant call for one or the other. Yet it is entirely possible that a significant percentage of HPH customers do not order pancakes, or prefer fruit or another topping instead. The greater this percentage, the less meaningful any statistic about the level of customer satisfaction among all of HPH's Southwestern customers as an indicator of preference for butter or margarine.

Thirdly, the speaker unfairly assumes that HPH customers unhappy with the change generally complain about it. Perhaps many such customers express their displeasure simply by not returning to the restaurant. The greater the percentage of such customers, the weaker the argument's evidence as a sign of customer satisfaction with the change.

C Two additional problems specifically involve the reports from "many" servers that "a number" of customers asking for butter do not complain when served margarine

The key to GRE Argument flaws **A**–**F** *can be found on page 289.*

instead. Since the speaker fails to indicate the percentage of servers reporting or customers who have not complained to servers, this evidence is far too vague to be meaningful. Also, the speaker omits any mention of reports from servers about customers who have complained. Since the anecdotal evidence is one-sided, it is inadequate to assess overall customer satisfaction with the change.

Finally, even if HPH's Southwest customers are happy with the change, the speaker unfairly assumes that customers in other regions will respond similarly to it. Perhaps Southwesterners are generally less concerned than other people about whether they eat margarine or butter. Or perhaps Southwesterners actually prefer margarine to butter, in contrast to prevailing tastes elsewhere. Or perhaps Southwesterners have relatively few choices when it comes to pancake restaurants.

In sum, the speaker's argument is weak. To better assess it I would need to know: (1) how long the change has been in effect in the Southwest, (2) what percentage of HPH servers and managers have received customer complaints about the change, and (3) the number of such complaints as a percentage of the total number of HPH customers who order meals calling for either butter or margarine. To strengthen the argument, the speaker must provide clear evidence—perhaps by way of a reliable survey—that HPH customers in other regions are likely to be happy with the change and continue to patronize HPH after the change.

Argument:
Homework assignments and academic performance

The speaker argues that if the state board of education required that homework be assigned to high school students no more than twice per week academic performance would improve. To support this assertion the speaker cites a statewide survey of math and science teachers. According to the survey, students in the Marlee district, who are assigned homework no more than once per week, achieve better grades and are less likely to repeat a school year than students in the Sanlee district, who are assigned homework every night. Close scrutiny reveals, however, that this evidence provides little credible support for the speaker's assertion.

To begin with, the survey appears to suffer from two statistical problems, either of which renders the survey's results unreliable. First, the speaker relies on statistics from only two districts; however, it is entirely possible that these two districts are not representative of the state's school districts overall. Second, the survey involved only math and science teachers. Yet the speaker draws a broad recommendation for all teachers based on the survey's results.

In addition, the speaker's recommendation relies on the assumption that the amount of homework assigned to students is the only possible reason for the comparative academic performance between students in the two districts. However, in all likelihood this is simply not the case. Perhaps Sanlee teachers are stricter graders then Marlee teachers. Or perhaps Sanlee teachers are less effective than Marlee teachers, and therefore Sanlee students would perform more poorly regardless of homework schedule.

Or perhaps fewer Sanlee students than Marlee students actually do their assigned homework. In short, in order to properly conclude that fewer homework assignments results in better academic performance, the speaker must first rule out all other feasible explanations for the disparity in academic performance between the two districts.

C Finally, the survey results as reported by the speaker are too vague to support any firm conclusion. The speaker reports that Sanlee students receive lower grades and are more likely to repeat a school year then Marlee students. Yet the speaker does not indicate whether this fact applies to Sanlee and Marlee students generally, or just to math and science students. The speaker's recommendation for all high school students might be defensible in the former case, but not in the latter case.

In conclusion, the recommendation that all high school students be assigned homework once per week at most is indefensible based on the evidence. To strengthen the argument, the speaker must show that the reported correlation in the areas of math and science is also found among most other academic subjects. The speaker must also rule out other factors that might determine the students' grades and their likelihood of repeating a year. Finally, to better assess the argument we would need to know whether the reported disparity in academic performance between Sanlee and Marlee students involved only math and science students or all students.

Argument:
Maintaining profits at **Hyper-Go Toy Company**

In this memo, the president of Hyper-Go Toy Company (HG) argues that in order to maintain profitability the company should discontinue its complete line of action toys and focus exclusively on a new line of educational toys. To support this argument the president cites the dramatic decline in sales of HG's Fierce Fighter (FF) toy airplane, which during the previous three years had been a top seller, and an HG customer survey indicating increasing concern among parents about youth violence and for improving their children's education. The president also points out that several other toy companies have begun marketing educational toys and report a 200% increase in overall sales, and that the average family income is growing. The president's argument relies on several doubtful assumptions and is therefore unpersuasive.

First, the president's assumption that parental concern about youth violence is the cause of declining FF sales might be unwarranted. The decline might have been caused by one or more other factors—such as supply or distribution problems, new competing products from other toy companies, or a waning of interest in FF among children. Without ruling out these and other possible reasons for the decline, the president's argument seems ill conceived.

Secondly, the results of HG's customer survey are not necessarily representative of the overall population of toy-buying parents. Perhaps HG's current customers are more concerned about youth violence and education than most parents. If so, then the president has overlooked the possibility that a substantial portion of HG's target market would not react favorably to the proposed changes.

The key to GRE Argument flaws **A** – **F** *can be found on page 289.*

Thirdly, perhaps sales of HG's other action toys remained stable or even increased last year. In fact, it is entirely possible that some of HG's other toys are becoming very popular and will soon replace FF as top sellers. If so, then discontinuing the entire line would be ill advised indeed.

Fourth, assuming the toy companies that saw a 200% sales increase last year are statistically representative of toy companies in general, that increase might be due to action-toy sales rather than to educational-toy sales. If so, then the statistic would amount to scant support for the proposed course of action.

C Finally, the mere fact that average family income is growing provides little assurance that the proposed changes would increase HG's sales. Perhaps the average income of families without young children is growing, but for families with young children who buy toys it is shrinking. For that matter, perhaps average family expenses are also growing, so that families have even less discretionary income than before. Without ruling out these possibilities, the president cannot justify the proposed changes on the basis of the growth of average family income.

In sum, the president's argument is unconvincing as it stands. To strengthen it the president must show that parents in general, not just HG customers, are concerned about youth violence and education, and that these concerns are the reason for declining FF sales. To better assess the argument I would need more information about sales trends of HG's other action toys, and about the types of toys that have contributed to the 200% increase in sales for the other toy companies.

Argument:
A jazz club for **Monroe**

This loan applicant claims that a jazz club in Monroe would be a profitable venture. To support this claim the applicant points out that Monroe has no other jazz clubs. He also cites various other evidence that jazz is popular among Monroe residents. Careful examination of this supporting evidence, however, reveals that it lends little credible support to the applicant's claim.

D First of all, if the demand for a live jazz club in Monroe were as great as the applicant claims, it seems that Monroe would already have one or more such clubs. The fact that the closest jazz club is 65 miles away suggests a lack of interest among Monroe residents in a local jazz club. Since the applicant has not adequately responded to this concern, his claim that the proposed club would be profitable is untenable.

D The popularity of Monroe's annual jazz festival and of its nightly jazz radio show might appear to lend support to the applicant's claim. However, it is entirely possible that the vast majority of festival attendees are out-of-town visitors. Moreover, the author provides no evidence that radio listeners would be interested in going out to hear live jazz. For that matter, the radio program might actually pose competition for the C-Note club, especially considering that the program airs during the evening.

D Nor does the mere fact that several well-known jazz musicians live in Monroe lend significant support to the applicant's claim. It is entirely possible that these musicians perform elsewhere, perhaps at the club located 65 miles away. This would go a long way toward explaining why Monroe does not currently have a jazz club, and it would weaken the applicant's assertion that the C-Note would be profitable.

Finally, the nationwide study showing that the average jazz fan spends $1,000 each year on jazz entertainment would lend support to the applicant's claim only if Monroe residents typify jazz fans nationwide. However, the applicant provides no credible evidence that this is the case.

In conclusion, the loan applicant's argument is not persuasive. To bolster it he must provide clearer evidence that Monroe residents would patronize the C-Note on a regular basis. Such evidence might include the following: statistics showing that a significant number of Monroe residents attend the jazz festival each year; a survey showing that fans of Monroe's jazz radio program would go out to hear live jazz if they had the chance; and assurances from well-known local jazz musicians that they would play at the C-Note if given the opportunity.

Argument:
The **price of milk**

This editorial recommends that Batavia's government regulate milk prices because profits from milk sales are excessive given the apparently adequate supply. The editorial also claims that price regulation would help ensure an adequate supply of milk. To support these assertions the author cites the fact that over the past ten years the number of dairy farms in Batavia has increased by 25% while at Excello Food Market milk prices have increased by 100%. However, the argument relies on a series of unsubstantiated assumptions, which render it unconvincing as it stands.

First of all, the author assumes that Excello's milk prices reflect those throughout Batavia. However, the author provides no evidence that this is the case. To the extent that Excello's milk prices currently exceed nationwide averages the author's argument for government regulation of milk prices would be undermined.

D In the second place, even if Excello's milk prices reflect those in Batavia generally, in claiming that milk prices are particularly "excessive" the author assumes that milk-sale profits exceed profits from the sale of other goods in Batavia to a significant degree. But the author provides no evidence to substantiate this assumption. Perhaps other prices have risen commensurably, or perhaps even more on a percentage basis, during the same time period. Moreover, perhaps profit margins from the sale of other goods are even greater than profits from milk sales. In either event, the author could not justifiably rely on the mere fact that milk prices have increased by 100% to support the claim that milk-sale profits are excessive.

In the third place, the author assumes that an increase in milk prices results in increased profits. However, this is not necessarily the case. It is entirely possible that the costs associated with producing and delivering milk have increased as well over the last ten years. Thus, the strength of the author's claim of excessive milk-sale profits depends on a cost benefit analysis that the author does not provide.

The key to GRE Argument flaws **A**–**F** *can be found on page 289.*

In the fourth place, based on the fact that the number of dairy farms has increased the author infers that the supply of milk has also increased. However, this is not necessarily the case. It is possible that dairy farm production has shifted away from milk to other dairy products, and that the supply of milk has actually declined over this time period. To the extent that this is the case, then the author's supply-and-demand argument that milk prices are excessive is unconvincing.

Finally, in asserting that price regulation would help ensure an adequate supply of milk the author overlooks the possibility that milk producers would respond to the regulation by producing less milk, depending on the extent to which demand increases as a result of lower milk prices. If regulation has the effect of lowering profits, then common sense tells me that milk producers might be less inclined to produce milk. Without ruling out this possible scenario, the author cannot convince me that the recommendation would help ensure an adequate supply of milk.

In conclusion, the recommendation for regulation of milk prices is not well supported. To convince me that the proposed regulation is needed to ensure a reasonably priced milk supply, the author must provide clear statistical evidence that Excello's milk prices reflect nationwide milk prices and that profits from milk sales are in fact excessive. To better evaluate the recommendation, I would need more information about how the proposed regulation would effect both the supply of milk and the demand for milk in Batavia.

Argument:
Worker safety at **Alta Manufacturing**

This editorial recommends that Alta Manufacturing reduce its work shifts by one hour each in order to reduce its on-the-job accident rate and thereby increase Alta's productivity. To support this recommendation the author points out that last year the number of accidents at Alta was 30% greater than at Panoply Industries, where work shifts were one hour shorter. The author also cites certain experts who believe that many on-the-job accidents are caused by fatigue and sleep deprivation. I find this the argument unconvincing for several reasons.

First and foremost, the author provides absolutely no evidence that overall worker productivity is attributable in part to the number of on-the-job accidents. Although common sense informs me that such a relationship exists, the author must provide some evidence of this cause-and-effect relationship before I can accept the author's final conclusion that the proposed course of action would in fact increase Alta's productivity.

Secondly, the author assumes that some accidents at Alta are caused by fatigue or sleep deprivation. However, the author overlooks other possible causes, such as inadequate equipment maintenance or worker training, or the inherent hazards of Alta's manufacturing processes. By the same token, Panoply's comparatively low accident rate might be attributable not to the length of its work shifts but rather to other factors, such as superior equipment maintenance or worker training. In other words, without ruling out alternative causes of on-the-job accidents at both companies, the author cannot justifiably conclude that merely by emulating Panoply's work-shift policy Alta would reduce the number of such accidents.

Thirdly, even assuming that Alta's workers are fatigued or sleep-deprived, and that this is the cause of some of Alta's on-the-job accidents, in order to accept the author's solution to this problem we must assume that Alta's workers would use the additional hour of free time to sleep or rest. However, the author provides no evidence that they would use the time in this manner. It is entirely possible that Alta's workers would use that extra hour to engage in some other fatiguing activity. Without ruling out this possibility the author cannot convincingly conclude that reducing Alta's work shifts by one hour would reduce Alta's accident rate.

D Finally, a series of problems with the argument arise from the scant statistical information on which it relies. In comparing the number of accidents at Alta and Panoply, the author fails to consider that the per-worker accident rate might reveal that Alta is actually safer than Panoply, depending on the total number of workers at each company. Second, perhaps accident rates at the two companies last year were aberrations, and during other years Alta's accident rate was no greater, or even lower, than Panoply's rate. Or perhaps Panoply is not representative of industrial companies generally, and that other companies with shorter work shifts have even higher accident rates. In short, since the argument relies on very limited statistical information I cannot take the author's recommendation seriously.

In conclusion, the recommendation for emulating Panoply's work-shift policy is not well supported. To convince me that shorter work shifts would reduce Alta's on-the-job accident rate, the author must provide clear evidence that work-shift length is responsible for some of Alta's accidents. The author must also supply evidence to support her final conclusion that a lower accident rate would in fact increase overall worker productivity.

Argument:
Local merchants and a new **ski resort**

This editorial concludes that a new ski resort should be developed north of town because it would attract tourism and therefore be an economic boon to local merchants. To support this claim the author, a local merchant, points out that those opposed to the project do not live in the area and that a bank has agreed to fund the project. The argument suffers from several critical flaws and is therefore unpersuasive as it stands.

D First of all, that mere fact that environmentalists who oppose the development do not live in the town lends no credible support to the editorial's conclusion. In essence, the author attempts to argue for one position by attacking his opponents based on potentially irrelevant considerations. We are not informed about the environmentalists' specific reasons for their position. Besides, although they do not live in the town they

---

The key to GRE Argument flaws **A**–**F** *can be found on page 289.*

might operate businesses or own property in the area; thus, their opposition might be based on economic grounds entirely relevant to the argument.

D Secondly, the editorial provides no firm evidence to justify the assertion that a new ski resort north of town will in fact benefit the town's merchants. It is entirely possible that the resort might have the opposite effect, by drawing business away from local merchants, especially if the resort includes facilities such as apparel shops, restaurants, and grocery stores. Besides, we are not informed how far from town the resort would be located or how tourists would reach the resort. It is possible, for example, that the resort would be situated where visitors would take a route that does not pass through the town. Without ruling out these possibilities the editorial cannot justify its assertion that the resort would be a boon for local merchants.

Thirdly, the editorial's conclusion relies partly on the fact that a bank has agreed to fund the resort's development. However, this fact alone does not lend support to the assertion that local merchants will benefit. Common sense tells me that the bank agreed to fund the project because it believes the resort will be profitable, not because it believes other local merchants will benefit. In fact, a profitable ski resort might very well draw business away from local merchants.

In conclusion, the argument is untenable as it stands. To strengthen it, the editorial's author must provide clear evidence that the resort would increase business for the town's merchants rather than drawing business away from these merchants. To better evaluate the argument, we would need more information about the bank's reasons for agreeing to fund the project—especially whether the bank also lends to existing local merchants whose interests would be affected by the resort.

Argument:
Comparing **cold medications**

This argument concludes that Cold-Away is a more effective non-prescription cold medication than Coldex. The argument points out that each one has a distinct unwanted side effect: Cold-Away causes drowsiness, while Coldex contributes to existing high blood pressure. To support its conclusion, the argument points out that Cold-Away has been on the market considerably longer, and that it is used by more hospitals than Coldex. I find the argument unconvincing for three reasons.

D First, the mere fact that Cold-Away has been on the market longer than Coldex is scant evidence of their comparative effectiveness. Well-established products are not necessarily better than newer ones. Moreover, in my observation newer medicines often make use of newer pharmaceutical developments than competing products; thus it can be argued that since Cold-Away has been on the market longer than Coldex it is likely to be less, not more, effective than Coldex.

Secondly, the argument unfairly assumes that hospitals prefer Cold-Away because of its comparative effectiveness as a cold medication. It is entirely possible that hospitals do not consider drowsiness an undesirable side effect for their patients. For that matter, perhaps hospitals use Cold-Away primarily for this effect rather than as a cold medication.

A third problem with the argument involves Coldex's side effect: high blood pressure. Admittedly, people who already have a serious blood pressure problem would probably be well advised to use Cold-Away instead. However, only those people are susceptible to this side effect. Thus, for all other people—the vast majority of cold-medicine users—Coldex's side effect is irrelevant in choosing between the two products. Moreover, if a person without high blood pressure wishes to avoid drowsiness, Coldex would seem to be the preferable medication.

In sum, the argument is unconvincing as it stands. To strengthen it, the argument's proponent must provide clear evidence that hospitals prefer Cold-Away because of its effectiveness in treating colds. To better assess the argument, I would need better evidence comparing the effectiveness of the two products—perhaps through clinical studies or reliable surveys of the general population.

Argument:
A fitness-gym **franchise** opportunity

This brochure for Power-Lift Gym claims that by investing in a Power-Lift franchise an investor will earn a quick profit. To support this claim the brochure cites a variety of statistics about the current popularity of physical fitness and of Power-Lift Gyms in particular. However, careful scrutiny of this evidence reveals that it lends no credible support to the claim.

D One problem with the brochure's claim involves its reliance on the bare fact that revenue from last year's sales of health books and magazines totaled $50 million. This statistic in itself proves nothing. Health magazines do not all focus on weightlifting or even physical fitness; it is possible that very few sales were of those that do. Besides, it is entirely possible that in previous years total sales were even higher and that sales are actually declining. Either scenario, if true, would serve to weaken the brochure's claim rather than support it.

D Another problem with the brochure's claim involves the fact that more and more consumers are purchasing home gyms. It is entirely possible that consumers are using home gyms as a substitute for commercial gyms, and that the number of Power-Lift memberships will decline as a result. Without ruling out this possibility, the brochure cannot convince me that a new Power-Lift franchise would be profitable.

D A third problem with the brochure's claim involves its reliance on the fact that 500 Power-Lift franchises are now in existence. It is entirely possible that the market has become saturated, and that additional Power-Lift gyms will not be as successful as current ones. Moreover, it is possible that the number of competing gyms has also increased in tandem with the general interest in health and fitness. Without addressing this supply-and-demand issue, the brochure cannot justify its conclusion that a new Power-Lift franchise would be a sound investment.

The key to GRE Argument flaws **A**—**F** *can be found on page 289.*

In conclusion, the brochure is unpersuasive as it stands. To strengthen its claim that a new Power-Lift franchise would be profitable, the brochure should provide stronger evidence that the general interest in physical fitness, and weightlifting in particular, will continue unabated in the foreseeable future. The brochure must also provide evidence that home gyms are not serving as substitutes for commercial gyms. Finally, to better evaluate the argument we would need more information about the extent to which the fitness-gym market has become saturated, not only by Power-Lift franchises but by competing gyms as well.

Argument:
Writing for books vs. **writing for television**

This article cites a recent study showing that during a typical day people make an average of 23 references to watching television but only one reference to reading fiction. From these statistics the author reasons that the television industry must be far more profitable than the book-publishing industry, then concludes that people seeking careers in writing should acquire training and experience in television writing. This argument is flawed in several critical respects.

First of all, the article's author has not shown the study upon which the argument depends to be statistically reliable. The people studied must be representative of the overall population of people who buy books and watch television; otherwise the author cannot draw any firm conclusions about the comparative profitability of the television and book-publishing industries based on the study's results.

Secondly, the author's argument depends on the assumption that the frequency with which a person refers in conversation to television, or to fiction books, is a good indication of how much television a person watches, or how many fiction books a person reads. Yet this is not necessarily the case. Perhaps people tend to refer many times in daily conversation to the same television show. If so, then the statistics cited would overstate the amount of television people watch compared to the number of fiction books they read.

Thirdly, even if the statistics cited accurately reflect the amount of television people watch compared to the number of fiction books they read, it would be hasty to infer based merely on this fact that the television industry is more profitable than the book-publishing industry. To begin with, the study's results excluded any data about nonfiction books—a category that might very well constitute book publishers' main profit source. Moreover, the author has not shown any correlation, let alone a cause-and-effect relationship, between the number of hours a person spends watching television and that industry's profits. In any event, lacking financial statistics about the profitability of the two industries the editorial's author cannot convince me that writers should follow the author's recommendation.

D Finally, even assuming that the television industry is more profitable than the book-publishing industry, the author's implicit claim that television writers enjoy more secure and lucrative careers than book writers is without support. It is entirely possible that television writers are paid comparatively low wages; in fact, low writer compensation might partially explain why the television industry is relatively profitable. Without better evidence that television writers are better off then book writers it might be folly to follow the author's recommendation.

In sum, the argument relies on several poor assumptions and is therefore unconvincing as it stands. To strengthen it the article's author must provide clear evidence that the study's subjects reflect the overall population, and that their conversational habits accurately reflect how much television they watch compared to how many books they read. The author must also show that the disparity between the two contributes to far greater financial rewards for the television industry, as well as for its writers, than for the book-publishing industry and its writers.

Argument:
The relationship between **sleep apnea** and weight gain

In this argument, the speaker concludes that any person who snores should try to eat less and exercise more than the average person. To justify this conclusion the speaker points out that many snorers awaken frequently during sleep—often so briefly that they are unaware that they are awake—in order to catch their breath (a condition called sleep apnea), and as a result are too tired during normal waking hours to exercise. The speaker also cites data collected during a recent study, suggesting that snorers are more likely to gain weight than other people. This argument is flawed in several critical respects.

First, the speaker provides no assurances that the recently collected data suggesting a correlation between snoring and weight gain are statistically reliable. Perhaps the study's subjects were unrepresentative of the overall population—in terms of other traits and habits that might affect body weight. Lacking such evidence the speaker simply cannot draw any firm conclusions based on the study about the relationship between snoring and weight gain.

Even assuming a strong correlation between snoring and weight gain among the general population, the speaker has not adequately shown that sleep apnea causes weight gain. A correlation is one indication of a causal relationship, but in itself does not suffice to prove such a relationship. It is entirely possible that some other medical condition, or some other trait or habit, that causes snoring also causes weight gain. Without establishing clearly that snoring at least contributes to weight gain, the speaker cannot convince me that snorers should either eat less or exercise more than the average person.

E Even if many snorers suffer from sleep apnea and tend to gain weight as a result, the speaker's advice that "anyone who snores" should try to eat less and to exercise is nevertheless unwarranted. It is entirely possible that some—or perhaps even most— snorers do not suffer from sleep apnea, or are not too tired to exercise, or do not in any event tend to gain weight. Without ruling out these possibilities, the speaker must expressly limit the advice to those snorers whose snoring causes weight gain.

The key to GRE Argument flaws **A** – **F** *can be found on page 289.*

F Even if the speaker's advice were modified as indicated above, the advice to exercise would still be logically unsound. If a person with sleep apnea is too tired to exercise as a result, then simply advising that person to exercise begs the question: What should the person do to eliminate the cause of the tiredness? Thus, the speaker should determine the cause of sleep apnea and modify the advice so that it targets that cause. Of course, if it turns out that weight gain is one cause of snoring and sleep apnea, then the speaker's advice that snorers should try to eat less would have considerable merit.

Yet, without any evidence that this is the case, the speaker's advice might be at least partially ineffective in counteracting a snorer's tendency to gain weight.

In sum, the speaker's advice for "any" snorer is ill conceived and poorly supported. To lend credibility to this advice the speaker should provide evidence that the recently collected data reflect the general population. To better assess the argument it would be useful to know all the possible causes of snoring and of sleep apnea.

In sum, the argument is unconvincing as it stands. To strengthen it the author must show that charging beach-access fees would reduce the number of beachgoers, but not to the extent of undermining the goal of raising sufficient funds to maintain an attractive coastal area. The author must also provide better evidence that replenishing sand would indeed protect nearby buildings, and that the net result would be the enhancement of Tria's tourist industry.

Argument:
Promofoods' recall of its cans of tuna

This magazine article concludes that the 8 million cans of tuna Promofoods recalled, due to complaints about nausea and dizziness, do not after all contain any chemicals that pose a health risk. To support this conclusion the author cites the fact that five of eight chemicals commonly causing these symptoms were not found in the recalled cans, while the other three also occur naturally in other canned foods. For several reasons, this evidence lends little credible support to the author's conclusion.

To begin with, the author relies partly on the fact that, although three of the eight chemicals most commonly blamed for nausea and dizziness appeared in Promofoods' recalled tuna, these chemicals also occur naturally in other canned foods. However, this fact alone lends no support to the author's conclusion, for two reasons. First, the author might be ignoring an important distinction between "naturally occurring" chemicals and those not occurring naturally. It is entirely possible that these three chemicals do not occur naturally in Promofoods' tuna, and that it is for this reason that the chemicals cause nausea and dizziness. Secondly, it is entirely possible that even when they occur naturally these chemicals cause the same symptoms. Unless the author rules out both possibilities, he cannot reliably conclude that the recalled tuna would not cause these symptoms.

E Another problem with the argument is that the author's conclusion is too broad. Based on evidence about certain chemicals that might cause two particular heath-related symptoms, the author concludes that the recalled tuna contains no chemicals that pose a health risk. However, the author fails to account for the myriad of other possible health risks that the recalled tuna might potentially pose. Without ruling out all other such risks, the author cannot justifiably reach his conclusion.

A third problem with the argument involves that fact that the eight particular chemicals with which the test was concerned are only the eight "most commonly blamed" for nausea and dizziness. It is entirely possibly that other chemicals might also cause these symptoms, and that one or more of these other chemicals actually caused the symptoms. Without ruling out this possibility, the author cannot justifiably conclude that the recalled tuna would not cause nausea and dizziness.

A final problem with the argument involves the testing procedure itself. The author provides no information about the number of recalled cans tested or the selection method used. Unless the number of cans is a sufficiently large sample and is statistically representative of all the recalled cans, the study's results are not statistically reliable.

In conclusion, the article is unconvincing as it stands. To strengthen the assertion that the recalled tuna would not cause nausea and dizziness, the author must provide evidence that the three chemicals mentioned that occur naturally in other canned foods also appear naturally in Promofoods' tuna. The author must also provide evidence that ingesting other canned foods containing these three chemicals does not cause these symptoms. To better evaluate the argument, we would need to know whether the sample used in the tests was statistically significant and representative of all the recalled tuna. We would also need to know what other chemicals in the recalled tuna might pose any health risk at all.

Argument:
The **Mozart School of Music**

This argument concludes that the Mozart School should be the first choice of any music student aware of its reputation for (1) its intensive practice requirements for students of all ages; (2) its outstanding facilities, up-to-date equipment, and distinguished faculty; and (3) the accomplishments of its graduates. Although the evidence provided strongly suggests that this school would be an excellent choice for certain prospective students, the conclusion that it should be the first choice for any prospective music student is indefensible—in three respects.

E First, the fact that the Mozart School is known for its intensive practice and training regimen for even the youngest students suggests that the school might be suitable for certain child protégées, but perhaps not for children for whom a more balanced education would be more prudent. For that matter, many older students with other interests and activities would no doubt find the intensity and time commitment that the Mozart program requires unfeasible or undesirable.

Secondly, in all likelihood the outstanding facilities, equipment, and faculty come at a considerable price to students—in the form of high tuition. Thus, the argument seems to assume that for all prospective music students money is no object when it

The key to GRE Argument flaws **A** – **F** *can be found on page 289.*

comes to musical training. Yet common sense informs me that many students would place a higher priority on affordable training than on the specific features that the argument touts.

E Thirdly, although the fact that many famous performers and highly paid performers are among the school's graduates might be relevant to students with the requisite natural talent and motivation to attain these lofty goals, for others this feature would not be relevant. For example, some prospective students would no doubt wish to focus their study on musicology, theory, composition, or even performance—not to become famous or highly paid performers but rather to prepare for careers in music education. Other prospective students might not aspire to make music their eventual vocation at all. Thus, some other school—one with a less rigorous performance-oriented approach—might be a better choice for less-gifted students and for those with other aspirations.

In sum, the Mozart School's features do not justify the argument's sweeping conclusion that the school should be the first choice for every music student. To strengthen the argument, its proponent must show at the very least that the school would be affordable to any prospective student. To better assess the argument I would need more information about what non-performance music programs the school offers, and whether Mozart students of various ages have any choice in how intensely they are required to practice and train.

Argument:
Clearview: An ideal place **for retirement**

This article argues that anyone seeking a place to retire should choose Clearview. To support this argument the article cites Clearview's consistent climate and natural beauty; it's falling housing costs; its low property taxes compared to nearby towns; and the mayor's promise to improve schools, streets, and services. The article also claims that retirees can expect excellent health care because the number of physicians in Clearview greatly exceeds the national average. This argument is flawed in several critical respects.

E To begin with, although consistent climate and natural beauty might be attractive to many retirees, these features are probably not important to all retirees. For many retirees it is probably more important to live near relatives, or even to enjoy changing seasons. Thus, I cannot accept the author's sweeping recommendation for all retirees on this basis.

E Also, Clearview's declining housing costs do not necessarily make Clearview the best place to retire—for two reasons. First, despite the decline Clearview's housing costs might be high compared to housing costs in other cities. Secondly, for wealthier retirees housing costs are not likely to be a factor in choosing a place to retire. Thus, the mere fact that housing costs have been in decline lends scant support to the recommendation.

E The article's reliance on Clearview's property-tax rates is also problematic in two respects. First, retirees obviously have innumerable choices about where to retire besides Clearview and nearby towns. Secondly, for retirees who are well off financially property taxes are not likely to be an important concern in choosing a place to retire. Thus, it is unfair to infer from Clearview's property-tax rates that retirees would prefer Clearview.

Yet another problem with the argument involves the mayor's promises. In light of Clearview's low property-tax rates, whether the mayor can follow through on those promises is highly questionable. Absent any explanation of how the city can spend more money in the areas cited without raising property taxes, I simply cannot accept the editorial's recommendation on the basis of those promises. Besides, even if the city makes the improvements promised, those improvements—particularly the ones to schools—would not necessarily be important to retirees.

Finally, although the number of physicians in Clearview is relatively high, the per capita number might be relatively low. Moreover, it would be fairer to compare this per capita number with the per capita number for other attractive retirement towns—rather than the national average. After all, retirees are likely to place a relatively heavy burden on health-care resources. Besides, the article provides no assurances that the number of physicians in Clearview will remain high in the foreseeable future.

In conclusion, the recommendation is poorly supported. To strengthen it the author must convince me—perhaps by way of a reliable survey—that the key features that the vast majority of retirees look for in choosing a place to live are consistent climate, natural beauty, and low housing costs. The author must also provide better evidence that Clearview's property taxes are lower than the those of cities in other areas. The author must also explain how the city can make its promised improvements without raising property taxes. Finally, to better assess the argument I would need to now how the per capita number of physicians in Clearview would compare to the national average in the future.

Argument:
New housing for **Claitown University** students

This argument recommends commissioning a famous architect known for futuristic and experimental designs as the best means of providing new affordable housing for Claitown University students. The argument's line of reasoning is that the building will attract paying tourists, new students, and donations from alumni—all of which will help raise the funds needed for the project. However, the argument is problematic in several critical respects.

First of all, a famous architect might charge a substantial fee for the project, in which case the funds raised by charging tourists and through alumni donations might be offset to the point of rendering the entire project unfeasible financially. The argument's proponent must address this issue before I can accept the argument's conclusion.

The key to GRE Argument flaws **A**–**F** *can be found on page 289.*

Secondly, the argument relies on the tenuous assumption that tourists will be interested in paying for tours of a building used for a purpose as mundane as student housing. It is entirely possible that once the building is in use, tourists will not be willing to pay for tours. Besides, perhaps the appeal of this architect's buildings lies primarily in their exteriors, in which case tourists would be able to appreciate the new building's salient architectural features without paying for a tour. In either case, the argument's claim that the architect's notoriety and the building itself will generate the funds needed for its construction would be dubious at best.

F Thirdly, the argument fails to explain how the University will be able to pay for construction when it will not begin to receive the revenue it needs until after construction is complete. Unless the architect and contractors agree to be paid later, the argument's proponent cannot convince me that the recommended course of action will achieve the University's goals.

Finally, the argument assumes without justification that a futuristic or experimental building will attract alumni donations and students. While this might be true, it is also possible that instead the University's alumni and students strongly prefer the architectural status quo at their campus; in fact, the appeal of the campus' predominant architectural styles might be one of the key attractions for students and alumni dollars. Thus, I would need some evidence to substantiate this assumption before I can accept the argument's conclusion.

In sum, as it stands the argument is not well supported. To strengthen it, the argument's proponent must supply clear evidence—perhaps involving other college buildings designed by famous architects—that tourists will be willing to pay for tours of the building once it is completed and is in use as student housing. To better assess the argument I would need detailed and realistic financial projections, accounting for the architect's fees, to determine the project's financial feasibility. I would also need to know—perhaps by way of a reliable survey—the extent to which students and alumni would be likely to support the project.

Argument:
Replacing **Bayhead Public Library**'s books

In this argument the speaker supports Bayhead Public Library's plan to replace books that are borrowed less frequently than once per year with additional copies of recent novels. In support of this position, the speaker suggests that seldom-borrowed books amount to wasted shelf space because people who want to read recent novels frequently find the library's only copy checked out. In further support of this position, the speaker points out that only thirty people have protested the plan. I find the speaker's position unjustified in several critical respects.

First of all, the speaker ignores the possibility that replacing less popular books with more copies of popular new novels will undermine the library's primary function as a repository of a wide variety of books for free public access. New books are available at bookstores, whereas older, less popular ones are not. Thus, the library might lose the patronage of a large percentage of the community should it adopt the plan.

F Secondly, the speaker unfairly implies that the library has only two options: to maintain the status quo or to follow the proposed plan. Some other alternative—one that would appease protesters while preserving community support—might provide an optimal long-term solution. For example, perhaps the library can remove books that have not been borrowed for three years or for five years, rather than for one year. Although this alternate plan would free up less shelf space than the current plan, it would nevertheless make room for the most popular new books.

Finally, the mere fact that only thirty people have protested the plan accomplishes little toward supporting the speaker's argument—for two reasons. First, this statistic is scant evidence that the community at large would support the plan; it is entirely possible that many opponents have simply not voiced their opposition. Second, the thirty protesters might very well be in a position to influence many other people; or they might be among the library's most significant financial patrons. In either event, ignoring these protesters might result in the ultimate loss of community or financial support the library needs to thrive, or even survive.

In sum, the library's plan seems neither well reasoned nor well-supported. To strengthen her position, the speaker must convince me that the plan is the only viable option to maintaining the status quo. To better assess the plan's impact on the library's value as a community resource, I would need to know what percentage of the library's current inventory would be replaced under the plan. I would also need to know the extent of influence among the thirty protesters, and the extent of support for the plan among the vast majority of community members who have not voiced their opinions about it.

Argument:
Distance-learning courses at **Xanadu College**

In this letter a Xanadu College professor asserts that the development of an extensive distance-learning program would enhance the college's reputation, as well as increase total enrollment and therefore total tuition income. To support this assertion the professor points out that in last year's trial program two traditional courses were easily adapted for distance learning. Next, the professor reasons that with more free time faculty could engage in extensive research, which in turn would enhance the college's reputation. The argument is flawed in several critical respects.

First of all, the professor's claim that an increase in enrollment would result in an increase in tuition income is warranted only if Xanadu students would be willing to pay a sufficiently high fee for distance-learning courses. However, it is entirely possible that Xanadu's distance-learning courses would not command as high a fee as its traditional courses, and that Xanadu's total tuition income would actually decline if this less-expensive alternative were available to Xanadu students.

The key to GRE Argument flaws **A**—**F** *can be found on page 289.*

F Secondly, the professor's dual claims about distance learning—that it would enhance Xanadu's reputation and that it would increase enrollment and income—might very well be mutually exclusive alternatives. The availability of distance-learning courses might actually diminish Xanadu's overall reputation for quality education. Without addressing this issue the professor cannot justifiably conclude that the distance-learning alternative would achieve both goals.

A third problem with the argument involves last year's trial project. Despite the fact that two particular courses were easily adapted to distance learning, other courses might not be as adaptable. Common sense informs me that certain courses, especially in the arts, require hands-on learning to be effective. Thus, the professor cannot justify her claim on the basis of the trial project.

Finally, the professor's claim that distance learning would afford Xanadu faculty more free time to engage in extensive research raises two problems. First, it is possible that the time needed for faculty to adapt their courses for distance learning would equal or even exceed the time they would save by not teaching traditional classes. Second, even if a net time savings does result, the professor provides no evidence that Xanadu faculty would actually use this extra free time for research, or that additional research would in fact enhance Xanadu's reputation.

In conclusion, the argument is indefensible as it stands. To strengthen it the professor must provide specific information about Xanadu's current reputation, and provide clear evidence that distance learning would in fact enhance this reputation. The professor must also convince us that the two courses in the trial project were representative of Xanadu's other courses—in terms of the ease with which the faculty could adapt their courses to distance learning. Finally, to better assess the argument we would need a detailed analysis comparing loss in tuition from traditional-course enrollment with expected gains in tuition from distance-learning enrollment.

Argument:
The benefits of merging two **townships**

This editorial recommends the merger of Roseville and West Roseville. The author claims that the merger would (1) eliminate confusion among both townships' residents about which authority to call for services, (2) reduce aggregate administrative costs by eliminating duplicative jobs and services, and (3) attract business investment as did the merger of Hamden and North Hamden ten years ago. The author claims further that the merger would result in certain job reassignments but not in the loss of any jobs for current municipal employees. I find these claims problematic in several respects.

First, although a merger might be necessary to eliminate current confusion about which authority to contact for services, the editorial overlooks the possibility that the merger will not in itself suffice to eliminate this confusion. Specifically, until the residents of both communities are apprised of the change and learn how to respond appropriately, confusion will continue—and perhaps even increase in the short term.

Thus, some measure of community awareness and responsiveness might also be required for the elimination of confusion.

F Secondly, the editorial seems to make two irreconcilable claims. One is that the merger will result in the elimination of certain duplicative jobs; the other is that no current municipal employee will become unemployed as a result of the merger. The editorial fails to consider that eliminating duplicative jobs would decrease the aggregate number of current municipal employees unless enough new jobs are created to offset the decrease, and that new jobs would in turn add to administrative costs. Thus, as it stands the argument is self-contradictory, and the author must either modify it by choosing between two competing objectives—preserving current employment levels and cutting costs—or somehow reconcile these two objectives.

Thirdly, the author's claim that the merger will attract business investment relies on the hasty assumption that the newly merged Roseville would be similar to Hamden in every way, affecting their attractiveness to business investment. Perhaps Hamden's business tax rates, labor pool, or even climate are more attractive than the newly merged Roseville's would be. If so, then the proposed merger in itself might accomplish little toward attracting business investment to Roseville. In other words, without evidence that Hamden and the newly merged Roseville would be equally attractive to business investments I cannot accept the author's conclusion that a merger will carry the same result for Roseville as for Hamden.

In sum, the editorial not only is logically unsound but also relies on several doubtful assumptions. To strengthen the argument the author must modify the recommendation to account for other measures needed to eliminate the confusion mentioned in the editorial. The author must also provide a cost-benefit analysis that accounts for the costs of creating new jobs to offset the elimination of duplicative jobs. Finally, the author must show that the new Roseville would be just as attractive to business investment as the new Hamden has been. Argument:

Argument:
Choosing a **paving** contractor

The vice president of a company that builds shopping malls argues here that the company should hire Appian rather than McAdam to build access roads for the company. To support this argument the vice president points out that a certain area of Route 101 that McAdam repaved two years ago has deteriorated significantly, while a certain stretch of Route 66 that Appian repaved four years ago remains in good condition. The vice president also points out that Appian recently acquired new state-of-the-art paving equipment and hired a new quality-control manager. I find the vice president's argument logically unconvincing—in several respects.

First of all, it is unfair to infer based solely on the comparison between the two stretches of highway that Appian does better work than McAdam. The inference relies on the poor assumption that the comparative quality of two contractors' work, rather than some other phenomenon, was responsible for the comparative condition of the two

The key to GRE Argument flaws **A** – **F** *can be found on page 289.*

stretches of pavement. Perhaps the stretch that McAdam repaved is located in an area whose extremes in climate or high traffic volume serve to erode and damage pavement very quickly. For that matter, perhaps soil or other geological conditions in that area were primarily responsible for deterioration of the pavement along that stretch. In short, without showing that all other conditions in the two areas have been essentially the same, the vice president cannot convince me that the quality of McAdam's and Appian's repaving work was responsible for the difference in how well the two stretches of pavement have held up.

Secondly, it is unfair to conclude based on Appian's recent equipment acquisition and personnel decision that Appian will do a better job than McAdam. Perhaps McAdam has also acquired the same type of equipment. Moreover, perhaps McAdam's quality-control manager is far more experienced than Appian's new manager, and as a result McAdam's product is likely to be better than Appian's. Besides, equipment and on-site management are only two of many factors affecting the quality of a pavement job. Other such factors include the experience and competence of other workers, and the paving material used. Without showing that the two firms are similar in these and other respects, the vice president cannot justify his recommendation of Appian over McAdam.

F Finally, the vice president's recommendation rests on the unlikely assumption that the company has only two alternatives—McAdam and Appian. In all likelihood the company can engage one of many other paving contractors instead. Thus, to the extent the vice president recommends Appian over not just McAdam but over any other contractor the recommendation is unwarranted.

In sum, the vice president has not convinced me that the company should hire Appian. To strengthen the argument the vice president must provide clear evidence that it was the quality of McAdam's and Appian's work—rather than one or more other factors—that resulted in the difference between how well the two stretches of pavement have held up over time. The vice president must also provide better evidence that Appian's new equipment and new manager will enhance, or at least maintain, the quality of Appian's overall work—at a higher level than McAdam's overall work. Finally, to better assess the argument I would need to know what other paving contractors the company could hire, and the quality of those contractors' work compared to McAdam's and Appian's.

Argument:
A new dormitory for **Buckingham College**

In this memo, a dean at Buckingham College recommends that in order to meet expected enrollment increases the college should build an additional dormitory. To support this recommendation the dean points out that rental rates for off-campus apartments have been increasing, thus making it more difficult for students to afford this housing option. The dean also points out that a new dormitory would attract prospective students to the college. This argument is problematic in several respects.

A threshold problem with the argument involves the statistical reliability of the reports about off-campus rental rates. The dean indicates only that "student leaders" reported these statistics; the dean provides no information about how these students collected their data. It is entirely possible that the report was based on an insufficiently small sample, or a sample that was unrepresentative of the town's overall student rental market.

Secondly, the dean assumes that this current trend in rental rates will continue in the future; yet the dean offers no evidence to substantiate this assumption. These rates are a function of supply and demand, and it is entirely possible that construction of apartment houses will increase in the future, thereby reducing rental rates along with the need for an additional dormitory. Without considering this possible scenario, the dean cannot justifiably conclude that an additional dormitory is needed to meet future demand.

Thirdly, the dean assumes that as enrollment increases the demand for student housing will also increase. While this might be the case, the dean ignores the possibility that the increased enrollment will be the result of an increase in the number of students commuting to Buckingham from their parents' homes. This scenario, if true, would render the dean's argument for building a new dormitory untenable.

F Yet another problem with the argument involves the dean's final claim that an attractive new dormitory would attract prospective students to Buckingham. Even assuming students in fact choose colleges on this basis, by relying on this evidence the dean essentially provides an argument against building the new dormitory. If an attractive new dormitory would increase demand for dormitory space, this fact would only serve to undermine the dean's conflicting claim that the new dormitory would help meet increasing demand for dormitory space.

In conclusion, the dean's recommendation is not well supported. To strengthen it the dean must provide clear evidence that average rental rates for off-campus student apartments have in fact been increasing, that this trend will continue in the future, and that this trend will in fact result in an increased demand for dormitory housing.

The key to GRE Argument flaws **A**–**F** *can be found on page 289.*

About the Author

Mark Alan Stewart (B.A., Economics; J.D., University of California at Los Angeles) is an attorney and a preeminent authority and top-selling author on the subject of graduate-level entrance exams. For more than a decade, Mr. Stewart served as consultant to schools in the University of California and California State University systems in graduate-level entrance exam programs. His books on LSAT, GRE, and GMAT preparation are perennial top sellers among aspiring law, business, and graduate students. His other book-length publications for graduate-level admission include the following (all published by Peterson's): *Master the GMAT, GRE-LSAT Logic Workbook, GRE Answers to the Real Essay Questions, GRE-LSAT-GMAT-MCAT Reading Comprehension Workbook, Words for Smart Test Takers, Math for Smart Test Takers,* and *How to Write the Perfect Personal Statement.*